SCIENCE AND ENGINEERING FOR GRADES 6–12

Investigation and Design at the Center

D1526364

Brett Moulding, Nancy Songer, and Kerry Brenner, Editors

Committee on Science Investigations and Engineering
Design Experiences in Grades 6–12

Board on Science Education
Division of Behavioral and Social Sciences and Education
National Academy of Engineering

A Consensus Study Report of

The National Academies of
SCIENCES · ENGINEERING · MEDICINE

THE NATIONAL ACADEMIES PRESS
Washington, DC
www.nap.edu

Ron—
Here's hoping
we have
more
STEM
adventures
ahead.
Nancy

THE NATIONAL ACADEMIES PRESS   500 Fifth Street, NW   Washington, DC 20001

This activity was supported by contracts between the National Academy of Sciences and Carnegie Corporation of New York (#G-16-53835) and Amgen Foundation (#204944891). Any opinions, findings, conclusions, or recommendations expressed in this publication do not necessarily reflect the views of any organization or agency that provided support for the project.

International Standard Book Number-13: 978-0-309-48260-8
International Standard Book Number-10: 0-309-48260-7
Digital Object Identifier: https://doi.org/10.17226/25216
Library of Congress Control Number: 2019931123

Additional copies of this publication are available for sale from the National Academies Press, 500 Fifth Street, NW, Keck 360, Washington, DC 20001; (800) 624-6242 or (202) 334-3313; http://www.nap.edu.

Suggested citation: National Academies of Sciences, Engineering, and Medicine. (2019). *Science and Engineering for Grades 6–12: Investigation and Design at the Center*. Washington, DC: The National Academies Press. doi: https://doi.org/10.17226/25216.

The National Academies of
SCIENCES · ENGINEERING · MEDICINE

The **National Academy of Sciences** was established in 1863 by an Act of Congress, signed by President Lincoln, as a private, nongovernmental institution to advise the nation on issues related to science and technology. Members are elected by their peers for outstanding contributions to research. Dr. Marcia McNutt is president.

The **National Academy of Engineering** was established in 1964 under the charter of the National Academy of Sciences to bring the practices of engineering to advising the nation. Members are elected by their peers for extraordinary contributions to engineering. Dr. C. D. Mote, Jr., is president.

The **National Academy of Medicine** (formerly the Institute of Medicine) was established in 1970 under the charter of the National Academy of Sciences to advise the nation on medical and health issues. Members are elected by their peers for distinguished contributions to medicine and health. Dr. Victor J. Dzau is president.

The three Academies work together as the **National Academies of Sciences, Engineering, and Medicine** to provide independent, objective analysis and advice to the nation and conduct other activities to solve complex problems and inform public policy decisions. The National Academies also encourage education and research, recognize outstanding contributions to knowledge, and increase public understanding in matters of science, engineering, and medicine.

Learn more about the National Academies of Sciences, Engineering, and Medicine at **www.nationalacademies.org**.

The National Academies of
SCIENCES · ENGINEERING · MEDICINE

Preface

S tudents learn by doing. Science investigation and engineering design provide an opportunity for students to *do*. When students engage in science investigation and engineering design, they are able to engage deeply with phenomena as they ask questions, collect and analyze data, generate and utilize evidence, and develop models to support explanations and solutions. Research studies demonstrate that deeper engagement leads to stronger conceptual understandings of science content than what is demonstrated through more traditional, memorization-intensive approaches. Investigations provide the evidence that students need to construct explanations for the causes of phenomena. Constructing understanding by actively engaging in investigation and design also creates meaningful and memorable learning experiences for all students. These experiences pique students' curiosity and lead to greater interest and identity in science.

Science is a way of knowing based on the collection and analysis of empirical data in relation to a scientific question. The growing inclusion of engineering design in K–12 classrooms presents an opportunity for students to learn yet another way of interacting with the natural and designed world around them. When investigation and design are at the center of learning, students can gather evidence and take ownership of the evidence they have gathered. This process contributes to student agency as they make sense of phenomena and designs and extend their understanding of the natural and designed world.

Learning is more meaningful when investigation and design are relevant to student lives. Investigation and design that are connected to students' culture and place tend to increase student interest in learning. Culturally responsive teaching requires teachers to understand the students' culture and place, use inclusive pedagogies to meet the needs of all their students, and adapt instruction by using phenomena and challenges that are linked to students' place and culture.

The introduction of *A Framework for K–12 Science Education*, the Next Generation Science Standards, and state standards consistent with the *Framework* provide a structure for rethinking how students engage in science and engineering and how they can use investigation/design to gather and analyze data to support explanations of the causes of phenomena and to design solutions. They focus on three-dimensional learning (via performances that integrate crosscutting concepts, scientific and engineering practices, and core disciplinary ideas) and provide a new ambitious vision for the classroom, in which students engage in meaningful learning. The new approaches provide an opportunity for teaching and learning to improve via the use of new instructional strategies and resources that foster, guide, and evaluate teaching and learning. They create an impetus for professional learning in which educators experience, practice, and reflect upon the new approaches as they prepare to engage students in science investigation and engineering design.

To reiterate, the goal of education reform is to improve student learning. Student learning occurs as teachers work day by day to help students learn to engage in doing science and engineering. Science investigation and engineering design provide a structure and a vision for meaningful student learning. This report describes ways teaching and learning can shift toward investigation/design that builds from current research in how students learn toward the realization of the new vision in the classroom.

Brett Moulding and Nancy Songer, *Cochairs*
Committee on Science Investigations and
Engineering Design Experiences in Grades 6–12

Acknowledgments

This Consensus Study Report reflects the invaluable contributions of many individuals, including those who served on the committee, the staff of the National Academies of Sciences, Engineering, and Medicine, and many other experts.

This report was made possible by sponsorships from the Amgen Foundation and the Carnegie Corporation of New York. We first thank both Scott Heimlich, vice president at Amgen Foundation, and Jim Short, Carnegie Corporation's program director of leadership and teaching to advance learning, for requesting the study and providing insight to the committee.

Over the course of the study, the committee held public fact-finding meetings, including a public workshop, and members of the committee greatly benefited from presentations by, and discussions with, the many individuals who participated in these meetings: Megan Bang, University of Washington, Seattle; Lizette Burks, Kansas State Department of Education; Al Byers, National Science Teachers Association; Ravit Golan Duncan, Rutgers University; Richard Duschl, Pennsylvania State University; Rowhea Elmesky, Washington University in St. Louis; Susan Gomez-Zwiep, California State University, Long Beach; John Kamal, Science Leadership Academy @ Center City; Matthew Kloser, University of Notre Dame; Scott McDonald, Pennsylvania State University; Tamara Moore, Purdue University; Tiffany Neill, Council of State Science Supervisors and Oklahoma State Department of Education; Christian Schunn, University of Pittsburgh; Kimberly Scott, Arizona State University; Stacey van der Veen, NGSSPD Consultants; Wil van der Veen, Raritan Valley Community College; Donna

Williams-Barrett, Georgia Science Teachers Association and Fulton County Schools; and Christopher Wright, Drexel University.

The committee is also grateful for the efforts of the following authors who prepared background papers for the committee's use in drafting the report:

- Matthew Kloser, on the nature of the teacher's role in supporting student investigation;
- Joseph Michaelis, on the role of interest and motivation in the learning of science and engineering;
- Felicia Moore Mensah and Kristen Larson, on inclusive pedagogies for science investigation and engineering design;
- William Penuel and Brian Reiser, on designing science curriculum materials for three-dimensional learning;
- Senay Purzer, on epistemic, disciplinary practices in engineering and the integration of engineering and science in secondary classrooms;
- Victor Lee and Michelle Wilkerson, on the state of data and technology use to support learning for middle and high school students; and
- Dan Aladjem and Alisha Butler (Policy Studies Associates) who prepared a literature review to inform the study.

This Consensus Study Report was reviewed in draft form by individuals chosen for their diverse perspectives and technical expertise. The purpose of this independent review is to provide candid and critical comments that will assist the institution in making its published report as sound as possible and to make certain that the report meets institutional standards for objectivity, evidence, and responsiveness to the charge. The review comments and draft manuscript remain confidential to protect the integrity of the deliberative process.

We thank the following individuals for their review of this report: Mary M. Atwater, Department of Mathematics and Science Education, University of Georgia; Brenda L. Bass, University of Utah School of Medicine; Monica E. Cardella, Engineering Education, Purdue University; Dianne Chong, Assembly, Factory & Support Technology (retired), Boeing Research and Technology; Edith M. Flanigen (retired), Union Carbide Corporation, Honeywell UOP; Amelia Wenk Gotwals, Department of Teacher Education, Michigan State University; Carolyn Higgins, Warwick Public Schools, Warwick, Rhode Island; Adam Johnston, Department of Physics, Weber State University; Lauren J. Kaupp, Office of Curriculum, Instructional Design, State of Hawaii; Catherine Mackey, Science Program, Dawson Education Cooperative, Arkansas Department of Education; Scott McDonald, Krause Innovation Studio, Pennsylvania State University; Stephen L. Pruitt,

President's Office, Southern Region Education Board; Bruce Wellman, Olathe Northwest High School, Olathe, Kansas; Mark Windschitl, College of Education, University of Washington; Susan Gomez-Zweip, Department of Science Education, California State University, Long Beach.

Although the reviewers listed above provided many constructive comments and suggestions, they were not asked to endorse the content of the report nor did they see the final draft of the report before its release. The review of this report was overseen by Melanie Cooper, Colleges of Education and Natural Science, Michigan State University and Paul R. Gray, executive vice chancellor and provost (emeritus), University of California, Berkeley. They were responsible for making certain that an independent examination of this report was carried out in accordance with the standards of the National Academies and that all review comments were carefully considered. Responsibility for the final content rests entirely with the authoring committee and the National Academies.

Thanks are also due to the project staff. Kerry Brenner of the Board on Science Education (BOSE) directed the study and played a key role in the report drafting and review process. Amy Stephens (program officer, BOSE) and Tiffany Taylor (Christine Mirzayan science and technology policy fellow [2017] and research associate, BOSE) provided critical assistance in project direction, organizing the report, and revising the writing. Greg Pearson (scholar, National Academy of Engineering) contributed thoughtful insight and suggestions for the coverage of engineering within the report. Heidi Schweingruber (director, BOSE) provided infinite wisdom and oversight throughout the entire study. We are also extremely grateful to Natalie Nielson (consultant) who contributed to the writing of the report. We also thank Anne Simonis (Christine Mirzayan science and technology policy fellow [2018]) who assisted with information gathering during the report writing process. Coreetha Entzminger (former program assistant, BOSE) managed the first three meeting's logistical and administrative needs. Erik Saari (administrative assistant, Division on Engineering and Physical Sciences) stepped in to help with the administrative and logistical needs of the fourth committee meeting, and Jessica Covington (senior program assistant, BOSE) managed the rest of the study's logistical and administrative needs, along with manuscript preparation.

Finally, we thank Paula Whitacre (independent consultant) who provided invaluable editorial direction and Kirsten Sampson Snyder (Division of Behavioral and Social Sciences and Education) who expertly guided us through the National Academies review process. The committee also wishes to express its sincere appreciation to the National Academies Research Center staff for their assistance with fact checking the report.

Contents

Summary

It is essential for today's students to learn about science and engineering in order to make sense of the world around them and participate as informed members of a democratic society. The skills and ways of thinking that are developed and honed through engaging in scientific and engineering endeavors can be used to engage with evidence in making personal decisions, to participate responsibly in civic life, and to improve and maintain the health of the environment, as well as to prepare for careers that use science and technology.

The majority of Americans learn most of what they know about science and engineering as middle and high school students. During these years of rapid change for students' knowledge, attitudes, and interests, they can be engaged in learning science and engineering through schoolwork that piques their curiosity about the phenomena around them in ways that are relevant to their local surroundings and to their culture. Many decades of education research provide strong evidence for effective practices in teaching and learning of science and engineering. One of the effective practices that helps students learn is to engage in science investigation and engineering design. Broad implementation of science investigation and engineering design and other evidence-based practices in middle and high schools can help address present-day and future national challenges, including broadening access to science and engineering for communities who have traditionally been underrepresented and improving students' educational and life experiences.

The National Academies of Sciences, Engineering, and Medicine convened the Committee on Science Investigations and Engineering Design

Experiences for Grades 6–12, under the guidance of the Board on Science Education, to address the following statement of task:

> The committee will review research on science investigations and engineering design for middle and high school students conducted since publication of *America's Lab Report* (National Research Council, 2006) and use this research to inform the revision of the original report. The review of research will include research and evaluations of innovative approaches, such as computer modeling or use of large on-line data sets that have become more widely available since publication of the original report. The committee will provide guidance for designing and implementing science investigations and engineering design for middle and high school students that takes into account the new vision for science education embodied in the *Framework for K–12 Science Education* (National Research Council, 2012) and standards based upon it.

Over the past decade, there has been a shift in the thinking about the role of the teacher and about the nature of student work. Instead of receiving knowledge from the teacher, students make sense of phenomena through exploration, reflection, and discussion. Instead of students learning science content and methods for doing science separately, they engage simultaneously with three dimensions: science and engineering practices, disciplinary core ideas, and crosscutting concepts as part of curriculum, instruction, and assessment. These three dimensions and much of this approach were introduced in *A Framework for K–12 Science Education* (hereafter referred to as the *Framework*; National Research Council, 2012). Learning in the style described in the *Framework* is often referred to as three-dimensional learning: that is, learning where students incorporate aspects from all three dimensions as they make sense of the natural and engineered world around them. The *Framework's* presentation of engineering as part of what K–12 students should learn is another shift in the last decade. Instead of seeing engineering as separate from science, students can see the ways science and engineering each serve the other.

The current report revisits *America's Lab Report: Investigations in High School Science* (National Research Council, 2006) in order to consider its discussion of laboratory experiences and teacher and school readiness in an updated context. It considers how to engage today's middle and high school students in doing science and engineering through an analysis of evidence and examples. It provides guidance for teachers, administrators, creators of instructional resources, and leaders in teacher professional learning on how to support students as they make sense of phenomena, gather and analyze data/information, construct explanations and design solutions, and communicate reasoning to self and others during science investigation and engineering design. It provides guidance to help educators get started with designing, implementing, and assessing investigation and design. Science investigation and engineering design are driven by questions about phenomena and engineering challenges and include multiple connected coherent experiences. These experiences allow students to engage deeply with the ideas and ways of thinking used in science and engineering and to make sense of themselves as learners as they draw on their own ideas and identities in the process of doing science and engineering.

Some previous attempts to reform science education focused on the students expected to join the future scientific and technical workforce and intentionally or unintentionally excluded others. This report recognizes the extensive inequities in science education that currently exist and acknowledges that while some previous attempts to improve science education have *called* for science for all students, they ultimately failed to meet *all* students, teachers, schools, and districts where they were. Many previous reform efforts incorrectly assumed that all students and all schools begin at an even starting point for change, but this is generally not the case. For example, because schools that served primarily students of low social and economic status began at a disadvantage, they were not in a position to fully benefit from reform efforts. Likewise, many students from groups underrepresented in science and engineering have not had the advantages of students from other groups. Therefore, providing equal resources to students and to schools that started out at a disadvantage could not result in equitable outcomes. Equitable outcomes require development and use of instructional strategies intended to make education more inclusive of students from many types of diverse backgrounds and cultures, as well as attention to distribution of resources and the ways educators think about student access, inclusion, engagement, motivation, interest, and identity.

Engaging all students in learning science and engineering through investigation and design will require a system that supports instructional approaches that (1) situate phenomena in culturally and locally relevant contexts, (2) provide a platform for developing meaningful understanding of three-dimensional science and engineering knowledge, and (3) provide an opportunity for the use of evidence to make sense of the natural and engineered world beyond the classroom. These are big changes to the status quo and will require significant and sustained work by teachers, administrators, leaders in professional learning, those designing instructional resources and assessment tools, as well as policy makers. This report discusses key aspects that need to be considered to improve experiences for all students as they investigate science and engineering in the classroom, in the laboratory, in the field, online, and beyond their time in school.

CONCLUSIONS AND RECOMMENDATIONS

Conclusions

In reviewing the evidence, the committee noted many factors and contexts that influence the learning of science and engineering in middle and high schools today and made the following conclusions and recommendations.

CONCLUSION 1: Engaging students in learning about natural phenomena and engineering challenges via science investigation and engineering design increases their understanding of how the world works. Investigation and design are more effective for supporting learning than traditional teaching methods. They engage students in doing science and engineering, increase their conceptual knowledge of science and engineering, and improve their reasoning and problem-solving skills.

CONCLUSION 2: Teachers can use students' curiosity to motivate learning by choosing phenomena and design challenges that are interesting and engaging to students, including those that are locally and/or culturally relevant. Science investigation and engineering design give middle and high school students opportunities to engage in the wider world in new ways by providing agency for them to develop questions and establish the direction for their own learning experiences.

CONCLUSION 3: Science investigation and engineering design entail a dramatic shift in the classroom dynamic. Students ask questions, participate in discussions, create artifacts and models to show their reasoning, and continuously reflect and revise their thinking. Teachers guide, frame, and facilitate the learning environment to allow student engagement and learning.

CONCLUSION 4: Inclusive pedagogies can support the learning of all students by situating differences as assets, building on students' identities and life experiences, and leveraging local and dynamic views of cultural life for the study of science and engineering.

CONCLUSION 5: Centering classes on science investigation and engineering design means that teachers provide multiple opportunities for students to demonstrate their reasoning and show understanding of scientific explanations about the natural world. Providing opportunities for teachers to observe student learning and embed assessment into the flow of learning experiences allows students as well as teachers to reflect on learning.

CONCLUSION 6: Instructional resources are key to facilitating the careful sequencing of phenomena and design challenges across units and grade levels in order to increase coherence as students become increasingly sophisticated science and engineering learners.

CONCLUSION 7: Teachers' ability to guide student learning can be improved by preservice education on strategies for investigation and design as well as opportunities for professional learning at many stages of their in-service teaching careers. Intentionally designed and sustained professional learning experiences that extend over months can help teachers prepare, implement, and refine approaches to investigation and design.

CONCLUSION 8: Engaging students in investigation and design requires attention to facilities, budgets, human resources, technology, equipment, and supplies. These resources can impact the quantity and quality of investigation and design experiences in the classroom and the students who have access to them.

CONCLUSION 9: Changes in the teaching and learning of science and engineering in middle and high schools are occurring within a complex set of systems. Classroom-level change is impacted in various and sometimes conflicting ways by issues related to funding and resources, local community priorities, state standards, graduation requirements, college admission requirements, and local, state, and national assessments. When incentives do not align, successful implementation of investigation and design is hindered.

CONCLUSION 10: There are notable inequities within and among schools today in terms of access to educational experiences that engage students in science investigation and engineering design. Many policies and structures tend to perpetuate these inequities, such as disparities in facilities and teacher expectations, experiences, and qualifications across schools and districts.

Recommendations

RECOMMENDATION 1: Science investigation and engineering design should be the central approach for teaching and learning science and engineering.

- Teachers should arrange their instruction around interesting phenomena or design projects and use their students' curiosity to engage them in learning science and engineering.

- Administrators should support teachers in implementation of science investigation and engineering design. This may include providing teachers with appropriate instructional resources, opportunities to engage in sustained professional learning experiences and work collaboratively to design learning sequences, choose phenomena with contexts relevant to their students, and time to engage in and learn about inclusive pedagogies to promote equitable participation in science investigation and engineering design.

RECOMMENDATION 2: Instruction should provide multiple embedded opportunities for students to engage in three-dimensional science and engineering performances.

- Teachers should monitor student learning through ongoing, embedded, and post-instruction assessment as students make sense of phenomena and design solutions to challenges.
- Teachers should use formative assessment tasks and discourse strategies to encourage students to share their ideas, and to develop and revise their ideas with other students.
- Teachers should use evidence from formative assessment to guide instructional choices and guide students to reflect on their own learning.

RECOMMENDATION 3: Instructional resources to support science investigation and engineering design need to use approaches consistent with knowledge about how students learn and consistent with the *Framework* to provide a selection of options suitable for many local conditions.

- Teachers and designers of instructional resources should work in teams to develop coherent sequences of lessons that include phenomena carefully chosen to engage students in the science or engineering to be learned. Instructional resources should include information on strategies and options teachers can use to craft and implement lessons relevant to their students' backgrounds, cultures, and place.
- Administrators should provide teachers with access to high-quality instructional resources, space, equipment, and supplies that support the use of *Framework*-aligned approaches to science investigation and engineering design.

RECOMMENDATION 4: High-quality, sustained, professional learning opportunities are needed to engage teachers as professionals with effective evidence-based instructional practices and models for instruction in science and engineering. Administrators should identify and encourage participation in sustained and meaningful professional learning opportunities for teachers to learn and develop successful approaches to effective science and engineering teaching and learning.

- Professional development leaders should provide teachers with the opportunity to learn in the manner in which they are expected to teach, by using *Framework*-aligned methods during professional learning experiences. Teachers should receive feedback from peers and other experts while working throughout their career to improve their skills, knowledge, and dispositions with these instructional approaches.
- Professional development leaders should prepare and empower teachers to make informed and professional decisions about adapting lessons to their students and the local environment.
- Administrators and education leaders should provide opportunities for teachers to implement and reflect on the use of *Framework*-aligned approaches to teaching and learning.

RECOMMENDATION 5: Undergraduate learning experiences need to serve as models for prospective teachers, in which they experience investigation and design as learners.

- College and university faculty should design and teach science classes that model the use of evidence-based principles for learning and immerse students in *Framework*-aligned approaches to science and engineering learning.
- Faculty should design and teach courses on pedagogy of science and engineering that use instructional strategies consistent with the *Framework*.
- College and university administrators should support and incentivize design of new courses or redesign of existing courses that use evidence-based principles and align with the ideas of the *Framework*.

RECOMMENDATION 6: Administrators should take steps to address the deep history of inequities in which not all students have been offered a full and rigorous sequence of science and engineering learning opportunities, by implementing science investigation and engineering design approaches in all science courses for all students.

- School and district staff should systematically review policies that impact the ability to offer science investigation and engineering design opportunities to all students. They should monitor and analyze differences in course offerings and content between schools, as well as patterns of enrollment and success in science and engineering courses at all schools. This effort should include particular attention to differential student outcomes, especially in areas in which inequality and inequity have been well documented (e.g., gender, socioeconomic status, race, and culture). Administrators should use this information to construct specific, concrete, and positive plans to address the disparities.

- State and national legislatures and departments of education should provide additional resources to schools with significant populations of underserved students to broaden access/opportunity and allow all students to participate in science investigation and engineering design.

RECOMMENDATION 7: For all students to engage in meaningful science investigation and engineering design, the many components of the system must become better aligned. This will require changes to existing policies and procedures. As policies and procedures are revised, care must be taken not to exacerbate existing inequities.

- State, regional, and district leaders should commission and use valid and reliable summative assessment tools that mirror how teachers measure three-dimensional learning.
- States, regions, and districts should provide resources to support the implementation of investigation and engineering design-based approaches to science and engineering instruction across all grades and in all schools, and should track and manage progress toward full implementation. State, regional, and district leaders should ensure that the staff in their own offices who oversee science instruction or science educators have a deep knowledge of *Framework*-aligned approaches to teaching and learning.

1

Introduction

T he impacts of science and engineering are evident in how scientific and technological advances have proliferated and now permeate most aspects of life in the 21st century. It is increasingly important that all members of a democracy are able to rely on the skills developed and honed through engaging in scientific and engineering endeavors to make evidence-based decisions affecting a civic way of life. Additionally, learning how to construct explanations for the causes of phenomena[1] or designing evidence-based solutions to challenges can serve students well as a way of thinking about future personal and societal issues and needs. These students can then contribute to decisions, such as those about health care or about the use of engineering solutions to improve energy efficiency in the home and community.

Because of the focus on reading and mathematics at the elementary level and uneven access to outside-of-school science and engineering experiences, the majority of Americans learn most of what they know about science and engineering as middle and high school students (Pianta et al., 2007). *A Framework for K–12 Science Education* (hereafter referred to as the *Framework*; National Research Council, 2012) calls for educators to consider the progression of student learning of science and engineering from kindergarten through grade 12. The committee recognizes the key role that *Framework*-aligned instructional approaches should play in engaging and preparing elementary students, who have been shown to be capable

---

[1] Throughout this report, the term "phenomena" is used to refer to natural science events and processes as well as human-engineered solutions.

of learning and understanding surprisingly complex science and engineering ideas. As the focus of this committee is on the middle and high school years, we hope that others will take on future work that focuses on learning by younger students. In considering our charge, the committee recognizes the importance of attention to the middle and high school years as they are a key time to foster students' agency in their own learning in association with their developing identities, connections to the larger world, and thoughts for their futures (Meeus, 2011). Middle and high school students can become engaged with and identify with science and engineering in a practical and meaningful way through substantive experiences with doing science and engineering (Hirsch et al., 2007). These grades are generally the first time students have teachers and courses where the central focus is on science and engineering subjects. Learning how to strengthen their abilities to ask productive questions, analyze data, and design solutions helps students to make sense of the world around them and provides useful skills for gathering, evaluating, and engaging with evidence when they make decisions as adults. Students' school-based experiences during these important formative years can shape their future interactions with science and engineering, including the ways they interact with data and evidence in their daily lives, whether they choose to pursue additional educational opportunities in science, and the types of careers that they may choose to pursue (Maltese and Tai, 2010; Tai et al., 2006). In addition, learning science and engineering can contribute to their understanding of the world and enjoyment of life.

Many decades of education research provide strong evidence for effective practices in teaching and learning of science and engineering that can be used in teaching science and engineering (Blumenfeld et al., 1991; Duschl and Osborne, 2002; Elby, 2000; Gay, 2010; Krajcik, 2015; Ladson-Billings, 2006; Michaels and O'Connor, 2012; Miller and Krajcik, 2015; Reiser, 2004; Rosebery, Warren, and Conant, 1992; Watkins et al., 2018; Wild and Pfannkuch, 1999; Windschitl et al., 2012). Adoption of evidence-based practices in middle and high schools can help address present-day and future national challenges, including broadening access to science and engineering for communities who have traditionally been excluded or neglected, as well as fostering the development of students' ability to think critically, question deeply, engage with others to refine ideas together, and draw from evidence in all aspects of their educational and life experiences. As will be discussed in Chapter 5, educators have the opportunity to use instructional approaches that make learning more relevant, meaningful, and enduring for all students. Student-centered, inclusive approaches to science and engineering provide students with interesting and engaging opportunities. This report offers guidance on designing appropriate classroom experiences and how to prepare and support teachers in their implementation.

CURRENT CONTEXT OF SCIENCE EDUCATION

Recent years have seen advances in the understanding of how students learn that have contributed to changes in how science is taught. Learning research provides more information on what motivates students and how to foster deep engagement in learning science and engineering (Krapp and Prenzel, 2011). This report presents ways that science investigation and engineering design can provide students with learning opportunities where they use their knowledge and skills to engage in ongoing systems of exploration, production of artifacts, discussion, and reflection to facilitate deep conceptual understanding of the natural and constructed world. Science investigation and engineering design can allow students to participate in science as a social enterprise and help them to connect science and engineering concepts and principles to their own experiences and ideas. It should be noted that the term investigation is used in this report in a broader sense than the practice of "planning and carrying out investigations" described in the *Framework* (National Research Council, 2012). In this broad interpretation of investigation, students work together to ask questions and draw on evidence as they make sense of science and engineering and develop deeper understanding of the nature of their own learning and interests. Specific aspects of science investigation and engineering design are discussed in the later chapters of this report, for example, in Tables 4-2 and 5-1.

Many recent efforts to improve science education in schools are based on the ideas described in the *Framework* (National Research Council, 2012), which describes a way of teaching and learning science and engineering grounded in evidence from the education research literature. In this approach, students participate in science and engineering learning by making sense of phenomena through exploration, reflection, and discussion, in a process that involves the interactions of three dimensions[2] that are defined as

- science and engineering practices,
- disciplinary core ideas, and
- crosscutting concepts.

The 2006 precursor to the current study, *America's Lab Report: Investigations in High School Science* (National Research Council, 2006),

---

[2]The three dimensions of the *Framework* describe knowledge and practices scientists use to learn about the natural world and engineers use to build models and solutions (practices), ideas that apply across the disciplines of science such as patterns, structure/function, change, energy (crosscutting concepts) and important organizing concepts or key tools relevant to physical science, life science, earth and space science, or engineering, technology and applications of science (disciplinary core ideas).

is based on much of the same literature as the *Framework*, but does not use the same language about the three dimensions because it predates the *Framework* by about 6 years. *America's Lab Report* helped science educators shape their instruction by linking evidence-based teaching approaches to desired student outcomes. Over the past decade, there has been a shift in the way the education community thinks about the role of the teacher and about the nature of student work. In addition, the *Framework* brought engineering into the conversation as a fundamental discipline complementary to science that should be included in K–12 education. The centerpiece of the vision of the *Framework* is engaging students in making sense of phenomena and designing solutions to meet human needs, and that is the focus of this current report.

The current report revisits the issues discussed in *America's Lab Report*. It builds on the approach of the *Framework*, includes recent changes in thinking about science education, and provides guidance for classroom-based investigations and design projects and the role they should play in helping middle and high school students learn science and engineering. It expands the scope of *America's Lab Report* to include middle schools and engineering design as well as high school science.

THE IMPORTANCE OF EQUITY

As discussed further in Chapter 2, some previous attempts to reform science education focused on the students who were expected to become the future scientific and technical workforce and intentionally or unintentionally excluded others. Beginning in the late 1980s, reports began to include language about educating all students, but they fell short of providing strategies for inclusiveness or failed to recognize that not all students start from an equal footing. Many reform efforts did not consider the significant ways in which expectations and institutional structures would need to change in order to provide opportunity to all students, nor did they consider how the complex context outside of the classroom could limit efforts to make quality educational experiences and preparation for technical careers accessible to all. The way that society thinks about equity, especially in regard to race, gender, ethnicity, and disabilities, is undergoing a shift. These changes go beyond noting the increasing diversity of the country and especially the school-age population and extend to the recognition that concerted action is needed to include all students because of the growing recognition that the historical and current inequities of broader society are still reflected in schools and other institutional structures.

Our work attempts to explicitly recognize the extensive inequities in science education that currently exist and acknowledges that previous attempts to improve science education may have *called* for science for all students, but ultimately failed to meet *all* students, teachers, schools, and districts where they were. Many previous reform efforts incorrectly assumed that all students and all schools begin at an even starting point for change, but this is generally not the case for students from groups historically underrepresented in science and for students from families of low social and economic status. Students from these groups have not been in a position to fully benefit from reform efforts. Therefore, providing equal resources to students and to schools that started out at a disadvantage could not result in equitable outcomes. Equitable outcomes require attention to how people think about student access, inclusion, engagement, motivation, interest, and identity, and about the actions and investments required to achieve such outcomes.

This report includes information on using inclusive pedagogies to improve education so all students in all schools can fully participate in learning science and engineering through engaging in high-quality experiences with science investigation and engineering design to make sense of the natural and designed world. Inclusion is often discussed in relation to including special education students in general education classes, but our use of the term is much broader. This report uses the term "inclusive pedagogies" when discussing instructional strategies that are designed to make education more inclusive of students from many types of diverse backgrounds and cultures. Engagement in science investigation and engineering design can help to prepare students to better participate as informed members of society in daily decisions (such as those related to their own health care, the environment, and use of technology), to contribute to civic life of their community and government, and to prepare the next generation of science and engineering professionals. To ensure that these opportunities and pathways are open to all interested students, the committee addresses issues related to providing science investigation and engineering design to all students at all grade levels, including both boys and girls and those from all ethnic and racial groups, those who are English language learners, and those with disabilities. Mechanisms for ensuring these opportunities are available to all extends beyond the scope of this report and includes topics such as the decisions about which students attend which schools, the science learning experiences available to students before they enter middle school, and opportunities for outside-of-school experiences in science and engineering (National Research Council, 2009).

SCIENCE INVESTIGATION AND ENGINEERING DESIGN

Throughout this report, the committee addresses the rationale for engaging students in three-dimensional science and engineering performances in order to achieve three-dimensional science and engineering learning;

during these performances, students make sense of phenomena through exploration, reflection, and discussion that simultaneously involves science and engineering practices, disciplinary core ideas, and crosscutting concepts.[3] This approach draws on decades of research about how students learn (National Research Council, 2000, 2012). Involving and encouraging students to engage in productive struggle helps them make sense of the natural and engineered world—to know that not all questions lead to one clean or "right" answer, that development of multiple models can be useful for understanding a single phenomenon, and that most engineering challenges are amenable to multiple design solutions. Engaging in science investigation and engineering design can *challenge* students, and in doing so, result in an enduring understanding of science and engineering and of the natural and designed world. Teachers, administrators, professional development providers, and curriculum developers can benefit from guidance on how to implement and support these approaches to learning science and engineering. Meaningful and ongoing teacher professional learning focused on experiences specific to three-dimensional learning via science investigation and engineering design, along with support from administrators, professional development providers, and policy makers, can provide the resources and conditions necessary for change.

Consistent with the evidence-based vision for science education set forth in the *Framework*, our committee envisions students asking questions as they work to make sense of phenomena and human problems. Students ask questions as part of sustained and relevant investigation to acquire the ability to make sense of the natural and designed world beyond the classroom. They can apply this experience to the challenges they encounter and issues they value in their daily lives to participate in discussion and action related to the societal complexities important to a democracy.

Engaging all students in learning science and engineering through investigation and design benefits from a system that supports instructional approaches that (1) choose phenomena that are interesting to students, for example those that can be examined in contexts relevant to students; (2) provide a platform for developing understanding of three-dimensional science and engineering knowledge; and (3) provide an opportunity for using evidence to make sense of the natural and engineered world beyond the classroom. These approaches can build on students' natural curiosity

---

[3] Three-dimensional science learning is used here in the same way as the National Research Council report *Developing Assessment for the Next Generation Science Standards* to refer to the integration of these dimensions; that report explained, "It describes not the process of learning, but the kind of thinking and understanding that science education should foster" (National Research Council, 2014, p. 2). Although we do not explicitly state that investigation and design is three-dimensional each time we use the terms, this report considers the inclusion of three-dimensional learning to be an essential aspect of their definitions.

and wonder and support students in developing a useful understanding of the nature of science. Implementation of investigation and design in the classroom using the identified instructional approaches will require significant and sustained work by teachers, teacher preparation programs, and administrators who can facilitate professional learning experiences. Professional learning that is designed to be coherent, sustained, and consistent with science professional learning standards can equip teachers to effectively engage students in science and engineering performances consistent with how students learn. In this report, we provide guidance for the many interconnected stakeholders in efforts to improve middle and high school science and engineering.

CHARGE TO THE COMMITTEE

The Amgen Foundation and the Carnegie Corporation of New York requested that the National Academies of Sciences, Engineering, and Medicine convene a committee to revisit the 2006 report of the National Research Council, *America's Lab Report: Investigations in High School Science*. The committee was asked to consider the influence of the 2012 publication of the *Framework*, the 2013 introduction of the *Next Generation Science Standards: For States, By States*[4] (NGSS Lead States, 2013), and the expanded evidence base in this field over the last decade. Additionally, this committee was asked to consider the middle school context, as opposed to just high school, and to explore the ways that both engineering and science are taught to students at these grade levels. The National Academies convened the Committee on Science Investigations and Engineering Design Experiences in Grades 6–12, under the guidance of the Board on Science Education, to address the following charge (see Box 1-1).

The landscape of science education has changed since publishing the original report in 2006. The approaches to teaching and learning science described in the *Framework* have shifted the conversation toward a larger vision of what and how students should learn in order to engage in science. However, in many ways the perspectives of the committee who authored the 2006 report remain true today. The 2006 *America's Lab Report* study noted a growing shift away from viewing laboratory experiences as separate from the flow of classroom science instruction in which students engage in exercises that demonstrate already-proven facts. They concluded that more

---

[4]The Next Generation Science Standards were developed through a state-led process where state policy leaders, higher-education leaders, K–12 teachers, the science and business community and others worked together to agree on science standards that describe a coherent progression of performance expectations for students to learn. They used the vision and the three dimensions of the *Framework* to inform their work.

BOX 1-1
Committee Charge

The committee will review research on science investigation and engineering design for middle and high school students conducted since publication of *America's Lab Report* (National Research Council, 2006) and use this research to inform the revision of the original report. The review of research will include research and evaluations of innovative approaches, such as computer modeling or use of large on-line data sets that have become more widely available since publication of the original report. The committee will provide guidance for designing and implementing science investigations and engineering design for middle and high school students that takes into account the new vision for science education embodied in *A Framework for K–12 Science Education* (National Research Council, 2012) and standards based upon it.

---

integrated laboratories were needed and described necessary steps to initiate that change away from traditional standalone laboratory exercises. In the first chapter of *America's Lab Report*, that committee explicitly addressed the many possible meanings of the phrase "science laboratories," which appeared in their charge. To clarify the scope of their work, they used the term "laboratory experiences," which they defined as follows:

> Laboratory experiences provide opportunities for students to interact directly with the material world (or with data drawn from the material world), using the tools, data collection techniques, models and theories of science (National Research Council, 2006, p. 31).

They then provided five student activities that would qualify as laboratory experiences: (1) physical manipulation of real-world materials or systems, (2) interaction with simulations and models, (3) interaction with data drawn from the real world, (4) access to large databases, and (5) remote access to scientific instruments. All of these activities can be included in science investigation or engineering design if they are components of examining phenomena or designing solutions in order to learn science and engineering.

The current committee is charged with providing an update to that 2006 report, and thus, we return to this definition in order to frame the scope of our work. Our charge addresses not *laboratories*, but *science investigation and engineering design*—this change in language represents the significant shift toward thinking about science education as described in the *Framework*. Work in laboratories is still relevant but it is a component of the larger investigation or design and not a standalone activity. The

Framework (p. 45) stated that when investigating, ". . . scientists determine what needs to be measured; observe phenomena; plan experiments, programs of observation, and methods of data collection; build instruments; engage in disciplined fieldwork; and identify sources of uncertainty." In bringing the concept of investigations into the classroom, the report further stated (p. 25) that students must "be actively involved in the kinds of learning opportunities that classroom research suggests are important for (1) their understanding of science concepts, (2) their identities as learners of science, and (3) their appreciation of science practices and crosscutting concepts." Investigation is *purposeful*: it is driven by questions about phenomena and engineering challenges. Through engagement in three-dimensional learning via science investigation and engineering design, students make sense of the world around them and also learn about themselves as learners. Because of the inclusion of engineering in the *Framework*, this committee's charge includes engineering design as well as more traditional science topics and disciplines. Learning about and experiencing the way that engineers study the world and work to design, develop, and test solutions to meet human needs is another tool for engaging middle and high school students in science and engineering and helping them to see relevance to their lives.

INFORMATION GATHERING

To address our charge, the committee evaluated the existing evidence on middle and high school science and engineering. We approached the task iteratively, gathering information in multiple ways and cycles to inform discussion and deliberation. In building upon the work of the 2006 report, the committee held three public fact-finding meetings, including a public workshop, and commissioned a literature review and six papers[5] prepared by experts in the field, as described below. In preparing this report, we carefully considered all these sources of information in light of our own extensive experience and expertise in education. (See Appendix E for committee members and staff biographical sketches.)

Early in the deliberations, the committee decided that an initial mapping of the secondary science education landscape over the last decade would be helpful in laying the groundwork for the study. Therefore, we consulted Policy Study Associates, Inc. to prepare and present a review of the literature, highlighting research areas relevant to the committee's charge in science and engineering. From the literature reviewed, Policy Study Associates, Inc. identified the following notable strands where they were able to find a body of literature to share with the committee: the potential

---

[5]The commissioned papers are available at http://sites.nationalacademies.org/dbasse/bose/science-investigations-and-design/index.htm [December 2018].

of inquiry-based, laboratory instruction to increase students' knowledge, interest, and motivation for science; strategies to implement laboratory science; engagement of students from underserved and underrepresented communities; and teacher education and professional development. Additionally, at its first fact-finding meeting, the following individuals informed the committee about the core needs of practitioners and the current state of the field: Tiffany Neill, Council of State Science Supervisors and Oklahoma State Department of Education; Al Byers, National Science Teachers Association; and Donna Williams-Barrett, Georgia Science Teachers Association and Fulton County Schools.

Prior to the second meeting, the committee wrestled with the ways in which issues related to equity would be represented in the report. The committee took several steps to expand information within this domain and invited three researchers to present evidence for how to attend to equity in middle and high school science and engineering. Christopher Wright (Drexel University) presented work on the link between engineering and identity in students of color, Rowhea Elmesky (Washington University in St. Louis) discussed the role of science education within culturally marginalized and economically disadvantaged student populations, and Kimberly Scott (Arizona State University) discussed the representation of girls in STEM. Additionally, at the second meeting, Richard Duschl (Pennsylvania State University) shared his expertise on investigations and the nature of science with the committee. Insights from these presentations were used to inform the commissioning of three papers on the following topics: interest and motivation in the learning of science and engineering (Joseph Michaelis, University of Wisconsin–Madison), inclusive pedagogy and investigations (Felicia Mensah and Kristen Larson, Teachers College, Columbia University), and engineering approaches to problem solving and design (Senay Purzer, Purdue University).

Between the second and third meetings, the committee identified other areas in which members could benefit from additional information on science and engineering education in U.S. middle and high schools. This resulted in the commissioning of three final papers on (1) the nature of the teacher's role (Matthew Kloser, University of Notre Dame), (2) the shifts in the design of curricula in the era of the *Framework* (Bill Penuel, University of Colorado Boulder, and Brian Reiser, Northwestern University), and (3) the potential affordances through the use of data and technology in investigations (Michelle Wilkerson, University of California, Berkeley, and Victor Lee, Utah State University). At its third and final fact-finding meeting, the committee held a public workshop (see Appendix D for the agenda) where invited presenters and audience participants shared their expert knowledge on a variety of factors influencing science investigation and engineering design in middle and high school. The public workshop was a pivotal component of the information-gathering process. Taken together, all of these efforts enabled the committee to address the charge with fidelity.

At its fourth meeting, the committee carefully vetted and discussed overall findings and conclusions. Consequently, the content of the report and its conclusions and recommendations are the result of an extensive process designed to provide guidance to the field.

In carrying out our charge, the committee examined and synthesized research on the teaching and learning of science and engineering, with a focus on student engagement in doing science and engineering. The committee also consulted the literature and theoretical work on how people learn and adolescent development. In some areas studies were scarce, and the committee therefore examined related research that was not specific to science and engineering or included students younger or older than grades 6–12. We also drew on the broader literature on professional learning, curriculum, assessment, leadership, community connections, education policy, and school reform and improvement efforts.

The bodies of research we reviewed comprise many types of studies, from qualitative case studies, ethnographic and field studies, and interview studies to large-scale surveys and randomized controlled trials. When weighing the evidence from this research, we adopted the stance of an earlier committee that "a wide variety of legitimate scientific designs are available for education research" (National Research Council, 2002, p. 6). According to *Scientific Research in Education*, to be scientific,

> . . . the design must allow direct, empirical investigation of an important question, [use methods that permit direct investigation of the question], account for the context in which the study is carried out, align with a conceptual framework, reflect careful and thorough reasoning, and disclose results to encourage debate in the scientific community.

Recognizing the value of many types of research, we used different types of evidence to achieve different aims related to our charge. We did not automatically exclude studies with certain designs from consideration; rather, we examined the appropriateness of the design to the questions posed, whether the research methods were sufficiently explicated, and whether conclusions were warranted based on the design and available evidence. To provide descriptive summaries and conclusions about the students and teachers involved in science and engineering education in grades 6–12, we relied on all types of research and on state- and national-level survey and administrative data. Descriptive evidence often is essential for understanding current conditions, in preparation for contemplating change. Identifying what changes are needed, however, requires research that goes beyond description to indicate what new outcomes would be expected to emerge as a result of the changes being considered.

Regardless of the methods used, we considered the quality of the study design and the fidelity with which that design was carried out. To gain additional information, the committee also sought out richly descriptive work. Although case studies and other interpretive work did not lead us to draw causal conclusions, they did help us understand the roles of students, teachers, assessment, curricula, and technology.

CONTENT OF THE REPORT

This report provides guidance for middle and high school teachers, administrators, curriculum designers, professional development providers, and others. It provides ideas and resources they can use to help middle and high school students build on their inherent curiosity about the natural world so that they can learn via engaging in science and engineering to investigate phenomena and design solutions to human challenges. The report focuses on ways to make this education accessible to all students, especially those who are members of groups that have been previously excluded. It explains why doing science and engineering is beneficial for students and details productive attributes of inclusive learning environments, curricula, and instructional approaches that use relevance to foster student engagement in science investigation and engineering design. It builds upon *A Framework for K–12 Science Education* (National Research Council, 2012) and its three dimensions: science and engineering practices, disciplinary core ideas, and crosscutting concepts. Immersing students in the doing of science and engineering affords invaluable opportunities for students to deepen their knowledge of science and engineering practices, crosscutting concepts, and disciplinary core ideas in ways that go far beyond the memorization of facts or vocabulary, or the repetition of prescribed laboratory exercises. Students learn to use the three dimensions together to make sense of the complex world around them in a way that is inclusive and relevant to their daily lives. This learning can help them grow into adults who are able to make confident decisions based on a deep understanding of the evolving world around them.

This report explores many issues related to science investigation and engineering design to provide a resource for teachers, professional development providers, teacher education programs, administrators, policy makers, and others so that they can use this information to improve experiences for all students as they investigate science and engineering in the classroom, in the laboratory, in the field, online, and beyond students' time in school.

Chapter 2 describes the current context of science and engineering education in middle and high schools, including the lack of equal and equitable access and opportunity for all students to engage in science investigation and engineering design. In Chapter 3, we address how students learn and what motivates them. Chapter 4 describes the nature of putting science investigation and engineering design at the center of middle and high school classes. Chapter 5 focuses on instruction and how the role of the teacher has shifted, whereas Chapter 6 delves into instructional resources. Chapter 7 discusses professional learning for teachers engaged in this new way of supporting student learning, and in Chapter 8, we look at issues related to space, time, resources, and safety. Chapter 9 discusses the educational systems that impact science education reform. The report ends with conclusions and recommendations for practice and questions for researchers to develop better information to guide future decisions.

REFERENCES

Blumenfeld, P., Soloway, E., Marx, R., Krajcik, J.S., Guzdial, M., and Palincsar, A. (1991). Motivating project-based learning: Sustaining the doing, supporting the learning. *Educational Psychologist, 26*(3 & 4), 369–398.

Duschl, R.A., and Osborne, J.F. (2002). Supporting and promoting argumentation discourse in science education. *Studies in Science Education, 38*, 39–72.

Elby, A. (2000). What students' learning of representations tells us about constructivism. *The Journal of Mathematical Behavior, 19*(4), 481–502.

Gay, G. (2010). *Culturally Responsive Teaching: Theory, Research, and Practice* (2nd ed.). New York: Teachers College Press.

Hirsch, L.S., Carpinelli, J.D., Kimmel, J., Rockland, R., and Bloom, J. (2007). *The Differential Effects of Pre-Engineering Curricula on Middle School Students' Attitudes to and Knowledge of Engineering Careers.* Presented at the 37th ASEE/IEEE Frontiers in Education Conference, Milwaukee. Available: https://ieeexplore.ieee.org/stamp/stamp.jsp?arnumber=4417918 [September 2018].

Krajcik, J.S. (2015). Three-dimensional instruction: Using a new type of teaching in the science classroom. *Science and Children, 53*(3), 6–8.

Krapp, A., and Prenzel, M. (2011). Research on interest in science: Theories, methods, and findings. *International Journal of Science Education, 33*(1), 27–50.

Ladson-Billings, G. (2006). Yes, but how do we do it? Practicing culturally relevant pedagogy. In J. Landsman and C.W. Lewis (Eds.), *White Teachers/Diverse Classrooms: A Guide to Building Inclusive Schools, Promoting High Expectations and Eliminating Racism* (pp. 29–42). Sterling, VA: Stylus.

Maltese, A.V., and Tai, R.H. (2010). Eyeballs in the fridge: Sources of early interest in science. *International Journal of Science Education, 32*(5), 669–685.

Meeus, W. (2011). The study of adolescent identity formation 2000–2010: A review of longitudinal research. *Journal of Research on Adolescence, 21*(1), 75–94.

Michaels, S., and O'Connor, C. (2012). *Talk Science Primer.* Available: https://inquiryproject.terc.edu/shared/pd/TalkScience_Primer.pdf [September 2018].

Miller, E., and Krajcik, J. (2015). Reflecting on instruction to promote alignment to the NGSS and equity. In O. Lee, E. Miller, and R. Januszyk (Eds.), *Next Generation Science Standards: All Standards, All Students.* Arlington, VA: National Science Teachers Association.

National Research Council. (2000). *How People Learn: Brain, Mind, Experience, and School: Expanded Edition.* Washington, DC: National Academy Press.

National Research Council. (2002). *Scientific Research in Education.* Washington, DC: National Academy Press.

National Research Council. (2006). *America's Lab Report: Investigations in High School Science.* Washington, DC: The National Academies Press.

National Research Council. (2009). *Learning Science in Informal Environments: People, Places, and Pursuits.* Washington, DC: The National Academies Press.

National Research Council. (2012). *A Framework for K-12 Science Education: Practices, Crosscutting Concepts, and Core Ideas.* Washington, DC: The National Academies Press.

National Research Council. (2014). *Developing Assessments for the Next Generation Science Standards.* Committee on Developing Assessments of Science Proficiency in K–12. Board on Testing and Assessment and Board on Science Education, J.W. Pellegrino, M.R. Wilson, J.A. Koenig, and A.S. Beatty, Editors. Division of Behavioral and Social Sciences and Education. Washington, DC: The National Academies Press.

NGSS Lead States. (2013). *Next Generation Science Standards: For States, By States.* Washington, DC: The National Academies Press.

Pianta, R.C., Belsky, J., Houts, R., Morrison, F., and the National Institute of Child Health and Human Development Early Child Care Research Network. (2007). Opportunities to learn in America's elementary classrooms. *Science, 315*(5820), 1795–1796.

Reiser, B.J. (2004). Scaffolding complex learning: The mechanisms of structuring and problematizing student work. *The Journal of the Learning Sciences, 13*(3), 273–304.

Rosebery, A., Warren, B., and Conant, F. (1992). Appropriating scientific discourse: Findings from language minority classrooms. *The Journal of the Learning Sciences, 2,* 61–94.

Tai, R.H., Liu, C.Q., Maltese, A.V., and Fan, X. (2006). Planning early for careers in science. *Science, 312*(5777), 1143–1144.

Watkins, J., Hammer, D., Radoff, J., Jaber, L.Z., and Phillips, A.M. (2018). Positioning as not-understanding: The value of showing uncertainty for engaging in science. *Journal of Research in Science Teaching.* doi: 10.1002/tea.21431.

Wild, C.J., and Pfannkuch, M. (1999). Statistical thinking in empirical inquiry (with discussion). *International Statistical Review, 67*(3), 223–265.

Windschitl, M., Thompson, J., Braaten, M., and Stroupe, D. (2012). Proposing a core set of instructional practices and tools for teachers of science. *Science Education, 96*(5), 878–903.

2

K–12 Science Education Past and Present: The Changing Role and Focus of Investigations

S cience became a formal focus of the curriculum in the late 19th century to address changing societal contexts and subsequent concerns, such as communicable diseases in densely populated areas and manufacturing changes spurred by the Industrial Revolution (DeBoer, 1991). Ever since that time, the goals and focus of K–12 science education have periodically shifted in response to changing societal context. Through these changes, the laboratory has remained a constant feature of science education and has traditionally been used to develop students' inductive reasoning, provide experiences for conducting observations of nature and quantitative laboratory work, and facilitate students' understanding of the nature of scientific investigations and the generation of scientific knowledge (DeBoer, 1991).

As we discuss in this chapter, recent developments in K–12 science education represent a significant departure from previous reform efforts. These current efforts draw extensively on research from the learning sciences, cognitive psychology, and education as they aim to convey the nature of science and engineering about how scientists and engineers think and work. Science investigation and engineering design as the central approach for teaching and learning science and engineering in middle and high schools is compatible with both the current reform efforts and what is known about how students learn. When investigations are at the core of science instruction, all students engage in the three-dimensional learning described in *A Framework for K–12 Science Education* (hereafter referred to as the *Framework*; National Research Council, 2012) in which they engage with scientific and engineering practices, crosscutting concepts, and disciplinary core ideas. Foregrounding investigation and design is in keeping with the current efforts that intentionally focus on all students regardless of their race,[1] ethnicity, gender, socioeconomic status, level of English proficiency, or disability status.

Although this more research-based and inclusive approach to science education represents a marked shift from the past and a hopeful direction for the future, the structures and approaches of earlier eras that focused on preparing the future technical workforce and concentrated more on educating students who were socioeconomically advantaged (from historical/cultural perspectives, this would mean white) and/or identified as gifted still constrain today's students and today's reform. In this chapter, we provide an overview of some features of science education and science education reform, the greater focus over time on making that education more equitable, and the recent shifts toward standards based on the *Framework* (National Research Council, 2012) that frame learning around engaging students in the three dimensions of science and engineering performance. We also identify some implications for equity and opportunities to promote more inclusiveness in science and engineering education.

A BRIEF HISTORY OF THE GOALS OF K–12 SCIENCE EDUCATION AND ROLE OF INVESTIGATIONS

There are several traditional, prevalent, and often unquestioned views about education in the United States: Individuals can succeed if they work hard and the provision of a free public education is a great equalizer, with the vehicle for upward mobility and betterment chief among them (Giroux, 1989). A critical examination of U.S. education, both historically and contemporarily, shows these perceptions about the utility of public education are realities for some but are unattainable aspirations for many. For example, many jobs in science, technology, engineering, and mathematics (STEM)[2] fields require postsecondary (or specialized) education. STEM jobs are the fastest growing sector in the United States, and the national average wage for all STEM occupations was $87,570 in 2015, nearly double that for non-STEM occupations (Fayer, Lacey, and Watson, 2017). Consequently,

---

[1] Throughout the report, the committee attempts to use terms for racial and ethnic groups that reflect the terms used in the literature, reference, or study being discussed. For example, the National Assessment of Educational Progress (NAEP) uses white, black, Asian/Pacific Islander, and Hispanic to describe specific population groups so when we discuss NAEP data we also use those terms. The committee recognizes that there are notable disparities within specific population groups (e.g., Asian and Pacific Islanders) and that the use of these groups and terms raises many issues that extend beyond the scope of our work.

[2] This report focuses on science and engineering, in keeping with the *Framework* and the NGSS. However, other components of STEM such as mathematics and computer science are, of course, relevant to carrying out investigation and design.

securing a STEM job could contribute greatly to upward mobility and betterment. However, the reality of who has access to high-quality education
in order to prepare and compete for these jobs substantially differs from
the prevalent belief that these job opportunities are equally available to all.

The existing societal contexts at the time that many far-reaching decisions were made included a society that was hierarchically structured by
factors, such as socioeconomics, race, gender, and language. This impacted
the design of education in the United States in ways that meant not all
students were served equally (Webb, 2006). It was not the intent to include
everyone; subsequently, the education system excluded and marginalized
populations. Although historians of science education often describe reforms with an emphasis on their content, these reforms did not exist in isolation from the society in which they occurred. The inequalities, inequities,
exclusion, and marginalization of populations that existed in society, and
in education generally, also permeated science education: this was operative
then and it is operative now. The inequalities and inequities, intentionally
produced throughout the history of U.S. education, endure and are ever-
present challenges for realizing the *Framework*-guided vision for science
education in the 21st century for which inclusion is a goal. A critical view
of the current state of affairs indicates science education is not inclusive and
more work remains, but a brief review of history shows progress.

Inclusiveness and Equity over Time

An examination of the history of science education in the United States
shows that although inequality and inequity have been hallmarks of education and subsequently science education throughout U.S. history, they went
unacknowledged in science education reform until the mid-1980s. Early
formal science instruction was for whites only.[3] In the mid to late 1800s,
education was initially available and accessible only to the wealthy, but later
expanded to include the poor for the purposes of socialization and vocational
skill development. For a brief period during Reconstruction, after the Civil
War to 1877, the education system included blacks, but what blacks could
study and resources to fund those schools were severely limited (DuBois
and Dill, 1911; Lee and Slaughter-Defoe, 1995). Special schools designed
to assimilate Native Americans also existed during this time (Webb, 2006).

In a similar vein, the recommended directives for science curriculum
and instruction from the early to mid-1900s—and efforts to implement

---

[3] Tolley (1996, 2014) contended that educators in the late 18th and early 19th centuries
deemed science as an appropriate study for girls. Educators and others viewed the study of
science as preparing girls for their social roles of mother, wife, and teacher; this was in lieu of
the study of classics, which was prominently valued and reserved for boys.

those directives—were targeted at those who were recognized as citizens and entitled to the full rights of citizenship, to the exclusion of all others. Groups viewed as incapable of benefitting from educational advances were relegated to separate schools and less ambitious educational goals. For example, blacks were educated mostly in schools established by northern missionary organizations, foundations, and formerly enslaved African Americans. The manual training model, similar to present-day vocational tracks, dominated their education during this time (Anderson, 1978, 1990; Lee and Slaughter-Defoe, 1995; Webb, 2006). Government-sponsored boarding schools and on-reservation day schools for Native Americans sought to assimilate Native Americans into white culture (Webb, 2006). In these schools, academic subjects and religious instruction constituted half of the day and vocational and agricultural training comprised the other half (Hale, 2002). Laws and policies allowed and buttressed such unequal and inequitable education until the landmark *Brown v. Board of Education* decision in 1954 ushered in a new era.

Although the passage of the Civil Rights Act of 1964 and the Elementary and Secondary Education Act of 1965 facilitated the desegregation of schools, racial segregation of schools continued into the 1970s, with whites receiving an education of higher quality (Orfield and Lee, 2004). Because of differences in access to resources and quality instruction, blacks and Hispanics were among the groups who did not enjoy the full measure of positive results from science curriculum reforms in the 1970s. Only in the 1980s, with the emergence of *Science for All Americans* (American Association for the Advancement of Science, 1989), was the inclusive goal of "science for all" made explicit; however, as we discuss below under "Inclusiveness and Equity over Time," this goal has not yet become reality.

Many significant and historic events have influenced science education. The imprint of the emphases and efforts in more recent times are readily evident in present-day science education. These events include the Cold War, launching of Sputnik, standards-based reform movement, and federal policy such as the *No Child Left Behind Act*. Even though the content of these reforms are featured, it is important to note these events and their impact on science education did not significantly ameliorate the seemingly intractable exclusion, inequality, and inequity related to certain populations. The inequities and inequalities persisted throughout changes and reforms, impacting the parents and grandparents of today's middle and high school students.

In 1946, President Truman created the President's Scientific Research Board (DeBoer, 1991). Declaring science as paramount to the military strength and economic prosperity of the nation, the board advanced recommendations to remedy personnel shortages in the sciences at all levels of education with college/university a major priority, promote high-quality precollege science programs that would foster an early interest in science and increase the pool of potential scientists, and develop an appreciation and understanding of science among the general populace. These recommendations gave rise to a science curriculum that most closely resembles today's structure of general science courses in the disciplines with requirements including 1 year of general physical science, 1 year of general biology, and 1 year of general science for all, and 3 years of specialized study for students with an aptitude in science (DeBoer, 1991).

Curricula developed by scientists and science education faculty initially featured the content areas of physics, biology, and chemistry demarcated in the previous era's formalization of science curriculum. They included laboratory experiments and student laboratory guides, with the goal of using the laboratory to facilitate student understanding about the nature of scientific investigations and the generation of scientific knowledge. Later, the National Science Foundation (NSF) funded other curriculum projects in earth science, engineering, physical sciences, and elementary science; these projects followed the logic of the earlier curriculum efforts.

The influence of this science education curriculum reform movement continued into the 1970s, when the discourse in science education shifted from understanding the structures and principles of the scientific disciplines to developing scientific literacy. Scientific literacy gained prominence when the National Science Teachers Association (1971) declared it to be the most important goal of science education. Scientific literacy involved people's uses of science—its content, processes, and related values—to make everyday decisions as they interacted with the world around them and with others in the world.

Science Education and Investigations in the Era of Standards-Based Reform[4]

The standards-based reform movement arose from the report *A Nation at Risk* (National Commission on Excellence in Education, 1983). During this era, several national science education reform documents identified broad goals for science education that were eventually reflected in many state curricula as subject area learning standards. These documents include *Science for All Americans* (American Association for the Advancement of Science, 1989) and *Benchmarks for Science Literacy* (American Association for the Advancement of Science [AAAS], 1993) from Project 2061 of AAAS, and the *National Science Education Standards* (National Research Council, 1996).

Although these documents differ in their scope and focus, they all emphasize the content knowledge and skills necessary for developing a

---

[4]This section draws heavily on *America's Lab Report* (National Research Council, 2006).

scientifically literate society. *Science for All Americans*, for example, advocated the importance of scientific literacy for all U.S. high school students, to increase their awareness and understanding of science and the natural world and to develop their ability to think scientifically (American Association for the Advancement of Science, 1989). Four years later, the AAAS published *Benchmarks for Science Literacy*, which identified expected competencies at each school grade level in each of the earlier report's 10 areas of scientific literacy (American Association for the Advancement of Science, 1993).

The NRC's *National Science Education Standards* (National Research Council, 1996) shared this focus on science literacy for all and emphasized the underpinnings of cognitive science and how students learn (Forman and Cazden, 1985; Frederiksen, 1984). The NRC proposed national science standards for high school students designed to help all students develop (1) abilities necessary to do scientific inquiry and (2) understandings about scientific inquiry (National Research Council, 1996, p. 173). In the standards, the NRC suggested a new approach to laboratories that went beyond simply engaging students in experiments. It explicitly recognized that laboratory investigations should be learning experiences, stating that high school students must "actively participate in scientific investigations, and . . . use the cognitive and manipulative skills associated with the formulation of scientific explanations" (National Research Council, 1996, p. 173). The standards presaged the practices of science by emphasizing the need for students to use evidence, apply logic, and construct scientific arguments and explanations for observations made during investigations.

Alongside the goal of scientific literacy for all, a secondary goal for science education emerged in the early 2000s of preparing the future scientific and technical workforce. In 2004, the National Science Board called for improvements in science education that would increase the number of U.S. citizens who become scientists and engineers (National Science Foundation, 2004). At the same time, there was a growing awareness that secure, well-paying jobs that did not require postsecondary education nonetheless required abilities that may be developed through scientific investigations. These included the ability to use inductive and deductive reasoning to arrive at valid conclusions, distinguish among facts and opinions, identify false premises in an argument, and use mathematics to solve problems (American Diploma Project, 2004).

In 2001, the *Elementary and Secondary Education Act* was reauthorized as the *No Child Left Behind Act*. This legislation increased the national focus on accountability and placed a heavy emphasis on academic performance in core subjects such as mathematics and English language arts. It also mandated that test scores be disaggregated so that achievement disparities among racial, ethnic, and socioeconomic groups would be visible to stakeholders. To satisfy the requirements of *No Child Left Behind*, many states used achievement scores in relation to benchmarks of adequate yearly progress to categorize schools and publicized the classifications. An unintended consequence of the emphasis on reading and mathematics scores was that science was largely squeezed out of the curriculum, especially in the elementary grades (National Research Council, 2011). Critics of *No Child Left Behind* also argue that curricula and instruction driven by standardized testing did little to advance science as inquiry, the science education envisioned in the *National Science Education Standards* (Anderson, 2012).

INFLUENCE OF THE FRAMEWORK ON K–12 SCIENCE EDUCATION

As discussed in Chapter 1, the *Framework* (National Research Council, 2012) has dramatically influenced the current thinking about science teaching and learning. It differs from previous reform efforts by bringing the science practices into the heart of the discussion, not presenting them as a separate goal, and by including engineering practices as part of the conversation. The *Framework's* three-dimensional learning moves away from a presentation of discrete facts in different disciplines and "toward a coherent set of ideas that can provide a foundation for further thought and exploration in the discipline" (Passmore, 2014).

This integrative approach signifies the importance of emphasizing the contexts internal (what occurs inside the learner's mind) and external (varied and layered contexts that impact learning and learners) to the learner that facilitate learning and the application of that knowledge. Learning is seen as a progressive process in which learners equipped with existing knowledge and myriad abilities from their interactions with the social and physical world refine and develop more in-depth and sophisticated understandings about and competencies around phenomena over time as they continue to make sense of phenomena or solve new problems. This includes learning that takes place as part of a community: that is, the collective learning in classrooms that accompany the individual learning (Bereiter and Scardamalia, 2014). An important goal is to guide knowledge toward a more scientifically based and coherent view of the sciences and engineering, as well as of the ways in which they are pursued and how their results can be used.

The *Framework* served as the basis for the state-developed Next Generation Science Standards (NGSS), which set expectations for what students should know and be able to do (NGSS Lead States, 2013). As of 2018, 19 states, along with the District of Columbia, have adopted the NGSS. Many other states have adopted their own new standards based on the

Framework. In this report, we refer to "science standards" as science standards consistent with the *Framework*, and we direct our advice to states, districts, and schools seeking to implement *Framework*-aligned standards. We do so because the research on learning that underpins the original 2006 *America's Lab Report* and the 2012 *Framework*, as well as in the updated *How People Learn* II (National Academies of Sciences, Engineering, and Medicine, 2018), provides evidence that the new direction for science education holds the best promise for more effective and equitable science and engineering education.

Investigation and Three-Dimensional Learning

As described in Chapter 1, the *Framework* emphasizes that learning science and engineering involves fostering three kinds of scientific knowledge and skills at the same time: scientific content (core ideas and crosscutting concepts) and the practices needed to engage in science investigation and engineering design. Classroom instruction consistent with the *Framework* engages students in investigation as a strategy for developing students' knowledge and skills to make sense of natural phenomena and understand engineered solutions to human problems beyond the classroom. During science investigations, the learner's internal processes, learning contexts, and task engagement converge to foster practices, crosscutting concepts, and disciplinary core ideas into science performances for attaining the major goal of science education articulated in the *Framework*—for all learners to use knowledge in preparation for their individual lives and for their roles as citizens in this technology-rich and scientifically complex world.

This instructional stance aligns with and extends findings from Chapter 3 of the 2006 *America's Lab Report*, which defines "Integrated Instructional Units" as those that engage students in doing science investigations or other "hands-on" science activity that are integrated into the content learning (National Research Council, 2006). A review of research for the 2006 report showed that these "Integrated Instructional Units" are more beneficial for student learning and for student interest in science than the "Typical Laboratory Experience" in science instruction, where lab work consists mostly of following predefined procedures and is a separate activity from the remainder of the science teaching sequence.

The 2006 report and related National Research Council studies on science learning—*Taking Science to School* (2007); the *Framework* (2012); and *Learning Science in Informal Environments* (2009)—are supported by a growing body of evidence that engaging students in science performances is more effective than simply memorizing and engaging in activities to demonstrate accepted science theories and a description of "the scientific method," along with pre-planned laboratory exercises (Furtak et al., 2012;

Penuel et al., 2015; Songer, Kelcey, and Gotwals, 2009; Weiss et al., 2003). In line with the theories of learning discussed in Chapter 3 of this report, interacting with real-world phenomena may enable instructional choices that facilitate students making connections among new concepts (Carey, 1986; Glaser, 1984) and prior knowledge, foster episodic linkages with lived and vicarious experiences, relate abstractions to concrete objects and experiences (Fyfe et al., 2014; Moreno, Ozogul, and Reisslein, 2011; Stice, 1987), promote the transfer of concept understanding to new situations (Gobert and Buckley, 2000; Schwartz and Martin, 2004), and cultivate actions and perceptions that align with the goals of science education.

Operating from an initial premise of context and content as conjoined, science investigations can leverage students' familiar contexts in promoting and achieving three-dimensional learning for all learners, regardless of the learners' demography or prior experiences with science (Krajcik and Shin, 2014). Research has shown that context familiarity, particularly as it relates to culture, activates prior knowledge and thus enhances comprehension. For example, a recent study conducted by Song and Bruning (2016) on climate change showed that when American and Korean students were given passages couching global warming in different cultural contexts, learners recalled and elaborated more from their respective native cultural contexts (American and Korean). The familiar context activates schemata, which is an elaborate web of connected concepts (Freebody and Anderson, 1983; Pritchard, 1990; Reynolds et al., 1981). As discussed in Chapter 3, because learners have a limited amount of novel information that they can hold onto, the activated schemata can lessen cognitive load.

Science investigation and engineering design offer a promising vehicle for anchoring student learning in meaningful contexts. Interacting with real-word phenomena allows instructional choices that better connect to students' lives, experiences, and cultural backgrounds than science instruction that is focused on discrete facts organized by discipline. Learners can apply their own assets and experiences to cognitively challenging tasks. When students problematize data, measurement, and observation obtained during an investigation they get a more accurate representation of how science and engineering are done in the real world, instead of using standard canned activities where students all receive the same materials and always arrive at the right answer (Duschl and Bybee, 2014). The presence of a productive struggle as a part of doing science helps keep learners from leaving school with a naïve notion that obtaining results from investigations and developing scientific knowledge are straightforward and nonproblematic. Student engagement in deciding, developing, and documenting lead students to acquire conceptual and epistemic knowledge and help them to attain problematic images of the nature of science. The *Framework* (National Research Council, 2012) argues that understanding of how science functions requires a synthesis of content, procedural, and epistemic knowledge. Epistemic knowledge is fostered in a classroom through critiques and arguments about which ideas are worth pursuing further and are values intrinsic to learning science.

In such environments, science ideas emerge as needed to solve problems or make sense of phenomena. Investigations also provide opportunities for inclusion and support of language learners by engaging students in experiences of realistic classroom discourse (Lee, Quinn, and Valdés, 2013). In these ways, investigation also provides opportunity for meaningful learning of science to be enjoyable and memorable for all students and, ideally, to stimulate their longer-term interest and engagement.

The *Framework*'s Influence on Our Update of *America's Lab Report*

As discussed in Chapter 1, several aspects of *Framework*-aligned standards represent notable differences from the context in which the 2006 report was written and have implications for the conceptualization of investigation and its role in the curriculum. First, the *Framework* called for the inclusion of engineering as one of the core disciplines to reflect the importance of understanding the human-built world and to recognize the value of better integrating the teaching and learning of STEM disciplines (p. 8). *Framework*-aligned standards include the engagement of students in engineering design projects to produce solutions to actual societal problems as well as science investigations to support students in developing explanations of real-world phenomena.

Second, the *Framework* and other studies have concluded (partly on the basis of the 2006 report) that the idea of the "science lab" should be generalized to include a broader concept of investigation, which refers to all aspects of engaging in the scientific and engineering practices, whether in the laboratory or outside of it. Thus, in this report, instead of using the term "laboratory," we use "investigation" to describe both the three-dimensional student science and engineering performances and the central focus of what students are doing in science classrooms to learn. While some aspect of investigation in K–12 education may include doing an experiment in a traditional science lab, investigation consistent with the *Framework* includes various ways that students can obtain data and information to make sense of phenomena. The emphasis is on carrying out the full suite of science or engineering practices, calling on the crosscutting concepts as tools for problem solving and applying one's developing understanding of the disciplinary core ideas in order to develop models and explanations of phenomena and the systems in which they occur, or to engineer designs that solve a meaningful problem. Through this work, students are developing the capacity to incorporate the science and engineering ideas, concepts, and practices that they are learning into their everyday thinking and problem solving, and to communicate these results to others.

Third, as noted, *Framework*-aligned standards assume that a progression in science learning and student growth through middle and high school is fostered through the learning that occurs in elementary science (National Research Council, 2007). As implementation of *Framework*-aligned standards matures, students will enter middle school with some basic skill in using all of the science and engineering practices (NGSS Lead States, 2013, App. F), some facility in applying crosscutting concepts, and some fundamental understandings of all the disciplinary core ideas. By the time they reach high school, students will be expected to design and carry out increasingly sophisticated investigations, in which they "identify questions to be researched . . . decide what data are to be gathered, what variables should be controlled, what tools or instruments are needed to gather and record data in an appropriate format, and eventually to consider how to incorporate measurement error in analyzing data" (National Research Council, 2012, p. 61). These expectations and the K–12 learning progression influenced the decision to add middle school investigations to this update of the 2006 *America's Lab Report*. While this report does not address elementary students, it also is important to note that successful efforts to improve science and engineering education must begin before students enter middle school so that they are prepared to engage in science investigation and engineering design in the manner described here.

Current Views of Investigation

The context of this study in 2018 is significantly different from that of the 2006 *America's Lab Report*. At the time of the original report, the research base and understanding of how students learn was strong, but not widely used as the basis for science instruction. The effects of the accountability movement on the science curriculum and focus of instruction were just beginning to be felt. Demographics in the United States were shifting, and *No Child Left Behind* was prompting conversations about the performance of different student groups and the need for educational equity. In 2018, our committee is comfortable making recommendations for science and engineering learning that build on the robust literature on how students learn and with making a more explicit acknowledgement that the struggle to overcome a long history of inequity and inequality in opportunities for the learning of science in U.S. schools is far from over.

Although the actuality of science classrooms has changed little since 2006, the descriptions of effective science teaching and learning are significantly different now, and science and engineering are showing signs of increasing prominence in the curriculum. The new thinking no longer includes labs as something that supports classroom endeavors; instead, science investigation and engineering design are the center of how science and engineering are taught and learned and the way that students make sense of the world. The three dimensions of the *Framework* form the process for learning via investigation and design, whereas traditional labs saw inquiry skills and the steps of the "scientific method" as separate steps and goals from the content knowledge that was being fostered in the lab. While the thinking about science education and investigation have shifted dramatically since 2006, the experiences of students in middle and high school classrooms have changed to a much smaller degree. Here we briefly discuss the context of science instruction in middle and high schools into which changes will be introduced to put investigation and design at the center. Aspects of this context related to resources are further addressed in Chapter 8, and the way that investigation and design fit into the larger education system are discussed in Chapter 9.

TODAY'S MIDDLE AND HIGH SCHOOLS

Most middle school students fall into the early adolescent range (ages 10–13), and most high school students are adolescents (teenagers). These developmental stages represent times of profound and rapid physical growth, cognitive development, and social change (Piaget, 1977). These transformations are especially pronounced in middle school.

The transition to middle school itself is a significant adjustment because the structure of the school day differs greatly from elementary schools. In many settings, students are no longer in self-contained classes. At the same time, students of this age are beginning to form their own identities— defining themselves and starting to make more of their own choices about friends, sports and other extracurricular activities, and school (Darling, Caldwell, and Smith, 2005; Eccles, 1999; Meeus, 2011). Adolescents may experience considerable self-doubt about all aspects of their lives, from their appearance to their intellect. As a result, the more challenging academic work in middle school can become a source of stress and anxiety (Eccles, 1999; Romero et al., 2014). Bullying by peers also increases during middle school, and social influence becomes excessively important. Peer influences can drive many of the choices students make about their engagement and participation in academics and other activities that potentially compete for their time and attention (Albert, Chein, and Steinberg, 2013; Eccles, 1999).

Adolescence is a time of great uncertainty during the transition from childhood to adulthood. As they go through adolescence, high school (and many upper middle school) students mature physically and further develop their identities and personalities. These rapid physical, cognitive, and emotional changes can be overwhelming, and adolescence is typically marked by self-consciousness and sensitivity (Harter, 1990). Peers still exert a strong influence, and teenagers also begin exploring other interests as they search for and establish a stronger sense of themselves. Because these interests might or might not be related to academics, they can take attention away from school. Examples include sports competitions, music performances, and part-time jobs. Also, during adolescence, young people begin thinking more about their future plans for school and work. While these plans can be a source of stress and anxiety, they begin to shape the decisions students make about taking future courses and participating in other activities that align with their burgeoning interests (Bandura et al., 2001; Eccles and Wigfield, 2002).

Alongside these physical and developmental changes, cognitive capacities of young people also change rapidly during middle and high school. For example, early adolescents begin to transition from concrete thinking to more complex thinking during their middle school years (Eccles, Wigfield, and Byrnes, 2003). During adolescence, students develop (1) more advanced reasoning skills, (2) the capacity to think abstractly, and (3) an ability to consider multiple points of view. They also become more metacognitive (able to think about their thinking) (Keating, 1990). The development of these capacities has implications for how science and engineering investigations are designed at the middle and high school levels.

Middle School

Middle schools typically include grades 6–8, 7–8, or 7–9. The average U.S. middle school science class has 23.6 students, but there is considerable variation by locality. For example, in 2013, 20 percent of U.S. middle grades science classes had 30 or more students and 23 percent had fewer than 20 students, according to the National Survey of Science and Mathematics Education (Banilower et al., 2013).[5] Because middle school is such a tumultuous time for early adolescents, many schools and districts have adopted different structural approaches to promote the engagement and success of these students. Some notable examples include creating teams or cohorts of students that progress through middle school together, and looping, or having teachers and students stay together for 2 or more years. In looped middle schools, students have different teachers for each subject area, but they stay with the same subject area teachers over a period of multiple years. These and other approaches are designed to foster relationships

---

[5]This section is excerpted, with minimal changes, from Chapter 3 of the 2015 National Academies of Sciences, Engineering, and Medicine report *Science Teachers' Learning*. It summarizes the results of the nationally representative 2012 National Survey of Science and Mathematics Education (Banilower et al., 2013).

and promote a sense of belonging so that middle school students do not fall through the cracks, become disaffected, and drop out of school.

Most middle schools have dedicated science teachers, and students participate in science class daily or every other day (National Academies of Sciences, Engineering, and Medicine, 2015). Middle schools spend about twice as much per pupil for science equipment and supplies than elementary schools and provide more instructional resources for science teaching (National Academies of Sciences, Engineering, and Medicine, 2015). During the *No Child Left Behind* era, science was largely squeezed out of the curriculum in grades K–5 (National Research Council, 2011), so it is not surprising that middle schools across the country allocate more time in the curriculum and other resources for science learning than elementary schools. The 2012 National Survey of Science and Mathematics Education found that 57 percent of middle school teachers indicated that their facilities were adequate, and about one-half viewed their equipment as adequate. About 40 percent viewed their consumable supplies and instructional technology as adequate (Banilower et al., 2013).

The most frequent instructional techniques reported by middle school science teachers were the teacher explaining science ideas, whole-class discussions, and students working in small groups (Banilower et al., 2013). Middle school science teachers also reported that at least once a week their students were asked to

- supply evidence in support of their claims (64%);
- engage in hands-on/laboratory activities (62%);
- represent and/or analyze data using tables, charts, or graphs (54%); and
- read from a science textbook or other material (56%).

Reflecting the increasing emphasis on testing and accountability at higher grade levels, science tests and quizzes are more common in middle school, including short-answer tests and tests requiring constructed responses (National Academies of Sciences, Engineering, and Medicine, 2015).

Based on the 2013 data, middle school science classes do not incorporate instructional technology (e.g., computers, calculators, probes, and sensors) to a great extent (Banilower et al., 2013). Only 30 percent of middle school teachers reported that they had used instructional technology in their most recent lesson. Most middle school teachers (80%) use commercially published textbooks or modules as the basis for instruction (Banilower et al., 2013), and about one-half use these texts or modules for 50 percent or more of their science instructional time. They also supplement these materials with other resources or skip parts they deem unimportant.

High School

The grades served by high schools depend on their feeder middle schools, and either include grades 9–12 or 10–12. The average U.S. high school science class size is 21.7 students, which is smaller than in middle school. Fifteen percent of high school science classes have more than 30 students, and 36 percent have fewer than 20 students (Banilower et al., 2013).

The following discussion focuses on comprehensive high schools as opposed to the few hundred STEM-focused high schools in the United States (Means et al., 2008). STEM-focused schools are organized around one or more of the STEM disciplines and may or may not have selective admissions criteria. They are generally characterized by expert teachers, advanced curricula, and sophisticated laboratory equipment; the schools with selective admissions criteria also often feature apprenticeships with scientists (National Research Council, 2011). By design, the science and engineering experiences in these STEM-focused schools differ from those in comprehensive high schools.

Similar to middle school, the most frequent instructional approaches in high school are the teacher explaining science ideas to the whole class, students working in small groups, and whole-class discussions (Banilower et al., 2013). Relative to middle school teachers, high school teachers are more likely to ask students, at least once a week, to do hands-on laboratory investigations (70% versus 62% in middle school) and to represent or analyze data using tables, charts, or graphs (58% versus 54% in middle school).

As at the middle school level, most high school teachers report that their classes have access to the Internet, personal computers, and non-graphing calculators. However, high school teachers have greater access to more sophisticated scientific equipment, including microscopes, probes for collecting data, and graphing calculators (Banilower et al., 2013). This greater access to scientific equipment is reflected in higher percentages of high school teachers, relative to middle school teachers, who rate their facilities, equipment, consumable supplies, and instructional technology as adequate. However, still less than one-half (48%) of high school teachers rated their instructional technology as adequate, which may explain, in part, why only about one-third of high school science teachers reported using instructional technology in their most recent lesson.

Most middle school (80%) and high school (77%) science teachers use commercially published textbooks or modules as the basis for instruction (Banilower et al., 2013, Table 6.1). Yet, high school science teachers use textbooks and modules less extensively than middle school science teachers do: less than one-third of high school teachers use them for 50 percent or more of their science instructional time compared to approximately 50 percent of middle school teachers (Banilower et al., 2013, Table 6.11). Like middle school teachers, high school teachers often supplement textbooks and modules with other resources or skip parts they deem unimportant.

STUDENTS, INVESTIGATION AND DESIGN, AND THE NATURE OF SCIENCE AND ENGINEERING

Middle and high school students are adolescents who are shifting their perspectives to engage more with the wider world. Their interest in science may change during the course of these school years in reaction to their experiences in and out of school. They enter with existing views about what science is and who scientists are; these views can be influenced by their involvement in science education and how it shows them the nature of science and engineering.

As the historical discussion in this chapter illustrates, having students understand the nature of science has long been a goal of K–12 science education. With the inclusion of practices and core ideas related to engineering, technology, and the applications of science in the *Framework*, this goal broadens to include an understanding of the role of engineering and the interplay between science and engineering in the development of new technologies and in developing solutions to real-world problems.

Prior research on teaching and learning the nature of science has identified eight ideas about science that all students should come to understand (NGSS Lead States, 2013, App. H):

(1) Scientific investigations use a variety of methods.
(2) Scientific knowledge is based on empirical evidence.
(3) Scientific knowledge is open to revision in light of new evidence.
(4) Scientific models, laws, mechanisms, and theories explain natural phenomena.
(5) Science is a way of knowing.
(6) Scientific knowledge assumes an order and consistency in natural systems.
(7) Science is a human endeavor.
(8) Science addresses questions about the natural and material world.

These are metacognitive ideas that students do not generally recognize without explicit or guided learning, that is students do not come to understand these ideas by simply doing science projects, particularly those of the traditional science lab experiment. However, engaging in investigation can provide context and experiential basis for students to begin understanding the nature of science and engineering. This understanding allows students to distinguish science and engineering ways of knowing from other ways of knowing, such as those used in the humanities. Classroom discourse and guided reflection can help students see the value of empirical evidence as a powerful tool for understanding the world.

Following from the ideas of the *Framework*, the core idea of engineering design includes the following three component ideas (NGSS Lead States, 2013, App. I):

(1) Defining and delimiting engineering problems involves stating the problem to be solved as clearly as possible in terms of criteria for success and constraints or limits.

(2) Designing solutions to engineering problems begins with generating a number of different possible solutions, then evaluating potential solutions to see which ones best meet the criteria and constraints of the problem.

(3) Optimizing the design solution involves a process in which solutions are systematically tested and refined and the final design is improved by trading off less important features for those that are more important.

Student Views of Science and Engineering

More than 60 years of research on students' perceptions of scientists "has demonstrated that students do not have a clear perception of what science has to offer them or what scientists do" (Wyss, Huelskamp, and Siebert, 2012, p. 503). This body of research reveals that although the perception of women as scientists has increased over time (Miller et al., 2018), an enduring perception persists of scientists as "old, white males working in a laboratory performing dangerous experiments" (Wyss, Huelskamp, and Siebert, 2012, p. 503), especially as the students get older. Particularly as demographics in the United States continue to shift, these perceptions mean that an ever-larger swath of the population does not see science as relevant to them or as including them.

Although considerably less research exists on middle and high school students' perceptions of engineering, the existing research also suggests an incomplete understanding of the field. For example, in one sizable study of middle school students, a large proportion of the students "have no perception of engineering. Others frequently perceive engineers as working outdoors in manual labor" (Fralick et al., 2009, p. 60). Other perceptions held by elementary and middle students are that the engineering process includes making or working on vehicles or building structures (Cunningham, 2018; Fralick et al., 2009). However, other studies suggest that middle school students view engineers as creative, future-oriented, and artistic problem finders and solvers (English, Dawes, and Hudson, 2011).

Incomplete or inaccurate perceptions of the practitioners and practices of science and engineering can preclude students from making informed determinations about their interest and competencies in these fields. A better understanding of what scientists and engineers do—gained in part through science and engineering investigation—might help middle and high school students to see these fields as relevant to them.

Student Perceptions of Themselves as Scientists and Engineers

Views of science and mathematics as difficult, only for smart students, or more appropriate for males can pose a barrier to the pursuit and enjoyment of science and engineering as early as elementary school; these views arise from many sources and can inadvertently be reinforced by teacher anxieties (Beilock et al., 2010). Considerable research has been conducted to understand the development of confidence and interest in science, as well as young people's science experiences and career interests (Aschbacher, Li, and Roth, 2010; some of this research is described in greater detail in Chapter 3 of this volume). Given persistent gender imbalances in the STEM workforce, much of this attention has focused on gender differences, including factors that influence females' choices to pursue—or not—majors and careers in these fields (Maltese and Cooper, 2017).

Broadly speaking, there is a science "identity gap" between males and females, especially for females from groups that are underrepresented in science and engineering (Tan et al., 2013). Regardless of test scores or performance, in general, high school and college females do not identify with science or enjoy science and mathematics as much as their male peers (Riegele-Crumb, Moore, and Ramos-Wada, 2011). One study of ACT test takers did show that similar proportions of females (47%) and males (50%) expressed interest in STEM, but noted that gender gaps in STEM-related attainment remain (ACT, 2017). More specifically, "girls often perceive science as difficult, uninteresting, or leading to an unattractive lifestyle" (Brotman and Moore, 2008, p. 978). Some studies have shown that even when girls do enjoy science and mathematics, they are less confident in their abilities in those subjects than males (Brotman and Moore, 2008; Riegele-Crumb, Moore, and Ramos-Wada, 2011).

In addition to these broad differences, females and males also identify with different disciplines because of the social importance placed on the field or because of differences in self-efficacy (Maltese and Cooper, 2017). Males are typically more interested in physics, engineering, and technology; females are more interested in biology, health, and medicine; and both sexes express similar degrees of interest in chemistry (Baram-Tasbari and Yarden, 2011; Sadler et al., 2012). The courses students take and activities they engage in during middle and high school can both reflect and reinforce these preferences and identities.

Less research has examined other groups that are underrepresented in science and engineering, such as African Americans and Hispanics. Moreover, the relationship between students' interest and their ongoing participation in science and engineering is less clear. For example, despite the marked underrepresentation of African Americans and Hispanics in the science and engineering workforce, some research suggests that high school students from these groups are as interested or more interested in pursuing STEM majors in college than their white peers (Anderson and Kim, 2006; Hanson, 2004). Research on attitudes toward science and mathematics has similarly revealed that African American and Hispanic students expressed views of these subjects that were as positive or more positive than those of white students (Muller, Stage, and Kinzie, 2001).

Student Interest in Science and Engineering

Many of the changes students experience during early adolescence and adolescence directly or indirectly affect their overall interest in school, and their specific interest in science and engineering. Indeed, research has documented general losses of interest and engagement in school during transitions to middle and high school, with especially pronounced effects for boys, students from lower socioeconomic groups, and historically underrepresented groups (Wigfield et al., 2006). Studies of public schools in New York and Florida also have revealed overall declines in test scores at these same transition points (Rockoff and Lockwood, 2010; West and Schwerdt, 2012).

Interest in the STEM subjects also declines in middle and high school (George, 2006; Sadler et al., 2012). Some research points to high school as an especially important time for the development of science and engineering-related career intentions (Riegle-Crumb, Moore, and Ramos-Wada, 2011; Sadler et al., 2012). Others argue the process of shaping opinions about science occupations begins much earlier (Bandura et al., 2001). Indeed, the work of Tai and Maltese (Maltese and Tai, 2010; Tai et al., 2006) suggests that students in grade 8 who express an interest in STEM are three times as likely to pursue STEM degrees than their peers who do not express an interest.

There are also gender-related differences in interest over time. One review, for example, found that ". . . girls' overall attitudes toward science are either less positive than boys' or decline more significantly with age" (Brotman and Moore, 2008, p. 978). Another study similarly revealed that the proportion of females interested in STEM careers declined during high school, with no such decrease for males (Sadler et al., 2012).

Loss of interest in science, mathematics, and engineering during middle and high school has important longer-term implications because the choices students begin to make about science and engineering course-taking in high school and in college, as well as choices of science and engineering-related activities, could affect their future options. Interests and motivations in science and engineering are shaped by a complex and socially constructed interaction of individual, family, community, peer, and school-related factors (see Aschbacher, Li, and Roth, 2010, for a discussion of these factors). Chapter 3 further discusses learning and motivation as it applies to adolescent students and their engagement with investigation and design.

INCLUSIVENESS AND EQUITY IN THE CURRENT CONTEXT

As mentioned, a notable change from the 2006 context to the present is an explicit recognition of the need for science and engineering to be more inclusive, and to ensure that students from groups that have been excluded or marginalized in the past have equal and equitable access to quality K–12 science and engineering learning opportunities. For example, very few students had access to learning about engineering unless they had a family member or other close contact who was an engineer or if they had access to an afterschool/summer/weekend engineering outreach program (National Academy of Engineering and National Research Council, 2009). Significant changes inside (inclusive pedagogies; see Chapter 5) and outside the classroom (e.g., policies, facilities, resources; see Chapter 8) could increase the inclusion of traditionally excluded groups in these opportunities. Such opportunities provide a base for making life and community decisions that depend on scientific and technological understanding. Furthermore, they allow students to develop skills and interests that greatly broaden their perspectives on career opportunities and possibilities and that open the doors to make those opportunities real.

This explicit focus on broadening these opportunities to include all students is especially timely because of demographic changes in the United States since the 2006 report. In 2014, the percentage of students of color (i.e., Hispanic, African American, Asian/Pacific Islander, American Indian/Alaska Native) enrolled in public elementary and secondary schools was 50.5 percent, reflecting the first time that the percentage of students who were white was less than 50 percent. Additionally, it is projected that the number of white students will continue to decrease, falling to 45 percent in 2026, while enrollments of Hispanic students and Asian/Pacific Islander students, in particular, will continue to increase (McFarland et al., 2017). Although the current goals for science education are more inclusive and responsive to current conditions, inequities persist in several important areas: participation in the STEM workforce, opportunities to learn science and mathematics, and achievement.

While Hispanic, African American, and American Indian/Alaska Native people together make up 27 percent of the U.S. population (looking at people ages 21 and older), they comprise only 11 percent of those employed in STEM occupations (National Science Board, 2018a). Asians account for 21 percent of employed STEM workers, despite comprising only 6 percent of the U.S. population ages 21 and older; however, the majority are employed in engineering fields and less so in other science disciplines. Gender representation in the STEM workforce is also important, and while an increase in the representation of women in the STEM workforce has been observed, as with Asians, disparities remain, particularly by discipline. In 2015, women were highly employed within the social sciences (60%) and life sciences (48%) fields, but largely underrepresented in engineering (15%), computer and mathematical sciences (26%), and physical sciences (28%) occupations (National Science Board, 2018a).

Even though courts acted to dismantle formerly lawful segregation, segregation has persisted in ways that did not reach the legal threshold for intervention and in the legally permissible form of segregation resulting from factors such as housing restrictions and local zoning ordinances. Consequently, racially segregated schools, separate and unequal, still exist today. A report issued by the Government Accountability Office (2016) showed an increase from 9 percent in 2000–2001 to 16 percent in 2013–2014 in schools classified as high-minority enrollment schools, defined as 75 percent or greater black and Hispanic student enrollments. In contrast, the percentage of schools comprised of fewer black and Hispanic students decreased by one-half during the same period. Schools with large proportions of black and Hispanic students, English learners, and/or students in poverty are often under-resourced (see Box 2-1) (Morgan and Amerikaner, 2018; Ushomirsky and Williams, 2015). Consequently, they typically offer fewer math and science courses and course sequences and fewer certified

---

BOX 2-1
Unequal Funding to School Districts

Analyzing data from 2010–2012, Ushomirsky and Williams (2015) reported that nationwide, the highest-poverty school districts in the United States receive approximately 10 percent or $1,200 per student less in state and local funding than the lowest-poverty school districts. School districts serving the most students of color nationally receive about 15 percent or $2,000 per student less in state and local funding than those districts serving the fewest. For a middle school of 500 students and a high school of 1,000 students, this funding gap translates into $600,000 and $1.2 million shortfalls per year, respectively, for high-poverty districts and $1 million and $2 million shortfalls, respectively, for districts with high enrollments of students of color.

teachers in science content areas—particularly in physics and chemistry—
than schools serving predominantly white and higher-income students
(U.S. Department of Education, 2014). Moreover, because science classrooms and related equipment are expensive to establish and maintain, these
schools also are less likely to have high-grade space and equipment for science (Banilower et al., 2013, p. 105 [Table 6.21], and p. 108 [Table 6.26];
Filardo, 2016, pp. 6–7). Tracking of students into fewer and less rigorous
science and mathematics courses has excluded or marginalized many low-
income and historically underrepresented students (Burris, Welner, and
Bezoza, 2009; Oakes, 2005).

In the United States, student performance on the National Assessment
of Educational Progress (NAEP) in science is slowly increasing across all
ethnic groups, though gaps in opportunities to learn and achievement
among various groups remain. As shown in Figure 2-1, NAEP results reveal

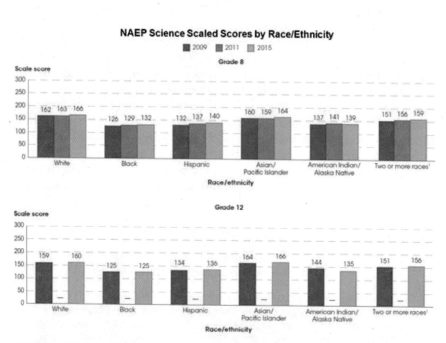

FIGURE 2-1 8th- and 12th-grade science NAEP scores, 2009–2015.
SOURCE: U.S. Department of Education, National Center for Education Statistics (2016).
NOTES: Bars indicate the average NAEP science scale scores of 8th- and 12th-grade students,
by race/ethnicity: 2009, 2011, and 2015.
"—" indicates data that are not available. In 2009, students in the "Two or more races"
category were categorized as "Unclassified." Includes public and private schools. Scale ranges
from 0 to 300 for all grades, but scores cannot be compared across grades. Assessment was
not conducted for grade 12 in 2011. Race categories exclude persons of Hispanic ethnicity.

significant racial and ethnic disparities, with persistent 34–36 point gaps between white and black students at both 8th and 12th grades, and 24–26 point gaps between white and Hispanic students at both grade levels. The most significant narrowing of the gap was in 8th grade between white and Hispanic students, from 30 points in 2009 to 26 points in 2015 (U.S. Department of Education, 2016).

Socioeconomic status continues to be one of the leading causes of variation in student performance, as illustrated in Table 2-1, which shows differences in NAEP science scores between 8th- and 12th-grade students who are eligible for the school lunch program and those who are not.

The 2015 NAEP results show a 13-point to 27-point difference in performance between students eligible and not eligible for the free or reduced-price lunch program. For both 8th and 12th grade, the largest gaps between eligible and non-eligible students were seen within the Asian and Pacific Islander race/ethnic group (National Science Board, 2018a).

SUMMARY

Current reform efforts in K–12 science and engineering education are largely based on the *Framework* and focus on engaging all students in the understanding of how science and engineering work; these reform efforts represent a departure from previous ones. Centering science instruction around investigation and design can improve instruction in middle and high schools and help students to learn to make sense of phenomena and develop solutions. However, structures and approaches of earlier eras still constrain the opportunities afforded to today's students. Through the use of an integrative framework for learning, teachers are able to leverage the assets that students bring to the classroom through engaging with phenomenon and engineering design. This is primarily because science investigation and engineering design offer a promising vehicle for anchoring student learning in meaningful contexts.

Moreover, adolescence represents a period of adjustment in students' lives. They are navigating rapid physical growth, cognitive development, and social change. It is a time in which engaging students in science investigation and engineering design might shape their identity and their future identity as a potential scientist or engineer. This is particularly crucial for females and other students from traditionally underrepresented populations. Leveraging science investigation and engineering design could allow students to develop skills and interests that greatly broaden their perspectives on career opportunities and possibilities as well as provide a base for making life and community decisions that depend on scientific and technological understanding.

TABLE 2-1 2015 NAEP Science Scores of 8th and 12th Graders by Socioeconomic Status within Race or Ethnicity

Race or Ethnicity	Eligible for Free or Reduced-Price Lunch	Not Eligible for Free or Reduced-Price Lunch	Numerical Gap (not eligible – eligible)
8th Grade			
White	153	171	18
Black	127	146	19
Hispanic	135	154	19
Asian or Pacific Islander	148	174	26
American Indian or Alaska Native	134	155	21
More than one race	146	170	24
12th Grade			
White	146	164	18
Black	119	136	17
Hispanic	132	145	13
Asian or Pacific Islander	150	177	27
American Indian or Alaska Native	suppressed for reasons of confidentiality and/or reliability	suppressed for reasons of confidentiality and/or reliability	--
More than one race	145	162	17

SOURCE: National Science Board (2018b).
NOTES: NAEP uses eligibility for the federal National School Lunch Program (NSLP) as a measure of socioeconomic status. NSLP is a federally assisted meal program that provides low-cost or free lunches to eligible students. It is sometimes referred to as the free or reduced-price lunch program. The overall scale for the assessments is 0 to 300, the effective score range of these tests is about 90 points: 80 percent of 8th graders scored between 109 and 195, and 80 percent of 12th graders scored between 103 and 196.

REFERENCES

ACT. (2017). *STEM Education in the U.S.: Where We Are and What We Can Do.* Available: https://www.act.org/content/dam/act/unsecured/documents/STEM/2017/STEM-Education-in-the-US-2017.pdf [September 2018].

Albert, D., Chein, J., and Steinberg, L. (2013). The teenage brain: Peer influences on adolescent decision making. *Current Directions in Psychological Science, 22*(2), 114–120.

American Association for the Advancement of Science. (1989). *Science for All Americans: A Project 2061 Report on Literacy Goals in Science, Mathematics, and Technology.* Washington, DC: Author.

American Association for the Advancement of Science. (1993). *Benchmarks for Science Literacy.* New York: Oxford University Press.

American Diploma Project. (2004). *Ready or Not: Creating a High School Diploma That Counts: Executive Summary.* American Diploma Project, Achieve. Available: https://www.achieve.org/publications/ready-or-not-creating-high-school-diploma-counts [October 2018].

Anderson, E. (1990). *Streetwise: Race, Class, and Change in an Urban Community.* Chicago: University of Chicago Press.

Anderson, E., and Kim, D. (2006). *Increasing the Success of Minority Students in Science and Technology.* Washington, DC: American Council on Education.

Anderson, J.D. (1978) Northern foundations and the shaping of southern, Black rural education: 1902–1935. *History of Educational Quarterly, 18*(4), 371–396.

Anderson, K.J.B. (2012). Science education and test-based accountability: Reviewing their relationship and exploring implications for future policy. *Science Education, 96*(1), 104–129.

Aschbacher, P.R., Li, E., and Roth, E.J. (2010). Is science me? High school students' identities, participation and aspirations in science, engineering, and medicine. *Journal of Research in Science Teaching, 47*(5), 564–582.

Bandura, A., Barbaranelli, C., Caprara, G.V., and Pastorelli, C. (2001). Self-efficacy beliefs as shapers of children's aspirations and career trajectories. *Child Development, 72,* 187–206.

Banilower, E.R., Smith, P.S., Weiss, I.R., Malzahn, K.A., Campbell, K.M., and Weis, A.M. (2013). *Report of the 2012 National Survey of Science and Mathematics Education.* Chapel Hill, NC: Horizon Research. Available: http://www.horizon-research.com/2012nssme/research-products/reports/technical-report/ [October 2018].

Baram-Tsabari, A., and Yarden, A. (2011). Quantifying the gender gap in science interests. *International Journal of Science and Mathematics Education, 9,* 523–550.

Beilock, S.L., Gunderson, E.A., Ramirez, G., Levine, S.C. (2010). Female teachers' math anxiety affects girls' math achievement. *Proceedings of the National Academy of Sciences, 107,* 1860–1863. doi: 10.1073/pnas.0910967107.

Bereiter, C., and Scardamalia, M. (2014). Knowledge building and knowledge creation: One concept, two hills to climb. In S.C. Tan, H.J. So, and J. Yeo (Eds.), *Knowledge Creation in Education* (pp. 35–52). Singapore: Springer.

Brotman, J.S., and Moore, F.M. (2008). Girls and science: A review of four themes in science education literature. *Journal of Research in Science Teaching, 45,* 971–1002.

Burris, C.C., Welner, K.G., and Bezoza, J.W. (2009). *Universal Access to a Quality Education: Research and Recommendations for the Elimination of Curricular Stratification.* Boulder, CO: National Education Policy Center. Available: http://nepc.colorado.edu/files/Epic-Epru_LB-UnivAcc-FINAL.pdf/ [September 2018].

Carey, S. (1986). Cognitive science and science education. *American Psychologist, 41*(10), 1123.

Cunningham, C.M. (2018). *Engineering in Elementary STEM Education: Curriculum Design, Instruction, Learning, and Assessment.* New York: Teachers College Press.

Darling, N., Caldwell, L.L., and Smith, R. (2005). Participation in school-based extracurricular activities and adolescent adjustment. *Journal of Leisure Research, 37*(1), 51–76.

DeBoer, G.E. (1991). *A History of Ideas in Science Education: Implications for Practice.* New York: Teachers College Press.

DuBois, W.E.B., and Dill, A.G. (1911). *The Common School and the Negro American. The Atlanta University Publications, No. 16.* Atlanta, GA: The Atlanta University Press.

Duschl, R.A., and Bybee, R.W. (2014). Planning and carrying out investigations: an entry to learning and to teacher professional development around NGSS science and engineering practices. *International Journal of STEM Education, 1*(1), 12.

Eccles, J.S. (1999). The development of children ages 6 to 14. *The Future of Children, 9*(2), 30–44.

Eccles, J.S., and Wigfield, A. (2002). Motivational beliefs, values, and goals. *Annual Review of Psychology, 53,* 109–132.

Eccles, J.S., Wigfield, A., and Byrnes, J. (2003). Cognitive development in adolescence. In R.M. Lerner, M.A. Esterbrooks, and J. Mistry (Eds.), *Handbook of Psychology: Developmental Psychology Volume 6* (pp. 325–350). Hoboken, NJ: John Wiley & Sons.

English, L., Hudson, B., and Dawes, L. (2011). Middle school students' perceptions of engineering. Science, Technology, Engineering and Mathematics in Education Conference. In P.B. Hudson and V. Chandra (Eds.), *STEM in Education Conference: Science, Technology, Engineering and Mathematics in Education Conference.* Queensland University of Technology, Queensland University of Technology, Brisbane. Available: file:///C:/Users/ywise/Downloads/Middle_school_students_perceptions_of_engineering.pdf [December 2018].

Fayer, S., Lacey, A., and Watson, A. (2017). *BLS Spotlight on Statistics: STEM Occupations-Past, Present, and Future.* Washington, DC: U.S. Department of Labor, Bureau of Labor Statistics.

Filardo, M. (2016). *State of Our Schools: America's K–12 Facilities 2016.* Washington, DC: 21st Century School Fund.

Forman, E.A., and Cazden, C.B. (1985). Exploring Vygotskian perspectives in education: The cognitive value of peer interaction. In J. Wertsch (Ed.), *Culture, Communication, and Cognition: Vygotskian Perspectives.* Cambridge: Cambridge University Press.

Fralick, B., Kearn, J., Thompson, S., and Lyons, J. (2009). How middle schoolers draw engineers and scientists. *Journal of Science Education and Technology, 18,* 60–73.

Frederiksen, N. (1984). Implications of cognitive theory for instruction in problem solving. *ETS Research Report Series, 1983*(1), 363–407.

Freebody, P., and Anderson, R.C. (1983). Effects of vocabulary difficulty, text cohesion, and schema availability on reading comprehension. *Reading Research Quarterly, 18,* 277–294.

Furtak, E.M., Seidel, T., Iverson, H., and Briggs, D.C. (2012). Experimental and quasi-experimental studies of inquiry-based science teaching: A meta-analysis. *Review of Educational Research, 82,* 300–329. doi: 10.3102/0034654312457206

Fyfe, E.R., McNeil, N.M., Son, J.Y., and Goldstone, R.L. (2014). Concreteness fading in mathematics and science instruction: A systematic review. *Educational Psychology Review, 26*(1), 9–25.

George, R. (2006) A cross-domain analysis of change in students' attitudes toward science and attitudes about the utility of science. *International Journal of Science Education, 28*(6), 571–589.

Giroux, H. (1989). Schooling as a form of cultural politics: Toward a pedagogy of and for difference. In H. Giroux and P. McLaren (Eds.), *Critical Pedagogy, the State and Cultural Struggle* (pp. 125–151). Albany, NY: State University of New York Press.

Glaser, R. (1984). Education and thinking: The role of knowledge. *American Psychologist*, 39(2), 93.

Gobert, J.D., and Buckley, B.C. (2000). Introduction to model-based teaching and learning in science education. *International Journal of Science Education*, 22(9), 891–894.

Government Accountability Office. (2016). *K-12 Education: Better Use of Information Could Help Agencies Identify Disparities and Address Racial Discrimination, Report to Congressional Requesters, GAO-16-345 Student Diversity*. Washington, DC: Author.

Hale, L. (2002). *Native American Education: A Reference Handbook*. Santa Barbara, CA: ABC-CLIO.

Hanson, S.L. (2004). African American women in science: Experiences from high school through the post-secondary years and beyond. In J. Bystydzienski and S. Bird (Eds.), *Removing Barriers: Women in Academic Science, Technology, Engineering, and Mathematics*. Bloomington, IN: Indiana University Press.

Harter, S. (1990). Self and identity development. In S.S Feldman and G.R. Elliott (Eds.), *At the Threshold: The Developing Adolescent* (pp. 352–387). Cambridge, MA: Harvard University Press.

Keating, D.P. (1990). Adolescent thinking. In S.S. Feldman and G.R. Elliott (Eds.), *At the Threshold: The Developing Adolescent* (pp. 54–89). Cambridge, MA: Harvard University Press.

Krajcik, J.S., and Shin, N. (2014). Project-based learning. In R.K. Sawyer (Ed.), *The Cambridge Handbook of the Learning Sciences, Second Edition* (pp. 275–297). New York: Cambridge University Press.

Lee, C., and Slaughter-Defoe, D. (1995). Historical socio-cultural influences in African American education. In J. Banks and C. Banks (Eds.), *Handbook of Research on Multicultural Education* (pp. 348–371). New York: Macmillan.

Lee, O., Quinn, H., and Valdés, G. (2013). Science and language for English language learners in relation to Next Generation Science Standards and with implications for Common Core State Standards for English Language Arts and Mathematics. *Educational Researcher*, 42(4), 223–233.

Maltese, A.V., and Cooper, C.S. (2017). *STEM Pathways: Do Men and Women Differ in Why They Enter and Exit?* AERA Open. doi: 10.1177/2332858417727276.

Maltese, A.V., and Tai, R.H. (2010). Eyeballs in the fridge: Sources of early interest in science. *International Journal of Science Education*, 32(5), 669–685.

McFarland, J., Hussar, B., de Brey, C., Snyder, T., Wang, X., Wilkinson-Flicker, S., Gebrekristos, S., Zhang, J., Rathbun, A., Barmer, A., Bullock Mann, F., and Hinz, S. (2017). *The Condition of Education 2017*. Washington, DC: U.S. Department of Education, National Center for Education Statistics. Available: https://nces.ed.gov/pubsearch/pubsinfo.asp?pubid=2017144 [March 2018].

Means, B., Confrey, J., House, A., and Bhanot, R. (2008). *STEM High Schools. Specialized Science Technology Engineering and Mathematics Secondary Schools in the U.S.* Menlo Park, CA: SRI International.

Meeus, W. (2011). The study of adolescent identity formation 2000–2010: A review of longitudinal research. *Journal of Research on Adolescence*, 21(1), 75–94.

Miller, D.I., Nolla, K.M., Eagly, A.H., and Uttal, D.H. (2018). The development of children's gender-science stereotypes: A meta-analysis of 5 decades of U.S. draw-a-scientist studies. *Child Development*, 1–13. Available: https://onlinelibrary.wiley.com/doi/full/10.1111/cdev.13039 [October 2018].

Moreno, R., Ozogul, G., and Reisslein, M. (2011). Teaching with concrete and abstract visual representations: Effects on students' problem solving, problem representations, and learning perceptions. *Journal of Educational Psychology*, 103(1), 32–47.

Morgan, I., and Amerikaner, A. (2018). *Funding Gaps 2018: An Analysis of School Funding Equity Across the U.S. and Within Each State*. Washington, DC: The Education Trust.

Muller, P.A., Stage, F.K., and Kinzie, J. (2001). Science achievement growth trajectories: Understanding factors related to gender and racial-ethnic differences in precollege science achievement. *American Education Research Journal, 38*, 981–1012.

National Academies of Sciences, Engineering, and Medicine. (2015). *Science Teachers' Learning: Enhancing Opportunities, Creating Supportive Contexts*. Washington, DC: The National Academies Press.

National Academies of Sciences, Engineering, and Medicine. (2018). *How People Learn II: Learners, Contexts, and Cultures*. Washington, DC: The National Academies Press.

National Academy of Engineering and National Research Council. (2009). *Engineering in K–12 Education*. Washington, DC: The National Academies Press.

National Commission on Excellence in Education. (1983). *A Nation at Risk: The Imperative for Educational Reform*. Washington, DC: U.S. Department of Education.

National Research Council. (1996). *National Science Education Standards*. Washington, DC: National Academy Press.

National Research Council. (2006). *America's Lab Report: Investigations in High School Science*. Washington, DC: The National Academies Press.

National Research Council. (2007). *Taking Science to School: Learning and Teaching Science in Grades K-8*. Washington, DC: The National Academies Press.

National Research Council. (2009). *Learning Science in Informal Environments: People, Places, and Pursuits*. Washington, DC: The National Academies Press.

National Research Council. (2011). *Successful K-12 STEM Education: Identifying Effective Approaches in Science, Technology, Engineering, and Mathematics*. Washington, DC: The National Academies Press.

National Research Council. (2012). *A Framework for K-12 Science Education: Practices, Crosscutting Concepts, and Core Ideas*. Washington, DC: The National Academies Press.

National Science Board. (2018a). *Science and Engineering Indicators 2018*. NSB-2018-1. Alexandria, VA: National Science Foundation. Available: https://www.nsf.gov/statistics/indicators/ [October 2018].

National Science Board. (2018b). NAEP 2015 *Science Assessment, Elementary and Secondary Mathematics and Science Education*. Alexandria, VA: National Science Foundation. Available: https://nsf.gov/statistics/2018/nsb20181/report/sections/elementary-and-secondary-mathematics-and-science-education/highlights [December 2018].

National Science Foundation. (2004). *An Emerging and Critical Problem of the Science and Engineering Workforce*. Arlington, VA: Author. Available: http://www.nsf.gov/sbe/srs/nsb0407/start.htm [October 2018].

National Science Teachers Association. (1971). NSTA position statement on school science education for the 70's. *The Science Teacher, 38*, 46–51.

NGSS Lead States. (2013). *Next Generation Science Standards: For States, by States*. Washington, DC: The National Academies Press.

Oakes, J. (2005). *Keeping Track: How Schools Structure Inequality (2nd edition)*. New Haven, CT: Yale University Press.

Orfield, G., and Lee, C. (2004). *Brown at 50: King's Dream or Plessy's Nightmare?* Cambridge, MA: The Civil Rights Project at Harvard University.

Passmore, C. (2014). *Implementing NGSS: How Your Classroom Is Framed Is as Important as What You Do in It: NSTA Blog*. Available: http://nstacommunities.org/blog/2014/11/10/implementing-the-next-generation-science-standards-how-your-classroom-is-framed-is-as-important-as-what-you-do-in-it/ [October 2018].

Penuel, W.R., Harris, C.J., D'Angelo, C., DeBarger, A.H., Gallagher, L.P., Kennedy, C.A., Cheng, B.H., and Krajcik, J.S. (2015). Impact of project-based curriculum materials on student learning in science: Results of a randomized controlled trial. *Journal of Research in Science Teaching, 52*(10), 1362–1385.

Piaget, J. (1977). *Epistemology and psychology of functions.* Dordrecht, Netherlands: D. Reidel.

Pritchard, R. (1990). The effects of cultural schemata on reading processing strategies. *Reading Research Quarterly, 25*(4), 273–295.

Reynolds, R.E., Taylor, M., Steffensen, M.S., Shirey, L.L., and Anderson, R.C. (1981). *Cultural Schemata and Reading Comprehension.* Technical Report No. 201. Urbana, IL: University of Illinois, Center for the Study of Reading.

Riegle-Crumb, C., Moore, C., and Ramos Wada, A. (2011). Who wants to have a career in science or math? Exploring adolescents' future aspirations by gender and race/ethnicity. *Science Education, 95*(3), 458–476.

Rockoff, J.E., and Lockwood, B.B. (2010). Stuck in the middle: Impacts of grade configuration in public schools. *Journal of Public Economics, 94*(11-12), 1051–1061.

Romero, C., Master, A., Paunesku, D., Dweck, C., and Gross, J.J. (2014). Academic and emotional functioning in middle school: The role of implicit theories. *Emotion, 14*(2), 227–234.

Sadler, P.M., Sonnert, G., Hazari, Z., and Tai, R. (2012). Stability and volatility of STEM career interest in high school: A gender study. *Science Education, 96*(3), 411–427.

Schwartz, D.L., and Martin, T. (2004). Inventing to prepare for future learning: The hidden efficiency of encouraging original student production in statistics instruction. *Cognition and Instruction, 22*(2), 129–184.

Song, M., and Bruning, R. (2016). Exploring the effects of background context familiarity and signaling on comprehension, recall, and cognitive load. *Educational Psychology: An International Journal of Experimental Educational Psychology, 36*(4), 691–718.

Songer, N.B., Kelcey, B., and Gotwals, A.W. (2009). How and when does complex reasoning occur? Empirically driven development of a learning progression focused on complex reasoning about biodiversity. *Journal of Research in Science Teaching, 46*(6), 610–631.

Stice, J.E. (1987). Using Kolb's learning cycle to improve student learning. *Engineering Education, 77*(5), 291–296.

Tai, R.H., Liu, C.Q., Maltese, A.V., and Fan, X. (2006). Planning early for careers in science. *Science, 312*(5777), 1143–1144.

Tan, E., Calabrese Barton, A., Kang, H., and O'Neill, T. (2013). Desiring a career in STEM-related fields: How middle school girls articulate and negotiate identities-in-practice in science. *Journal of Research in Science Teaching, 50*(10), 1143–1179.

Tolley, K. (1996). Science for ladies, classics for gentlemen: A comparative analysis of scientific subjects in the curricula of boys' and girls' secondary schools in the United States, 1794-1850. *History of Education Quarterly, 36*, 129–153. doi: 10.2307/369502.

Tolley, K. (2014). *The Science Education of American Girls: A Historical Perspective.* New York: Routledge Falmer.

U.S. Department of Education, National Center for Education Statistics. (2016). *National Assessment of Educational Progress (NAEP), 2009, 2011, and 2015 Science Assessment, NAEP Data Explorer.* Available: https://nces.ed.gov/programs/coe/indicator_cne.asp [October 2018].

U.S. Department of Education, Office for Civil Rights. (2014). *Civil Rights Data Collection Data Snapshot: Teacher Equity.* Available: https://www2.ed.gov/about/offices/list/ocr/docs/crdc-teacher-equity-snapshot.pdf [October 2018].

Ushomirsky, N., and Williams, D. (2015). *Funding Gaps: Too Many States Still Spend Less on Educating Students Who Need the Most*. Available: https://edtrust.org/wp-content/uploads/2014/09/FundingGaps2015_TheEducationTrust1.pdf [October 2018].

Webb, L.D. (2006). *The History of American Education: A Great American Experiment*. Upper Saddle River, NJ: Pearson Merrill Prentice Hall.

Weiss, I.R., Pasley, J.D., Smith, P.S., Banilower, E.R., and Heck, D.J. (2003). *Looking Inside the Classroom: A Study of K–12 Mathematics and Science Education in the United States*. Available: http://www.horizon-research.com/insidetheclassroom/reports/looking/complete.pdf [October 2018].

West, M., and Schwerdt, G. (2012). The middle school plunge: Achievement tumbles when young students change schools. *Education Next, 2*(12), 62–68.

Wigfield, A., Eccles, J.S., Schiefele, U., Roeser, R.W., and Kean, P.D. (2006). Development of achievement motivation. In W. Damon, R.M. Lerner, and N. Eisenberg (Eds.), *Handbook of Child Psychology, 6th Edition, Volume 3, Social, Emotional and Personality Development* (pp. 933–1002). New York: Wiley.

Wyss, V.L., Heulskamp, D., and Siebert, C.J. (2012.). Increasing middle school student interest in STEM careers with videos of scientists. *International Journal of Environmental and Science Education, 7*(4), 501–522.

3

Learning and Motivation

As described in Chapter 2, the changes that occur during middle and high school (learners experiencing rapid changes physically, socially, and cognitively) may directly or indirectly affect learners' overall interest in school, and their specific interest in science investigation and engineering design. Middle and high school students are beginning to form their own identities—as individuals and potential scientists and/or engineers. Peers can exert influences on the choices that learners make about their engagement and participation in academics and other activities that potentially compete for their time and attention (Eccles and Barber, 1999). Moreover, learners from traditionally underrepresented populations are also constructing their ethnic and racial identities at this time (Rivas-Drake et al., 2014), which may be affected by whether they see scientist or engineer as a plausible identity for a member of their group. As such, learning, interest, and motivation to learn are essential when considering students' involvement in science investigation and engineering design.

America's Lab Report (National Research Council, 2006) focused on many aspects of laboratory experiences, but the research on learning was narrowly discussed. Over the past decade, substantial progress has been made examining aspects of learning, interest, and motivation that facilitate student engagement in investigation and design (Blumenfeld, Kempler, and Krajcik, 2006; Lazowski and Hulleman, 2016; Linnenbrink-Garcia and Patall, 2016; Nieswandt and Horowitz, 2015). In particular, the contexts in which learning takes place are important because they can engage learners in authentic tasks that are culturally relevant and meaningfully support the development of connected knowledge (or deep learning) so that learners could then apply their knowledge to other situations (National Research Council, 2012). These contexts encourage learners to raise meaningful questions and facilitate their sustained learning on cognitively challenging tasks. When supports from a myriad of relevant contexts converge in the science classroom, science and engineering ideas emerge as needed to address challenges, design solutions, or make sense of phenomena.

Developing usable knowledge requires the learner to actively engage in making sense of human challenges and natural phenomena about which they develop and refine questions, make predictions, and explain phenomena using repeatable and reliable evidence (National Research Council, 2012). For the knowledge to become more connected, learners need to apply their knowledge to new phenomena and design solutions by building from prior knowledge and experiences that allow for opportunities that reflect on their learning (Novak and Gowin, 1984). By using multiple representations of information (e.g., gestures, diagrams, graphs, equations) within diverse and meaningful contexts, learners' knowledge becomes more connected and more refined (Waldrip, Prain, and Carolan, 2010). Moreover, learning is enhanced within a collaborative and inclusive community in which discourses are used as tools to express knowledge and debate and come to resolution regarding ideas and the validity of evidence to support claims (Osborne, 2010).

This chapter begins with a discussion of the different theoretical perspectives about learning that have shaped science education. Several themes that are part of a rich learning context are then discussed. The chapter concludes with a discussion of the importance of interest and motivation for science investigation and engineering design.

DYNAMICS OF LEARNING

The cognitive perspective of learning is the traditional view of learning. A cognitive perspective treats the individual learner as the primary unit of analysis, highlighting the processes and structures hypothesized to operate in an individual's mind as he or she physically interacts with others, objects, and events or mentally imagines these interactions. The focus on the minds of individuals in the cognitive perspective is useful in understanding behavior and promoting change within an educational system that tracks performance achievements and gains of individual learners.

In contrast to the cognitive perspective, the sociocultural perspective of learning emphasizes context. Context is multifaceted and encompasses conditions directly and indirectly connected to the learner. At one extreme, it refers to the immediate settings in which learners are directly involved; the science classroom is an example of this facet of context. At the other extreme, context refers to conditions far removed from learners' direct participation but that nonetheless impact them: Institutional arrangements like state formulae for funding education and certification requirements for highly qualified science teachers exemplify this aspect of context. The general notion of context captures the relational nature of learning—the learner's relationship with others; the material resources available and experiences to facilitate learning; the learner's relation to the formal and informal protocols and procedures operative in the spaces in which learning occurs; and the learners' relation to arrangements and decisions often far removed from the learner that produce policies that influence learning and other experiences (Cole, 1995). Although the initial learning context that supported early learning might fade, and as learning progresses other contexts become more prominent, they are all critical to the process of learning, interest, and motivation.

Sociocultural perspectives are useful in considering and addressing large-scale, persistent patterns in education (e.g., underrepresentation of females in computational fields)—particularly in educational systems historically and intentionally designed to differentiate access to education by group membership. A sociocultural account of learning emphasizes the following: (1) what is learned (e.g., practices, symbol systems) and what facilitates learning (e.g., tools) are culturally determined; (2) this determination is socially mediated by and situated within historical and contemporary sociopolitical conditions; and (3) the internal processes of individual learning are influenced by these cultural determinations and social mediations.

A more comprehensive perspective of learning integrates the cognitive perspective with the sociocultural perspective. This holistic perspective of learning emphasizes both what is internal and what is external to the learner (Cobb, 1994) and may prove useful in realizing the vision of science education proposed in *A Framework for K–12 Science Education* (hereafter referred to as the *Framework*; National Research Council, 2012). With educating all learners in science and engineering as its first goal, an integrative approach is necessary to fulfill the aims of three-dimensional learning (see Chapters 1 and 2 for an explanation of the three dimensions), with particular attention to making these practices equitable and inclusive. This approach allows for an understanding of the collective nature of some types of learning in the classroom. For example, the sense-making of groups as they work together on a phenomenon of design solution shapes the learning of the individuals working together.

LEARNING THEORY THEMES

Our view of learning for this report synthesizes the views of a number of significant reports on science education that each offered compilations of the current learning sciences research showing that learning occurs within and is inseparable from contexts. As can be seen in Box 3-1 and elaborated

---

BOX 3-1
Themes in Learning Theory Used in Past
Science Education Reports

1. Learning involves making cognitive connections.
2. Learning is developmental.
3. Learning is embodied and involves changing actions and perceptions.
4. Learning involves social and emotional engagement in communities.
5. Learning is influenced by levels of engagement.
6. Learning is historical.
7. Learning occurs within and is inseparable from contexts.

---

on below, several common themes emerge from these reports. In addition, our view of learning in this report incorporates the importance of contexts reflected: Learning occurs within and is inseparable from contexts.

Learning Involves Making Cognitive Connections

In order to learn, it is necessary to form new connections among concepts and for knowledge to be useful in new contexts. Connections among concepts become formed and are enriched as learners interact with the world, respond to human needs, make decisions, and make sense of new experiences they encounter (Novak and Gowin, 1984). Some of the important types of connections learners make include connecting new concepts to prior knowledge and experiences, forming episodic connections to their lived experiences and the stories they hear, seeing analogies and contrasts between distinct concepts, and relating abstractions to concrete objects and experiences, either literally or metaphorically. As individuals use their knowledge, more connections are made among concepts.

Multiple and varied experiences enrich these connections (Chi, Feltovich, and Glaser, 1981; Ericsson et al., 2018; Goswami, 2012; National Academy of Engineering and National Research Council, 2014; National Research Council, 2000; Noble et al., 2012) such as through social and physical interactions with others and the world. These interactions provide rich, multisensory contexts that greatly aid memory and sense making. Social and physical interactions also help learners to develop metacognitive understanding of their own knowledge and ways of knowing, to reflect on what they do and do not understand, and to describe what they know through language (such as explanation and argumentation) and building and revising models (such as diagrams, systems of equations, physical prototypes, and computer programs). As a result, these interactions—making sense of phenomena, gathering and analyzing data/information, constructing explanations and design solutions, and communicating reasoning to self and others—are all critical to learning. Science investigations can therefore enhance learning by providing physically and socially rich experiences that reveal and help form meaningful connections among concepts and offer ways to change existing concepts in the face of contradictions and reflections on learning.

When knowledge is organized with numerous meaningful connections, individuals can access that knowledge to solve problems, make decisions, and learn more. Elaborated webs of connected concepts are referred to as schemata. Schemata play roles in comprehension, remembering, and learning (Freebody and Anderson, 1983; Pritchard, 1990; Reynolds et al., 1982). Developing schemata is critical to learning because when an investigation activates that web of knowledge, the cognitive load[1] is lower than if the activity is unrelated to previously acquired knowledge, allowing learners to learn more, learn faster, or figure out a new situation. Concepts that are not connected or connect in ways that do not allow access for problem solving and making sense of the world comprise inert knowledge, a knowledge that can be expressed but not utilized (Bransford et al., 1986; Gentner et al., 2009; Gick and Holyoak, 1980; Perkins, 1999; Renkl, Manid, and Gruber, 2010; Whitehead, 1929).

The evidence that meaningful learning has occurred is that individuals can use their knowledge in new situations, that is, transfer understanding of a concept to new experiences (National Research Council, 2000). In transferring understanding, connections between concepts become stronger and enriched. Transfer also relates to personal motivation when it supports learners in making connections from school learning to their values and lives outside of school (National Research Council, 2000). It is especially beneficial for learners and to societies in this scientifically and technologically advanced era when learning experiences facilitate the process of identity formation in which people come to think of themselves as engineering and science learners capable of doing investigation and design. The research is clear that usable knowledge—that is, learning that can be transferred to new situations—only occurs when individuals are actively making sense of the world (National Research Council, 2012).

Learning Is Developmental

Psychologists including Lev Vygotsky and Jean Piaget conceptualized learning in developmental terms with a primary emphasis on internal

---

[1] Cognitive load theory highlights the limited capacity of working memory when novel information is to be learned (Sweller, 2005).

mental structures (Piaget) and the interactions among internal processes and the social and physical world (Vygotsky).[2] Vygotsky (reprinted in Cole et al. [eds.], 1978) defined the *zone of proximal development* as the difference between a child's actual performance level from independent actions and the performance that is achieved when guided by a more capable other (e.g., a parent, teacher, or more experienced student). In an instructional setting, the zone of proximal development can be operationalized as *scaffolding* (Wood, Bruner, and Ross, 1976), where a more knowledgeable other provides social support within the child's zone of proximal development to master a cultural skill, practices, or knowledge. These scaffolds then fade as the student demonstrates greater autonomy (Puntambekar and Hubscher, 2005).

Developing and revising models, as well as constructing evidence-based explanations for phenomena and evidence-based solutions to challenges, are complex cognitive processes that need to be scaffolded in classrooms and developed over time—they cannot be contained in isolated 50-minute class periods. Instructional resources can provide scaffolds by reducing complexity and providing hints (see Chapter 6), and teachers scaffold work synergistically with supports provided in materials to enhance the learning situation (McNeill et al., 2009; Tabak, 2004). Therefore, students benefit from coherent curricula that help them connect material across classes and grade levels and in which they can revisit concepts and ideas at multiple ages (see Chapters 5 and 6).

Learning Is Embodied and Involves
Changing Actions and Perceptions

Actions are central to investigations. Experiencing phenomena and challenges and making sense of them through developing and revising models, arguing from evidence, planning and carrying out an investigation, or constructing an evidence-based explanation are critical to the aspect of doing science and engineering. Through actions, learners can improve their understanding of conceptual relations through such sense-making mechanisms as spatial metaphor and causal inference. Different strategies (e.g., contextualizing, spacing through repeated exposure, and providing variability) to deliberate practice (Ericsson, 2008) have been linked to increasing the learner's flexibility and retrieval of information.

---

[2]Neo-Piagetians examined cognitive development from other theoretical perspectives, like social cognitive theory, and considered other complexities, such as interactions between the learner and contexts (e.g., others, tools) surrounding the learner. In similar fashion, neo-Vygotskian scholars have shown that children can operate beyond their autonomous levels of performance when they receive assistance.

Moreover, more efficient learning is linked with informative and timely feedback (Hattie and Timperley, 2007; Healy and Sinclair, 1996; Karpicke and Roediger, 2008).

An equally important consideration is the ways learners use their perceptions, so that they can begin to see (and hear, feel, and smell) the world differently. Engaging learning in various multimodal experiences—reading and writing text, experiencing phenomena, using simulations, interpreting graphs—is essential for meaningful learning. Investigations may enhance science learning because they engage learners' embodied ways of knowing in service of perceptual, motoric, and procedural learning.

Learning Involves Social and Emotional Engagement in Communities

Learning is enhanced within a collaborative community in which language is used as a tool to express knowledge, argue explanations and solutions, and come to resolution regarding the validity of evidence to support or refute a proposed explanation (Osborne, 2010). Working with peers and knowledgeable others supports individuals' learning new ideas and skills that they could not learn on their own. The back-and-forth of using ideas builds new connections and reinforces previously made connections.

When learners argue the validity of their evidence and share diverse perspectives on these ideas with others, their interactions help them to form new connections among ideas or enrich previous connections. Knowledge becomes shared within the community. As such, collaborations promote learners building shared understandings of scientific ideas and of the nature of the discipline (Krajcik and Shin, 2014). Teachers or more knowledgeable others need to support learners in collaborating, including listening to others' ideas, being open to and respectful of others' ideas, making use of others' ideas, and pressing for more information.

Learning Is Influenced by Levels of Engagement

When students are cognitively engaged, they experience high levels of challenge, skill, and interest (Schneider et al., 2016) that will drive their learning (see the section "Interest and Motivation" below). Engagement relies upon learning principles, such as authentic situations, context, active engagement, choice, and collaboration to engage individuals and promote learning. Such environments engage learners in science investigations, collaborations, and artifact creation that represent their developing understanding. Not all environments promote cognitive engagement that sustain students in learning challenging ideas. More often than not, learning environments (i.e., traditional classrooms) do not push students to address challenges that are important to them, make sense of phenomena that are situated in their lives, or allow them to make decisions about the direction of an investigation. Such environments do not inspire students to invest effort or to persevere in learning challenging ideas.

Learning Is Historical

Science education reforms often situate learning as a present-day, here-and-now neutral event that primarily involves the teacher or other knowledgeable other, the learner, and the materials and tools for science learning. A sociocultural view of learning with a focus on context acknowledges the historical, sociocultural nature of learning. For example, advanced education for many families with multigeneration college completers is a complex event that is expected and endorsed by the families. This event is also facilitated by conditions that persist across generations. Individual learners' science learning can be a similar production.

BOX 3-2
Leonardi's Case: Teachers and Policies Can
Impact a Student's Motivation to Engage

As described by Rivera Maulucci and colleagues (2014), Leonardi was a student in a science inquiry program at an urban middle school. He had been struggling with motivation, but through this program, he was provided with opportunities to engage in the work that scientists and engineers do. The program—intended to be an intervention—resulted in Leonardi seeing himself as achieving success in science.

'Leonardi was an under-performing student selected for the program because the assistant principal thought it would be a good experience for him. He lived with his mother and little brother . . . his worst subject was science 'because you have to know . . . a lot of facts to find out what the meaning of it is.' One week into the authentic science inquiry program, Leonardi's teacher stopped Maria [the assistant principal] in the hall and said, 'I don't know why you picked him to be in your program, he doesn't deserve it.' We were pulling the students out of their regular afternoon classes in order to work on the inquiry projects and the teacher felt that his behavior in class did not warrant such a special privilege. She made it clear that she would have picked another student, and later, exercised her control by not allowing Leonardi to be excused from class to present at the District Science Exposition. Yet Leonardi was one of the most dedicated students in the program and during the final week, he stayed late after school to finish his project even though his partner could not stay to help. . . .

As stated earlier, the assistant principal chose Leonardi for the program as an intervention. Leonardi struggled with staying motivated in school and his academic performance and behavior were inconsistent. In the program, he took on the roles of a serious academic student and a scientist. It made him feel like a genius.

On one hand, sociocultural perspectives can cast science learning as a local social practice. It is a contested space where the larger institutional issues (e.g., funding, teacher quality, historical inequities in access) and histories embodied in social practice (e.g., beliefs about who can and cannot do science) intersect (Holland and Lave, 2001; Penuel et al., 2016). On the other hand, sociocultural perspectives can situate science learning within a complex activity system (Cole, 1996a,b; Engeström, 2009). This system view allows a specific individual's science learning at a particular moment in time to be examined in relation to the learner's past experiences and future aspirations and the past and present experiences and future aspirations of the learner's significant others. In addition, the complex activity system view allows for the consideration of science learning with respect to the learner's membership in a socially defined group (e.g., gender, race, disability) as it pertains to the group's historical and contemporary status in society generally and in the activity system in particular.

Learning as historical is illustrated in several ways in a case study about a young boy named Leonardi (see Box 3-2). For example, the case

The whole year following the program, whenever Leonardi saw Maria in hall or whenever his class came to the Lab, he would ask her if she was going to do the program again, because he wanted to be in it. In seventh grade, he finally got his chance. . . . As part of a unit on simple machines, Leonardi's teacher had students design and build Rube Goldberg machines. The groups were required to include at least three simple machines in their designs. They also had to test their designs and show the data for their test trials. Leonardi and his partner built an elaborate garbage disposal machine, and just as with the authentic science program, he showed dedication in making sure that his machine worked and that it had a purpose. He explained that his group had come up with many different machines, but they had no purpose and he wanted one that had a purpose. Leonardi's machine was selected as one of four projects to represent the school at the District Science Exposition that year, and his project was one of the highlights of the exposition. Students flocked to his project because they could try for themselves to see how it worked" (Rivera Maulucci et al., 2014, pp. 1134–1136).

The classification of Leonardi as an underperforming student surmises his past academic performance and his views about science implicates his past experiences with science. The underperforming label shaped how the assistant principal (Maria) and one of his teachers perceived him and what they expected of him. These perceptions and expectations of persons with authority influenced what experiences Leonardi could access. The assistant principal viewed his access to a high-quality science learning experience as a vehicle to alter his classification as an underperforming student, but his teacher believed he did not deserve the access—these contradictory perspectives feature the contested nature of social practice, a sociocultural perspective on the local end of the continuum.

SOURCE: Adapted from Rivera Maulucci et al. (2014, pp. 1134–1136).

highlights how the classification of Leonardi shaped the perceptions that teachers and school leaders had regarding his potential to engage with science learning. Learning as historical from the systems end of the sociocultural perspective continuum is implicit but nonetheless present in a myriad of ways: policy and resources around pull-out instruction, qualifications, and employment consistency of Leonardi's past and present teachers who taught science, and the quality of the facilities and equipment to build and test the machine models are just a few.

Learning Occurs Within and Is Inseparable from Contexts

Learning, conceived as forming connections among concepts and changing perceptions and actions, is intricately linked to contexts. There are numerous examples of context as an intermediary of learning, but consistent illustrations appear in the *Framework* committee's treatment of progression, the common element, distinctly sectioned throughout the report, to practices, crosscutting concepts, and core ideas, as excerpted here:

> In the earliest grades, as students begin to look for and analyze patterns—whether in their observations of the world or in the relationships between different quantities in data (e.g., the sizes of plants over time)—they can also begin to consider what might be causing these patterns and relationships and design tests that gather more evidence to support or refute their ideas. By the upper elementary grades, students should have developed the habit of routinely asking about cause-and-effect relationships in the systems they are studying, particularly when something occurs that is, for them, unexpected. The questions "How did that happen?" or "Why did that happen?" should move toward "What mechanisms caused that to happen?" and "What conditions were critical for that to happen?" In middle and high school, argumentation starting from students' own explanations of cause and effect can help them appreciate standard scientific theories that explain the causal mechanisms in the systems under study. Strategies for this type of instruction include asking students to argue from evidence when attributing an observed phenomenon to a specific cause. For example, students exploring why the population of a given species is shrinking will look for evidence in the ecosystem of factors that lead to food shortages, over-predation, or other factors in the habitat related to survival; they will provide an argument for how these and other observed changes affect the species of interest (National Research Council, 2012, pp. 88–89).

In addition to illustrating developmental influences, the above excerpt implicates contexts of learning in numerous ways that point out the synergy between sociocultural and cognitive perspectives on scientific reasoning.

The excerpt featured contexts as the setting (e.g., level of education, the stage for learning) in which student observations, questioning, and explanations occurred as they engage in investigation. Context is also implicit in the excerpt: fundamentals are not listed or clearly described but must be present for the described learning to occur. For example, contexts include the determination of the processes highlighted in the investigation and how these processes unfold; the materials needed to carry out the investigation (e.g., packaging and representation of phenomena for student examination); and more knowledgeable others to scaffold understandings (e.g., teachers employing instructional strategies). A change in any of the contexts—the settings, the tools used by learners, etc.—would alter the learning experience and the learning. The expansive nature of context (e.g., close proximity to and distant from the learner), the myriad manifestations of it (e.g., physical materials in classroom, policies that define what is valued, familiarity and value of the problem to the learner), and the integral function it plays in cognition and learning make context a critical tool in achieving inclusive excellence in science education and high-quality science learning for all learners.

INTEREST AND MOTIVATION

As illustrated in the previous section, developing a deep and usable understanding of science as envisioned by the *Framework* involves forming new connections among concepts and application of that knowledge in new contexts. Learning is a lifelong process as people construct foundational knowledge through formal schooling and then expand knowledge throughout their lives as they mindfully engage in problem solving and making sense of the world. People are able and willing to engage with science from infancy through adulthood only if they are motivated to do so. The contexts of learning are important factors, and finding opportunities to cultivate motivation and interest in science investigation and engineering design is key.

Motivation can evolve and change over time and elements of the student's learning environment can foster curiosity[3] and interest that supports the motivation to learn (Hidi and Renninger, 2006). In general, motivation has been found to be a key mechanism for enhancing student learning outcomes in science (Lazowski and Hulleman, 2016). For example, the evidence for underrepresented learners suggests that issues related to interest

---

[3] Curiosity is an additional construct often associated with motivational variables including interest. Like interest, curiosity can be thought of as a state induced by environmental factors, such as novelty and complexity, as well as a more stable trait (Silvia, 2012). However, curiosity is most often considered as an emotional factor (Renninger and Su, 2012), whereas most motivational variables consist of both emotional/affective and cognitive components.

and motivation may be the primary factor behind underrepresentation in certain STEM career tracks rather than ability (Wang, Eccles, and Kenny, 2013). However, the study of motivation in STEM learning is primarily supported by correlational or qualitative case studies (Lazowski and Hulleman, 2016) and as such, no direct mechanism has been specifically linked with motivated behavior and subsequent academic achievement (Linnenbrink-Garcia and Patall, 2016). To promote three-dimensional learning, creating meaningful environments that use various motivational constructs is essential.

Theories of Motivation

Due to the importance of interest and motivation for engagement in science investigation and engineering design and persistence in STEM more broadly, research has focused on student perceptions specific to science and engineering that can be barriers to motivation. In general, some learners have firm beliefs that they "just can't do" science or engineering; perceive stereotypes that exclude groups from feeling they *can* participate; have little experience with science or engineering outside of academic context; and/or feel that learning in science or engineering has little inherent value to them (e.g., "When will I ever use this?"). These barriers can be overcome through interventions that target specific or multiple motivational constructs; however, they are not necessarily able to address systemic exclusion of individuals or groups from participation in science and engineering (see Chapter 2). There are several different contemporary theories of motivation: expectancy-value, attribution, social-cognitive, goal orientation, and self-determination (Cook and Artino, 2016; Schunk, Meece, and Pintrich, 2014).

Eccles and Wigfield developed the ideas behind the theory of expectancy-value (Wigfield and Eccles, 2000). For this theory, motivation is a function of the expectation of success and perceived value. There are two pieces behind expectancy-value. The first concerns the expectation of success, which is the degree to which individuals believe they will be successful if they try. The second concerns the perceived task value, which is the degree to which individuals perceive the task as having personal importance (Cook and Artino, 2016).

Attribution theory, described by Weiner in 1985, explains why individuals differentially respond to a given experience. These different responses are thought to arise from the ways in which the individual perceives the cause of the initial outcome. There are three dimensions that can describe the "cause": (1) locus—whether it is internal or external to the learner, (2) stability—whether it is fixed or likely to change, and (3) controllability—whether it is within or outside of the individual's control (Cook and Artino, 2016). For example, Ziegler and Heller (2000) trained teachers of an 8th-grade physics class to give feedback on student work that emphasized that the students' efforts were responsible for their success. After 1 year of the physics classroom intervention, learners in a treatment group demonstrated increases in their belief of an internal attribution of success (i.e., success is attributed to effort) and achievement test scores as compared to a control group. Similar outcomes were found for high-achieving high school girls (although importantly, not for boys, who already had significantly higher beliefs in internal attributions of success) in chemistry who received attribution training through informational videos (Ziegler and Stoeger, 2004).

Social-cognitive theory of motivation is one that is also considered to be a theory of learning. It focuses on the reciprocal interactions among personal, behavioral, and environmental factors with self-efficacy being the primary driver of the motivated action (Cook and Artino, 2016). Bandura (1994) described self-efficacy as one's belief in one's ability to succeed in specific situations or accomplish a task. Interventions that target increasing student self-efficacy have also demonstrated a positive effect on motivation and achievement in science and engineering (Bong, Lee, and Woo, 2015; Linninbrink-Garcia and Patall, 2016). Promoting learners experiencing achievement appears to be the most common approach to positively influencing self-efficacy. Although this method of intervention does seem promising, there appear to be very few intervention studies aimed specifically at increasing self-efficacy in middle and high school science or engineering.

The theory of goal orientation focuses on whether learners tend to engage in tasks for mastering content (mastery goal), for doing better than others (performance-approach goal), or for avoiding failure (performance-avoidance goal) (Cook and Artino, 2016). Mastery goals are associated with interest and deep learning, whereas performance-goals are associated with better grades (Cook and Artino, 2016). Research has consistently shown that learners who demonstrate a strong belief that success in science is a result of effort are more likely to feel confident about their ability to engage with science, to persevere when the going gets tough, to retain what they have learned for long periods, to have generally positive attitudes toward science (Blackwell, Trzesniewski, and Dweck, 2007; Elliot, McGregor, and Gable, 1999), and to continue engaging with science after school (Fortus and Vedder-Weiss, 2014).

Self-determination theory, developed by Deci and Ryan, explores intrinsic and extrinsic motivational factors (Deci, Koestner, and Ryan, 1999). Intrinsic motivation is when a learner performs a particular activity for personal rewards, whereas extrinsic motivation is when a learner performs an activity to earn a reward or avoid a punishment. The relationship between intrinsic and extrinsic motivation with respect to learning is described in the next section. A major approach to interventions aimed at improving intrinsic motivation is to attempt to increase a student's sense of value or connection to science and engineering. Improving student's perceptions of what real science and engineering jobs are like has been linked with increases in the learner's value for the content being learned. Role models for learners can help inspire them to engage and achieve in science and engineering disciplines, and see themselves in these roles (Stout et al., 2011). Through a direct value intervention, Harackiewicz and colleagues (2012) used brochure mailings and a website to support parents' belief in the usefulness of taking high school science courses and to guide parents in talking to their children about the utility of math and science. Learners in this intervention demonstrated increased enrollment in high school science courses and increases in utility value of science courses if their mother's perception of utility value also increased. A follow-up study found that these same learners had higher math and science ACT scores and greater pursuit of STEM careers (Rozek et al., 2017).

Overall, it is important to provide opportunities for learners to challenge their own perceptions about science learning, which could lead to increased interest and motivation to learn; however, it should be acknowledged that these efforts may not be sufficient to overcome systemic institutional barriers such as racial and gender biases or inadequately resourced and supported learning experiences.

Intrinsic and Extrinsic Factors Influencing Interest and Motivation

The quality of learning during science investigation and engineering design is dependent, in part, on the student's interest and motivation to engage during the investigation (Blumenfeld, Kempler, and Krajcik, 2006). When learners are intrinsically motivated, they want to engage in an investigation because it is viewed as interesting and enjoyable. Learners are more intrinsically motivated when there is the perception of a high degree of autonomy rather than being externally controlled (Deci and Ryan, 2000). Moreover, as these learners willingly engage in investigation, they are more likely to perceive the challenges as within their abilities. On the other hand, external rewards may undermine the learner's perceptions of autonomy and control, decreasing intrinsic motivation and interest (Deci and Ryan, 1985). However, teaching strategies that use rewards to stimulate interest in a topic may provide learners with the encouragement needed to develop feelings of autonomy, competence, and academic achievement (Vansteenkist et al., 2004).

In education, the use of extrinsic motivation is still under debate (Linnenbrink-Garcia and Patall, 2016). Extrinsic motivation was once thought to be detrimental to long-term student motivation and have lasting negative consequences for learning, because it was thought to undermine intrinsic motivation (e.g., Deci, Koestner, and Ryan, 1999). However, research has suggested that extrinsic motivators such as rewards and grades may actually have important benefits to promote motivation, because they may be necessary to motivate learners who have less interest (Hidi and Harackiewicz, 2000). As such, intrinsic and extrinsic motivational factors can exist simultaneously, and their intersection can be beneficial for motivation and learning (Harackiewicz et al., 2002). For example, learners may attempt to pursue learning content material deeply to master course content and grow their knowledge of the subject (i.e., are intrinsically motivated) and simultaneously attempt to maximize their course grade (i.e., are extrinsically motivated) during learning in academic coursework.

Design Features to Promote Interest and Motivation through Science Investigation and Engineering Design

Classrooms can be structured to make particular goals more or less salient and can shift or reinforce learners' interests (Maehr and Midgley, 1996). Research in interest development has proposed several methods of maintaining and increasing interest that can be used to promote quality and sustained engagement in science investigation and engineering design (Nieswandt and Horowitz, 2015). In particular, the design principles include (1) providing choice or autonomy in learning, (2) promoting personal relevance, (3) presenting appropriately challenging material, and (4) situating the investigations in socially and culturally appropriate contexts.

Providing Choice or Autonomy

The first design principle focuses on providing choice or autonomy. Research on interest development suggests that allowing learners some autonomy to choose the direction or content of their learning (Patall, Cooper, and Wynn, 2010), particularly in science and engineering (Nieswandt and Horowitz, 2015), and having options that relate to one's interests (Azevedo, 2013; Walkington, 2013) can benefit interest development and learning. When learners are given the opportunity to make choices about their learning, they may gain a sense of competence, which may foster interest and motivation (Patall, Sylvester, and Han, 2014). However, too much choice, particularly with lack of knowledge about those choices, can have negative consequences that can lead to random choice or being overwhelmed (Katz and Assor, 2007). Overall, allowing learners to experience phenomena or challenges and then brainstorm related questions they can explore is an important aspect of providing choice. Teachers need to be mindful to structure the learning environments to scaffold the selection of choices and provide ones that connect to a variety of other possible student interests outside of the content being learned (see Chapter 5).

Promoting Personal Relevance

The second design principle involves tailoring science investigation and engineering design work to be relevant to the student and is important for engagement and learning (Järvelä and Renninger, 2014). One way that this can be accomplished is by situating the phenomena within the learner's local context (see the place-based learning discussion below). Alternatively, as described above, the student could be offered some choice about the topic so that he or she may choose a topic of inherent interest. To help learners see or make personal connections during an investigation, teachers can ask learners to describe how the work they are doing in the science and/ or engineering class is related to their lives. For example, Hulleman and Harackiewicz (2009) found that when learners self-describe the personal relevance of learning tasks, it can lead to improvements in interest and achievement as it allowed the learners to sense the value or make a connection between science and engineering and their own lives.

Funds of knowledge are broadly defined as the historically accumulated and culturally developed bodies of knowledge and skills essential for household or individual well-being (Gonzales, Moll, and Amanti, 2005). The concept of funds of knowledge emerged out of the qualitative work of teacher-researcher collaborations with families of students living on the United States-Mexico border; they are the valuable understandings, skills, and tools that students maintain as a part of their identity (Moll et al., 1992). Incorporating learners' funds of knowledge can increase their understanding of science and engineering concepts and increase their motivation. For example, Kellogg and colleagues (2016) examined the role of participatory bioexploration assays for American Indian and Alaska Native learners using medicinal plant knowledge as an entry point to support student engagement. Through the use of observational monitoring,[4] the study found that the integration of learners' cultural knowledge increased engagement during classroom discussions as well as during investigation and design activities.

Project-based learning (Krajcik and Shin, 2014), with its focus on engaging learners in finding solutions to questions anchored in phenomena that they find meaningful and opportunities to ask and explore questions, also provides this relevance. For example, Hoffman and Hausler (1998) found that situating a physics-related problem—the working of a pump—into a

---

[4]The STROBE method was used to measure in-class student engagement. That is, visible behaviors, such as looking at the instructor, writing, reading classroom content, or performing experiments were quantified and measured. The percentage of time that students exhibited disengaged (actively off task–talking or passively off task–sleeping) and engaged (listening/ watching/speaking, writing or reading, and hands-on activity) behaviors was calculated across the activity period (Kellogg et al., 2016).

real-world context—the type of pump used in heart surgery—resulted in significantly more interest for high school girls. Place-based learning (Sobel, 2005), often used in environmental education, offers another approach to increase personal relevance as the focus is on challenges and phenomena that exist in the local community. Learners are more likely to make personal connections and see science and engineering as more relevant to their lives by working on challenges with which they can directly identify. For learners from communities traditionally underrepresented in the sciences and engineering (low-income learners from urban and rural contexts, girls, and certain racial and ethnic groups), place-based education has the added potential to help learners see the relevance of science and engineering concepts in their daily lives and communities (Clark, Fuesting, and Diekman, 2016; Endreny, 2010).

Presenting Appropriately Challenging Material

The third set of design principles is based on creating lessons and tasks that are appropriately challenging for learners. Optimal difficulty and complexity of a task can lead to long-term individual interest development (Nieswandt and Horowitz, 2015). There is variability in the success of learners in challenging situations with some learners thriving (Renninger and Su, 2012) and others lacking perseverance (Sansone, Thoman, and Fraughton, 2015). For learners faced with an environment that is more challenging than they are comfortable with, it may be beneficial to provide some scaffolding to the investigation. Teachers can help the learner by highlighting the potential personal relevance to the learner, include more incremental steps to help the learner feel more comfortable and interested in the investigation, and provide feedback that conveys appreciation for the difficulty of the problem for the learner. These ideas are further expanded in Chapters 4, 5, and 6.

Socially and Culturally Situated Learning

The last design principle concerns socially and culturally situated learning. There has been an increase in the use of situated and sociocultural approaches with the intent to foster interest and motivation (Azevedo, 2013). To positively influence motivation, STEM lessons must be sensitive to the cultural and personal backgrounds of learners and leverage the power of social engagement to enhance interest development. Curriculum designed in this way can facilitate retention and reactivation of the learned content and develop interest (Häussler and Hoffman, 2002; see also Chapter 6).

Another method of utilizing socially or culturally situated learning is to design lessons to deliberately emphasize social and cultural connectedness.

Social connections support interest and learning in content by providing a shared experience and excitement for the work, access to information, and ideas about how and what to pursue next (Bergin, 2016). As noted in the discussion on the importance of context in learning earlier in this chapter, cultural connectedness enhances what is familiar to the learner. Cultural connectedness also affirms aspects of learners' identities by conveying the value of their backgrounds and experiences, as demonstrated in Dee and Prenner's (2017) research on cultural relevance by way of high school ethnic studies curriculum.

These social and cultural connections aid in internalizing values for the content (Deci and Ryan, 1991) through finding shared purpose, focus, and values (Rogoff, 1998). Promoting social and cultural connectedness can be achieved by creating investigations that make explicit connections between school-based learning and the real worlds that the learners live in (Pressick-Kilbourn, 2015), and intentionally pointing out the importance of these connections. It is important that the attempt to make these connections is culturally appropriate, authentic, and related to the real lives of the learners.

Students from Underrepresented Populations

Within the broad field of science education, as articulated in Chapter 2, a growing body of work draws attention to issues of equity. Chapter 2 highlights that there have been a number of systemic institutional barriers that have limited the opportunities that members of traditionally underrepresented groups have in science. The limit in opportunities may influence whether or not the learner might have eventually developed an interest in science and engineering topics. Girls, learners from backgrounds traditionally underrepresented in the sciences and engineering, English learners, and learners with physical and cognitive disabilities could benefit from instructional practices that encourage their participation in investigation and design that, in turn, have the potential to spark and strengthen their interests in pursuing science-related and/or engineering education at various levels. Many of the strategies just described have been successfully implemented to improve interest, motivation, and learning for students from these underrepresented groups (Alexakos, Jones, and Rodriguez, 2011; Calabrese Barton and Tan, 2018).

Learners' identities in science and engineering are shaped by their opportunities to engage meaningfully in science and engineering knowledge and practice, to be able to use that knowledge in combination with other forms of salient knowledge to take action on issues they care about, and to be recognized for their efforts by their teachers and other learners.

However, when any of these three components of identity work[5] are disrupted or limited, learners' identity work suffers (Calabrese Barton et al., 2013). For example, in a study that examined girls from grades 6–8, it was found that those learners who lost interest in STEM had limited opportunities to exercise agency in science or to be recognized for their efforts to do so (Tan et al., 2013).

Longitudinal and multisited ethnographic studies and design-based research document how youth from underrepresented backgrounds participate in and develop science identities over time (grades 6–9) and place (home, afterschool, school; Jiang et al., 2018; Tan et al., 2013). Having opportunities to create identities as "community science experts" (people who have deep knowledge of community and STEM and can merge them toward solving science-related problems) is one form of identity work that has been shown to support youth from historically underrepresented backgrounds in increasing their STEM knowledge and practice and in increasing their agency in STEM (Birmingham and Calabrese Barton, 2014; Calabrese Barton and Tan, 2010). That is, students walk away thinking "I can solve this problem collaboratively right here in my community, right now using what I know." Work by Calabrese Barton and Tan (Calabrese Barton and Tan, 2018) also shows that when youth are supported in taking up STEM practices in ways that reflect deep and critical knowledge of the needs communities face, they persist in STEM learning toward more robust STEM/engineering designs.

An additional factor to be addressed for those groups traditionally underrepresented in science and engineering are persistent gendered and racial stereotypes in these fields (Buck et al., 2008; Museus et al., 2011). One method of attacking the common stereotypical image of white males in science and engineering fields is to provide role models. Researchers have found that rather than simply matching student demographics, presenting science and engineering as disciplines made of a multitude of real and diverse people is effective in developing interest and motivation in these fields (Cheryan et al., 2011). In a study of role models for girls, Buck et al. (2008) reported that learners want both male and female role models from a variety of racial backgrounds with whom they can make personal and real connections, rather than one who is "perfect." Betz and Sekaquaptewa (2012) found that presenting overtly feminine STEM role models had a negative effect on promoting interest in science and math for girls with lower interest. Moore (2006) also pointed out that there is an important part for

---

[5] Calabrese Barton and colleagues (2013) define identity work as "the actions that individuals take and the relationships they form (and the resources they leverage to do so) at any given moment and as constrained by the historically, culturally, and socially legitimized norms, rules, and expectations that operate within the spaces in which such work takes place" (p. 38).

family role models to play in developing interest in STEM areas as they can play a critical role in the career decision process (e.g., the role model can articulate the struggles, provide assistance, and support during learning). By providing role models, students' eyes are open to the possibility that they can become involved in science and engineering themselves. This can aid learners in seeing congruence between their content-based identity as a doer of science and engineering, and other identities such as gender and race.

However, larger societal and institutional issues related to inequities and biases (such as those discussed in Chapter 2) play a key role in underrepresented student motivation that create external barriers for these learners, and these external barriers must be addressed. (For a comprehensive review of this issue, see DeCuir-Gunby and Schutz, 2016.) For underrepresented students, persistence in science and engineering learning requires "substantial financial resources, as well as ongoing social and educational support, to make the transition from interest in engineering to a college major and a career in an engineering field" (Bystydzienski, Eisenhart, and Bruning, 2015, p. 94). In relation to in-the-moment classroom learning, adding social supports may be one area classroom educators can focus on to remove external barriers to success for underrepresented students. Teachers, as well as parents and peers, can resist setting lowered expectations and offer encouragement to engage in science and engineering learning as social supports for underrepresented students (Yu, Corkin, and Martin, 2016). Classroom environments must also actively pursue *positive intergroup relations*, where all individuals are given equal status, support from authority, and a voice in creating common goals (Kumar, Karabenick, and Warnke, 2017).

SUMMARY

The *Framework* and the resulting Next Generation Science Standards and state standards provide a rigorous set of standards and expectations for all learners in grades K–12. Learners are expected to use their knowledge to solve problems and make sense of phenomena by using disciplinary core ideas, crosscutting concepts, and science and engineering practices. The science education community can use what is known about student learning and motivation to inform efforts, while also conducting further research to expand understanding of learning and motivation.

Learning and motivation work together to promote usable knowledge in learners. There is a wealth of theoretical models describing how to develop and maintain interest and motivation in science and engineering and how this increased motivation is linked to increased learning and achievement. It is known how to characterize the goals of learners and aspects of the learning environment that can be harnessed to promote the formation of usable knowledge. While empirical classroom-based research is lacking that compares motivational interventions to control conditions that could be used to change STEM education, there is some evidence to suggest that interventions designed to address intrinsic motivation in science and engineering are effective (Deci, Koestner, and Ryan, 1999).

Several design guidelines from interest development research can be integrated into science and engineering learning environments to effectively increase learning during investigation and design activities. These guidelines include (1) providing choice or autonomy in learning, (2) promoting personal relevance, (3) presenting appropriately challenging material, and (4) situating the investigations in socially and culturally appropriate contexts. They can be a useful starting point for researchers to evaluate the effectiveness of specific instructional innovations, but also speak to teachers and designers about how to design effective learning environments. Motivation-based interventions offer a path to improve the representation of women, people of color, and other underrepresented groups in science and engineering. Additional information could be gained from longitudinal studies and theoretical frameworks sensitive to examining factors—ones internal to individuals as highlighted by a cognitive perspective on learning and ones external to individuals centralized in a sociocultural view of learning—that influence participation and persistence of underrepresented groups in science and engineering in three-dimensional context.

REFERENCES

Alexakos, K., Jones, J.K., and Rodriguez, V.H. (2011). Fictive kinship as it mediates learning, resiliency, perseverance, and social learning of inner-city high school students of color in a college physics class. *Cultural Studies of Science Education*, 6(4), 847–870.

Azevedo, F.S. (2013). The tailored practice of hobbies and its implication for the design of interest-based learning environments. *Journal of the Learning Sciences*, 22(3), 462–510.

Bandura, A. (1994). Self-efficacy. In V.S. Ramachaudran (Ed.), *Encyclopedia of Human Behavior Volume 4* (pp. 71–81). New York: Academic Press.

Bergin, D. (2016). Social influences on interest. *Educational Psychologist* 51(1), 7–22.

Betz, D.E., and Sekaquaptewa, D. (2012). My fair physicist? Feminine math and science role models demotivate young girls. *Social Psychological and Personality Science*, 3(6), 738–746.

Birmingham, D., and Calabrese Barton, A. (2014). Putting on a green carnival: Youth taking educated action on socioscientific issues. *Journal of Research in Science Teaching* 51(3), 286–314. doi: 10.1002/tea.21127.

Blackwell, L.S., Trzesniewski, K.H., and Dweck, C.S. (2007). Implicit theories of intelligence predict achievement across an adolescent transition: A longitudinal study and an intervention. *Child Development*, 78, 246–263.

Blumenfeld, P.C., Kempler, T.M., and Krajcik, J.S. (2006). Motivation and cognitive engagement in learning environments. In R.K. Sawyer (Ed.), *Cambridge Handbook of the Learning Sciences*. New York: Cambridge University Press.

Bong, M., Lee, S., and Woo, Y. (2015). The roles of interest and self-efficacy in the decision to pursue mathematics and science. In K. Renninger, M. Nieswandt, and S. Hidi (Eds.), *Interest in Mathematics and Science Learning* (pp. 33–48). Washington, DC: American Educational Research Association.

Bransford, J., Sherwood, R., Vye, N., and Rieser, J. (1986). Teaching thinking and problem solving: Research foundations. *American Psychologist, 41*(10), 1078–1089.

Buck, G.A., Plano Clark, V.L., Leslie-Pelecky, D., Lu, Y. and Cerda-Lizarraga, P. (2008). Examining the cognitive processes used by adolescent girls and women scientists in identifying science role models: A feminist approach. *Science Education, 92*(4), 688–707.

Bystydzienski, J.M., Eisenhart, M., and Bruning, M. (2015). High school is not too late: Developing girls' interest and engagement in engineering careers. *The Career Development Quarterly, 63*(1), 88–95.

Calabrese Barton, A., and Tan, E. (2010). We be burnin: Agency, identity and learning in a green energy program. *Journal of the Learning Sciences, 19*(2), 187–229.

Calabrese Barton, A., and Tan, E. (2018). A longitudinal study of equity-oriented STEM-rich making among youth from historically marginalized communities. *American Education Research Journal*.

Calabrese Barton, A., Kang, H., Tan, E., O'Neill, T., and Brecklin, C. (2013). Crafting a future in science: Tracing middle school girls' identity work over time and space. *American Education Research Journal, 50*(1). doi: 10.3102/0002831212458142.

Cheryan S., Siy J.O., Vichayapai M., Drury B., and Kim S. (2011). Do female and male role models who embody STEM stereotypes hinder women's anticipated success in STEM? *Social Psychological and Personality Science, 2*, 656–664.

Chi, M.T.H., Feltovich, P.J., and Glaser, R. (1981). Categorization and representation of physics problems by experts and novices. *Cognitive Science, 5*(2),121–152.

Clark E. K., Fuesting M.A., and Diekman, A.B. (2016). Enhancing interest in science: Exemplars as cues to communal affordances of science. *Journal of Applied Social Psychology, 46*, 641–654.

Cobb, P. (1994). Where is the mind? Constructivist and sociocultural perspectives on mathematical development. *Educational Researcher, 23*(7), 13–20.

Cole, M. (1995). Culture and cognitive development: From cross-cultural research to creating systems of cultural mediation. *Culture & Psychology 1*(1), 25–54.

Cole, M. (1996a). *Cultural Psychology: A Once and Future Discipline*. Cambridge, MA: The Belknap Press of Harvard University Press.

Cole, M. (1996b). Interacting minds in a lifespan perspective: A cultural historical approach to culture and cognitive development. In P.B. Baltes and U.M. Staudinger (Eds.), *Interactive Minds: Life-Span Perspectives on the Social Foundation of Cognition* (pp. 59–87). New York: Cambridge University Press.

Cole, M., John-Steiner, V., Souberman, J., and Scribner, S. (Eds.) (1978). *L.S. Vygotsky Mind in Society: The Development of Higher Psychological Processes*. Cambridge, MA: Harvard University Press.

Cook, D.A., and Artino, Jr., A.R. (2016). Motivation to learn: An overview of contemporary theories. *Medical Education, 50*(10), 997–1014. Available: https://onlinelibrary.wiley.com/doi/epdf/10.1111/medu.13074 [October 2018].

Deci, E.L., and Ryan, R.M. (1985). *Intrinsic Motivation and Self-Determination in Human Behavior*. New York: Plenum.

Deci, E.L., and Ryan, R.M. (1991). A motivational approach to self: Integration in personality. In R. Dienstbier (Ed.), *Nebraska Symposium on Motivation: Volume 38. Perspectives on Motivation* (pp. 237–288). Lincoln: University of Nebraska Press.

Deci, E.L., and Ryan, R.M. (2000). The "what" and "why" of goal pursuits: Human needs and the self-determination of behavior. *Psychological Inquiry, 11*, 227–268.

Deci, E.L., Koestner, R., and Ryan, R.M. (1999). A meta-analytic review of experiments examining the effects of extrinsic rewards on intrinsic motivation. *Psychological Bulletin, 125*(6), 627–668.

DeCuir-Gunby, J., and Schutz, P. (Eds.). (2016). *Race and Ethnicity in the Study of Motivation in Education.* New York: Routledge.

Dee, T.S., and Penner, E.K. (2017). The causal effects of cultural relevance: Evidence from an ethnic studies curriculum. *American Educational Research Journal, 54*(1), 127–166.

Eccles, J.S., and Barber, B.L. (1999). Student council, volunteering, basketball, or marching band: What kind of extracurricular involvement matters? *Journal of Adolescent Research, 14*(1), 10–43.

Elliot, A.J., McGregor, H.A., and Gable, S. (1999). Achievement goals, study strategies, and exam performance: A mediational analysis. *Journal of Educational Psychology, 91*(3), 549–563.

Endreny, A.H. (2010). Urban 5th graders conceptions during a place-based inquiry unit on watersheds. *Journal of Research in Science Teaching, 47*(5), 501–517.

Engeström, Y. (2009). From learning environments and implementation to activity systems and expansive learning. *Actio: An International Journal of Human Activity Theory, 2*, 17–33.

Ericsson, K.A. (2008). Deliberate practice and acquisition of expert performance: A general overview. *Academic Emergency Medicine, 15*, 988–994.

Ericsson, K.A., Hoffman, R.R., Kozbelt, A., and Williams, A.M. (Eds.). (2018). *The Cambridge Handbook of Expertise and Expert Performance.* New York: Cambridge University Press.

Fortus, D., and Vedder-Weiss, D. (2014). Measuring students continuing motivation for science learning. *Journal of Research in Science Teaching, 51*(4), 497–522.

Freebody, P., and Anderson, R.C. (1983). Effects of vocabulary difficulty, text cohesion, and schema availability on reading comprehension. *Reading Research Quarterly, 18*, 277–294.

Gentner, D., Loewestein, J., Thompson, L., and Fortus, K.D. (2009). Reviving inert knowledge: Analogical abstraction supports relational retrieval of past events. *Cognitive Science, 33*, 1343–1382.

Gick, M.L., and Holyoak, K.J. (1980). Analogical problem solving. *Cognitive Psychology, 12*(3), 306–355.

Gonzales, N., Moll, L., and Amanti, C. (Eds.). (2005). *Funds of Knowledge.* Mahwah, NJ: L. Erlbaum Associates.

Goswami, U. (2012). Principles of learning, implications for teaching? Cognitive neuroscience and the classroom. In S.D. Sala and M. Anderson (Eds.), *Neuroscience in Education: The Good, the Bad, and the Ugly* (pp. 47–61). Oxford, UK: Oxford University Press.

Harackiewicz, J.M., Barron, K.E., Pintrich, P.R., Elliot, A.J., and Thrash, T.M. (2002). Revision of achievement goal theory: Necessary and illuminating. *Journal of Educational Psychology, 94*(3), 638–645.

Harackiewicz, J.M., Rozek, C.S., Hulleman, C.S., and Hyde, J.S. (2012). Helping parents to motivate adolescents in mathematics and science: An experimental test of a utility-value intervention. *Psychological Science, 23*, 899–906.

Hattie, J., and Timperley, H. (2007). The power of feedback. *Review of Educational Research, 77*(1), 81–112.

Häussler, P., and Hoffmann, L. (2002). An intervention study to enhance girls' interest, self-concept, and achievement in physics classes. *Journal of Research in Science Teaching, 39*, 870–888.

Healy, A.F., and Sinclair, G.P. (1996). The long-term retention of training and instruction. In E.L. Bjork and R.A. Bjork (Eds.), *Memory* (pp. 525–564). San Diego, CA: Academic Press.

Hidi, S., and Harackiewicz, J.M. (2000). Motivating the academically unmotivated: A critical issue for the 21st century. *Review of Educational Research, 70*(2), 151–179.

Hidi, S., and Renninger, K.A. (2006). The four-phase model of interest development. *Educational Psychologist, 41*, 111–127.

Hoffmann, L., and Häussler, P. (1998). An intervention project promoting girls' and boys' interest in physics. In L. Hoffmann, A. Krapp, K.A. Renninger, and J. Baumert (Eds.), *Interest and Learning: Proceedings of the Second Conference on Interest and Gender* (pp. 301–316). Kiel, Germany: IPN.

Holland, D., and Lave, J. (Eds.). (2001). *History-in-Person: Enduring Struggles, Contentious Practice, Intimate Identities.* Santa Fe, NM: School of American Research Press.

Hulleman C.S., and Harackiewicz, J.M. (2009). Promoting interest and performance in high school science classes. *Science, 326*, 1410–1412.

Järvelä, S., and Renninger, K.A. (2014). Designing for learning: Interest, motivation, and engagement. In D.K. Sawyer (Ed.), *Cambridge Handbook of the Learning Sciences, Second Edition* (pp. 668–685). New York: Cambridge University Press.

Jiang, S., Shen, J., Smith, B.E., and Kibler, K.W. (2018). *Examining Sixth Graders' Science Identity Development in a Multimodal Composing Environment.* Available: https://www.researchgate.net/publication/323549782_Examining_Sixth_Graders'_Science_Identity_Development_in_a_Multimodal_Composing_Environment [October 2018]

Karpicke, J.D., and Roediger, H. L. (2008). The critical importance of retrieval for learning. *Science, 319*, 966–968.

Katz, I., and Assor, A. (2007). When choice motivates and when it does not. *Educational Psychology Review, 19*(4), 429–442.

Kellogg, J., Plundrich, N.J., Lila, M., Croom, D.B., Taylor, R.F., Graf, B., and Raskin, I. (2016). Engaging American Indian/Alaska Native (AI/AN) students with participatory bioexploration assays 1. *NACTA Journal, 60*(1), 42–50.

Krajcik, J.S., and Shin, N. (2014). Project-based learning. In R.K. Sawyer (Ed.), *The Cambridge Handbook of the Learning Sciences, Second Edition* (pp. 275–297). New York: Cambridge University Press.

Kumar, R., Karabenick, S.A., and Warnke, J.H. (2017). Role of culture and proximal minority/majority status in adolescent identity negotiations. In P. Schutz and J. DeCuir-Gunby (Eds.), *Researching Race and Ethnicity in the Study of Learning and Motivation in Social and Cultural Contexts* (pp. 152–167). New York: Routledge.

Lazowski, R.A., and Hulleman, C.S. (2016). Motivation interventions in education: A meta-analytic review. *Review of Educational Research, 86*(2), 602–640.

Linnenbrink-Garcia, L., and Patall, E.A. (2016). Motivation. In E. Anderman and L. Corno, (Eds.), *Handbook of Educational Psychology, 3rd ed.* (pp. 91–103). New York: Taylor & Francis.

Maehr, M.L., and Midgley, C. (1996). *Transforming School Cultures. Lives in Context Series.* Boulder, CO: Westview Press.

McNeill, K., Lizotte, D., Krajcik, J., and Marx, R. (2009). Supporting students' construction of scientific explanations by fading scaffolds in instructional materials. *Journal of the Learning Sciences, 15*(2), 153–191.

Moll, L.C., Amanti, C., Neff, D., and Gonzalez, N. (1992). Funds of knowledge for teaching: Using a qualitative approach to connect homes and classrooms. *Theory into Practice, 31*(2), 132–141.

Moore, J.L., III. (2006). A qualitative investigation of African American males' career trajectory in engineering: Implications for teachers, school counselors, and parents. *Teachers College Record, 108*(2), 246–266.

Museus, S.D., Palmer, R.T., Davis, R.J., and Maramba, D. (2011). Special issue: Racial and ethnic minority students' success in STEM education. *ASHE Higher Education Report,* 36(6), 1–140.

National Academy of Engineering and National Research Council. (2014). *STEM Integration in K-12 Education: Status, Prospects, and an Agenda for Research.* Washington, DC: The National Academies Press.

National Research Council. (2000). *How People Learn: Brain, Mind, Experience, and School: Expanded Edition.* Washington, DC: National Academy Press.

National Research Council. (2006). *America's Lab Report: Investigations in High School Science.* Washington, DC: The National Academies Press.

National Research Council. (2012). *A Framework for K-12 Science Education: Practices, Crosscutting Concepts, and Core Ideas.* Washington, DC: The National Academies Press.

Nieswandt, M., and Horowitz, G. (2015). Undergraduate students' interest in chemistry: the roles of task and choice. In K. Renninger, M. Nieswandt, and S. Hidi (Eds.), *Interest in Mathematics and Science Learning* (pp. 225–242). Washington, DC: American Educational Research Association.

Noble, K.G., Houston, S.M., Kan, E., and Sowell, E.R. (2012). Neural correlates of socioeconomic status in the developing human brain. *Developmental Science,* 15(4), 516–527.

Novak, J.D., and Gowin, D.B. (1984). *Learning How to Learn.* Cambridge, UK: Cambridge University Press.

Osborne, J. (2010) Arguing to learn in science: The role of collaborative, critical discourse. *Science* 328(5977), 463–466.

Patall, E.A., Cooper, H., and Wynn, S.R. (2010). The effectiveness and relative importance of choice in the classroom. *Journal of Educational Psychology, 102,* 896–915.

Patall, E.A., Sylvester, B.J., and Han, C. (2014). The role of competence in the effects of choice on motivation. *Journal of Experimental Social Psychology, 50,* 27–44.

Penuel, W., DiGiacomo, D.K., Horne, K.U., and Kirsher, B. (2016). A social practice theory of learning and becoming across contexts and time. *Frontline Learning Research, 4*(4), 30–38.

Perkins, D. (1999). The many faces of constructivism. *Educational Leadership, 57*(3), 6–11.

Pressick-Kilborn, K. (2015). Canalization and connectedness in the development of science interest. In K. Renninger, M. Nieswandt, and S. Hidi (Eds.), *Interest in Mathematics and Science Learning* (pp. 353–368). Washington, DC: American Educational Research Association.

Pritchard, R. (1990). The effects of cultural schemata on reading processing strategies. *Reading Research Quarterly, 25,* 273–295.

Puntambekar, S., and Hubscher, R. (2005). Tools for scaffolding students in a complex learning environment: What have we gained and what have we missed? *Educational Psychologist, 40*(1), 1–12.

Renkl, A., Mandi, H., and Gruber, H. (1996). Inert knowledge: Analyses and remedies. *Educational Psychologist, 31*(2), 115–121.

Renninger, K.A., and Su, S. (2012). Interest and its development. In R.M. Ryan (Ed.), *Oxford Library of Psychology. The Oxford Handbook of Human Motivation* (pp. 167–187). New York: Oxford University Press.

Reynolds, R.E., Taylor, M.A., Steffensen, M.S., Shirey, L.L., and Anderson, R.C. (1982). Cultural schemata and reading comprehension. *Reading Research Quarterly, 17,* 353–366.

Rivas-Drake, D., Seaton, E. K., Markstrom, C., Quintana, S., et al. (2014). Ethnic and racial identity in adolescence: Implications for psychosocial, academic, and health outcomes. *Child Development, 85*(1), 40–57. doi: 10.1111/cdev.12200.

Rivera Maulucci, M.S., Brown, B.A., Grey, S.T., and Sullivan, S. (2014). Urban middle school students' reflections on authentic science inquiry. *Journal of Research in Science Teaching, 51*, 1119–1149.

Rogoff, B. (1998). Cognition as a collaborative process. In W. Damon (Ed.), *Handbook of Child Psychology: Vol. 2. Cognition, Perception, and Language* (pp. 679–744). Hoboken, NJ: John Wiley & Sons.

Rozek, C., Svoboda, R., Harackiewicz, J., Hulleman, C., and Hyde J. (2017). Utility-value intervention with parents increases students' STEM preparation and career pursuit. *Proceedings of the National Academy of Sciences, 114*(5), 909–914.

Sansone, C., Thoman, D.B., and Fraughton, T. (2015). The relation between interest and self-regulation in mathematics and science. In K.A. Renninger, M. Neiswandt, and S. Hidi (Eds.), *Interest in K-16 Mathematics and Science Learning and Related Activity*. Washington, DC: American Educational Research Association.

Schneider, B., Krajcik, J., Lavonen, J., Salmela-Aro, K., Broda, M., Spicer, J., Bruner, J., Moeller, J., Linnansaari, J., Juuti, K., and Viljaranta, J. (2016). Investigating optimal learning moments in U.S. and Finnish science classes. *Journal of Research in Science Teaching, 53*, 400–421. doi: 10.1002/tea.21306.

Schunk, D.H., Meece, J.R., and Pintrich, P.R. (2014). *Motivation in Education: Theory, Research, and Applications, 4th Edition*. Boston, MA: Pearson.

Silvia, P.J. (2012). Human emotions and aesthetic experience: An overview of empirical aesthetics. In A.P. Shimamura and S.E. Palmer (Eds.), *Aesthetic Science: Connecting Minds, Brains, and Experience* (pp. 250–275). New York: Oxford University Press.

Sobel, D. (2005). *Place-Based Education: Connecting Classrooms & Communities*. (2nd ed). Great Barrington, MA: Orion Society.

Stout, J. G., Dasgupta, N., Hunsinger, M., and McManus, M. (2011). STEMing the tide: Using ingroup experts to inoculate women's self-concept and professional goals in science, technology, engineering, and mathematics (STEM). *Journal of Personality and Social Psychology, 100*, 255–270.

Sweller, J. (2005). Cognitive load theory, learning difficulty, and instructional design. In R.E. Mayer (Ed.), *The Cambridge Handbook of Multimedia Learning* (pp. 19–30). New York: Cambridge University Press.

Tabak, I. (2004). Synergy: A complement to emerging patterns of distributed scaffolding. *Journal of the Learning Sciences, 12*(3), 305–335.

Tan, E., Kang, H. O'Neill, T., and Calabrese Barton, A. (2013). Desiring a career in STEM-related fields: How middle school girls articulate and negotiate between their narrated and embodied identities in considering a STEM trajectory. *Journal of Research in Science Teaching, 50*(10), 1143–1179. doi: 10.1002/tea.21123.

Vansteenkiste, M., Simons, J., Lens, W., Sheldon, K.M., and Deci, E.L. (2004). Motivating learning, performance, and persistence: the synergistic effects of intrinsic goal contents and autonomy-supportive contexts. *Journal of Personality and Social Psychology, 87*(2), 246–260.

Vygotsky, L.S. (1978). *Mind in Society: The Development of Higher Psychological Processes*. Cambridge, MA: Harvard University Press.

Waldrip, B., Prain, V., and Carolan, J. (2010). Using multi-modal representations to improve learning in junior secondary science. *Research in Science Education, 40*, 65–80.

Walkington, C.A. (2013). Using adaptive learning technologies to personalize instruction to student interests: The impact of relevant contexts on performance and learning outcomes. *Journal of Educational Psychology. 105*, 932–945.

Wang, M., Eccles, J., and Kenny, S. (2013). Not lack of ability but more choice: Individual and gender differences in choice of careers in science, technology, engineering, and mathematics. *Psychological Science, 24*(5), 770–775.

Weiner, B. (1985). An attributional theory of achievement motivation and emotion. *Psychology Review*, 92, 548–573.

Whitehead, A.N. (1929). *The Aims of Education & Other Essays*. New York: The Macmillan Company.

Wigfield, A., and Eccles, J.S. (2000). Expectancy-value theory of achievement motivation. *Contemporary Educational Psychology*, 25, 68–81.

Wood, D.J., Bruner, J.S., and Ross, G. (1976). The role of tutoring in problem solving. *Journal of Child Psychiatry and Psychology*, 17(2), 89–100.

Yu, S.L., Corkin, D.M., and Martin, J. P. (2016). STEM motivation and persistence among underrepresented minority students: A social cognitive perspective. In J.T. DeCuir-Gunby and P.A. Schutz (Eds.), *Race and Ethnicity in the Study of Motivation in Education* (pp. 67–81). New York: Routledge.

Ziegler, A., and Heller, K.A. (2000). Effects of an attribution retraining with female students gifted in physics. *Journal for the Education of the Gifted*, 23(2), 217–243.

Ziegler, A., and Stoeger, H. (2004). Evaluation of an attributional retraining (modeling technique) to reduce gender differences in chemistry instruction. *High Ability Studies*, 15(1), 63–83.

4

How Students Engage with Investigation and Design

The vision articulated in *A Framework for K–12 Science Education* (hereafter referred to as the *Framework*; National Research Council, 2012) and supported by research contrasts sharply with the more traditional approach to learning science. In the traditional model, classes often begin with the teacher sharing scientific terminology and ideas, whereas in the *Framework* approach the students begin by asking questions and constructing explanations as they use the three dimensions (scientific and engineering practices, disciplinary core ideas, and cross-cutting concepts) together to make sense of phenomena and design solutions. The teacher structures the instruction and supports student learning instead of providing information to the students. Our committee advocates putting science investigation and engineering design at the center of teaching and learning science and building classes around students investigating phenomena and designing solutions by working to make sense of the causes of phenomena or solve challenges in a way that uses all three dimensions of the *Framework* (see the second footnote in Chapter 1 for an explanation of the three dimensions) in an increasingly deeper, more connected, and sophisticated manner. The ability of students to achieve this deeper, more connected, and sophisticated understanding begins to form in elementary school as students are exposed to the start of the progressions. The examples presented here focus on implementation in middle and high schools, in keeping with the charge to the committee.

For example, here are some student experiences that illustrate investigation or design at the center:

- Students **develop a design** (a practice) for a device (crosscutting concept: structure and function) that collects plastics that have made their way to a local waterway and are **causing** native marine life to die prematurely (crosscutting concept: cause/effect).
- Students **develop a model** (a practice) to show how the flow of energy into an ecosystem (disciplinary core idea) causes **change** (a crosscutting concept) in the seasonal rate of growth of grass.
- Students **construct an explanation** (a practice) for how **changes in the quantity** (a crosscutting concept) of grass cause **changes** (a crosscutting concept) in the population of deer mice in the sand hills of Nebraska.

The core ideas about energy and ecosystems and the crosscutting concepts of causality, changes in systems in terms of matter and energy, and changes in populations help students make sense of phenomena via three-dimensional learning.

In order to demonstrate the nature of classrooms with investigation and design at the center, this chapter focuses on what students do during investigation and design. Chapters 5 then focuses on instruction and how teachers can implement the ideas. Chapter 6 discusses the role of instructional resources.

Specifically, Chapter 4 highlights the shifts from traditional to proposed approaches, explains how investigation and design give structure to inquiry, presents five features of student engagement in investigation and design, and uses vignettes to demonstrate the classroom experience and to discuss and illustrate these features.[1]

PUTTING INVESTIGATION AND DESIGN AT THE CENTER

America's Lab Report (National Research Council, 2006) set up many of the ideas of the *Framework* and recommended that laboratory experiences move into the main flow of the class experience. We advocate going further and using the three dimensions of the *Framework* to transform the laboratory experience into the centerpiece of what students do to learn science and engineering. Science and engineering courses would be organized around science investigation and engineering design, and the students would focus on making sense of phenomena and designing solutions to meet human needs. More specifically, they would ask questions about the

---

[1]This chapter includes content drawn from a paper commissioned by the committee—*Designing NGSS-Aligned Curriculum Materials* by Brian Reiser and Bill Penuel. The commissioned papers are available at http://www.nas.edu/Science-Investigation-and-Design [December 2018].

causes of phenomena, gather evidence to support explanations of the causes of the phenomena or find solutions to human needs, and communicate their reasoning to themselves and others. Investigation and design may take a number of different paths, but each path would take students in search of finding evidence to support their explanations and/or a solution.

Shifts in Approach When Investigation and Design Are at the Center

In a class centered on investigation and design, there are many shifts from the traditional model of science instruction, where a laboratory was just one of many activities in which the students and teachers engaged. Figure 4-1 presents some examples of these shifts. On the left-hand side of Figure 4-1 are listed some traditional activities carried out in science classes that no longer exist in the same form when classes center on investigation

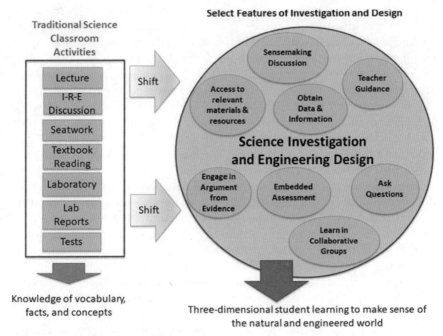

FIGURE 4-1 Select features of science investigation and engineering design and how they differ from activities in traditional science classrooms.
NOTE: The boxes in the list on the left contain examples of approaches used in traditional science classrooms. The small circles on the right represent examples of features of learning via investigation and design. The examples are not exhaustive, and many other approaches are possible within investigation and design.

and design. In the traditional class, these activities each stand alone; they are not part of a laboratory experience. On the right-hand side, the figure shows examples of student experiences that contribute to investigation and design, which is now at the center of classroom activity. The labels within the circles on the right indicate some of the features discussed in this report, but there are many other possible features that could be included in classes centered on science investigation and engineering design. Some of the new features illustrated in the circles on the right, such as engaging in argument from evidence, were not represented in traditional classrooms, while others have a stronger connection to traditional activities. The arrows from left to right highlight the shift that takes place from traditional approaches to having investigation and design at the center of science and engineering courses.

There is not a one-to-one correspondence between the old activities and new features, but examples of contrasts can help clarify the nature of the changes. For example, standalone, confirmatory laboratory exercises disappear entirely, but students still gather data and information as part of investigation and design. The Initiate-Response-Evaluate (I-R-E) teaching model,[2] in which teachers ask questions and evaluate student responses, is not a part of investigation and design, but students do participate in sense-making discussions in which teachers facilitate student conversations about phenomena and students ask questions, leverage their everyday experiences, make sense of data, and engage in developing explanations and argumentation from evidence. In this new approach, teacher guidance for understanding is prominent and lectures are rare. Traditional individual seat work disappears; students participate in cooperative group work, where they work collaboratively to engage with data and to share their ideas, explanations, and thinking with each other. The interaction of students with each other and collaborative efforts to gather reliable sources of information and discuss evidence is key to investigation and design and a central mechanism for student learning. Textbooks do not necessarily disappear, but their central role is lost. They become one of many sources of information, and reading of text is done for the purpose of gathering relevant timely information to support explanations. Students become proficient at accessing and evaluating relevant materials and resources as they seek evidence to support explanations in investigations or solutions to design challenges.

Table 4-1 presents shifts implied by the *Framework* that impact what happens in science education generally and during investigation and design specifically. Examples include how the students can drive learning and investigation by asking questions, gathering information, evaluating evidence,

---

[2] The I-R-E model is a teacher-directed approach to classroom interactions. The teacher asks a simple question that requires a straightforward answer from a student. The teacher then says whether the answer is correct or not (Cazden, 1986).

TABLE 4-1 Implications of the Vision of the *Framework* and the NGSS

Science Education Will Involve Less	Science Education Will Involve More
Rote memorization of facts and terminology	Facts and terminology learned as needed while developing explanations and designing solutions supported by evidence-based arguments and reasoning
Learning of ideas disconnected from questions about phenomena	Systems thinking and modeling to explain phenomena and to give a context for the ideas to be learned
Teachers providing information to the whole class	Students conducting investigations, solving problems, and engaging in discussions with teachers' guidance
Teachers posing questions with only one right answer	Students discussing open-ended questions that focus on the strength of the evidence used to generate claims
Students reading textbooks and answering questions at the end of the chapter	Students reading multiple sources, including science-related magazines, journal articles, and web-based resources; Students developing summaries of information
Preplanned outcomes for "cookbook" laboratories or hands-on activities	Multiple investigations driven by students' questions with a range of possible outcomes that collectively lead to a deep understanding of established core scientific ideas
Worksheets	Students writing journals, reports, posters, media presentations that explain and argue
Oversimplification of activities for students who are perceived to be less able to do science and engineering	Providing supports so that all students can engage in sophisticated science and engineering practices

SOURCE: Reprinted from Table 1-1 of *Guide to Implementing the Next Generation Science Standards* (National Research Council, 2015).

and developing explanations. The table uses "investigations" in accordance with the *Framework's* scientific and engineering practice of "planning and carrying out investigations," whereas elsewhere in our report we use investigation in the larger sense of what students do to make sense of natural and engineered phenomena. The actions of the students as part of investigation and design encompass multiple scientific and engineering practices as well as crosscutting concepts and disciplinary core ideas.

Investigation and design take time, as students construct their own understanding instead of accepting information provided by the teacher. Investigations can be "messy" as they incorporate students' real questions, which do not have clean answers and sometimes raise questions that lead the class in unexpected new directions as they try to make sense of the complex and interconnected world around them. However, teachers can organize investigation and design around clear and well-described three-dimensional learning goals so that they lead to deeper understanding of the science and engineering concepts and core ideas that are the chosen focus of the unit. This contrast illustrates one of the ways that the role of the teacher shifts: The teacher becomes responsible for selecting phenomena, providing scientifically accurate resources, guiding discourse, considering how the investigation and design topics help students build on their previous courses and experiences to make sense of the universe, and setting a tone of respect and inclusion to support students as they engage in investigation and design to learn science and engineering. The change in the teacher role is addressed in greater depth in Chapter 5.

How Do Scientific Investigation and Engineering Design Relate to Inquiry?

The word "inquiry" is widely used throughout science education. Despite good intentions, however, confusion still exists about what constitutes effective inquiry (Crawford, 2014; Furtak et al., 2012; Osborne, 2014). For example, inquiry sometimes has been conflated with any hands-on experience. But hands-on activities do not necessarily result in meaningful experiences that help students engage in the conceptual, epistemic, and social aspects of science (American Association for the Advancement of Science, 1993). In fact, inquiry is not a single construct but rather a continuum that ranges from confirmatory activities that are teacher-led and traditional in nature to discovery-based and student-led tasks (Banchi and Bell, 2008; Furtak et al., 2012; Schwab, 1962). The inquiry continuum includes a broad range of interactions that go beyond scientific investigations. For example, students may engage in inquiry through historical case studies or the comparison of different texts without engaging in material activity or data collection.

Science investigation and engineering design do not *replace* inquiry, but they "articulate more clearly what inquiry looks like in building scientific knowledge" (Schwarz, Passmore, and Reiser, 2017, p. 5). An inquiry activity may be related to a question identified by the class, it may deal with empirical evidence, but it may not get to the end result of sense-making through discourse and modeling that contributes to building up of understanding over time. How the core ideas and crosscutting concepts play out across the series is key to student understanding, the structure of instruction engages students in a series of investigations on similar but different phenomena, students gather information they need to make sense of a phenomenon and then use that learning to apply to the next phenomenon in the series. For example, a series of carefully chosen performances connected by a shared core idea might use phenomena related to three different kinds of animals in which students ask questions about the animals' physical features and construct explanations about the relationships between each type of animal and its environment. As the students see similar patterns across types of animals, they may be able to develop and use a model to communicate how the structures organisms have changed over time because of the specific environment in which they live and improve their understanding of evolution. For each of the performances, students apply the same or similar core ideas and crosscutting concepts to make sense of a series of phenomena. An engineering design approach might have students consider solutions for deep sea travel that utilize properties observed in and adapted from the physiology of deep sea creatures.

In science investigation and engineering design, learners develop deep conceptual understandings by engaging with a carefully chosen sequence of three-dimensional science performances across a series of phenomena and/or design challenges. Returning to similar or related topics in subsequent classes or grades can provide efficiencies as the students build from previous exposure and experience and more quickly engage deeply with the approaches and ideas. These topics can be introduced beginning in elementary school and then students can build on them in middle and high school courses. In each investigation or design sequence, the student engages in gathering the information, data, and ideas needed to support explanations for the causes of phenomena and then finds various means to communicate explanations or solutions. Attention to the choices made about phenomena and challenges across a curriculum can allow a series of investigations to create opportunities to develop deeper understanding as students apply their three-dimensional learning to increasingly complex phenomena. Creating this kind of coherence within a grade and across grade levels is a challenging task and is discussed further in the sections on coherence in Chapters 5 and 6.

STUDENTS ENGAGE IN INVESTIGATION AND DESIGN

Engaging in science investigation and engineering design exposes students to how science and engineering produce knowledge and solutions. Here we describe features of the student experience using vignettes and examples to illustrate how they play out in the classroom. Features of experiences the students participate in as part of investigation and design are listed in Table 4-2. There is no prescribed order for using these features during investigation and design; rather, they are incorporated as appropriate to the phenomenon or challenge being examined. Each feature may be used multiple times during a single investigation when students revisit their

TABLE 4-2 Student Experiences during Investigation and Design

Examples of Student Experiences while Learning through Phenomena and Design Challenges (organized by features of science investigation and engineering design)

Make Sense of Phenomena and Design Challenge	Gather and Analyze Data and Information	Construct Explanations and Design Solutions	Communicate Reasoning to Self and Others	Connect Learning through Multiple Contexts
- Develop and ask questions about the causes of phenomena - Define engineering challenges by identifying stakeholders, goals, constraints, and criteria for evaluations of solutions	- Collect and organize data and seek patterns - Analyze data and evaluate information for evidence	- Develop models of the relationships among components within and between systems - Develop arguments for how the evidence supports or refutes an explanation for the causes of phenomena - Design solutions based on evidence and test the solutions to see how they meet the challenge	- Develop models and artifacts to communicate reasoning - Engage in productive and respectful discourse - Reflect on learning	- Use three-dimensional learning to make sense of phenomena across grades - Apply learning to make sense of phenomena beyond the classroom

questions, ideas, and models as they gain increasing understanding of the natural and designed world around them. These features each expand on the practices in the *Framework*, and the following sections illustrate that they can be incorporated in three-dimensional ways into investigation and design.

Table 4-2 can be seen as a potential progression of a science or engineering performance where a student engages in investigation or design. Students can encounter these features in many possible orders as they ask questions, collect and evaluate data, and make new models to increase their understanding. For example, in many investigations, students gather data to address a question, analyze that data and generate an explanation, then go back and do more analysis and generate a new explanation before they communicate their work. It is important to note that this is quite different from the formulaic scientific method that was previously taught, in part because it is not a highly regulated, stepwise sequence. Investigation and design involve many steps, but they do not occur in a prespecified order. Student performances can include iteration of individual features and revisiting of features that were previously used in the same investigation. Students often start by making observations, but they must return to observe in more strategic ways after they formulate their questions, so that they know what type of information they are seeking to gather through their observations.

During investigation and design, students **make sense of phenomena and design challenges** by using observations, building on their prior knowledge and experiences, and developing and asking questions about how these phenomena work in the natural and engineered world. They **gather and analyze data and information** to seek patterns and evaluate information for evidence. They build on and apply their knowledge of disciplinary core ideas and crosscutting concepts gained via previous investigations. For example, if the phenomenon is the variation in the rate of grass growing, students must apply their understanding of the core idea about photosynthesis to make sense of the role of genetic variation in how individual plants process energy from the sun. They need to understand crosscutting concepts to explain the cycling of matter and the flow of energy in the system and to see that the variation in the structure of the grass plants affect how well each plant is adapted to the environment in which it is growing. The use of core ideas and crosscutting concepts is what makes the practice of analyzing data three-dimensional.

Students **construct explanations** for the causes of phenomena and develop models for the relationships among the components of the systems, and they develop arguments for how the evidence gathered in the investigations supports the explanation. They **design solutions** that build on their understanding of relationships between components and test those solutions. They **communicate reasoning to self and others** through models and arguments to show how the evidence they have developed supports the explanation and/or solution. They use artifacts and representations that communicate reasoning and respond to others' ideas as they engage in productive discourse. Students **connect learning through multiple contexts** by reflecting on their own learning and seeing links between what they do during investigation and design experiences with phenomena and challenges beyond the classroom. As a result of engaging in science investigation and engineering design, students can learn the "system of thought, discourse, and practice—all in an inter-connected and social context—to accomplish the goal of working with and understanding scientific ideas" (National Research Council, 2012, p. 252).

A vignette provides a window into the nature of investigation and design in the classroom that we then use to unpack and discuss the ways the students participate. It helps to illustrate the interconnections of the system of thought, discourse, and practice in a social context of illness and medical treatment. Ms. Martinez opens class with a short video of a girl, Addie, who has been hospitalized because she has a bacterial infection that is resistant to antibiotic treatment (NGSS Storylines, 2017). Using information from the video and their prior knowledge, students generate and prioritize as a class a list of questions that they need to answer to explain what is going on with Addie. In the initial lesson, students write questions individually and in small groups, and they identify experiences they have had that might help them understand what is going on. As a class, students first build a timeline of the events that they see in the video and then draw an initial model to explain what they think is going on in small groups. This leads students to generate questions about parts they cannot explain (see Figure 4-2A). The class together assembles these questions and organizes them into major categories, recording them on an artifact called the Driving Question Board (Blumenfeld et al., 1991; Weizman, Schwartz, and Fortus, 2010). For each of the questions, the class brainstorms an initial list of investigations they might conduct in class to help them answer these questions (see Figure 4-2B).

Student investigation in this vignette is driven by the phenomenon of a girl named Addie who has been hospitalized due to a bacterial infection resistant to many antibiotics (Reiser and Penuel, 2017). Students try to make sense of this phenomenon by asking questions, organizing information, and forming potential explanations. They extend their learning by designing investigations of bacterial growth in the presence and absence of antibiotics. The data they collect are used to make models that could explain Addie's illness and treatment. Throughout the multiday lesson, the students produce artifacts and share their ideas with each other as they learn about the role of natural selection in antibiotic resistance. Our focus in providing this vignette is to provide the entire arc or storyline of a learning experience centered on student investigations into an anchoring phenomenon, to foreground the ways students engage in discussion and create artifacts as they engage in those investigations, and to highlight the ways that everyday assessment supports teachers in gathering information on an ongoing basis to support student learning throughout the unit. (More information on embedded assessment can be found in Chapter 5 and in Appendix A.)

After constructing their initial models and organizing their questions, students begin growing their own bacteria to try to figure out answers to some of their questions about where bacteria come from, how they grow, and how they can be killed. Students develop their larger questions into more focused investigations of bacterial growth that help them add to their models of what is going on with Addie. They create plans and protocols for data collection, and draw sketches and diagrams showing what happens to bacteria under different conditions over time. The students describe patterns they observe in their data and how the patterns support particular

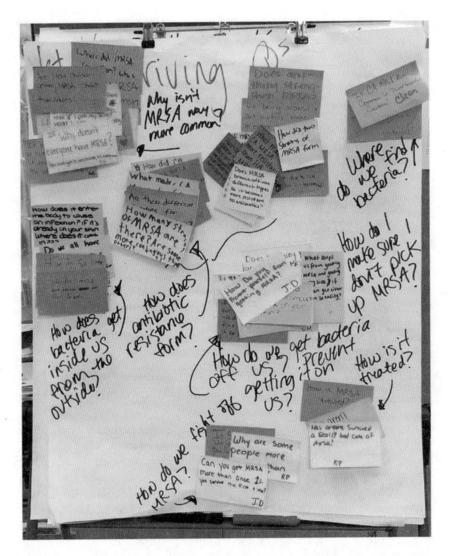

FIGURE 4-2A Example of class-generated Driving Questions Board showing how students grouped related questions by clustering of sticky notes on the larger page about driving questions.
SOURCE: Reiser and Penuel (2017).

Organizing Question Constructed by the Class	Example student questions
Why isn't MRSA way more common?	• Why doesn't everyone have MRSA? • Where did MRSA come from?
Where do we find bacteria?	• Is MRSA more common in third world countries? • How long does MRSA live outside in a public community area without people? • Can animals get MRSA? Can they give it to people?
How do I make sure I don't pick up MRSA?	• Does everything you handle have MRSA? • What keeps us from getting MRSA and getting very sick if you can get it so easily?
How do we fight off MRSA?	• Why are some people more sensitive than others? • Do the things we use to clean wounds like alcohol/peroxide kill MRSA?
How does antibiotic resistance form?	• How does different types of staph form? • Does being around antibiotics make it easier to form?
How does bacteria get from the inside to the outside?	• How does it enter the body to cause an infection? If it's already on your skin where does it get in? • Do you have to have a cut or scab to get MRSA? If not how does it get inside someone's body?

FIGURE 4-2B Example of class-generated list (derived from the class-generated Driving Questions Board in Figure 4-2A).
SOURCE: Reiser and Penuel (2017).

claims or "answers" to their questions. They make revised models to explain what might be going on with Addie and the bacteria (see Figure 4-3). Students share their plans and protocols with each other informally or via a peer review process. Through the sharing process, they develop increasingly sophisticated understandings of and explanations for how the bacteria population could change. At the conclusion of each lesson, Ms. Martinez invites students to reflect publicly on what they have figured out related to one or more of the questions on the Driving Questions Board. They submit electronic exit tickets that she can review to decide what ideas might need further discussion and development, as well as to analyze student perceptions of the lesson's personal relevance (Penuel et al., 2016). The class also reflects via a group discussion that produces a list of hypotheses or conjectures about what is going on that the class is considering at the moment, but about which there is not yet agreement. That discussion clarifies for the class precisely what they agree on so far, as well as where there are disagreements and provides ideas for what they should do next (Reiser and Penuel, 2017).

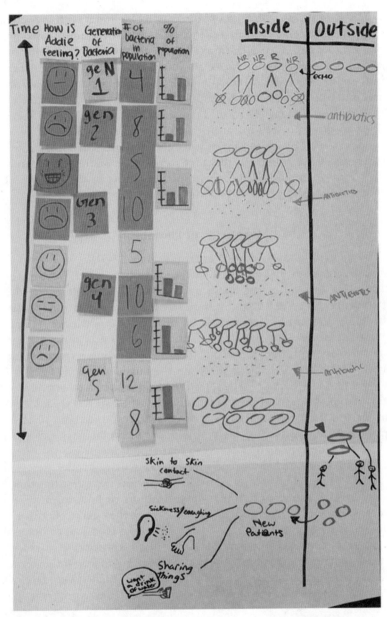

FIGURE 4-3 A small group's revised model to explain how Addie's condition changed as the bacteria changed within her.
NOTE: The model is organized into how Addie is feeling, the generation of bacteria, size of the resistant (R) and nonresistant (NR) bacteria population, and what is happening inside and outside Addie's body.
SOURCE: Reiser and Penuel (2017)

The vignette illustrates many features of a classroom with investigation and design at the center where students engage in three-dimensional performances that lead to science learning. The students engage with phenomena related to illness and bacteria, ask questions, gather data, construct explanations and make claims, develop models, produce artifacts, engage in discourse, and reflect on their learning. Students could also be asked to build on their question about "How do I make sure I don't pick up MRSA?" by working to design a solution using their engineering skills. For example, the students could work to design ways to minimize spread of bacteria in their school locker rooms. In the next sections we address the features in Table 4-2 in order, and discuss them in the context of the vignette above or another example.

Make Sense of Phenomena

The vignette about Addie (Reiser and Penuel, 2017) shows how students can engage in making sense of relevant phenomena through careful observations and the use of questions. It uses the example of an ill child that students can relate to, and it builds on the students' prior experiences with illness and antibiotics as well as their prior knowledge of bacteria as causes of disease. It presents a situation with a bit of mystery that can pique curiosity and motivate engagement. The students explore questions such as, "How do the bacteria get from the outside to the inside?" "Why don't we all have MRSA?" The questions help students to organize information about the parts of the phenomena that they do not yet understand. Learning to formulate empirically answerable questions about phenomena helps move students toward the development of preliminary explanations that can provide explanatory answers. Here the students use the questions as a starting point for developing investigations that includes experiments looking at bacterial growth. The students develop the questions that lead to their investigations and co-plan investigations of how to answer their questions. As part of their collaboration process, they make plans for what to do and how to gather and analyze the resulting data and evaluate their evidence. The key milestones are laid out in advance in the instructional sequence to help students build the important components of the key ideas. Using the prompts in the curriculum materials, the teacher is able to involve the students in working through the logic of how to make progress on their questions.

An essential component of learning for students is how interesting they find the phenomena or design challenge. Choosing topics that have relevance to their daily lives (such as bacterial infections) can help heighten interest, but there are many other ways to provide meaningful instruction. The guidelines described in Chapter 3 can be helpful: (1) providing choice or autonomy in learning, (2) promoting personal relevance, (3) presenting appropriately challenging material, and (4) situating the investigations in socially and culturally appropriate contexts. As we have discussed, science instruction where learners explore solutions to questions and design challenges (National Research Council, 2000, 2012) that are meaningful and relevant to their lives can motivate their learning (Krajcik and Blumenfeld, 2006; Rivet and Krajcik, 2008). Investigation and design provide opportunities to connect classroom experiences to learners' communities, culture, and experiences, and to real-world issues (Miller and Krajcik, 2015). To promote learning, more than initial interest is necessary; the topic needs to sustain student engagement and learning over a period of time, perhaps multiple class periods or even a full semester.

Contextualized phenomena can promote questions among students and the opportunity to address these questions in various ways (Krajcik and Czerniak, 2018; Windschitl, Thompson, and Braaten, 2008). Relevant, contextualized experiences connect underrepresented populations in STEM and English learners to the science community (Tolbert et al., 2014). These types of phenomena extend well beyond the classroom and can include real issues in the larger community such as the growth of antibiotic-resistant bacteria and their connection to human health and agriculture. Questions are the first step to sense-making of phenomena and design challenges (Schwarz et al., 2017). Starting this way entails some level of negotiation that elicits students' questions, design challenges, and initial ideas about a phenomenon in the natural or engineered world. It is often set up as an initial "question-gathering" where students brainstorm questions and record them. Unlike a traditional class—even those that are "inquiry-based"—the procedures are not fully provided to students.

Gather and Analyze Data and Information

The students in the vignette collect data on the bacterial growth on agar plates under different conditions to address their questions and gather information about the role of antibiotics and environmental conditions (such as those kept at body temperature versus room temperature). They analyze the data and look for patterns to start to construct explanations and develop models. Students explore the relationship between Addie's illness and the growth of bacteria.

An important component of preparing to investigate is to determine with students what they will document as evidence and how they will keep track of what they are figuring out (Schwarz et al., 2017). Compendia and reviews (Garfield and Ben-Zvi, 2007; Lovett and Shah, 2007) emphasize that reasoning about data involves understanding several related features of data, as well as how those features connect to a question that drives the data collection and the contexts from which those data were collected. For example, students should understand how data are constructed through measurement and sampling—what is being measured; how those measurements reflect the system under study; and how much, how often, or where measurements are collected. They should make sense of a dataset's characteristics such as distribution, patterns, or trends, as well as the variability within the data and its sources—for example, reasoning about whether variation and covariation in data reflect natural variability, errors, and biases in measurement, causal relationships, between- and within-group differences, and so on. All of this information about the nature and features of data should inform what explanations and claims students make from available data about a population or a phenomenon.

Measurement and sampling can be done in many different ways depending on the circumstances of an investigation and the technology available in the classroom. Students can count bacterial colonies by hand or use automated probes to track temperature. They can graph results on paper or using spreadsheets. They can simulate bacterial growth or examine plates from an incubator at the next class. New tools and technologies can be used to facilitate investigation, but new tools and technologies do not inherently improve an investigation. The manner in which the tools are used to support learning is key. Technology issues related to data are discussed further in Chapters 5 and 6, in the context of teachers' choices about instruction and the role of instructional resources.

Construct Explanations

After their bacterial experiments, the students create models to explain their data and understanding, such as Figure 4-3 about the timing of Addie's symptoms and correlations to the growth of the bacteria making her ill. The model shown here has a chronological set of measures and organizes and displays valuable information about the interconnections between illness and medical treatment.

The students use models in the manner described in the *Framework*, as a tool for thinking with, making predictions, and making sense of experience (Gouvea and Passmore, 2017; National Research Council, 2012, p. 56). Students should focus on using the analysis of data as evidence to support the formulation of explanations. Argumentation is the use of reasoning for how the evidence they have collected supports or refutes their explanation/claim. This vignette illustrates that explanation and argumentation do not need to be introduced as goals. They can emerge from the ongoing activity of the class to make sense of the overarching phenomena, as well as the investigations they conduct to help them answer their questions (Manz, 2015; Passmore and Svoboda, 2012).

A central aspect of engaging in investigation and design is to construct and revise models that explain phenomena. Defining a system and constructing a model of that system allows scientists and engineers to show the interaction among components in a system or between systems that cause an observed phenomenon. A key aspect of investigation and design is the exploration of systems and system modeling (Damelin et al., 2017). Dynamic modeling tools allow learners to construct and revise models to provide explanation of phenomena and test their ideas. For example, students can create complex system dynamic models including water quality, climate change, kinetic molecular theory and gas behavior, magnetic forces, collisions, forces, energy, evaporation air quality, environmental effects on disease, and weather patterns. Computer-based modeling tools can provide students with various supports and an easy-to-use visual and qualitative interface to scaffold the construction and revision of models. Students can construct models to explain phenomena by building quantitative relationships between identified variables using qualitative language accompanied by detailed descriptions that explain these relationships. Modeling tools differ from simulations in that students construct models—they specify the components and the relationships between the components and then test to see whether these relationships explain the phenomena. In simulations, students change the independent variable and observe what happens to the dependent variable. Constructing and revising models allows the students themselves to build on what is happening.

Communicate Reasoning to Self and Others

Just as a key component of the work of scientists and engineers is the sharing of ideas, experiments, and solutions with colleagues and the public, the sharing of reasoning with others is key to investigation and design. Students produce artifacts and engage in discourse and assessment for learning. The artifacts the students produce during the vignette above are not traditional laboratory reports, but rather plans and protocols for data collection, sketches, and diagrams showing what happens to bacteria under different conditions over time, and elaborated descriptions of how patterns they observed in data support particular claims or "answers" to their questions. The creation and development of these kinds of artifacts are tasks that push student learning and provide tangible representations of student understanding. They can be produced individually or in groups, on paper or digitally, all ways that make thinking visible (Bell and Linn, 2000; Berland and Reiser, 2009; Brown, 1997). The resulting artifacts (whether conveyed by models, explanations, writing, and/or speaking) represent learners' emerging understanding. These artifacts can be used by teachers to assess student understanding and by students to reflect on their own learning. In addition, students share their reasoning with each other through artifacts as well as through engaging in discourse.

The students participating in the investigation above engage in discourse as they formulate their questions, share their prior experiences, work together to plan their protocols for growing bacteria and gathering data, and reflect on their learning. They reflect via a group discussion and together produce a list of hypotheses or conjectures about what is going on. This allows them to highlight the ideas that the class is considering at the moment, but about which there is not yet agreement. Discourse is a key aspect of putting investigation and design at the center of classrooms, as students hold each other accountable to both each other's ideas, as well as the standards of a discipline (Engle and Conant, 2002).

Artifacts and Representations

Artifacts include writings, models, reports, videos, blogs, computer programs, and the like. Artifacts serve as external, intellectual products and as genuine products of students' exploration and knowledge-building activities (Krajcik and Czerniak, 2014). Artifacts have long been considered as "objects-to-think-with" (Papert, 1993) because artifacts are concrete and explicit and serve as tools of learning. Artifacts of learning and thinking are necessary products of investigation and design, and students learn the work by producing and reflecting on the artifacts. They can communicate their thinking using models, explanations, writing, and/or speaking. The artifacts and products they develop also allow them to reflect on their own learning, including the connections between what they do during investigation and design and novel phenomena beyond the classroom.

New computer-based technology, multimedia documents, and paper-based tools support students in communicating their findings from a scientific investigation. Creating multimedia documents allow students to link different media together, representing their understanding in multiple ways. Students can link graphs, tables, and various images (such as photos of their investigation or their data) or video with text that describe the graphs and videos. These technology tools both help student to communicate their findings as well as provide sophisticated ways for students to analyze data and reason the relationship among variables.

Discourse

Productive discourse or scientific talk has been promoted for several decades (at least as far back as Lemke, 1990) as a major means for improving students' sense-making of core science ideas. The goal of scientific talk is to foster uptake of students' ideas. Uptake occurs when a student puts forth an idea and other students address that idea instead of offering a new one. This engagement in others' ideas results in negotiated ideas and better-supported claims. Teachers and students often draw on productive talk that push for clarification and elaboration, allow students to agree or disagree with an idea, and privilege evidence over opinion (Chin, 2007).

We present here another vignette to explore student-led discourse in more detail. This example (see Box 4-1) shows students engaging and talking to each other as they are engaging in an engineering design project to explore temperature and the role of insulation. This vignette does not explore all of the possible angles with which students could engage in engineering design. For example, in another scenario, students could define a problem and consider a range of ways of addressing the challenge. The example presented here illustrates how student discourse can support scientific knowledge construction through engineering.

Box 4-1 contains three short examples of discourse among students sharing their designs and their scientific ideas as they engage in the process of engineering design. Students make their design decisions with each other explicit ("Foam would be a good idea") as well as the scientific reasons for doing so (because "it would hold the most heat"). The teacher comes in to ask students to justify what they are doing, but overall, the students are holding ongoing conversations with each other throughout the process of design. The students are also interacting around both scientific language ("less dense or more dense?") and everyday ways of describing those scientific ideas ("the insulation in walls are more like fluffy feel." "Yeah, thick. Thicker."). These interactions between everyday and scientific ideas, as well as connections between scientific concepts and design decisions, are emergent co-constructions as students engage in scientific reasoning and engineering design (Selcen Guzey and Aranda, 2017). The students could then move on to address the system and work to find solutions that would allow for maintaining the temperature within a defined range.

An important part of engaging in productive discourse is learning to respond to others' ideas, as shown in Box 4-1. This type of interaction requires that teachers and students establish norms that guide both general behaviors—how students interact physically in groups and socially through talk (Magnusson, Palincsar, and Templin, 2006)—and discipline-specific behaviors, defined in science in part through science and engineering practices (National Research Council, 2012). The disciplinary norms include the types of questions that science and engineering do and do not explore, how evidence is privileged when making and supporting claims, and how the community helps monitor the quality and accuracy of findings. A further example illustrating how teachers can elicit student thinking via engagement in discourse is presented in Chapter 5 in the discussion of the implosion of a tanker (Windschitl, Thompson, and Braaten, 2018). The teacher's

BOX 4-1
Discourse in an Engineering Unit

Selcen Guzey and Aranda (2017) studied decision-making processes and verbal interactions of 8th-grade students as they engaged in an engineering design-based science unit. Their work includes description of Mr. Harrison teaching 8th-grade students in a small, rural town in the midwestern United States. Mr. Harrison developed an engineering design-based unit after participating in a 3-week summer workshop supported by his state department of education. His intention was to engage students in the processes of engineering design as they applied scientific knowledge, such as heat transfer and the thermal properties of insulation materials, as they constructed, tested, evaluated, and redesigned an energy-efficient and cost-effective greenhouse made from a cardboard box and various insulating materials. The unit took twelve 50-minute class periods. He began the unit by showing the students materials for experimental testing and how they worked. The students then planned and sketched designs, tested prototypes, analyzed the strengths and weaknesses of the initial prototypes, redesigned and retested, and did additional analysis and evaluation.

The design challenge was initially posed to students as follows:

> Your job as a member of Heat Trappers, Inc., is to work with a team of engineers (your fellow students) to create as warm an environment as possible for some miniature tropical plants that were just acquired for your school's new botanical garden. Your team will modify a (shoe) box to make a greenhouse. You can add features such as a window and insulation. To test your design, you will insert a temperature probe inside your greenhouse and place it under the heat lamp and record temperatures of it for 10 minutes. . . . The school has a budget that they are trying to meet. You will receive higher consideration for your design if you stay within budget and get the largest temperature change (Selcen Guzey and Aranda, p. 591).

Mr. Harrison constrained the budget through the materials he provided to his students, which each cost a different amount. The materials included tape, felt, construction paper, bubble wrap, metallic construction paper, aluminum foil, and recycled materials (plastic, cloth, bubble wrap, and cardboard).

Throughout this unit, Mr. Harrison's students worked primarily in small teams of three or four. As students talked during the unit, they shared ideas with each other. They also related causal ideas about the materials used in their design and their scientific knowledge about insulators and heat transfer.

Student 1: Foam would be a good idea. It would hold the most heat.

Student 2: Where would we put it?

Student 1: I do not know.

Student 3: Where would it be located?

Student 1: In the center. Let's change our design. Here is the probe [showing where the probe will be inserted to measure temperature change]. We have our transparency here [referring to the window on top of the house] and the shiny stuff [referring to metallic reflective construction paper] here [under the transparency].

As the students discussed their design, Mr. Harrison joined the group and asked them about the design decisions they were making.

Mr. Harrison: What are you thinking about?

Student 1: It is kind of hard to draw. Here is the probe, and we have aluminum foil or something shiny so the sunlight will reflect off of this and we will put some black foam here so it will keep the heat.

When they made their decisions explicit, the students explained that the black foam was intended to trap air to minimize convection loss when placed in the center of the greenhouse, since they wanted to trap air to minimize convection loss. The students also decided to use a reflector made of shiny material to bounce extra light into the interior of the greenhouse, saying "reflecting light directly to the probe" would result in a higher temperature.

Once the group tested their initial design, they decided to continue to use foam in their redesign. In their discourse with each other, the students made their reasons for doing so explicit with each other.

Student 1: This [referring to their thick foam] is like insulation they put in homes.

Student 2: Somewhat.

Student 1: Yeah, the insulation in walls is more like fluffy feel.

Student 3: Yes, that is true. You want it less dense or more dense?

Student 1: Yeah, thick. Thicker.

Throughout their discussion, the group worked together to improve their knowledge as most of the members contributed to a conversation about foam as an insulation material. In the new design, however, they taped the corners and the sides of the cardboard around the window "so there is no heat escaping." Previously, in their initial design, students had not made explicit connections between the heat loss inside their house and the importance of sealing or taping to prevent air flow.

SOURCE: Selcen Guzey and Aranda (2017).

role in three-dimensional learning is to move understanding to accurate explanations; in this case, the teacher could use a three-dimensional prompt such as "How can you change your system to affect the transfer of heat energy into and out of the system?" instead of the more generic question "What are you thinking about?" This kind of language can focus and positively affect student thinking and reasoning so that the students continue a trajectory toward increased understanding of three-dimensional science.

Another interesting aspect of this vignette is that the sequence of tasks and questions has a carefully chosen and intentional order within the student experience. Prototype testing (the equivalent of explanations) is followed by redesign (the equivalent of data analysis) and retesting. The order of the activities is important, as is recognizing that there are and should often be multiple rounds of data analysis and design before a final explanation or solution.

Connect Learning Through Multiple Contexts

As students engage in science investigation and engineering design across many grades and courses, they begin to see the connections between what they have learned before and new investigation and design experiences. Teachers play a key role in helping students see these connections (see Chapter 5) and instructional resources can illustrate the connections and help students see and understand the overall coherence of science and engineering (see Chapter 6). Here we briefly point out some ways that students may see connections. For example, the vignette with Addie illustrates the phenomena of antibiotic resistance and evolution that may connect to students' previous school experiences as well as to their personal experiences with illness and medicine. For example, they may remember and reflect upon Addie the next time they or a family member have an illness that might need antibiotics. The ability to apply learning from one class unit to other situations inside and outside of school is a goal of investigation and design because it helps students to understand the ideas and concepts of science and engineering in a relevant way. The application of three-dimensional explanations and solutions to new phenomena could provide a way for student to internalize, conceptualize, and generalize the knowledge in ways that allow it to become part of how they see the natural and engineered world.

As discussed in Chapter 3, learning and motivation can be enhanced when culturally and socially relevant phenomena are selected and when connections are made to contexts familiar to students and to their prior knowledge. Teachers and administrators sometimes make the assumption that students from lower socioeconomic backgrounds, students from diverse linguistic backgrounds, and students of color do not have the prior experiences necessary to meaningfully engage in science investigation and engineering design (Gilbert and Yerrick, 2001; Nathan et al., 2010). These students, like all of their classmates, are not blank slates and their lived experiences can be leveraged to support their learning. The next example (see Box 4-2) shows how a student can apply her learning to her daily life, by discussing Teresa's repeated attempts to grow strawberries as part of an assignment to develop an engineering solution to a human need she identified and selected in her own community.

The preceding example illustrates an idea discussed in the *Framework*, of how engineering and technology provide a context in which students can test their own developing understanding and apply it to practical challenges. Doing so enhances their understanding of science—and, for many, their interest in science—as they recognize the interplay among science, engineering, and technology. The ideas students build upon can come from their everyday experiences, not just from science classrooms, and the experts that they draw upon can be family and community members, not just teachers, scientists, and engineers. It also shows that engagement in three-dimensional engineering design is as much a part of learning science as engagement in three-dimensional science learning (National Research Council, 2012). Application of learning requires deep, cognitive engagement rather than simply recalling information and reciting it. When students apply three-dimensional learning to making sense of novel phenomena, they must reason about the causes of the phenomena. The core ideas and crosscutting concepts students draw on in three-dimensional learning have, for the most part, been in existence for hundreds of years. These ideas and concepts do not need to be proven by students, but instead students apply the practices, core ideas, and crosscutting concepts through phenomena to make sense of their own world. The students need support from their teachers to make connections and learn via investigation and design, and the next chapter explores the role of the teacher in this new way of learning.

SUMMARY

Student participation in science investigation and engineering design is a dramatic shift from traditional approaches to science education. The classroom now centers on the features of investigation and design instead of on the presentation of known facts. During investigation and design students **make sense of phenomena and design challenges** by using observations, building on their prior knowledge and experiences, and developing and asking questions about how these phenomena work in the natural and engineered world. They **gather and analyze data and information** to seek patterns and evaluate information for evidence. They build on and apply their knowledge of disciplinary core ideas and crosscutting concepts gained

BOX 4-2
Growing Strawberries

Teresa, a high school student working on an engineering design project, attempted to address several factors she had learned at school as she tried to grow strawberries in a community garden. She and several of the other Hispanic youth working on the design project had many previous experiences growing home gardens, including many vegetables and fruit such as cucumbers, jalapenos, watermelon, cilantro, green chili, pumpkins, beans, garlic, raspberries, and strawberries. She and the other students working in her group had all had the experience where plants had not grown as they had expected. They tried out controlled experiments to diagnose and develop solutions to this problem. Some students noted that their family goat "basically ate all the garden," and others identified soil erosion, inadequate sunlight, infertile soil, and freezing temperatures.

Teresa described her own testing process as she tried growing strawberries over the course of several years: "If it doesn't turn out, then I go back in my mind and be like 'What was the part that I'm missing? Or what did I do wrong?'" One year she gave two different fertilizers to the plants to observe how each fertilizer affected their growth. However, during that same year, the plants were located in the path of rainwater that came out of a gutter. It seemed that the eroding soil, and not the fertilizer, was keeping the strawberries from growing, so she moved the strawberry plants to another part of her yard. However, despite her trying to use different kinds of fertilizers, the plants still were not growing as she expected. Teresa reflected on other possible causes for the plants' failure to grow and thrive, including the "bugs in the garden" that she had seen. Based on these experiences, she used pesticides on the strawberry plants in a later season, but then a family member ran over them with a car by accident. She noted that this inadvertent error limited her ability to conclude whether the pesticides had an influence on the growth of the strawberries. Throughout this process, while working in her home garden, Teresa had sought to design valid experiments in which she isolated single variables, made observations, developed tentative conjectures in regards to causation, redesigned experiments, and developed evidence-based explanations.

When they considered building a community garden for their engineering project, Teresa's group built on these prior experiences. The students noted that a community garden would need to be placed on flat land and in an area without too much water runoff so that water would not cause too much erosion. They noted that animal and human interference of many kinds were likely to occur but could be addressed through selecting a safe location and designing a fence. Teresa was unsure of a place in her community where a garden like this might be constructed, and so consulted her parents who acted as experts on community geography to help her to identify possible locations. Although the group ultimately abandoned the idea to produce a community garden, this experience illustrates the ways in which Teresa, as she engaged in the design process, activated multiple resources and leveraged her prior experiences, and those of her group members, toward the pursuit of her goal.

SOURCE: Adapted from Wilson-Lopez et al. (2018).

via previous investigations. Students **construct explanations** for the causes of phenomena and develop models for the relationships among the components of the systems, and they develop arguments for how the evidence gathered in the investigations and tests of the solutions to challenges supports the explanation. They **design solutions** that build on their understanding of relationships between components and test those solutions. They **communicate reasoning to self and others** through models and arguments to show how the evidence they have developed supports the explanation and/or solution. They use artifacts and representations that communicate reasoning and respond to others' ideas as they engage in productive discourse. Students **connect learning through multiple contexts** by reflecting on their own learning and seeing links between what they do during investigation and design experiences with phenomena and issues beyond the classroom.

REFERENCES

American Association for the Advancement of Science. (1993). *Benchmarks for Science Literacy.* New York: Oxford University Press.

Banchi, H., and Bell, R. (2008). The many levels of inquiry. *Science and Children, 46*(2), 26–29.

Bell, P., and Linn, M.C. (2000). Scientific arguments as learning artifacts: Designing for learning from the web with KIE. *International Journal of Science Education, 22*(8), 797–817.

Berland, L.K., and Reiser, B.J. (2009). Making sense of argumentation and explanation. *Science Education, 93*(1), 26–55.

Blumenfeld, P., Soloway, E., Marx, R., Krajcik, J.S., Guzdial, M., and Palincsar, A.S. (1991). Motivating project-based learning: Sustaining the doing, supporting the learning. *Educational Psychologist, 26*, 369–398.

Brown, A.L. (1997). Transforming schools into communities of thinking and learning about serious matters. *American Psychologist, 52*(4), 399.

Cazden, C. (1986). Classroom discourse. In M.C. Wittrock (Ed.), *Handbook of Research on Teaching, 3rd ed.* New York: Macmillan.

Chin, C. (2007). Teacher questioning in science classrooms: Approaches that stimulate productive thinking. *Journal of Research in Science Teaching, 44*(6), 815–843.

Crawford, B.A. (2014). From inquiry to scientific practices in the science classroom. In N.L. Lederman and S.K. Abell (Eds.), *Handbook of Research on Science Education* (vol. 2, pp. 515–541). New York, NY: Routledge.

Damelin, D., Krajcik, J., McIntyre, C., and Bielik, T. (2017). Students making system models: An accessible approach. *Science Scope, 40*(5), 78–82.

Engle, R.A., and Conant, F.R. (2002). Guiding principles for fostering productive disciplinary engagement: Explaining an emergent argument in a community of learners classroom. *Cognition and Instruction, 20*(4), 399–483. doi: 10.1207/S1532690xci2004_1.

Furtak, E.M., Seidel, T., Iverson, H., and Briggs, D.C. (2012). Experimental and quasi-experimental studies of inquiry-based science teaching: A meta-analysis. *Review of Educational Research, 82*(3), 300–329. doi: 10.3102/0034654312457206.

Garfield, J.B., and Ben-Zvi, D. (2007). How students learn statistics revisited: A current review of research on teaching and learning statistics. *International Statistical Review, 75*(3), 372–396. doi: 10.1111/j.1751-5823.2007.00029.x.

Gilbert, A., and Yerrick, R. (2001). Same school, separate worlds: A sociocultural study of identity, resistance, and negotiation in a rural, lower track science classroom. *Journal of Research in Science Teaching, 38*(5), 574–598.

Gouvea, J., and Passmore, C. (2017). 'Models of' versus 'models for': Toward an agent-based conception of modeling in the science classroom. *Science & Education, 26*, 49. doi:

Krajcik, J.S., and Blumenfeld, P. (2006). Project-based learning. In R.K. Sawyer (Ed.), *The Cambridge Handbook of the Learning Sciences* (pp. 317–333). New York: Cambridge University Press.

Krajcik, J.S., and Czerniak, C.M. (2014). *Teaching Science in Elementary and Middle School: A Project-Based Approach* (4th ed.). London: Routledge.

Krajcik, J.S., and Czerniak, C.M. (2018). *Teaching Science in Elementary and Middle School: A Project-Based Approach* (5th ed.). London: Routledge.

Lemke, J.L. (1990). *Talking Science: Language, Learning, and Values*. Norwood, NJ: Ablex.

Lovett, M.C., and Shah, P. (2007). *Thinking with Data*. Mahwah, NJ: Lawrence Erlbaum Associates.

Magnusson, S.J., Palincsar, A.S., and Templin, M. (2006). Community, culture, and conversation in inquiry based science instruction. In L.B. Flick and N.G. Lederman (Eds.), *Scientific Inquiry and Nature of Science: Implications for Teaching, Learning, and Teacher Education* (pp. 131–155). Dordrecht, Netherlands: Springer.

Manz, E. (2015). Representing student argumentation as functionally emergent from scientific activity. *Review of Educational Research, 85*(4), 553–590. doi: 10.3102/0034654314558490.

Miller, E., and Krajcik, J. (2015). Reflecting on instruction to promote equity and alignment to the NGSS. In O. Lee, E. Miller, and R. Janusyzk (Eds.), *NGSS for All Students* (p. 181). Arlington, VA: NSTA Press.

Nathan, M.J., Tran, N.A., Atwood, A.K., Prevost, A.M.Y., and Phelps, L.A. (2010). Beliefs and expectations about engineering preparation exhibited by high school STEM teachers. *Journal of Engineering Education, 99*(4), 409–426.

National Research Council. (2000). *Inquiry and the National Science Education Standards: A Guide for Teaching and Learning*. Washington, DC: National Academy Press.

National Research Council. (2006). *America's Lab Report: Investigations in High School Science*. Washington, DC: The National Academies Press.

National Research Council. (2012). *A Framework for K-12 Science Education: Practices, Crosscutting Concepts, and Core Ideas*. Washington, DC: The National Academies Press.

NGSS Storylines. (2017). *Why Don't Antibiotics Work Like They Used To?* (Curriculum materials.) Available: http://www.nextgenstorylines.org/whydont-antibiotics-work-like-they-used-to [October 2018].

Osborne, J. (2014). Teaching scientific practices: Meeting the challenge of change. *Journal of Science Teacher Education, 25*(2), 177–196.

Papert, S. (1993). *The Children's Machine: Rethinking Schools in the Age of the Computer*. New York: Basic Books.

Passmore, C.M., and Svoboda, J. (2012). Exploring opportunities for argumentation in modelling classrooms. *International Journal of Science Education, 34*(10), 1535–1554. doi: 10.1080/09500693.2011.577842.

Passmore, C., Schwarz, C., and Mankowski, J. (2017). Developing and using models, In C.V. Schwarz, C. Passmore, and B.J. Reiser (Eds.), *Helping Students Make Sense of the World: Using Next Generation Science and Engineering Practices* (pp. 109–134). Arlington, VA: NSTA Press.

Penuel, W.R., Van Horne, K., Severance, S., Quigley, D., and Sumner, T. (2016). Students' responses to curricular activities as indicator of coherence in project based science. In C.K. Looi, J.L. Polman, U. Cress, and P. Reimann (Eds.), *Transforming Learning, Empowering Learners: The International Conference of the Learning Sciences (ICLS) 2016* (vol. 2, pp. 855–858). Singapore: International Society of the Learning Sciences.

Reiser, B., and Penuel, B. (2017). *Designing NGSS-Aligned Curriculum Materials.* Paper commissioned for the Committee on Science Investigations and Engineering Design Experiences in Grades 6-12. Board on Science Education, Division of Behavioral and Social Sciences and Education. National Academies of Sciences, Engineering, and Medicine. Available: http://www.nas.edu/Science-Investigation-and-Design [October 2018].

Rivet, A.E., and Krajcik, J.S. (2008). Contextualizing instruction: Leveraging students' prior knowledge and experiences to foster understanding of middle school science. *Journal of Research in Science Teaching, 45*(1), 79–100.

Schwab, J. (1962). The teaching of science as enquiry. In J.J. Schwab and P.F. Brandwein, (Eds.), *The Teaching of Science* (pp. 1–103). New York: Simon and Schuster.

Schwarz, C.V., Passmore, C., and Reiser, B.J. (2017). Moving beyond "knowing about" science to making sense of the world. In C.V. Schwarz, C. Passmore, and B.J. Reiser (Eds.), *Helping Students Make Sense of the World Using Next Generation Science and Engineering Practices* (pp. 3–21). Arlington, VA: NSTA Press.

Selcen Guzey, S., and Aranda, M. (2017). Student participation in engineering practices and discourse: An exploratory case study. *Journal of Engineering Education, 106*(4), 585–606. doi: 10.1002/jee.20176.

Tolbert, S., Stoddart, T., Lyon, E.G., and Solís, J. (2014). The Next Generation Science Standards, Common Core State Standards, and English learners: Using the SSTELLA Framework to prepare secondary science teachers. *Issues in Teacher Education, 23*(1), 65–90.

Weizman, A., Shwartz, Y., and Fortus, D. (2010). Developing students' sense of purpose with a driving question board. In R.E. Yager (Ed.), *Exemplary Science for Resolving Societal Challenges* (pp. 110–130). Arlington, VA: NSTA Press.

Wilson-Lopez, A., Sias, C., Smithee, A., and Hasbún, I.M. (2018). Forms of science capital mobilized in adolescents' engineering projects. *Journal of Research in Science Teaching, 55*(2), 246–270. doi: 10.1002/tea.21418.

Windschitl, M., Thompson, J., and Braaten, M. (2008). Beyond the scientific method: Model-based inquiry as a new paradigm of preference for school science investigations. *Science Education, 92*(5), 941–967. doi: 10.1002/sce.20259.

Windschitl, M., Thompson, J., and Braaten, M. (2018). *Ambitious Science Teaching.* Cambridge, MA: Harvard Education Press.

5

How Teachers Support
Investigation and Design

The previous chapter focused on investigation and design from the student perspective. This chapter focuses on the teacher's role in engaging students in investigation and design. As discussed in *Guide to Implementing the NGSS* (National Research Council, 2015), instruction is the experiences that teachers organize in their classroom in order for students to learn, not the information teachers deliver to students. "[D]ay-to-day instruction is carried out by teachers who are making continual decisions about what best meets their students' needs along a learning path" (National Research Council, 2015, p. 24). This chapter discusses how teachers can guide students in each of the features of investigation and design covered in Chapter 4.[1] It includes an expanded consideration of assessment and an illustrative example of the features coming together in a classroom as well as discussion of fostering an inclusive classroom, using inclusive pedagogy, and planning for coherence. Chapter 6 discusses how instructional resources can help by providing materials and guidance for carrying out the instruction.

---

[1] This chapter includes content drawn from five papers commissioned by the committee: *Designing NGSS-Aligned Curriculum Materials* by Brian Reiser and Bill Penuel; *Data Use by Middle and Secondary Students in the Digital Age: A Status Report and Future Prospects* by Victor Lee and Michelle Wilkerson; *The Nature of the Teacher's Role in Supporting Student Investigations in Middle and High School Science Classrooms: Creating and Participating in a Community of Practice* by Matthew Kloser; *Engineering Approaches to Problem Solving and Design in Secondary School Science: Teachers as Design Coaches* by Senay Purzer; and *A Summary of Inclusive Pedagogies for Science Education* by Felicia Mensah and Kristen Larson. The commissioned papers are available at http://www.nas.edu/Science-Investigation-and-Design.

Multiple groups of researchers have identified sets of core instructional practices for science teachers (Kloser, 2014; Windschitl et al., 2012). Windschitl et al. (2012) noted that "classrooms are now being viewed as working communities in which the teacher's principal task is to mediate increasingly sophisticated forms of *academic conversation and activity by the students*, rather than have students memorize and reproduce textbook explanations or merely expose them to activities. . . . This mediation . . . promotes robust forms of reasoning about complex concepts . . . and engages learners in the characteristic practices of the discipline" (p. 886, emphasis ours). In addition to the teacher's crucial role in the day-to-day structuring of instruction, another important role is to facilitate discourse in ways that draw on students' ideas, attend to existing theories and evidence to shape those ideas, and equitably promote uptake of students' ideas amongst each other (Kloser, 2014).

Table 5-1 shows the ideas first presented in Table 4-2, but now from the perspective of a teacher thinking about instruction rather than the students' experiences with investigation and design. Many of the same ideas are important to the teacher, but the teacher has additional responsibilities. For example, the teacher selects and presents phenomena and engages the students in making sense of them via guided questions and observations. In making this selection, the teacher considers the students' background knowledge and their perspectives, as well as the local context, and seeks phenomena or design challenges that are likely to match student interests. The guidelines presented in Chapter 3 offer reminders to consider (1) providing choice or autonomy in learning, (2) promoting personal relevance, (3) presenting appropriately challenging material, and (4) situating the investigations in socially and culturally appropriate contexts. The phenomenon or challenge needs to provide more than just a hook to interest students, it must spark many questions that can be used to drive learning via investigation and design. In addition, the teacher helps the students determine which information counts as evidence and how it can be used to construct explanations or design solutions and to advance three-dimensional understanding. A key role of the teacher is in assessing student learning. This does not mean just giving tests; it includes helping students to reflect on their learning and the learning process and to productively share their ideas with each other in various formats. The teacher plays a key role in the students making connections to their prior knowledge and to phenomena they will encounter in the future. With the help of instructional resources (see Chapter 6), the teacher is responsible for creating a coherent experience for students where they can see these connections and apply their learning.

TABLE 5-1 Teacher Guidance during Investigation and Design

Examples of the Teacher's Role in Supporting Student Learning
(organized by features of science investigation and engineering design)

Make Sense of Phenomena and Design Challenge	Gather and Analyze Data and Information	Construct Explanations and Design Solutions	Communicate Reasoning to Self and Others	Connect Learning through Multiple Contexts
- Select and present real and relevant phenomena or challenges	- Communicate clear expectations for use of information as evidence	- Communicate clear expectations for students to develop evidence-based explanations and models	- Provide opportunities for students to produce multiple models and other artifacts that communicate their reasoning	- Highlight connections to experiences and phenomena students have encountered in previous units, courses, or in earlier school grades
- Guide observation and development of student questions	- Facilitate connections between relevant core ideas and crosscutting concepts related to the phenomena or challenge	- Set clear expectations for students to develop arguments for how their evidence supports explanations	- Establish a classroom culture of respect and guide productive and inclusive discourse	- Plan coherent support for students to connect learning to phenomena beyond the classroom
- Facilitate students developing and using meaningful and relevant questions		- Support design and testing of solutions to challenges, including redesign and retesting as students refine their approach	- Reflect on student and teacher learning	

MAKE SENSE OF PHENOMENA

Contextualized, real-world phenomena or human challenges are the heart of student engagement in science investigation and engineering design. When contextualized and situated, investigations can help students learn and use prior knowledge to explain or model novel phenomena. This way of focusing on investigation and design is a fundamental shift from the *America's Lab Report* (National Research Council, 2006), in which integrated instructional units brought the laboratory experience into the flow of the class to highlight connections, but the investigation itself was not the center of the unit. Investigation and design make contextualized, real-world phenomena the overarching and unifying driving force for all of the students' activity in the science classroom.

Teachers are integrally involved in partnering with students to identify and use contextualized phenomena that promote questions among students and the opportunity to address these questions in various ways (Krajcik and Czerniak, 2014; Windschitl, Thompson, and Braaten, 2018). To establish relevance, there needs to be a connection to learners' interests, such as their communities, cultures, places, and experiences, and to realworld issues (Miller and Krajcik, 2015). When teachers choose phenomena or design challenges that are relevant to the community, the resulting student questions will also be relevant. To promote learning, more than relevance and an initial interest is necessary; the phenomena and questions need to maintain student interest and learning over a sustained period of time. Relevant questions are critical for creating engaging learning environments for all students, including both boys and girls, as well as those from different cultures, races, and socioeconomic backgrounds (see Box 5-1). As discussed in Chapter 3, students need to be motivated to seek solutions to a question and persist at finding solutions or responses when work becomes challenging or they experience setback or failure.

Teachers play a key role in selecting phenomena for investigation and design that engage the students and at the same time lead to learning of important science and engineering ideas and concepts. While the focus of science and engineering in practice is on investigating phenomena in nature and the designed world, some phenomena may not be directly relevant to students' daily lives because they are not observable or are so abstract or divorced from students' experiences that they do not capture student interest (Windschitl et al., 2012). The phenomena or design problems introduced should be carefully chosen to provide a context to engage students in using science ideas and concepts to explain what is occurring and to improve student understanding of the chosen science or engineering topic. Phenomena and design challenges provide a context and purpose for students' science learning. In order to prepare for these types of instructional experiences, teachers need to be able to collaborate with students, colleagues, and community members to identify contextualized phenomena to drive investigations. One example of a mechanism for community collaboration is provided by EPICS K–12,[2] which provides sample service-learning modules that connect engineering and the community. More generally, Krajcik (2015) proposed several approaches, drawing ideas from the local environment and context (e.g., relationships in local habitats or ecosystems), tapping into students' interests (e.g., sports or music), identifying current challenges that face the environment (e.g., global warming), or drawing on scientific issues. The focus on complex phenomena has equity implications. Relevant, contextualized experiences connect underrepresented populations

---

[2]For more information, see https://engineering.purdue.edu/EPICS/k12 [December 2018].

BOX 5-1
Design Challenge Topics

Christopher G. Wright (Drexel University) studies the interrelationship between engineering competencies and identities for African American males. Focusing on what Nasir and Hand (2008) referred to as "practice-linked identities," Wright works to identify real-world design challenges that could potentially engage this student demographic, while providing authentic opportunities to participate in engineering and science practices. This work can lead to an understanding of the ways in which learning contexts could potentially support the learning and identities of students who have been historically marginalized within STEM communities.

Wright has worked with middle school students to understand the relationship between learning and identity in these contexts. The complexity in this work is avoiding the essentializing of students by boiling them down to common stereotypes and assumptions in what might interest them, but to truly understand what it means to engage students by incorporating aspects of their lived experiences and community capital. Considering students' competencies and identities, teachers may consider a more expansive learning space where students can participate in and reconstruct meanings for their own engagement in learning engineering and scientific competencies. Wright suggests that teachers identify the kinds of engineering challenges (e.g. particular human problems, and engineering practices in order to address student interests, participation, engagement, and identity development).

In a recent pilot study, Wright has worked with middle school students to explore the question, *What role do engineers play in the design and analysis of sneakers?* In addressing this question, students explore why different types of sneakers are used in a variety of common sports, study how engineers analyze the needs of athletes, and explore how engineers engage in the design of sneakers in order to meet athletes' needs. Students have opportunities to analyze foot movement in a variety of different sports and develop design criteria for individual sports and/or athletes.

SOURCE: Adapted from material presented to the committee by Christopher Wright on July 24, 2017.

in STEM and English learners to the science community (Tolbert et al., 2014). Another important instructional consideration is related to the progression of core ideas across the grade levels: that is, an explanation for a phenomenon can change as student learning becomes increasingly sophisticated across grade levels (see Box 5-2).

Problematizing everyday phenomena for students—that is, inducing in students "perplexity, confusion, or doubt" (Dewey, 1910, p. 12) in relationship to those phenomena—is one strategy for sparking and sustaining interest (Engle, 2012) and for pushing students to go deeper and develop

BOX 5-2
Example of Increasingly Sophisticated Understanding of the Same Phenomenon at Later Grade Levels

The following provides an example of how investigation of the same phenomenon results in increasingly sophisticated student explanations across three grade bands.

Phenomenon: It is easier to walk on wet sand than on dry sand.

Student Performances
1. Use cups and plates of sand to **explore** differences in **structure** of wet sand and dry sand.
2. **Formulate questions** and **plan and carry out an investigation** to gather evidence for why **(causes)** and how (mechanism) a ball or marble responds differently to dry sand and wet sand.
3. **Construct an explanation** for why **(causes)** it is "easier" (requires less effort) to walk on wet sand than on dry sand.

Nature of Core Ideas Used in Student Explanations by Grade Level

Grades 3-5: *The explanation* centers on reasoning that it is easier to walk on wet sand than dry sand because water makes the grains of sand stick together. The wet sand sticks together just like building a sand castle. Students observe that a person does not move much sand with each step on wet sand but moves a lot of sand with each step on dry sand. Since it takes energy to move sand, it will take more energy to walk in dry sand than it will on wet sand.

Middle School: The explanation centers on core ideas about adhesion and cohesion and Newton's laws of motion. When a person pushes down on the sand, an equal and opposite force causes him or her to move forward. In wet sand the grains of sand adhere to each other forming a semisolid surface that distributes the force of the foot pushing down over a larger area, so the force acting on the sand appears to be less than in dry sand, causing less sand to be displaced. The evidence that students use to support their explanation includes that a marble bounces off the wet sand but sinks into the dry sand. They use evidence from running in wet and dry sand.

High School Physical Science: The explanations focus on how the water causes the sand grains to be held together by intermolecular forces, hydrogen bonding, and the ideas of work and energy. The dipolar nature of water causes water to stick to grains of sand and to each other. The water molecules form a layer around the grains of sand held together by hydrogen bonds that cause the grains of sand to stick together. This layer of water is not present in dry sand. Energy is needed to break these hydrogen bonds. Work is done on the grains of sand with each step, and this work results in energy being passed to the sand. Students use evidence from how a marble bounces on the sand and their knowledge of how water can be stacked on top of a penny to support their explanation that hydrogen bonding causes things to stick together.

SOURCE: Adapted from Moulding and Bybee (2018).

explanations for phenomena they may take for granted (Reiser, 2004; Reiser, Novak, and McGill, 2017b; Watkins et al., 2018). Students' questions are at the center of curiosity and engagement in phenomena. Curiosity motivates students to persist in seeking the solutions to problems and the explanations for phenomena. Such projects would

- create interest and student curiosity that lead to engagement in learning;
- be relevant to students' communities, culture, place, and experiences, and to real-world issues;
- present challenges with a variety of possible solutions; and
- involve criteria and constraints that are not only technical (associated with a disciplinary core idea), but also address economic, societal, or environmental aspects.

Core ideas and crosscutting concepts can be thought of as the intellectual resources students use to make sense of phenomena in their daily life beyond the classroom. Huff and Duschl (2018) suggest that before middle school teachers begin instruction, they should first contemplate how the instruction builds on students' prior learning and how instruction will lead to coherence in learning and a more sophisticated understanding of core ideas and crosscutting concepts. For example, in a middle school classroom, students may learn about the solar system and how planets are held in orbit around the sun by its gravitational pull on them. They use models to learn about motions and tilt of the Earth and how these phenomena relate to the changing seasons.

Approaches aligned with *A Framework for K–12 Science Education* (hereafter referred to as the *Framework*; National Research Council, 2012) are often driven by students' emergent questions and ideas, both at the beginning of units of instruction, as well as along the way as those instructional sequences unfold. In the past, a focus of traditional science instruction was to lecture to students and focus on "filling them up" with knowledge. Teachers often feel the need to "frontload" science instruction by telling students science facts; the evidence indicates that 40 percent of class time in middle schools and nearly one-half of class time in high schools is spent frontloading content (Banilower et al., 2013). Even when teachers open up space for students to share their background knowledge and ideas about the phenomenon under study, the questions asked often limit the ability of students to truly make their ideas known. As discussed in Chapter 4, investigation and design do not use the traditional I-R-E model in which teachers initiate (I) interaction by asking an individual student a question followed by the student's response (R) and the teacher's evaluation (E) of that response (see the discussion of Figure 4-1) (Cazden, 2001). This questioning pattern often fails to address the needs of the entire learning community and does not engage students as participants in the disciplinary community (Michaels and O'Connor, 2017). The techniques of productive discourse discussed later in this chapter can provide alternate strategies for teachers to engage student questions.

Given the many challenges facing teachers in adapting instruction to on-going changes in student thinking, researchers have explored new strategies and supports to better prepare teachers to notice student thinking in the moment (Johnson, Wendell, and Watkins, 2017; Richards and Robertson, 2016; Russ and Luna, 2013). Some have examined the ways in which learning progressions, as representations of student ideas, concepts, and practices, can support teachers in understanding the complex landscape of student learning and can support them as they navigate less-structured learning environments (Alonzo and Elby, 2014; Furtak, Morrison, and Kroog, 2014).

Teachers can work to partner with students in identifying the students' questions by using culturally relevant (Ladson-Billings, 2006) and culturally responsive (Gay, 2010) pedagogies to help to inform the ways in which these questions and phenomena might be identified (as discussed later in this chapter). Teachers who are using culturally *relevant* pedagogies are first aware of their own power, positioning, and social context (Ladson-Billings, 2006), and they help to identify phenomena and problem scenarios that are relevant to students' lived experience and build on those experiences. Taking this one step farther, culturally *responsive* pedagogies seek to critique or disrupt the status quo (Parsons and Wall, 2011). Teachers can promote inclusion by choosing phenomena that build deeply on the communities and knowledge students bring to the classroom.

GATHER AND ANALYZE DATA

As discussed in Chapter 4, what it means to work with data has changed significantly since the preparation and publication of *America's Lab Report* (National Research Council, 2006) in ways that impact students, educators, and how science is taught. This change is expressing itself most obviously in the abundance of data that can be collected and accessed by students and teachers. There are also notable changes in the types of data (e.g., GPS, network, and qualitative/verbal data) that are now readily available and the purposes for which data are collected and analyzed. These shifts have both generated enthusiasm and raised a number of questions for K–12 science educators as new science standards are being adopted across the United States. Research continues to show that students benefit from working with data when such work is connected to meaningful inquiry, and when students have opportunities to participate in the construction, representation, analysis, and use of data as evidence in a coherent manner, rather than as separated experiences. Over the past several decades, considerable research has explored learners' general understandings about the nature and purpose of quantitative data. There are several key points for teachers to keep in mind about how students conceive of data during investigation and design:

1. **Leverage data in the context of meaningful scientific pursuits.** Data competences examined outside of authentic contexts appear different from those that are situated in familiar and meaningful contexts. In the latter, students have more opportunities to demonstrate and develop sophistication, and to construct, use, and communicate data in ways that are meaningfully connected to other scientific practices.

2. **Consider datasets as aggregates rather than only collections of data points and use related statistical notions.** Students are better equipped to interpret and communicate about data when they have developed ideas of distribution and variability, and when they richly understand how to use measures of center as one of many ways to describe a dataset.

3. **Representations are an important part of interpreting and communicating about data.** Data representations can be frequently misunderstood, but those misunderstandings can be refined through reflection on how a given data representation works and corresponds to the situation being modeled. Interpretive work with data representations should emphasize distributions and variability in the dataset, and students may benefit from constructing and using data representations to support scientific explanation or argument.

4. **Data engagements in science can provide better connections to how topics of data and statistics are encountered in mathematics instruction.** Some specific connections may be made by encouraging students to compare multiple datasets and use data representations when making and justifying claims (thus leveraging notions of center, spread, and representation from mathematics instruction as part of making inferences from data).

Teachers play a key role in helping students to use the tools and techniques needed to gather data, and they establish clear standards for what is used as evidence (see Box 5-3). They work to elicit evidence-based reasoning from students (also see the extended example about a tanker implosion later in this chapter for more on eliciting ideas). Teachers help students find and bring in the connections to their prior knowledge and how an investigation links to crosscutting concepts or disciplinary core ideas they have encountered in previous courses.

BOX 5-3
How Healthy Is the Water in Our Stream?

Ms. Novak, a 7th-grade science teacher at Greenhills School in Ann Arbor, Michigan, starts a semester-long project by asking her students about their own water use, followed by explorations of where the water they use comes from, how it can be polluted, and how pollution affects organisms. She then takes her students on a stream walk so that they can make initial observations of the nearby stream—which feeds into the local water supply—and the surrounding area. She asks her students, "How healthy is the water in our stream?" "How do you think humans might impact the quality of the stream?" "How does the quality of the stream impact organisms that live in the stream?" Based on their observations of the stream and the surrounding land, Ms. Novak asks her students to generate questions they might be able to investigate to better understand how healthy the stream is. One pair of students poses the question, "Does the storm drain pipe coming into the stream affect its quality?" Another pair asks, "Some of the banks along the river are just dirt, with nothing growing on them. Does that affect the quality of the stream?" A third pair of students wonders, "The condominium complex right next to the stream has really nice lawns. How does that impact the stream?"

Ms. Novak posts the students' questions on the class question board, and then turns the discussion to how experts measure water quality. She states to the class, "We'll need to research to find out what tests water quality experts' conduct, what tools they use, and what the various tests mean. We can talk with local groups who know about the stream and/or water quality. And we can present our findings to the local community." The students conduct Internet searches to find out how water quality is measured, and then learn that they can make these

---

Early work in mathematics and science education has documented common difficulties students have with reading canonical representations that often show data (Leinhardt, Zaslavsky, and Stein, 1990). A well-known example is that Cartesian graphs of velocity of an object are often interpreted by students as indicating the trajectory of the object (Clement, 1989). Similarly, students may expect histograms with flatter distributions to indicate there is less variability in data or that the x-axis of histograms are meant to indicate time (Kaplan et al., 2014). They may also treat displays of data as simple illustrations, rather than as tools for reasoning about and describing data (Wild and Pfannkuch, 1999). This extends to non-graphical data representations, such as map-based data visualizations, which middle and secondary students may interpret as being an iconic picture rather than a product and source of data (Swenson and Kastens, 2011).

While some incorrect data interpretations are to be expected, there is growing consensus that these misinterpretations be viewed as non-normative products of still useful reasoning processes (Elby, 2000; Lee

same measurements—pH, temperature, conductivity, and dissolved oxygen—using sensors attached to portable digital devices. They learn how to use these sensors to collect data, by investigating questions such as, "What is the pH of everyday products people use outside?" Using their results, they can predict how these products might impact the pH of the stream.

Then the students, scaffolded with supports from Ms. Novak, develop a plan for collecting data systematically over 6 to 8 weeks. They divide the stream into sections, and each group of students adopts one section of the stream where they will collect data four times. In addition to collecting sensor-based data, they make observations about what they observe in and around the stream. After each data collection period, students share their data, and analyze them to look for patterns, trends, and potential cause-and-effect relationships, and discuss the results. Students use the patterns and trends in the data as evidence to construct an explanation that addresses the driving question, "How healthy is our stream for freshwater organisms and how do our actions on land potentially impact the stream and the organisms that live in it?" and they revise this explanation with each round of data collection. With each revision, Ms. Novak provides feedback and written guides to help student groups revise their explanation and synthesize the new data, although many students find this challenging when new evidence appears to contradict their explanations.

At the end of the semester, the students develop a formal presentation that includes an argument for how their data supports their explanation for the causes of changes in water quality, both in class and to the residents of a retirement community located alongside the stream.

SOURCE: Adapted from Novak and Krajcik (2018).

and Sherin, 2006). For example, many errors documented in students' understandings of representations are misapplications of otherwise useful conventions that can be remedied through reflection and comparison of the data to the context about which an investigation is being conducted, or they may arise from a case-versus-aggregate treatment of data (delMas, Garfield, and Ooms, 2005). With time and support, however, students may notice and begin to make mappings between important features within a representation and the situation being modeled, even treating the representation as a source of data that can be further manipulated in order to answer new questions (Laina and Wilkerson, 2016).

Data representations that are carefully selected and introduced can help scaffold students' understandings of conventional representations, as well as of key features of data—including developing aggregate conceptions of datasets; attending to measures of center, spread, and distribution; and making inferences from the data (Konold, 2012). Dot and scatter plots that clearly indicate each observation in a dataset relative to others, for example, have been found to be more accessible to students who are still developing graphical competencies, allowing users to visualize how data are concentrated in "modal clumps" (Konold et al., 2002) and build on intuitive ways of "seeing" data. Similarly, Kuhn, Ramseym, and Arvidsson (2015) found that although even adults exhibit difficulty engaging in multivariate reasoning, brief interventions in which middle school students collected, aggregated, and visualized data about topics that have complex causal factors (e.g., life expectancy, body mass index) using dot plots yielded promising findings.

CONSTRUCT EXPLANATIONS

At a national level, science instruction is re-orienting toward engaging students with science as epistemic practice. One consequence of this shift is that students are expected to construct understandings of content through engaging in a suite of scientific and engineering practices, including not only data analysis, but also developing models, asking questions, planning and carrying out investigations, constructing explanations and designing solutions, and developing arguments for how the evidence supports an explanation. It is fortunate that these practices are well-aligned with what the literature shows about how students' reasoning with data can be further developed—collecting data in service of understanding real-world phenomena, using data as evidence, engaging in argument from evidence, and communicating the reasoning about the meaning of data as it relates to causal explanations.

One of the most obvious ways in which students can work with data in sophisticated and meaningful ways to advance their own scientific inquiries is through measurement and modeling. Lehrer and Romberg (1996) have promoted "data modeling" in which the emphasized practices involve iterative cycles of posing questions, generating and selecting attributes that can be measured, constructing measures, structuring and representing data, and making inferences from data. Such work involves an iterative testing and refinement of student models of the system connected with the measurements they undertake and the data representations they develop.

Another clear connection between investigation and design and data is the role evidence from data plays in scientific explanation and argumentation. Science educators have long sought to better support students in using data as scientific evidence. Epistemic scaffolds that explicitly privilege the use of evidence in explanation have proved useful in this regard (McNeil and Kraijcik, 2011; Sandoval and Reiser, 2004). Students may give quantitative data higher epistemic status than other forms of evidence (Sandoval and Çam, 2011); however, as described above, they may also treat data as an objective report rather than an uncertain construction whose validity can be assessed and challenged. The ways in which students make use of data as evidence to support explanation and argument depends on the nature and complexity of the data. Using complex data to support explanations and argument can be a challenge to most students (Kerlin, McDonald, and Kelly, 2010).

A key role for teachers is to establish clear expectations for the construction of models and the development of arguments for how the evidence supports or refutes an explanation or claim. When students engage in engineering design challenges (see Box 5-4), the teacher serves an additional role as a design coach (Purzer, 2017).

COMMUNICATE REASONING TO SELF AND OTHERS

A key feature of instruction is the opportunity for students to reflect on their own reasoning and share it with fellow students and their teachers. This can be done via production of artifacts and representations and by engaging in productive discourse. The teacher plays an important role in providing multiple opportunities for students to demonstrate various types of reasoning, by eliciting ideas during discourse, and by setting an expectation for inclusion and respect. This communication also provides opportunities for assessment, as students reflect on their own work and teachers learn about the students' understanding and progress.

Artifacts and Representations

As discussed in the previous chapter, artifacts are tangible representations of student understanding that serve as external, intellectual products and as genuine products of students' exploration and knowledge-building activities (Blumenfeld et al., 1991; Lucas et al., 2005). Students' explanations of phenomena and their design solutions for challenges serve as artifacts that help make the learners' scientific thinking visible to themselves and others. Discussions in which teacher's elicit student ideas and lead discussions to explore the ideas are central to learning via investigation and design. Student-generated artifacts help students organize and share their thinking. These representations not only reveal students' initial ideas and experiences, but also track ongoing changes in their thinking (Windschitl et al., 2012). In this way, teachers not only facilitate learning experiences for students through classroom discourse, but also mediate this discourse by encouraging students to create artifacts that students generate as individuals, in small groups, and as a class. Artifacts are important, because a key aspect of making scientific practices central is that teachers and students hold each other accountable to being responsive to each other's ideas, as well as to norms they have collectively established for what counts as quality practice

BOX 5-4
Aeronautics and Wind Tunnel Testing

On the first day of the aerospace engineering unit at the Science Leadership Academy @ Center City, in Philadelphia, the students entering Mr. Kamal's 10th-grade engineering class are handed a piece of paper. On the board is the daily "Spark Plug": *What makes a paper airplane fly far? Use the provided paper to make your best airplane.* Students build, test, and compare their planes. The class then watches a video of the world champion paper airplane flight followed by detailed table discussions about similarities and differences between their planes and that of the champion.

In conjunction with NGSS, Mr. Kamal uses Understanding by Design curricular methodology to backwards-design his unit. Essential questions that students use to drive their inquiry include

- Why do aircraft stay aloft?
- Are scaled models valid testing tools?
- How do we know if a test's results are valid?

Mr. Kamal teaches that there are primarily four forces that control air flight: weight, lift, drag, and thrust. Students fill out a table hypothesizing the source of each force for a bird, a 747 airplane, a glider, a baseball in flight, a spacecraft out of fuel, and other things in flight. It is natural in this engineering class to be asked to use prior knowledge to guess at answers to questions like this, and students know that wrong answers are opportunities for learning.

Over the following days, students explore how humans have always sought to fly, but were only successful in the past 100 years. When looking at Leonardo da Vinci's notebook, Sara notices that his design ideas mimicked those in nature—bird wings and bat bones. She speculates that those were the only sources of information about flight available to humans, so they would naturally think about scaling up those concepts. Mr. Kamal responds by asking the question, "If every linear dimension of a bird were doubled, would it still be able to fly?" This is the hook that prompts students to seek a deeper understanding of flight dynamics and how they can be modeled.

Over the course of the next week, students learn that drag and lift on a plane are dependent on the area of the wings, whereas weight is proportional to the total volume of the craft. Students learn that the direction in which an aircraft accelerates is based on the vector that results from adding all four forces (weight, lift, drag, and thrust).

Now that students have a deeper understanding of the factors at work, Mr. Kamal repeats the question about scaling the bird. Table groups break off to discuss this question and Mr. Kamal circulates through the tables posing clarifying questions to help teams move their discussions forward. Finally, Mamadou shouts that his team understands it: if a bird is doubled, its wing area and therefore lift goes up by a factor of four, but its volume and therefore weight goes up by a factor of eight. The bird can't fly! Mr. Kamal puts a chart of bird sizes and wingspans on the board, and the class observes that Mamadou must be right. The students calculate the amount of wing area a person would need in order to fly, and Janiya observes that a person could never control a wing of that size.

In their next class session, Mr. Kamal announces the Benchmark Project (a challenging inquiry-based project that allows students to demonstrate their mastery of a subject). The Wind Tunnel Testing Benchmark places students in the role of entrepreneurs who have recently launched an aircraft test company. The query is, "What techniques can they and their partners use to measure the forces of flight, and how can they know if they are accurate?" Students are tasked with testing their new equipment and communicating the validity of their approach to their customers via an engineering report. Teams design and build a model plane, construct a test procedure using our homemade wind tunnel, measure the forces of flight, analyze their results, and prepare a comprehensive report for their clients.

Students are initially intimidated by the size of the project, the short timeline, and the exactitude of their final report format. They are being challenged to solve a real-world workplace problem and communicate at a professional level. The classroom becomes a hive of activity as teams divide into designers, builders, testers, analysts, and writers. Foam and sawdust fly as students create personalized aircraft they believe will produce valid test results. Instrumentation and data gathering present particular challenges, such as how to assure that one battery of tests doesn't interfere with the accuracy of another simultaneous test. A discussion organically ensues about the relationships between engineering design and the scientific method and how to use scientific test procedure during the prototyping phase of design.

The planes are finally ready for testing, and they exhibit a level of diversity that reflects the students in the class—fighter jets, a Wright Flyer, a fanciful plane of the future, and a condom-covered plane for aerodynamic effect. The agency students personally exhibit in the design of their craft helps make the project meaningful to them. During these final days of the project, wind tunnel tests are underway, and the results are broadcast live to families and friends via social media. Slow-motion videos show lines of water vapor slip over fuselage and wing. Data are collected and analyzed, and final reports are prepared.

In their reflections, students shared common themes:

- Building and testing is always harder than it first seems.
- Time grows short faster than expected.
- Intimidating equations can be broken down, understood, and applied.

SOURCE: Adapted from material presented to the committee by John Kamal on November 2, 2017.

(Engle, 2012; Engle and Conant, 2002; Michaels, O'Connor, and Resnick, 2007) For example, students might draw a model illustrating their understanding of how energy is transferred and transformed by a wind turbine, share their models with each other, ask each other probing questions to better understand each other's models, and provide feedback to each other on how those models might be improved (e.g., representing invisible processes, connecting micro- and macro-level phenomena, or using labels or legends to help others interpret what is being represented).

Eliciting and facilitating student talk occurs synchronously and iteratively with capturing and representing student ideas publicly. Student ideas are made visible in initial and revised models (Windschitl, Thompson, and Braaten, 2018). Claim-Evidence-Reasoning prompts (e.g., McNeill and Pimintel, 2010; McNeill et al., 2006) and other task scaffolds can make student thinking explicit (Kang, Thompson, and Windschitl, 2014) as a foundation for conversations about student ideas (Kang et al., 2016). The creation and development of artifacts are tasks that push student learning.

The audiences for artifacts students construct begin with the classroom and extend outward. Students are first accountable to making sense of data, ideas, and design solutions for themselves, publicly and to make those ideas available for others to work on and with (Engle, 2012). The classroom learning community itself is a key audience for products, that is, an audience of peers in a community that adheres to norms for how to hold one another accountable for supporting ideas with evidence, for listening to others and building ideas together, and for critiquing and asking questions about one's own and others' ideas (Berland and Reiser, 2011; Berland et al., 2016). For design challenges, the audience may be the wider community, especially when those challenges connect students to ongoing endeavors in the community that are applying science and engineering practices to solving problems (Birmingham et al., 2017; Calabrese Barton and Tan, 2010; Penuel, 2016).

Discourse

Studies of discourse-rich classrooms have indicated that engaging students in productive conversation promotes development of conceptual understanding of science content (e.g., Rosebery, Warren, and Conant, 1992), as well as their motivation to learn (e.g., Kiemer et al., 2015). In these discourse-rich classrooms, teachers can use open-ended questions to elevate students' private ideas into the public space and to develop the substance of student ideas (Engle and Conant, 2002). When public, student ideas can be deliberated and held accountable to the discipline and to classroom norms (Michaels, O'Connor, and Resnick, 2007). Ideally, making students' ideas public would allow the teacher to shape classroom instruction in ways that would result in students engaging in three-dimensional performances with investigation that lead to greater student learning.

Teachers guiding science investigation and engineering design facilitate classroom discourse in which students authentically participate in sharing, building on, and responding to each other's ideas. Teachers do this by presenting authentic phenomena and engaging student with questions that are genuine requests to understand the nature of student thinking (Cazden, 2001; Coffey et al., 2011) and which provide opportunities for the teacher and students to make sense of the student's reasoning (Windschitl et al., 2012). Furthermore, discourse serves a key function from the perspective of *formative* assessment: namely, that it provides ongoing, informal spaces in which the teacher may listen and attend to the nature and status of student ideas as they develop (Bennett, 2011; Ruiz-Primo and Furtak, 2006, 2007), providing key opportunities not available in students' written work (Furtak and Ruiz-Primo, 2008) to understand the substance of what students are saying (Coffey et al., 2011). The nature of the types of talk moves teachers use to orchestrate classroom discussions (Cartier et al., 2013) are essential to helping students share their ideas with each other (Michaels and O'Connor, 2017), as seen in Table 5-2. Often referred to as *talk moves* (O'Connor and Michaels, 1993, 1996; Van Zee and Minstrell, 1997), these types of questions are all focused on helping students make their ideas explicit to their peers (Engle and Conant, 2002), to expand student thinking (Van Zee and Minstrell, 1997), and to press students for deeper reasoning and for evidence-based explanations (Windschitl et al., 2012).

These talk moves indicate to the community that all members want to understand each other's thinking (Michaels and O'Connor, 2017). The role of the teacher is to support uptake and further discussion, providing students enough time to think, and avoiding evaluative responses by using productive phrases such as, "Interesting idea, who else would like to talk about that idea?" (Michaels and O'Connor, 2017). Importantly, when facilitating this type of discussion, teachers should also use talk moves that help students to continue to expand on their ideas, such as by saying "say more" (Michaels and O'Connor, 2017), rather than giving evaluative responses, which have the effect of shutting down student thinking and reasoning.

These kinds of discussions are wide-ranging and center on students' lived experiences. They involve teachers listening to student ideas, repeating what students have said, and encouraging students to make sense of scientific ideas. Even when investigating a contextualized phenomenon that is the anchor of a larger storyline for a three-dimensional learning experience, these discussions may focus in the moment on working out specific ideas or understandings relevant to the development of the ongoing scientific storyline. Later in this chapter, emergent conversation of this sort is illustrated

TABLE 5-2 Talk Moves

Talk Move	Purpose	Example
Marking: "That's an important point."	Pointing out to students what a student has said that is important given the teacher's current academic purposes	"Did everyone hear what Marisol just said? She made a comparison between this phenomenon and something she experienced with her family last summer. That's important because it shows that we're connecting what we're doing in school to what's happening in our everyday lives."
Challenging Students: "What do YOU think?"	Promoting academically rigorous conversation by challenging students and turning the responsibility for reasoning back to students	"That's a great question, Kwame. What does everyone else think?" "That's an interesting idea, is there a way we could possibly test it to see if it's true?" "Can you give an example?" "Does your explanation fit with other science ideas, like [state science concept]?"
Linking Contributions: "Who wants to add on . . . ?"	Helping students link their contributions to the ongoing conversation	"Who disagrees with Arjun?" "Who else wants to add on to what she just said?"
Building on Prior Knowledge: "How does this connect?"	Reminding students of knowledge they have access to, or connections to other elements of ongoing storylines	"Thinking back to what we have been working on for the past few weeks, what connections can you make?" "How does what we have been discussing today connect with other ideas from your everyday experiences?"
Verifying and Clarifying "So, you are saying . . ."	Repeating or "revoicing" what the student said and offering the student a chance to agree or disagree with the teacher's version of what the student has said	"So what I heard you say is that the oil tanker collapsed because . . ." "Aha, so Abdul thinks that a car overtaking another car in the left lane of the highway does *not* have the same velocity as the car it is passing."

TABLE 5-2 Continued

Talk Move	Purpose	Example
Pressing for Evidence-Based Reasoning: "Where can we find that?"	Holding students accountable for providing evidence and reasoning for the claims they are making	"Why do you think that is the case? "What evidence do we have that that is true?
Expanding Reasoning: "Say more"	Using wait time and explicitly asking students to say more to support their initial contributions	"That is an interesting idea, Min. Can you say more about that so we can really understand your thinking?"

NOTE: A figure describing a taxonomy of talk moves can also be found in Windschitl, Thompson, and Braaten (2018) at http://ambitiousscienceteaching.org/wp-content/uploads/2014/09/Discourse-Primer.pdf [December 2018].

SOURCES: Adapted from vanZee and Minstrell (1997), Windschitl et al. (2012), and Michaels and O'Connor (2017).

when a teacher picks up on her students' ideas and uses them as a basis for an extended discussion about the phenomena of a tanker implosion.

Research under the umbrella of "responsive teaching" (Robertson, Scherr, and Hammer, 2016) prioritizes teachers listening to and designing subsequent learning experiences around student ideas. This teaching practice is central to scientific investigations in the *Framework* vision as it is less about teachers eliciting student ideas for the purpose of determining their accuracy, and more about teachers trying to understand students' understanding and to make connections between students' ideas and scientific processes and practices (Coffey et al., 2011). Honoring the nature of student thinking allows teachers to follow the thread of students' learning, rather than forcing or pushing particular sequences that may not align or resonate with series of students' own questions. Questions such as these are essential tools for teachers to draw out and support students in expanding upon and making their ideas clear throughout science investigation and engineering design.

Embedded Assessment

The term *embedded assessment* refers to formative assessment for learning and processes that have been thoughtfully integrated into an instructional sequence (Penuel and Shepard, 2016). Embedding assessments in investigation and design allows them to be content-rich and to build on or be a part of the classwork. Instead of written tests, assessments can build on the collaborative nature of investigation and design with more interactive forms of assessment. The discussion and student writing that help make thinking visible are more powerful when within the context of an investigation or design. They can follow the "contours of practices" and reflect how scientists and engineers assess and evaluate one another's questions, investigations, models, explanations, and arguments (Ford, 2008; Ford and Forman, 2006). For example, they might be planned to take place at a particular "joint" (Shavelson et al., 2008) or "bend" (Penuel et al., 2018) in a three-dimensional performance sequence, when the teacher determines an appropriate place to check student progress toward a performance expectation/learning goal. To build deep, usable knowledge, students should engage in making sense of multiple similar phenomena using the same core ideas with variety of practices and crosscutting concepts within and across curriculum units.

Formative assessment tasks also need to integrate specific types of scaffolds to draw out student thinking so that students have support on how to share their thinking beyond a blank outcome space. Songer and Gotwals (2012) examined how integrating different types of scaffolds can help support the explanation construction of middle school students. These scaffolds can be faded over time to support students' development of scientific practices (McNeill et al., 2006). In addition to using contextualized phenomena, these scaffolds could include providing students with checklists that consist of characteristics relevant to a given scientific practice (e.g., a modeling checklist that asks students to include both visible and invisible aspects of a system; an explanation checklist that asks students to include claims and evidence to support those claims), vocabulary checklists, rubrics, sentence frames, and explanatory models in combination with written explanations (Kang, Thompson, and Windschitl, 2014). Other approaches have explored the ways in which helping teachers develop their own assessment tasks might similarly create space for students to express their thinking, whether questions on the assessment are open- or closed-ended, and the extent to which the information students provide on the assessment can be easily interpreted (e.g., Furtak and Ruiz-Primo, 2008).

This type of formative assessment becomes seamless with everyday instruction; instead of setting formative assessment apart from daily classroom activity, it embeds it in the course of every interaction the teacher has with students. While formative assessment is perhaps most commonly thought of as consisting of formal, written tasks embedded into instructional units, it encompasses the informal activities in which teachers attend on an ongoing, daily basis to the nature and quality of student ideas during the course of daily instruction. Embedded assessment can also be conceived as an ongoing, informal process of teachers taking opportunities to create space for students to share their thinking with each other and with their teacher so that they may better support and develop their ideas as learning unfolds (Pellegrino, 2014; Ruiz-Primo and Furtak, 2006, 2007). This involves teachers asking authentic questions when drawing out student thinking as a starting point for working with their ideas (Cazden, 2001), making inferences about what students know (Bennett, 2011), attending closely to the nature and substance of student thinking (Coffey et al., 2011), and supporting students in expanding on their ideas (Richards and Robertson, 2016). It also consists of teachers and students (and students with other students) pushing each other in their thinking (Windschtil et al., 2012).

Once teachers have given students an embedded formative assessment task, they need to interpret the student work, evaluate what students know based upon their responses to the task (Bennett, 2011; National Research Council, 2001), and think about next instructional steps to move students ahead in their learning (e.g., Heritage et al., 2009; Wiliam, 2007). For tasks embedded in instructional materials, this might involve going through student work and making judgments about the extent to which students have learned what they need to know in order to move on, or harvesting students' language and models to inform where an instructional sequence might go next. When teachers circulate and monitor student work during an investigation, they need to be prepared with questions to extend student thinking. These questions are closely aligned with the materials themselves, focus on the core ideas and crosscutting concepts, and are intended to expose specific student reasoning about their thinking. Establishing time and space for students to share their ideas and respond to others can function as immediate feedback happening during the course of regular instruction (Michaels, O'Connor, and Resnick, 2007). This can help students and teachers see the thinking process the student is using to make sense of the phenomenon and reflect on how the student is using evidence.

Establish and Maintain an Inclusive Learning Environment

A key dimension of engaging all students in investigation and design is creating equitable classrooms in which the class culture welcomes and expects participation from all students. Teachers need to be able to support students "as they explicate their ideas, make their thinking public and accessible to the group, use evidence, coordinate claims and evidence, and build on and critique one another's ideas" (Michaels and O'Connor, 2012, p. 7). Group norms of participation, respect for others, a willingness to revise one's ideas, and equity are all critical, and the norms of the classroom need to align with those of the best forms of collaborative scientific practice (Berland and Reiser, 2011; Bricker and Bell, 2008; Calabrese Barton and Tan, 2009; Duschl and Osborne, 2002; Osborne, Erduran, and Simon, 2004; Radinsky, Oliva, and Alamar, 2010).

Teachers can also facilitate classroom discussions with students to encourage and support them in critically reflecting on their own roles in science (Johnson, 2011). Facilitating productive talk can move forward not only disciplinary goals, but also equity goals, if teachers take active steps to include all students including those from traditionally underrepresented communities. Establishing an environment in which all students' voices are respected and in which students are encouraged and taught how to respectfully engage each other's ideas can shift the power dynamic in traditional classrooms from the teacher as the source of knowledge to the students bringing knowledge from their own backgrounds (Moll et al., 1992) and from material activity to conceptual models. However, merely helping students recognize the primary features of scientific discourse patterns may not help students from "nondominant" populations fully participate if their native discourse patterns are totally neglected or if they cannot use scientific language in meaningful contexts (Michaels and O'Connor, 2017).

Students' own language resources as well as scientific discourses can be drawn upon to help students construct explanations or models about scientific phenomena (Brown and Kloser, 2009). McNeill and Pimentel (2010) compared three case studies in urban environments in which discussion and argumentation were infused. They highlighted the differences observed in the teachers' roles across the classrooms, only one of which included student-to-student interactions. The teacher who fostered student-to-student interactions used more open-ended questions and allowed students to use both scientific and everyday language. By recognizing students' ideas and their language resources, this teacher encouraged the community to consider new ideas and reflect on thinking from their classmates. In another case study investigating how a high school science teacher engaged 54 students in science argumentation, almost one-half of whom were English language learners (ELLs), three instructional strategies were observed that supported students' engagement in the community of practice. First, the teacher validated the use of the students' primary language to ensure they could conceptually understand the core science ideas. Many students would speak in Spanish during pair and small group work before translating the ideas to English. Second, the teacher provided deliberate scaffolds such as expectations that each claim should be supported by two pieces of evidence. Finally, the teacher used small group work prior to whole-class discussion in order to provide ELLs the opportunity to share their ideas in low-pressure situations.

This work is difficult and unnatural for many teachers. In a case study in which a project-based investigative approach was used among a classroom community, 97 percent of whom were African American students, teachers were prepared to lead productive and equitable discussions. In practice, they reverted to traditional I-R-E-type patterns two-thirds of the time (Alozie, Moje, and Krajcik, 2010). The authors suggested that several structures could better help teachers realize their role in leading classroom discussions. These structures centered on curriculum guides that could provide more rationale for planned discussions, a set of open-ended questions that teachers could use, strategies for training young people to engage in discussion, and strategies for facilitating and not dominating discussions, especially for students unaccustomed to this type of discourse. More information on inclusive pedagogies can be found later in this chapter in the discussion about connecting learning in multiple contexts and providing coherence.

FEATURES COME TOGETHER FOR INVESTIGATION AND DESIGN[3]

The sections above discuss features of investigation and design separately, but they all interact in multiple ways in the classroom. Here we present an example that shows many of the features described and gives a sense of the nature of a classroom with investigation and design at the center. It centers on Bethany, a high school chemistry teacher, who introduces a new and puzzling phenomenon to engage her students in exploring how molecules move and how that movement relates to the pressure of gasses. Throughout the unit, students create and revise models that represent ongoing changes in their thinking as they proceed through a series of investigations that help them to understand the relationships between variables involved in the phenomenon, and to relate their developing understandings to initial, anchoring phenomenon. On the first day of the unit, Bethany showed students a slide of an oil tanker train car and read the scenario from the slide:

> The purpose is to investigate how gasses behave and what affects their behavior, and we're going to look at a scenario of this tank car. You have this tank train, and the interior of the tank was washed out and cleaned with steam. Then all the outlet valves were shut and the tank car was sealed. All of the workers went home for the evening and when they returned, this was what they found.

Bethany asked the students to predict what they found, and one student suggested it may have exploded, another thought maybe it might have compressed, and a third thought maybe there was some steam coming off of it. She then flipped to the next slide, and students exclaimed with surprise and shock as they saw the huge, steel oil tanker car completely crushed in on itself. "Whoa!" "Holy smokes!" "Why'd that happen?" "That's cool!"

---

[3] Adapted from Windschitl, Thompson, and Braaten (2018) and Ambitious Science Teaching at https://ambitiousscienceteaching.org/ [October 2018].

Bethany responded, "That's a good question, that's what we're trying to figure out." She then showed a video of the tanker crushing and, unprompted,
the students spontaneously started sharing suggestions for why the tanker
might have collapsed. "Is it because there's nothing inside of it?" "How'd
that happen?" For more of the student questions, see Box 5-5 on eliciting
student ideas via discourse.

Bethany asked the students to complete an individual brainstorm, writing down in their journals what was happening inside the tanker or outside
the tanker that made it crush, why the tanker crushed, and how the tanker
crushed. She encouraged students to think about what happened before,
during, and after, and to draw diagrams representing their thinking (individual models). A similar type of prompt for students to make initial models
of this phenomenon is shown in Figure 5-1 below.

With this "leaving question" about what causes the tanker to shrink
(see Box 5-5; Windschitl, Thompson, and Braaten, 2018), Bethany encouraged the group to continue their conversation after she left. Throughout
the exchange with this small group, Bethany used the students' model as
a medium to ask questions about students' ideas, and challenged the ideas
the students shared. For example, the students often returned to the idea
that steam or air had escaped when the tanker had crushed in, but Bethany

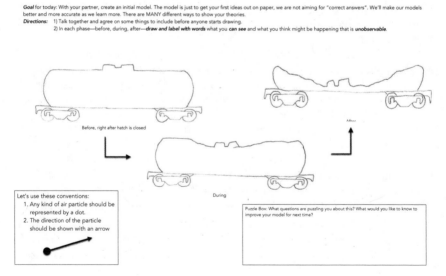

FIGURE 5-1 Initial template for student work on tanker explosion.
SOURCE: Windschitl, Thompson, and Braaten (2018, p. 123).

reminded them that the tanker had been sealed, setting the condition of a closed system. She helped them to identify and refine ideas about air temperature and pressure, and identify ideas about differences between the inside and outside of the tanker at different times. She similarly spoke to all of the groups in the class, encouraging them to refine their ideas and to represent those ideas on the three different times represented on their models.

The next day, Bethany guided the students as they built an initial consensus model as a whole class that combined elements of individual group models that they had presented at the end of the previous class period. As a warm-up activity, Bethany encouraged the students to think about three things the other groups had presented that they had not thought of, and then she used two guiding questions to help the students construct a whole-group model: first, to make a list of what is causing the tanker to crush; and second, to see if anything seemed to be linked together.

After assembling the whole-group consensus model, the students performed experiments in which they filled pop cans with water, heated the cans until the water was boiling, and then placed the hot cans into containers filled with ice water following a set of instructions that Bethany provided. They then used the empirical results they gathered to update the models they had already made. The results of these experiments helped the students to link a new observable phenomenon with phase changes and the speed of gas molecules. They then performed additional experiments that helped them to reason with the difference between pressure inside and outside a system and also performed readings. They used this information to better make sense of the anchoring phenomenon of the tanker implosion as they continued with their discourse on the next day of class.

In the conversation about crushing (see Box 5-6), Bethany explicitly helped students weave their findings from the can-crushing experiment to the oil tanker crushing, she drew out student ideas about multiple possible variables that might be involved, including temperature, size, air pressure, and whether the system was opened or closed. Then, Bethany encouraged students to connect these different variables that they would then directly test in an investigation to be conducted in class over the next days.

In the second activity with the pop can, students identified five discrete experiments to conduct based upon the possible relationships they identified:

- Experiment #1: Amount of water in the can
- Experiment #2: Temperature of the water bath
- Experiment #3: Amount of time on the hot plate
- Experiment #4: Volume of the can
- Experiment #5: Amount of seal

BOX 5-5
Eliciting and Supporting Student Ideas with Talk Moves

As part of the lesson described above on the tanker, students worked in small groups, having conversations in which they shared their ideas about what might have happened. After a few minutes of students talking and drawing their ideas, Bethany circulated to small groups, using talk moves to draw out and refine students' ideas and encouraging them to connect their drawings back to the phenomenon of the crushing tanker. An excerpt of the conversations is reprinted here.

Student: So we said that if it was like regular air in the beginning, this is air on the outside, and this is the air on the inside, and then when the steam, it was like bouncing the molecules . . . and then, um, what did we say? It's complicated.
Bethany: Because this looks empty now, is this empty?
Student: Well, I mean maybe it has some air in it.
Bethany: Because this is, they steam cleaned it, they closed all the valves . . .
Student: Oh so inside . . .
Bethany: So nothing can get in or out. So there still has to be something in here, what's in here?
Student: Just some air . . .
Bethany: What happened to the steam?
Student: It went out when it exploded.
Student: It didn't explode!
Student: I mean imploded 'cuz it like you know it broke, so now there's holes all over it so steam got out.
Bethany: So let's assume that it didn't break, that it just crushed. So like you know, ah . . .
Student: Then it, the steam, it's still there. . . .
Bethany: So the steam was still there, so how can you explain what happened?
Student: Maybe it comes in quickly.
Student: I forgot what I said . . .
Student: Like some phase change?
Student: . . . you said some, right?

After completing these experiments, Bethany guided students to begin creating a causal story, developing a rule that helped them to identify the ways that, as they manipulated one variable, it affected the amount the can crushed. Next, she supported students in reporting out and connecting their experimental findings, ultimately connecting their evolving ideas back to their initial models. Over the course of the unit, the students constructed a thorough explanation for the reason that the oil tanker had collapsed, and also extended this explanation to other, related phenomena. Bethany also helped the students to extend their ideas to less similar phenomena from

Student: Yes, I know.

Bethany: So it went back to liquid? So how can you show that in your picture?

Student: We can just draw some water . . .

Bethany: OK go ahead. And then I want you to think about, why was, what's going on here, when it turns to water, why would it cause this crushing? Why would it crush in?

Student: 'Cuz we learned that the heat that it expands so if it's cold I don't know why I think it's cold.

Student: I guess maybe it's just a reaction. . . .

Bethany: It was overnight, right?

Student: But it's cold, so . . . but it would not expand . . . like . : .

Student: Because it comes out.

Bethany: But it can't come out, it can't come out, it's sealed.

Student: But it's reverse like instead of just like coming into first liquid then gas. I guess it just reverses.

Bethany: OK, so you need to think about what would cause this to implode.

Student: So if it was for some reason the molecules are getting smaller . . . they don't change size, right?

Bethany: So what do they do?

Student: They're pulling in the sides of the tank.

Bethany: Remember if I have some steam and some water, which one takes up more space?

Student: The water, no, the steam.

Bethany: OK, so think about that. You have steam here, you said it's going all quickly, what is this doing to the outside of the container? The molecules that are moving in here, how are they in there?

Student: Pressure

Bethany: So they're putting pressure against the container here. You might want to draw, so you can show me pressure against the sides of the container. And then think about then, what causes this to shrink in? OK? So keep thinking about that. So why don't you add the pressure here.

NOTE: Multiple videos of teacher facilitation of class discussion are available at this Website.
SOURCE: Adapted from Windschitl, Thompson, and Braaten (2018) and Ambitious Science Teaching at https://ambitiousscienceteaching.org/video-series/ [October 2018].

the students' lived experiences, including modifications to tires or engines on race cars.

This example helps to illustrate not only the way that talk moves can help teachers to draw out and refine student ideas, but also the ways in which students' written models can serve as artifacts for making student ideas explicit and which can support conversations about student ideas. Throughout these 2 days of instruction, Bethany asked students to first write down their ideas in journals, then to share their ideas with each other and then draw those ideas into models. As she circulated around the room,

---

BOX 5-6
Eliciting Ideas and Constructing Explanations

On day 3 of the unit on the oil tanker, Bethany started class by posing the question, "How is the pop can similar to the crushing tanker? How is the pop can different from the crushing tanker?" With these questions, she encouraged students to make connections between the experiment they had completed the day before and the anchoring phenomenon for their unit. After allowing students to consider the questions individually in their journals, Bethany initiated a discussion with the class.

Bethany: OK, so let's go ahead and talk about this . . . what's one thing?
Student: Air pressure.
Bethany: Can you say more about the pressure thing?
Student: Um, I'm not really sure, well the steam causes the air pressure.
Bethany: OK so they both had steam, and that steam is linked to causing pressure.
Student: Mmhmm.
Bethany: Why do you think steam is linked to pressure?
Student: Because I don't know, it just does, or I guess there's an experiment. Yeah.
Bethany: OK, does somebody else have something that like, could, yeah?
Student: Because it's a gas, and gases don't like, really like to be contained?
Bethany: OK, and so, what does that have to do with pressure?
Student: It probably was pushing outward, causing more pressure on the can?
Bethany: OK, and do you think that was similar inside the tanker?
Student: Yeah.
Bethany: OK, what else is similar between the can and the tanker? Anything else? What about differences?
Student: They both started with gas and then they were liquid.
Bethany: They both started with gas and ended up with liquid. Do we know that that's what happened in the tanker or you're just, um, that's what you think was happening?
Student: That's what I think was happening.
Bethany: OK, we think that the same thing was happening in both, we couldn't see inside the tanker but we can kind of think that they're similar in that way.

In these exchanges, Bethany elicited and refined students' ideas about pressure, asking follow-up questions to refine and clarify their ideas. She then drew out additional ideas to identify additional variables that might be involved:

---

she interacted with students around the models, encouraging students to make micro-level processes more explicit, and to connect those processes back to the phenomenon at hand. She used talk moves to pick up on particular student ideas, revoicing student comments to be sure she understood what had been said (and, in some cases, students corrected her to be sure she had correctly understood them). The next day, she used similar talk

Bethany: What else? What else is different?

Student: Temperature.

Bethany: Temperature? What's different between that?

Student: Uh, they both needed something cold?

Bethany: OK, so that was something similar, they both needed a change in temperature. What's different about how the temperature changed for the two things?

Student: Um, the pop can was heated on a hot plate, and the tanker, we don't know if it was heated up or not, it was just outside.

Bethany: OK, what's our story about how the tanker, what did they do to the tanker?

Student: They steam cleaned it and then they sealed it off.

Bethany: OK, so if they were steam cleaning it, what could you assume about the temperature inside?

Student: It was hotter?

Bethany: OK, you're right, the way it was heated was different, and the way it was cooled off was different, right? OK, any other differences you can think of?

Student: The can wasn't sealed when we were heating it?

Bethany: OK, the can wasn't sealed when we were heating it, um, I don't know how tankers are steam cleaned, do you think it was sealed when they were heating it?

Student: There was probably steam still in it when it was sealed?

Bethany: Oh, OK, so that's another good thing to think about.

Bethany then summarized what the students had done the previous day when they wrote some questions about what they thought affects the can when it crushes and connected some of the statements the students had said in their contributions to the conversation they had just completed.

She provided a sentence starter on the board that said, "I think _____ might affect _____ because _____." Bethany let the students know the purpose of completing this sentence was to generate ideas about "what they might experiment with today . . . each group is going to test one of these so we can come up with a big picture of what affects how much this can is crushing."

SOURCE: Adapted from Windschitl, Thompson, and Braaten (2018) and Ambitious Science Teaching at https://ambitiousscienceteaching.org/video-series/ [October 2018]

moves in a whole-class format to highlight similarities across group models and to help the students assemble a whole-class model that they later refined after performing investigations in which they interacted with the same variables at play in the crushing of the oil tanker.

This example illustrating many features of investigation and design highlights the actions of the students as they conduct experiments, ask questions, make observations and engage discourse and produce artifacts. Boxes 5-5 and 5-6 show the prominent role of student discourse in learning. Discourse can leverage students' everyday vernacular and language as a part of science learning (Brown and Ryoo, 2008).

CONNECT LEARNING THROUGH MULTIPLE CONTEXTS

Teachers can consider thinking about core ideas and crosscutting concepts as the intellectual resources students use to make sense of phenomena in their daily life beyond the classroom. Moulding and Bybee (2018) suggested teachers use questions during classroom discourse that emphasize crosscutting concepts to help organize and focus students' thinking to make sense of the causes of phenomena. This approach can lead to students using the same types of questions when they encounter a novel phenomenon at a later time.

As discussed in Chapter 3, the transfer of knowledge to make sense of new phenomena is an important part of science learning. This transfer of knowledge serves to present insights into student understanding of underlying principles of science and to apply these ideas and concepts beyond the learning of specific facts and skills. Application of knowledge and skill across new situations requires students to generalize the knowledge (Bransford and Schwartz, 1999). Applying three-dimensional learning to new phenomena provides a way for students to internalize, conceptualize, and generalize the knowledge so that it becomes part of how they see the natural and engineered world. Teachers play a key role in helping students to make these connections between different course and different contexts.

For example, if a student is investigating a phenomenon in school such as how an ice cube on a countertop melts faster than an ice cube on a towel on the countertop, they can use core ideas (e.g., properties of insulators and conductors, thermal heat transfer) and crosscutting concepts (e.g., systems, change, energy) to construct explanations for the difference in the rate that ice melts. Most of these same ideas are needed to make sense of why it feels colder to sleep on the ground than on a blanket on the ground or why the cloth on a table feels warmer than the metal leg of a table, even though they are both at room temperature. The application of knowledge to make sense of novel phenomena helps student to conceptualize the learning so it becomes part of their daily way of viewing the world (National Research Council, 2012). As discussed in Chapter 4, during investigation and design, students develop not only the component skills and knowledge necessary to perform complex tasks, but also they practice combining and integrating them to develop greater fluency and automaticity. It is important for educators to develop conscious awareness of these elements of mastery so as to help students learn when and how to apply the skills and knowledge they have learned (Russ, Sherin, and Sherin, 2016). This can help provide coherence to the students' educational experiences. Inclusive pedagogies also provide mechanisms for connecting educational experiences to students' lived experiences (Calabrese Barton and Tan, 2009; Brown, 2017; Gay, 2010; Moll et al., 1992).

Inclusive Pedagogy

Inclusive pedagogies can be used to make science education more culturally and socially relevant. Science and engineering can be taught within broader sociocultural, sociohistorical, and sociopolitical contexts that invite multiple perspectives, knowledges, and understandings into the science classroom. Research on the broader field of inclusive education offers potential insights into approaches that involve students from a wide range of diverse backgrounds and abilities learning with their peers in school settings that have adapted and changed the way they work to meet the needs of all students (Loreman, 1999). These ways of teaching require support for teachers and schools to be able to learn, consider, and implement inclusive approaches. The notion of *empowering policies* (Mensah, 2010, p. 982) starts at the local level where success in working with schools and teachers to implement change and reform might occur, and then moves to higher levels, such as district, state, and nation-wide policies that support science education through inclusive pedagogies. There are challenges to these approaches (Young, 2010), but science and engineering education are uniquely situated to work toward inclusive practices that involve local and national efforts aimed at educational equity for all. There are many efforts to broaden the populations who have access to science investigation and engineering design, such as the work on culturally relevant engineering design curriculum for the Navajo Nation (Jordan et al., 2017). Efforts are also underway to increase universal design for instruction (Burgstahler, 2012a) and make science labs more accessible to students with disabilities (Burgstahler, 2012b). One issue is whether the teacher operates in a supportive environment that encourages adapting instructional strategies in favor of the strength of the students, as this can be of equal importance to making accommodations for students (Burgstahler, 2012a).

Broad topics and concepts traditionally taught in school science from elementary to high school, such as plants, water, pollution, and electricity, can be taught with inclusive pedagogies in mind. For example, if the idea of plants or water were taught in school science, how might these topics be addressed for cultural relevancy: where are plants grown, who has access to organic foods, where are "food deserts" within communities, is there harm from genetically modified foods? A question of "who has access to clean water" can be taught by studying recent cases from Flint, Michigan, or Newark, New Jersey, and extended to study global water crises with droughts in Somalia, water rationing in Rome, or flooding in Jakarta. Science can be studied to address issues such as, "Where do you find the majority of pollution producers? How does rising costs of health-care effect low-income families? What are alternative energy sources for my community?"

Science investigation and engineering design provide unique opportunities to use inclusive pedagogies to bring a broader spectrum of students into relevant and motivating learning environments with the potential to positively affect both student interest in and identity with science and engineering. There are various ways of thinking about inclusive pedagogies, and descriptions of several inclusive pedagogical approaches are described in Box 5-7. Though the pedagogies are distinctive, they share a similar framing in their potential to make science teaching and learning more inclusive to all students, and especially for students who have been traditionally

---

BOX 5-7
Inclusive Pedagogies

Culturally relevant pedagogy focuses on the teacher. The concept includes three important elements: how teachers view themselves and others, how they view knowledge, and how they structure social relations within the classroom (Ladson-Billings, 2006). Second, culturally relevant pedagogy also focuses on student learning with an aim toward social justice. Culturally relevant pedagogy differs from other culturally sensitive or responsive approaches in its criticality or purpose to interrogate and disrupt the status quo (Parsons and Wall, 2011).

Culturally responsive pedagogy rose out of "concerns for the racial and ethnic inequities that were apparent in learning opportunities and outcomes" (Gay, 2010, p. 28) that were brought to light with the rise of multicultural education. Culturally responsive pedagogy emphasizes teaching diverse students through their ethnic, linguistic, racial, experiential, and cultural identities. Culturally responsive pedagogy "validates, facilitates, liberates, and empowers ethnically diverse students by simultaneously cultivating their cultural integrity, individual abilities, and academic success" (p. 46).

Parsons, Travis, and Simpson (2005) defined **culturally congruent instruction** as instruction that "addresses the mismatch between institutional norms and values and those of the homes and communities of ethnic minorities" (p. 187). The aim of culturally congruent instruction is to incorporate the home and community cultures of children into schools and classrooms (Au and Kawakami, 1994).

Funds of knowledge are the valuable understandings, skills, and tools that students maintain as a part of their identity. They were developed in partnership with teachers, who served "as co- researchers using qualitative methods to study

marginalized in science education. The inclusive pedagogies described can be used to make the *Framework*-aligned instruction during investigation and design more culturally and socially relevant. These inclusive pedagogies recognize culture, identity, language, literacy, and community as valuable assets in the science classroom.

The potential benefits for inclusive pedagogies rest on how teachers implement them. Standard approaches are often missing attention to equity and diversity. Professional learning can assist teachers in how to focus on culturally relevant questions to support the inclusion of diverse perspectives and kinds of knowledge. In order to teach in these ways, preservice teachers and in-service teachers, with assistance and support from committed stakeholders, will need time and resources to work in collaborative partnerships to address equity, diversity, and social justice in science teaching. Professional learning about inclusive pedagogies is addressed further in

---

household knowledge, and drawing upon this knowledge to develop a participatory pedagogy" (Moll et al., 1992).

Third space is the notion that there is an in-between or hybrid spot between traditional community views and the academic world of science and engineering. The idea is that students bring their own experiences (funds of knowledge) from family, home, and community into their schools, which include disciplinary discourses of specialized content areas, and attempt to reconcile the different environments and types of discourse (Bhabha, 1994; Moje et al., 2004). This hybrid space can be used intentionally so that students can gain competency and expertise in negotiate differing discourse communities (Moje, 2004). In addition, this interaction of different funds of knowledge that emerge from the students' home communities can expand the boundaries of official school discourse, creating a space of cultural, social, and epistemological change where competing knowledges and discourses come together in "conversation" with each other (Moje, 2004).

Culturally sustaining pedagogy fosters "linguistic, literate, and cultural pluralism as part of the democratic project of schooling" (Paris, 2012, p. 93). He made the argument that culturally sustaining pedagogy is a necessary pushback against monocultural and monolingual social constructs perpetuated by education. He argued for a stance that "support[s] young people in sustaining the cultural and linguistic competence of their communities while simultaneously offering access to dominant cultural competence" (p. 95). The culturally sustaining pedagogy stance may be used to push students to understand and value their culture, language, and funds of knowledge while also navigating the dominant culture. In sum, culturally sustaining pedagogy has an explicit goal to support "multilingualism and multiculturalism in practice and perspective for students and teachers."

SOURCE: Mensah and Larson (2017).

Chapter 7. In addition, inclusive pedagogies for science education require both policy and administrative decision making to set structures that will allow these inclusive pedagogies to serve the best interests of all students (see the discussion of Systems in Chapter 9).

Coherence

In units that are designed to be coherent from the student point of view, students build new ideas that start from their own questions and initial ideas about phenomena (Reiser et al., 2016, 2017b; Severance et al., 2016). The flow of lessons is intended to help students build new ideas systematically and incrementally through their investigations of their questions. As discussed in Chapter 4, the choices of phenomena and the sequencing of investigation and design are important in providing students with opportunities to develop deeper understanding of increasingly complex ideas. Overall, the lessons build toward disciplinary understandings but the order of lessons reflects students' evolving sense in which these ideas emerged as their questions led to partial explanations, and then to new questions, rather than the order that a disciplinary expert might impose. If the order of lessons were to be organized around the logic of the discipline, engaging in practices to figure out key ideas may not make sense to students, this is sometimes referred to as an "expert blind spot." Thus, in a unit that is coherent from the student point of view, students are engaged in science and engineering practices because of a felt need to make progress in addressing questions or challenges they have identified.

To see the contrast between coherence from the disciplinary and student perspectives, consider the following example. Cell membranes are key to the structure and function of organisms, and biologists study how they serve as selective barriers to the movement of molecules. The study of cell membranes would fall under core idea LS1 of the *Framework* (National Research Council, 2012). Yet from a student's perspective, until the class has established that cells need to take in food and get rid of waste, and that these molecules need to cross the cell membrane to do that, there is no motivation to figure out how materials enter and exit cells. Establishing that cells need to obtain energy *then* raises the question about what could get into or out of a cell and motivates investigating what can get through a membrane. From an engineering design perspective, examples and challenges from bioengineering can be used as motivators. If an exoskeleton for a police bomb-sniffing dog that lost a limb must be designed, the question might be what would need to be done to ensure the cells that connect to the cybernetics will function properly and not die. Learners would need to track and regulate feeding and waste removal. Such bioengineering design challenges could be motivating for learners.

It is important to point out that attention to coherence from the students' perspective does not imply that teachers should follow students wherever their questions, prior conceptions, and interests take them (Krajcik et al., 2008; Reiser et al., 2017a,b). The goal is to help students develop useable knowledge, so turning over complete control to students could take the investigations too far afield. Moreover, it can leave gaps in understanding that prevent students from developing reasonable explanations of phenomena. Instead of providing questions to the students, the teacher guides and negotiates with students to co-develop questions about the phenomenon, so that students are partners in figuring out what to work on and how to proceed (Manz and Renga, 2017; Novak and Krajcik, 2018; Reiser, Novak, and McGill, 2017b). Thus, students see how engaging in the science and engineering practices will help them make progress on phenomena they are trying to explain or engineering challenges they are trying to address, even when developing the questions and planning the investigation includes important contributions from the teacher and other resources.

Taking coherence from the student point of view seriously demands careful consideration of inter-unit coherence as well. The *Framework* emphasizes the need to organize learning of core ideas, practices, and cross-cutting concepts around developmental progressions that students explore across multiple years, beginning with the elementary grades. It is not possible to support such learning through disconnected units; instructional resources developers must integrate coordinated supports among units to build student understanding over time (Fortus and Krajcik, 2012). Fortus and colleagues (2015) explored whether middle school students built on understandings of the concept of energy developed in early units in subsequent units. Using a set of curriculum-aligned tests, researchers examined student responses to multiple-choice questions related to energy (the items were not three-dimensional). The students had been participants in a field test of the resources. The analysis showed a strong predictive relationship between performance on earlier energy items and subsequent items associated with later units, providing supportive evidence of the value of inter-unit coherence. More specifically, the scores on energy unit test predicted 68 percent ($r = 0.82$) of the variance on the 7th-grade earth science test scores that occurred after the energy unit and 60 percent ($r = 0.78$) of the variance on the 8th-grade chemistry unit test that occurred the following year (Fortus et al., 2015).

Learning progressions are critical tools for building inter-unit coherence. Learning progressions are testable, empirically supported hypotheses about how student understanding develops toward specific disciplinary goals for learning (Corcoran, Mosher, and Rogat, 2009; National Research Council, 2007). They provide guides for possible routes for organizing student learning opportunities across different units. Inter-unit coherence does not entail covering the same territory over and over, however. Across units, students encounter different application of a core idea within different science and engineering practices, and they encounter crosscutting concepts across investigations of different core ideas. Over time, moreover, students' understanding of core ideas, science and engineering practices, and crosscutting concepts develops so that students can use this understanding to make sense of increasingly complex phenomena and design challenges, and their increasing grasp of practice supports their ability to engage with these phenomena and challenges. Importantly, in this endeavor the primary orientation is to focus on using students' ideas as resources and "stepping-stones" (Wiser et al., 2012) for developing more sophisticated understandings, rather than as misconceptions to be debugged (Campbell, Schwarz, and Windschitl, 2016; Smith, diSessa, and Roschelle, 1993/1994).

Crosscutting concepts when used consistently and accurately become common and familiar touchstones across the disciplines and grade levels, especially when introduced beginning in the elementary grades. As noted in the *Framework*, "explicit reference to the concepts, as well as their emergence in multiple disciplinary contexts, can help students develop a cumulative, coherent, and usable understanding of science and engineering" (National Research Council, 2012, p. 83). Across all of the disciplines, students' use of concepts of systems and system models provides coherence in how matter and energy flow into, out of, and within systems to cause changes. Whether students are investigating the flow of matter in ecosystems or the transfer and transformation of energy in a handheld generator they engineered, the use of crosscutting concepts to prompt student performances provides coherence to students' understanding of natural phenomena or design challenges. Instructional resources that prompt student performances using crosscutting concepts contribute to the coherence of learning science.

SUMMARY

Teachers provide guidance in many ways as student learn via science investigation and engineering design. They select and present interesting phenomena and challenges; facilitate connections between relevant core ideas and crosscutting concepts; communicate clear expectations for student use of data and evidence; provide opportunities for students to communicate their reasoning and learn from formative assessment; set the tone for respectful, welcoming, and inclusive classrooms; and provide coherence and linkages between topics, units, and courses. Engaging students in science investigation and engineering design is a strategy that can link student interest to academic learning, and this interest can increase motivation. New standards alone do very little to improve student learning, but they offer an opportunity to make significant and lasting changes to the structure and goals of instruction. Improving student science learning requires shifting instruction to focus on students reasoning about the causes of phenomena and using evidence to support their reasoning. Investigation and design can drive this shift. The shift comes in five parts: (1) engaging students in science performances and engineering design challenges during which they use each of the three dimensions to make sense of phenomena; (2) teachers valuing and cultivating students' curiosity about science phenomena and interest in addressing unmet needs; (3) developing student-centered culturally relevant learning environments; (4) students valuing and using science as a process of obtaining knowledge supported by empirical evidence; and (5) students valuing and using engineering as a process of using empirical evidence to create designs that address societal and environmental needs. The *Framework*-inspired standards are consistent with each of these shifts for science teaching and learning (NGSS Lead States, 2013).

REFERENCES

Alonzo, A.C., and Elby, A. (2014). The nature of student thinking and its implications for the use of learning progressions to inform classroom instruction. Available: https://create4stem.msu.edu/sites/default/files/discussions/attachments/2014_International_Conference_of_the_Learning_Sciences_2014_Alonzo.pdf [October 2018].

Alozie, N.M., Moje, E.B., and Krajcik, J.S. (2010). An analysis of the supports and constraints for scientific discussion in high school project-based science. *Science Education, 94*(3), 395–427.

Au, K.H., and Kawakami, A.J. (1994). Cultural congruence in instruction. In E.R. Hollins, J.E. King, and W.C. Hayman (Eds.), *Teaching Diverse Populations: Formulating a Knowledge Base* (pp. 5–23). Albany: State University of New York Press.

Banilower, E.R., Smith, P.S., Weiss, I.R., Malzahn, K.A., Campbell, K.M., and Weis, A.M. (2013). *Report of the 2012 National Survey of Science and Mathematics Education.* Chapel Hill, NC: Horizon Research. Available: http://www.horizon-research.com/2012nssme/research-products/reports/technical-report/ [October 2018].

Bennett, R.E. (2011). Formative assessment: A critical review. *Assessment in Education: Principles, Policy & Practice, 18,* 5–25. doi: 10.1080/0969594X.2010.513678.

Berland, L.K., and Reiser, B.J. (2011). Classroom communities' adaptations of the practice of scientific argumentation. *Science Education, 95*(2), 191–216. doi:10.1002/sce.20420.

Berland, L.K., Schwarz, C.V., Krist, C., Kenyon, L., Lo, A.S., and Reiser, B.J. (2016). Epistemologies in practice: Making scientific practices meaningful for students. *Journal of Research in Science Teaching, 53*(7), 1082–1112. doi:10.1002/tea.21257.

Bhabha, H.K. (1994). Of mimicry and man: The ambivalence of colonial discourse. In H.K. Bhabha (Ed.), *The Location of Culture* (pp. 85–92). New York: Routledge Press.

Birmingham, D., Calabrese Barton, A., McDaniel, A., Jones, J., Turner, C., and Rogers, A. (2017). "But the science we do here matters": Youth-authored cases of consequential learning. *Science Education, 101*(5), 818–844. doi: 10.1002/sce.21293.

Blumenfeld, P., Soloway, E., Marx, R., Krajcik, J.S., Guzdial, M., and Palincsar, A. (1991). Motivating project-based learning. *Educational Psychologist, 26*(3 & 4), 369–398.

Bransford, J.D., and Schwartz, D.L. (1999). Rethinking transfer: A simple proposal with multiple implications. *Review of Research in Education, 24*(40), 61–100.

Bricker, L.A., and Bell, P. (2008). Conceptualizations of argumentation from science studies and the learning sciences and their implications for the practices of science education. *Science Education, 92*(3), 473–498. doi: 10.1002/sce.20278.

Brown, B., and Ryoo, K. (2008). Teaching science as a language: A "content first" approach to science teaching. *Journal of Research in Science Teaching 45*(5), 529–553.

Brown, B.A., and Kloser, M. (2009). Conceptual continuity and the science of baseball: Using informal science literacy to promote students' science learning. *Cultural Studies of Science Education, 4*(4), 875–897.

Brown, J. (2017). A metasynthesis of the complementarity of culturally responsive and inquiry-based science education in K-12 settings: Implications for advancing equitable science teaching and learning. *Journal of Research in Science Teaching, 54*(9), 1143–1173.

Burgstahler, S. (2012a). *Equal Access: Universal Design of Instruction. A Checklist for Inclusive Teaching—(DO-IT)-Disabilities, Opportunities, Internetworking and Technology.* University of Washington, College of Engineering. Available: https://www.washington.edu/doit/sites/default/files/atoms/files/EA_Instruction.pdf [October 2018].

Burgstahler, S. (2012b). *Making Science Labs Accessible to Students with Disabilities: Application of Universal Design to a Science Lab—(DO-IT)-Disabilities, Opportunities, Internetworking and Technology.* University of Washington, College of Engineering. Available: https://www.washington.edu/doit/sites/default/files/atoms/files/Making-Science-Labs-Accessible-Students-Disabilities.pdf [October 2018].

Calabrese Barton, A., and Tan, E. (2009). Funds of knowledge and discourses and hybrid space. *Journal of Research in Science Teaching, 46*(1), 50–73. doi: 10.1002/tea.20269.

Calabrese Barton, A., and Tan, E. (2010). We be burnin: Agency, identity and learning in a green energy program. *Journal of the Learning Sciences, 19*(2), 187–229.

Campbell, T., Schwarz, C.V., and Windschitl, M. (2016). What we call misconceptions may be necessary stepping-stones toward making sense of the world. *Science and Children, 53*, 28–33.

Cartier, J.L., Smith, M.S., Stein, M.K., and Ross, D.K. (2013). *5 Practices for Orchestrating Productive Task-based Discussions in Science.* Reston, VA: National Council of Teachers of Mathematics.

Cazden, C.B. (2001). *Classroom Discourse: The Language of Teaching and Learning* (2nd ed.). Portsmouth: Heinemann.

Clement, J. (1989). The concept of variation and misconceptions in cartesian graphing. *Focus on Learning Problems in Mathematics, 11*(1–2), 77–87.

Coffey, J.E., Hammer, D., Levin, D.M., and Grant, T. (2011). The missing disciplinary substance of formative assessment. *Journal of Research in Science Teaching, 48*(10), 1109–1136. doi: 10.1002/tea.20440.

Corcoran, T., Mosher, F.A., and Rogat, A. (2009). *Learning Progressions in Science: An Evidence-Based Approach to Reform.* CPRE Research Report No. Rr-63. Consortium for Policy Research in Education, University of Pennsylvania. Available: http://www.cpre.org/sites/default/files/researchreport/829_lpsciencerr63.pdf [October 2018].

delMas, R., Garfield, J., and Ooms, A. (2005, July). *Using Assessment Items to Study Students' Difficulty with Reading and Interpreting Graphical Representations of Distributions.* Presented at the Fourth Forum on Statistical Reasoning, Thinking, and Literacy (SRTL-4), July 6, Auckland, New Zealand.

Dewey, J. (1910). *How We Think.* Boston, MA: Heath.

Duschl, R.A., and Osborne, J.F. (2002). Supporting and promoting argumentation discourse in science education. *Studies in Science Education, 38*, 39–72.

Elby, A. (2000). What students' learning of representations tells us about constructivism. *The Journal of Mathematical Behavior, 19*(4), 481–502.

Engle, R.A. (2012). The productive disciplinary engagement framework: Origins, key concepts, and developments. In Y. Dai (Ed.), *Design Research on Learning and Thinking in Educational Settings: Enhancing Intellectual Growth and Functioning* (pp. 161–200). New York, NY: Routledge.

Engle, R.A., and Conant, F. R. (2002). Guiding principles for fostering productive disciplinary engagement: Explaining an emergent argument in a community of learners classroom. *Cognition and Instruction, 20*(4), 399–483.

Ford, M.J. (2008). Disciplinary authority and accountability in scientific practice and learning. *Science Education, 92*(3), 404–423. doi:10.1002/sce.20263.

Ford, M.J., and Forman, E.A. (2006). Redefining disciplinary learning in classroom contexts. *Review of Research in Education, 30*, 1–32.

Fortus, D., and Krajcik, J.S. (2012). Curriculum coherence and learning progressions. In B.J. Fraser, K. Tobin, and C.J. McRobbie (Eds.), *Second International Handbook of Science Education* (pp. 783–798). Dordrecht, the Netherlands: Springer.

Fortus, D., Sutherland Adams, L.M., Krajcik, J., and Reiser, B. (2015). Assessing the role of curriculum coherence in student learning about energy. *Journal of Research in Science Teaching, 52*, 1408–1425. doi: 10.1002/tea.21261.

Furtak, E.M., and Ruiz-Primo, M.A. (2008). Making students' thinking explicit in writing and discussion: An analysis of formative assessment prompts. *Science Education, 92*(5), 799–824.

Furtak, E.M., Morrison, D., and Kroog, H. (2014). Investigating the link between learning progressions and classroom assessment. *Science Education, 98*(4), 640–673.

Gay, G. (2010). *Culturally Responsive Teaching: Theory, Research, and Practice* (2nd ed.). New York: Teachers College Press.

Heritage, M., Kim, J., Vendlinski, T., and Herman, J. (2009). From evidence to action: A seamless process in formative assessment? *Educational Measurement: Issues and Practice, 28*(3), 24–31.

Huff, K.L., and Duschl, R.A. (2018). Get in the game—Planning and implementing coherent learning progressions, sequences, and storylines. *The Science Teachers Bulletin, 81*(1), 26–38. Available: https://drive.google.com/drive/folders/16u64Ru9dgdV8GK9VvxCXrgD-y34mXkeT [October 2018].

Johnson, A.W., Wendell, K.B., and Watkins, J. (2017). Examining experienced teachers' noticing of and responses to students' engineering. *Journal of Pre-College Engineering Education Research, 7*(1), Article 2. Available: doi: 10.7771/2157-9288.1162 [October 2018].

Johnson, C. (2011). The road to culturally relevant science: Exploring how teachers navigate change in pedagogy. *Journal of Research in Science Teaching, 48*(2), 170–198. doi: 10.1002/tea.20405.

Jordan, S., White, K., Anderson, A., Betoney, C., Pangan, T., and Foster, C. (2017). Culturally-relevant engineering design curriculum for the Navajo Nation. In *Proceedings of the American Society for Engineering Education (ASEE) Annual Conference & Exposition*, Columbus, OH.

Kang, H., Thompson, J., and Windschitl, M. (2014). Creating opportunities for students to show what they know: The role of scaffolding in assessment tasks. *Science Education, 98*(4), 674–704. doi: 10.1002/sce.21123.

Kang, H., Windschitl, M., Stroupe, D., and Thompson, J. (2016). Designing, launching, and implementing high quality learning opportunities for students that advance scientific thinking. *Journal of Research in Science Teaching, 53*(9), 1316–1340.

Kaplan, J.J., Gabrosek, J.G., Curtiss, P., and Malone, C. (2014). Investigating student understanding of histograms. *Journal of Statistics Education, 22*(2).

Kerlin, S.C., McDonald, S.P., and Kelly, G.J. (2010). Complexity of secondary scientific data sources and students' argumentative discourse. *International Journal of Science Education, 32*(9), 1207–1225. doi: 10.1080/09500690902995632.

Kiemer, K., Gröschner, A., Schinderl, A.-K., and Seidel, T. (2015). Effects of a classroom discourse intervention on teachers' practice and students' motivation to learn mathematics and science. *Learning and Instruction, 35*, 94–103.

Kloser, M. (2014). Identifying a core set of science teaching practices: A Delphi expert panel approach. *Journal of Research on Science Teaching, 51*, 1185–1217.

Kloser, M. (2017). *The Nature of the Teacher's Role in Supporting Student Investigations in Middle and High School Science Classrooms: Creating and Participating in a Community of Practice.* Paper commissioned for the Committee on Science Investigations and Engineering Design Experiences in Grades 6–12. Board on Science Education, Division of Behavioral and Social Sciences and Education. National Academies of Sciences, Engineering, and Medicine.

Konold, C. (2012). Designing a data analysis tool for learners. In M. Lovett and P. Smith (Eds.), *Thinking with Data* (pp. 267–291). Abingdon, UK: Taylor & Francis. doi: 10.4324/9780203810057.

Konold, C., Robinson, A., Khalil, K., Pollatsek, A., Well, A., Wing, R., and Mayr, S. (2002). Students' use of modal clumps to summarize data. In *Proceedings of the Sixth International Conference on Teaching Statistics* (pp. 1–7). Available: https://iase-web.org/documents/papers/icots6/8b2_kono.pdf [October 2018].

Krajcik, J.S. (2015). Three-dimensional instruction: Using a new type of teaching in the science classroom. *Science and Children, 53*(3), 6–8.

Krajcik, J.S., McNeill, K.L., and Reiser, B.J. (2008). Learning-goals-driven design model: Developing curriculum materials that align with national standards and incorporate project-based pedagogy. *Science Education, 92*(1), 1–32. doi: 10.1002/sce.20240.

Krajcik, J.S., and Czerniak, C.M. (2014). *Teaching Science in Elementary and Middle School: A Project-Based Approach.* London: Routledge.

Kuhn, D., Ramsey, S., Arvidsson, T.S. (2015). Developing multivariable thinkers. *Cognitive Development, 35*, 92–11.

Ladson-Billings, G. (2006). Yes, but how do we do it? Practicing culturally relevant pedagogy. In J. Landsman and C.W. Lewis (Eds.), *White Teachers/Diverse Classrooms: A Guide to Building Inclusive Schools, Promoting High Expectations and Eliminating Racism* (pp. 29–42). Sterling, VA: Stylus.

Laina, V., and Wilkerson, M.H. (2016). Distributions, trends, and contradictions: A case study in sensemaking with interactive data visualizations. *Proceedings of International Conference of the Learning Sciences, ICLS, 2*, 934–937.

Lee, V.R., and Sherin, B. (2006). Beyond transparency: How students make representations meaningful. In *Proceedings of the 7th International Conference on Learning Sciences*, 397–403.

Lehrer, R., and Romberg, T. (1996). Exploring children's data modeling. *Cognition and Instruction, 14*(1), 69–108.

Leinhardt, G., Zaslavsky, O., and Stein, M.K. (1990). Functions, graphs, and graphing: Tasks, learning, and teaching. *Review of Educational Research, 60*(1), 1–63.

Loreman, T. (1999). Integration: Coming from the outside. *Interaction, 13*(1), 21–23.

Lucas, D., Broderick, N., Lehrer, R., and Bohanan, R. (2005). Making the grounds of scientific inquiry visible in the classroom. *Science Scope, 29*(3), 39–42.

Manz, E., and Renga, I.P. (2017). Understanding how teachers guide evidence construction conversations. *Science Education, 101*, 584–615. doi: 10.1002/sce.21282.

McNeill, K.L., and Pimentel, D.S. (2010). Scientific discourse in three urban classrooms: The role of the teacher in engaging high school students in argumentation. *Science Education, 94*(2), 203–229.

McNeill, K.L., Lizotte, D.J., Krajcik, J., and Marx, R.W. (2006). Supporting students' construction of scientific explanations by fading scaffolds in instructional materials. *Journal of the Learning Sciences, 15*(2), 153–191.

Mensah, F.M. (2010). Toward the mark of empowering policies in elementary school science programs and teacher professional development. *Cultural Studies of Science Education, 5*(4), 977–983.

Mensah, F.M., and Larson, K. (2017). *A Summary of Inclusive Pedagogies for Science Education.* Paper commissioned for the Committee on Science Investigations and Engineering Design Experiences in Grades 6–12. Board on Science Education, Division of Behavioral and Social Sciences and Education. National Academies of Sciences, Engineering, and Medicine.

Michaels, S., and O'Connor, C. (2012). *Talk Science Primer.* Available: https://inquiryproject. terc.edu/shared/pd/TalkScience_Primer.pdf [October 2018].

Michaels, S., and O'Connor, C. (2017). From recitation to reasoning: Supporting scientific and engineering practices through talk. In C.V. Schwartz, C. Passmore, and B.J. Reiser (Eds.), *Helping Students Make Sense of the World Using Next Generation Science and Engineering Practices* (pp. 311–366). Arlington, VA: NSTA Press.

Michaels, S., O'Connor, C., and Resnick, L.B. (2007). Deliberative discourse idealized and realized: accountable talk in the classroom and in civic life. *Studies in Philosophy and Education, 27,* 283.

Miller, E., and Krajcik, J. (2015). Reflecting on instruction to promote alignment to the NGSS and equity. In O. Lee, E. Miller, and R. Januszyk (Eds.), *Next Generation Science Standards: All Standards, All Students.* Arlington, VA: National Science Teachers Association.

Moje, E.B., Ciechanowski, K.M., Kramer, K., Ellis, L., Carrillo, R., and Collazo, T. (2004). Working toward third space in content area literacy: An examination of everyday funds of knowledge and discourse. *Reading Research Quarterly, 39*(1), 38–70.

Moll, L.C., Amanti, C., Neff, D., and Gonzalez, N. (1992). Funds of knowledge for teaching: Using a qualitative approach to connect homes and classrooms. *Theory Into Practice, 31*(2), 132–141. Available: http://www.jstor.org/stable/1476399 [October 2018].

Moulding, B., and Bybee, R. (2018). *Teaching Science Is Phenomenal.* Ogden, UT: ELM Tree.

Nasir, N.S., and Hand, V. (2008). From the court to the classroom: Opportunities for engagement, learning, and identity in basketball and classroom mathematics. *Journal of the Learning Sciences, 17,* 143–179.

National Research Council. (2001). *Knowing What Students Know: The Science and Design of Educational Assessment.* Washington, DC: National Academy Press.

National Research Council. (2006). *America's Lab Report: Investigations in High School Science.* Washington, DC: The National Academies Press.

National Research Council. (2007). *Taking Science to School: Learning and Teaching Science in Grades K-8.* Washington, DC: The National Academies Press.

National Research Council. (2012). *A Framework for K-12 Science Education: Practices, Crosscutting Concepts, and Core Ideas.* Washington, DC: The National Academies Press.

National Research Council. (2015). *Guide to Implementing the Next Generation Science Standards.* Washington, DC: The National Academies Press.

NGSS Lead States. (2013). *Next Generation Science Standards: For States, By States.* Washington, DC: The National Academies Press.

Novak, A.M., and Krajcik, J.S. (2018). A case study of project based learning of middle school students exploring water quality. In W. Hung, M. Moallem, and N. Dabbagh (Eds.), *Wiley Handbook of Problem-Based Learning.* Hoboken NJ: Wiley-Backwell.

O'Connor, M.C., and Michaels, S. (1993). Aligning academic task and participation status through revoicing: Analysis of a classroom discourse strategy. *Anthropology and Education Quarterly, 24*(4), 318–333.

O'Connor, M.C., and Michaels, S. (1996). Shifting participant frameworks: Orchestrating thinking practices in group discussion. In D. Hicks (Ed.), *Child Discourse and Social Learning* (pp. 63–102). Cambridge: Cambridge University Press.

Osborne, J.F., Erduran, S., and Simon, S. (2004). Enhancing the quality of argumentation in school science. *Journal of Research in Science Teaching, 41*(10), 994–1020.

Paris, D. (2012). Culturally sustaining pedagogy: A needed change in stance, terminology, and practice. *Educational Researcher, 41*(3), 93–97. doi: 10.3102/0013189X12441244.

Parsons, E.C., and Wall, S. (2011). Unpacking the critical in culturally relevant pedagogy: An illustration involving African Americans and Asian Americans. In L. Scherff and K. Spector (Eds.), *Culturally Relevant Pedagogy: Clashes and Confrontations* (pp. 15–34). New York: Rowman & Littlefield Education.

Parsons, E.C., Travis, C., and Simpson, J. (2005). The black cultural ethos, students' instructional context preferences, and student achievement: An examination of culturally congruent science instruction in eighth-grade classes of one African American and one Euro-American teacher. *Negro Educational Review, 56*, 183–204.

Pellegrino, J. (2014). Assessment as a positive influence on 21st century teaching and learning: A systems approach to progress. *Psicologia Educativa, 20*, 65–77.

Penuel, W.R. (2016). Studying science and engineering learning in practice. *Cultural Studies of Science Education, 11*(1), 89–104.

Penuel, W.R., and Shepard, L.A. (2016). Assessment and teaching. In D.H. Gitomer and C.A. Bell (Eds.), *Handbook of Research on Teaching* (pp. 787–851). Washington, DC: AERA.

Penuel, W.R., Reiser, B.J., Novak, M., McGill, T., Frumin, K., Van Horne, K., Sumner, T., and Adam Watkins, D. (2018). *Using Co-design to Test and Refine a Model for Three-Dimensional Science Curriculum That Connects to Students' Interests and Experiences.* Paper presented at the Annual Meeting of the American Education Research Association, New York. Available: http://learndbir.org/resources/Using-Co-Design-to-Test-and-Refine-a-Model-for-Three-Dimensional-Science-Curriculum.pdf [October 2018].

Purzer, S. (2017). *Engineering Approaches to Problem Solving and Design in Secondary School Science: Teachers as Design Coaches.* Paper commissioned for the Committee on Science Investigations and Engineering Design Experiences in Grades 6–12. Board on Science Education, Division of Behavioral and Social Sciences and Education. National Academies of Sciences, Engineering, and Medicine.

Radinsky, J., Oliva, S., and Alamar, K. (2010). Camila, the earth, and the sun: Constructing an idea as shared intellectual property. *Journal of Research in Science Teaching, 47*(6), 619–642.

Reiser, B.J. (2004). Scaffolding complex learning: The mechanisms of structuring and problematizing student work. *The Journal of the Learning Sciences, 13*(3), 273–304.

Reiser, B.J., Fumagalli, M., Novak, M., and Shelton, T. (2016). *Using Storylines to Design or Adapt Curriculum and Instruction to Make It Three-dimensional.* Paper presented at the NSTA National Conference on Science Education, Nashville, TN. Available: https://www.academia.edu/24083676/Using_Storylines_to_Design_or_Adapt_Curriculum_and_Instruction_to_Make_It_Three-Dimensional [October 2018].

Reiser, B.J., Brody, L., Novak, M., Tipton, K., and Sutherland Adams, L.M. (2017a). Asking questions. In C.V. Schwarz, C.M. Passmore, and B.J. Reiser (Eds.), *Helping Students Make Sense of the World Through Next Generation Science and Engineering Practices* (pp. 87–134). Arlington, VA: NSTA Press.

Reiser, B.J., Novak, M., and McGill, T.A.W. (2017b). *Coherence from the Students' Perspective: Why the Vision of the Framework for K-12 Science Requires More Than Simply "Combining" Three Dimensions of Science Learning.* Paper commissioned for the Board on Science Education workshop Instructional materials for the Next Generation Science Standards. Available: http://sites.nationalacademies.org/cs/groups/dbassesite/documents/webpage/dbasse_180270.pdf [October 2018].

Richards, J., and Robertson, A.D. (2016). A review of the research on responsive teaching in science and mathematics, In A.D. Robertson, R.E. Scherr, and D. Hammer (Eds.), *Responsive Teaching in Science and Mathematics* (pp. 227–247). New York: Routledge.

Robertson, A.D., Scherr, R.E., and Hammer, D. (2016). *Responsive Teaching in Science and Mathematics.* New York: Routledge.

Rosebery, A.S., Warren, B., and Conant, F.R. (1992). Appropriating scientific discourse: Findings from language minority classrooms. *The Journal of the Learning Sciences, 2*(1), 61–94.

Ruiz-Primo, M.A., and Furtak, E.M. (2006). Informal formative assessment and scientific inquiry: Exploring teachers' practices and student learning. *Educational Assessment, 11*(3–4), 205–235.

Ruiz-Primo, M.A., and Furtak, E.M. (2007). Exploring teachers' informal formative assessment practices and students' understanding in the context of scientific inquiry. *Journal of Research in Science Teaching, 44*(1), 57–84.

Russ, R.S., and Luna, M.J. (2013). Inferring teacher epistemological framing from local patterns in teacher noticing. *Journal of Research in Science Teaching, 50*(3), 284–314.

Russ, R.S., Sherin, B.L., and Sherin, M.G. (2016). What constitutes teacher learning? In D.H. Gitomer and C.A. Bell (Eds.), *Handbook of Research on Teaching* (fifth ed., pp. 391–438). Washington, DC: American Educational Research Association.

Sandoval, W.A., and Çam, A. (2011). Elementary children's judgments of the epistemic status of sources of justification. *Science Education, 95*(3), 383–408. doi: 10.1002/sce.20426.

Sandoval, W.A., and Reiser, B. J. (2004). Explanation-driven inquiry: Integrating conceptual and epistemic scaffolds for scientific inquiry. *Science Education, 88*(3), 345–372. doi: 10.1002/sce.10130.

Severance, S., Penuel, W.R., Sumner, T., and Leary, H. (2016). Organizing for teacher agency in curricular co-design. *Journal of the Learning Sciences, 25*(4), 531–564. doi: 10.1080/10508406.2016.1207541.

Shavelson, R.J., Young, D.B., Ayala, C.C., Brandon, P.R., Furtak, E.M., and Ruiz-Primo, M.A. (2008). On the impact of curriculum-embedded formative assessment on learning: A collaboration between curriculum and assessment developers. *Applied Measurement in Education, 21*, 295–314.

Smith, J.P., diSessa, A.A., and Roschelle, J. (1993/1994). Misconceptions reconceived: A constructivist analysis of knowledge in transition. *The Journal of the Learning Sciences, 3*(2), 115–163.

Songer, N.B., and Gotwals, A.W. (2012). Guiding explanation construction by children at the entry points of learning progressions. *Journal of Research in Science Teaching, 49*(2), 141–165.

Swenson, S., and Kastens, K. (2011). Student interpretation of a global elevation map: What it is, how it was made, and what it is useful for. *Geological Society of America Special Paper, 474*, 189–211.

Tolbert, S., Stoddart, T., Lyon, E.G., and Solís, J. (2014). The Next Generation Science Standards, Common Core State Standards, and English learners: Using the SSTELLA framework to prepare secondary science teachers. *Issues in Teacher Education, 23*(1), 65–90.

van Zee, E.H., and Minstrell, J. (1997). Using questioning to guide student thinking. *The Journal of the Learning Sciences, 6*(2), 227–269.

152   SCIENCE AND ENGINEERING FOR GRADES 6–12

Watkins, J., Hammer, D., Radoff, J., Jaber, L.Z., and Phillips, A.M. (2018). Positioning as not-understanding: The value of showing uncertainty for engaging in science. *Journal of Research in Science Teaching 55*(4), 573–599. doi: 10.1002/tea.21431.

Wild, C.J., and Pfannkuch, M. (1999). Statistical thinking in empirical Inquiry (with discussion). *International Statistical Review, 67*(3), 223–265.

Wiliam, D. (2007). Keeping learning on track: Classroom assessment and the regulation of learning. In F.K. Lester, Jr. (Ed.), *Second Handbook of Mathematics Teaching and Learning* (pp. 1053–1098). Greenwich, CT: Information Age.

Windschitl, M., Thompson, J., and Braaten, M. (2018). *Ambitious Science Teaching.* Cambridge, MA: Harvard Educational Press.

Windschitl, M., Thompson, J., Braaten, M., and Stroupe, D. (2012). Proposing a core set of instructional practices and tools for teachers of science. *Science Education Policy 96*(5), 878–903.

Wiser, M., Smith, C.L., Doubler, S., and Asbell-Clarke, J. (2012). *Learning Progressions as Tools for Curriculum Development: Lessons from the Inquiry Project.* Paper presented at the Learning Progressions in Science (LeaPS) Conference, June 2009, Iowa City, IA.

Young, E. (2010) Challenges to conceptualizing and actualizing culturally relevant pedagogy: How viable is the theory in classroom practice? *Journal of Teacher Education, 61*(3), 248–260.

6

Instructional Resources for Supporting Investigation and Design

Science investigation and engineering design rely upon effective instructional resources to guide teachers and facilitate student experiences. Instructional resources are key to providing coherence by presenting and revisiting phenomena throughout the year and making connections to these phenomena as instruction progresses to new topics, phenomena, or challenges. They help students see how they can use science and engineering to make sense of subsequent phenomena and their everyday world. Phenomena and design challenges should be at the center of all instructional resources, and they should provide opportunities for students to apply the science and engineering ideas and concepts learned in one investigation to help make sense of similar, but novel phenomena in and beyond the classroom.

Many types of tools and resources can support teacher instruction during science investigation and engineering design. This chapter discusses the role of instructional resources from the perspectives of the features presented in Chapters 4 and 5: making sense of phenomena; gathering and analyze data; constructing explanations; communicating reasoning to self and others; fostering an inclusive learning environment; connecting learning through multiple contexts; and fostering coherence in student experiences. It also discusses technology as an instructional resource for investigation and design, the inclusion of teachers in the teams that develop instructional resources, and the connection between instructional resources and professional learning.[1]

Ultimately, the purpose of instructional resources is to support teaching practices that help students either develop evidence to support explanatory models of phenomena through scientific investigations, or to design and test solutions to real-world challenges. Instructional resources can help students make personal connections and see science and engineering as more relevant to their lives by providing information on challenges they can directly identify with. As discussed in Chapter 3, learning theories support the idea that connecting science learning to students' experiences is essential to retain knowledge. Application of the science learned in school beyond the classroom provides a way to support meaningful science learning. Application of knowledge to new phenomena provides students with a fuller understanding of how science and engineering are used in life. Science is a practice that requires application for student to internalize and become a way of knowing. The application of science knowledge beyond the classroom requires making sense of novel phenomena and engineering solutions to new challenges. Instructional materials can facilitate science instruction to link multiple phenomena, with multiple core ideas to provide sufficient opportunities for students to apply learning to new contexts and conceptualize the science core ideas and crosscutting concepts beyond the classroom.

As discussed in Chapter 4, one of the primary ways to establish relevance is to use questions that students find meaningful (Krajcik and Mamlok-Naaman, 2006). It is a challenge to design instructional resources that help teachers engage all students. Both the inclusion of phenomena and design challenges that are likely to be interesting to a wide variety of students and highlighting the ways teachers can adapt and modify the phenomena and challenges to their own settings are important and beneficial. Adaptations and modifications by teachers can also be beneficial (Lee and Buxton, 2008; Suriel and Atwater, 2012). However, not all teachers will have the time and resources to make such adaptations. They can benefit from the support of instructional resources that point out options for modifications and from colleagues who share their own approaches to finding and creating relevant approaches.

The building of students' understanding across time differs from common instructional practices in several key ways. A key motivation for *A Framework for K–12 Science Education* (hereafter referred to as the *Framework*;

---

[1] This chapter includes content drawn from papers commissioned by the committee: *Designing NGSS-Aligned Curriculum Materials* by Brian Reiser and Bill Penuel and *Data Use by Middle and Secondary Students in the Digital Age: A Status Report and Future Prospects* by Victor Lee and Michelle Wilkerson. The commissioned papers are available at http://www.nas.edu/Science-Investigation-and-Design [January 2019].

National Research Council, 2012) and the Next Generation Science Standards (NGSS) was the "growing national consensus around the need for greater coherence—that is, a sense of unity—in K–12 science education. Too often, standards are long lists of detailed and disconnected facts, reinforcing the criticism that science curricula in the United States tend to be 'a mile wide and an inch deep'" (Schmidt, McKnight, and Raizen, 1997). The goal of the *Framework* is to organize standards so they reflect sensible learning sequences that support students in systematically building and connecting ideas across time. Analyses of standards and instructional resources reveal that traditional resources jump from topic to topic, without helping students build ideas piece by piece, putting them together over time, and making connections to other relevant ideas, and to their own experiences (BSCS, 2017; Kesidou and Roseman, 2002; Roseman, Stern, and Koppal, 2010; Schmidt, Wang, and McKnight, 2005; Stern and Roseman, 2004). Indeed, it is common today for teachers to adopt the strategy of assembling individual lessons on a topic from colleagues or downloading individual lesson plans from social networking sites (Greene, 2016; Hunter and Hall, 2018). While sharing instructional resources could be a valuable way to support professional learning, the types of individual lesson plans found in these venues may not reflect high-quality, independently evaluated material. Furthermore, cobbling together individual lesson plans is unlikely to result in supporting students in incrementally developing, extending, and refining their explanatory models.

The traditional paradigm of having textbooks or instructional resources simply present the central parts of disciplinary core ideas, and having students then explain them back or use them to achieve particular tasks fails to reflect this three-dimensional nature of lessons. While obtaining information (one of the science and engineering practices) may include reading a textbook or other resource to find out what experts know about a topic, this should be a part of a larger meaningful "ensemble of activity" in which students engage in practices such as argumentation from evidence or constructing explanations to put the pieces together and develop an explanation or model of the phenomenon being investigated that incorporates or applies that knowledge, rather than simply taking in a pre-packaged articulation of the concept. At the other end of the spectrum, inquiry activities in which students empirically explore relationships between variables but do not explain why those relationships hold also reflects a partial view of three-dimensional learning, since this activity leaves out the knowledge-building focus of the practices. Similarly, while science practices such as designing and conducting investigations may require instrumental skills, such as using a microscope or making a graph, simply learning these skills, isolated from an effort to make progress on making sense of the phenomena or design challenge and building knowledge of the three dimensions, would not reflect the intention of the *Framework* or what is meant by investigation and design. While a range of different pedagogical approaches may be possible to achieve three-dimensional learning, it is clear that certain pedagogical approaches leave little room for meaningful integration of the three dimensions to make sense of phenomena or solve challenges. The key features of instructional resources that support the *Framework* and NGSS are compared to features of prior instructional resources in Table 6-1.

As described in Chapter 5, the classroom envisioned by the *Framework* differs significantly from most current middle and high school science classrooms. Instructional resources adopted by districts, principals, and individual teachers are a primary driver of what goes on in the classroom, which means that changing the culture of the classroom requires changing instructional resources and supporting instructional resource developers in creating and maintaining excellent resources. Studies show that instructional resources make a difference in supporting students in developing the type of learning called for in the *Framework* and the NGSS (Harris et. al., 2014).

MAKE SENSE OF PHENOMENA

A key aspect of instructional resources for investigation and design is the selection of relevant phenomena. Explaining a phenomenon or solving a problem must require developing or applying key elements of disciplinary core ideas and crosscutting concepts. As discussed in Chapter 3, it is advantageous to connect phenomena and challenges to students' interests and everyday experiences where possible. Interest is a key catalyst for science learning in both the short and long term (Bathgate and Schunn, 2017; Bricker and Bell, 2014; Crowley et al., 2015). Presenting phenomena in ways that pique student curiosity about familiar phenomena allows students to make connections to everyday experiences, captivate their attention, and develop a sense of wonder. Utilizing multiple, but related phenomena helps address the diversity of student interests and experiences. Evidence related to the interest and personal relevance of phenomena can be used to select phenomena and design challenges, so as to facilitate broad student engagement (Penuel et al., 2017). Using place-based learning can be especially powerful when it is student driven: that is, the students identify the challenges (e.g., poor drinking water quality, human impacts that decrease local biodiversity) or phenomena (e.g., a change in depth water in a local aquifer, invasive species population increases as native species populations decrease in local ecosystem) to investigate. Place-based learning has had a positive influence on learning and motivation when collaborating with the surrounding community on environmental issues such as local air quality (Powers, 2004; Senechal, 2007; effect sizes not available).

To support three-dimensional learning, the phenomenon should provide a context in which students can gather and apply relevant science ideas and

TABLE 6-1 Shifting from Instructional Strategies Common in Prior Instructional Resources to Principles of Instructional Resources to Support Science Investigation and Engineering Design

---

Make sense of phenomena and design challenges.

• Separate treatment of content and process goals; curriculum and teachers explain and students apply ideas; phenomena as examples to illustrate ideas that have already been taught. • Topic focused.	• Making sense of phenomena and addressing design challenges. • Guiding and facilitating three-dimensional learning. • Relevant to the lives of learners. • Investigation and design focused.

Gather and analyze data and information.

• Using data to verify a scientific principle.	• Resources support the use of data as evidence to construct explanations and develop arguments to support explanations.

Construct explanations.

• Explanations provided by the teacher or found in the textbook.	• Resources support students as they develop arguments and make models for how the evidence supports an explanation or as they evaluate a proposed design solution.

Communicate reasoning to self and others.

• Worksheets and Lab Reports. • Supports include common "misconceptions" of students but not how to build on student ideas as resources. • Few supports beyond extension activities for students, little that addresses the need for connecting to students' experiences and identities or for ensuring equitable participation in classroom discussion.	• Units present students with multiple opportunities to build models and other artifacts that represent emerging understanding of the causes of phenomena or solution to challenges. • Embedded formative assessments provide teachers with multiple opportunities to elicit and interpret student thinking. • Supports for equitable participation are integrated.

---

continued

TABLE 6-1 Continued

Apply learning beyond the classroom.		
• Learning is specific and limited to the phenomena or challenges presented in the instructional unit. • Modular lessons and units; individual lessons mapped to standards; logic of instructional sequence clear to curriculum writers and teachers but not students.		• Establishes the expectation and opportunities for students to apply learning to novel phenomena and design challenges beyond the classroom. • Units present students with coherent investigation and design opportunities that support in incremental sense-making about the natural and engineered world.
Learning Goals		
• Learning goals are expressed with cognitive general verbs (e.g., identify, describe, explain, analyze) to describe learning expectations for science concepts or science process.		• Learning goals are expressed as three-dimensional performance expectations expressed with practices as the verb (e.g., develop models, analyze data, construct explanations).

crosscutting concepts to construct explanations for the causes of changes in systems, not simply as a context for teachers or instructional resources to demonstrate those ideas or explain them to students. A phenomenon that can be explained *without* reference to targeted core ideas or crosscutting concepts will not provide an adequate context for three-dimensional learning (Achieve, 2016). Similarly, a phenomenon that could be explained, in principle, by disciplinary ideas but does not engage students in applying these ideas to support an explanation of the causes of the phenomenon does not meet the criteria for instruction. For example, a teacher could show a 7th-grade classroom dry ice turning to gaseous carbon dioxide (which technically illustrates a phase change, the process of sublimation), but it is difficult to see how investigating this phenomenon will help the students develop the target ideas of the nature of matter, properties of solids and liquids, and the forces that hold them together.

Instructional resources can provide the links between phenomena and help teachers with how to sequence and draw out connections between the experiences. Science and engineering instruction that establishes the expectation that students apply what they learn deepens understanding by building on prior knowledge. Well-articulated instructional materials provide opportunities for students to apply what they have learned within the instructional sequence as well as beyond the classroom. The model of students making sense of one phenomenon and then transferring that same set of core ideas and crosscutting concepts to make sense of analogous phenomena is effective for science learning. Instructional materials can provide intentional instructional sequence that allow opportunities for application of students' three-dimensional learning to new contexts; more importantly, application of science knowledge to contexts beyond the classroom is an essential goal of science education. Instructional resources such as 5E or Gather, Reason, Communicate[2] provide instructional sequences, but many others, such as *Ambitious Science Teaching* (Windschitl, Thompson, and Braaten, 2018), provide resources and frameworks that are also useful for thinking about sequencing. When considering sequencing and the choice of phenomena or design challenges, teachers need to consider in advance whether there is enough depth to the examples chosen to connect the multiple learning goals or performance expectations to be met in the unit. Each investigation or design challenge requires investing extended classroom time so they should be chosen judiciously so that each one helps students meet learning goals, build student understanding incrementally, and help students see how ideas connect and relate to one another (Krajcik et al., 2014). Instructional resources should also provide a coherent structure and clear expectation for students to apply their science and engineering learning beyond the classroom.

Instructional resources can also help teachers to increase student interest by exposing students to concrete examples of the variety of work that real scientists and engineers do. This type of intervention challenges some of the stereotypical images of professionals in these fields, and students may then have a more concrete and complex picture of science work to relate to. Wyss, Heulskamp, and Siebert (2012) used this type of intervention in STEM learning by having students view video interviews with scientists about their careers; they found a positive influence on increasing interest in pursuing STEM careers for middle school children ($d = 0.52$), but no learning gains were measured. Another approach is instructional resources that provide strategies for adapting resources through place-based learning (Sobel, 2005). This method, often used in environmental science, focuses science and engineering investigations on challenges and phenomena that exist in the local community.

Instructional resource designers can attend to the ways phenomena and questions can support students in building deeper knowledge of the scientific and engineering practices, crosscutting concepts, and disciplinary

---

[2]The 5Es are engagement, exploration, explanation, elaboration, and evaluation. More information about the 5E instructional model can be found at https://bscs.org/bscs-5e-instructional-model [October 2018]. More information about the Gather, Reason, Communicate approach can be found in Moulding, Bybee, and Paulson (2015).

core ideas. Instructional resources support learners exploring solutions to questions (National Research Council, 2012) that are meaningful and relevant to their lives. Engineering design challenges and solutions are still novel to many teachers and many students. Developers of instructional resources can help teachers by anticipating student questions that will arise and demonstrating a sequence for exploring those questions that can help students build and test explanatory models or design and test solutions progressively over time. Research on design learning provides insight about cognition and can provide a framework for engaging students. A review by Crismond and Adams brings together information from many sources to inform engineering design approaches in the classroom (Crismond and Adams, 2012).

GATHER AND ANALYZE DATA AND CONSTRUCT EXPLANATIONS[3]

A central activity of science is to verify claims based upon evidence. In addition to the data that students gather themselves, they can now use data freely accessible on the web to answer important questions that will help them build knowledge of important useable knowledge aligned to performance expectations (standards). For example, they can access climate data, such as temperature and precipitation across years from the National Oceanic and Atmospheric Administration (NOAA); data about ocean acidification on such variables as dissolved carbon dioxide, pH, and oxygen (to name a few) from NOAA; water quality data from the United States Geological Survey (USGS); and astronomy data from Web sources such as Astronomical Data Sources on the Web. While a plethora of datasets exist for students to analyze, data are not evidence unless they can be used to provide support for scientific ideas or to support design decisions. Instructional resources can provide support for these efforts. And like any learning experience, the use and analysis of data must be used to support students in three-dimensional learning to build usable knowledge. Instructional resources can also provide structure for students to collect data and analyze data, driven by finding an answer to a question, and to use findings as evidence to support claims related to those questions.

Online data analysis tools, like Concord Consortium's Common Online Data Analysis Platform (CODAP), can allow students to analyze data that they collect as well as datasets that they might import from online sources.

---

[3]This section draws on the paper commissioned by the committee *Data Use by Middle and Secondary Students in the Digital Age: A Status Report and Future Prospects* by Victor Lee and Michelle Wilkerson. Available: http://www.nas.edu/Science-Investigation-and-Design [October 2018].

The Concord Consortium's Energy 3D tool could be utilized for engineering design (Xie et al., 2018). Such tools allow students to find patterns in data and test predictions. More advanced students can use various statistical calculations to find the best fit line or to test if one set of data is different from another set of data. While these online tools provide unprecedented power for students to analyze data, the tools must be used as a component of students' engagement in three-dimensional learning (i.e., a scientific investigation) and not just in isolation to carry out an activity.

Publicly accessible datasets and data visualizations are likely to become more commonly used in science classes in coming years and may affect the nature and use of data in classrooms. These datasets and visualizations are not necessarily constructed with pedagogical purposes in mind, and students do not have access to or full knowledge of how they were constructed. Complex, second-hand data are an increasingly common feature of science communication and practice and could be more explicitly integrated into middle and high school science. While public datasets have existed for years, their accessibility and visibility have exploded in the past decade. There are also a growing number of initiatives to make public data available for educational use (e.g., NOAA's *Data in the Classroom* initiative at dataintheclassroom.noaa.gov or NASA's *MyNASAData* project at mynasadata.larc.nasa.gov). While some of these efforts come with accompanying instructional resources and simplified data, early research suggests that students can benefit from interacting with complex, "messy" public data, perhaps even more than from textbook-like second-hand data. For example, Kerlin and colleagues (2010) found that students exploring earthquakes were more likely to engage in a full breadth of discourse related to data—including early theorizing, questioning the data collection process, exploring patterns, and predicting and evaluating—when working with "raw" data from the USGS, rather than when working with clean textbook data.

One particular challenge in using publicly available datasets in education concerns the many multivariate relationships that may be present. Students can become overwhelmed searching for meaningful relationships, or they can lose sight of the goals of inquiry as different patterns are revealed. Another challenge lies in manipulating these datasets so that they are appropriate for student-driven goals—which are likely to be quite different from the original motivations for assembling a given public dataset. However, early studies suggest that even young students are capable of some aspects of data wrangling—for example, merging datasets that may each address the same investigation, identifying subsets or specific parameters within a given dataset that are relevant for inquiry, or recalculating or recoding values so that they better align with a student or classroom's path of inquiry (Chick, Pfannkuch, and Watson, 2005; Wilkerson and Laina, n.d.; Wilkerson et al., 2018).

ASSESSMENT AND COMMUNICATING REASONING TO SELF AND OTHERS

Systems of embedded assessments in instructional resources thus need to include ways to assess students' explanatory models of phenomena and solutions to design challenges, as well as tasks that elicit students' ability to apply their understanding to reason about novel phenomena and challenges (Ruiz-Primo et al., 2002). Such tasks need to include scoring guides that help teachers interpret students' responses in light of the overall goal for unit learning, not just discrete elements of disciplinary core ideas, science and engineering practices, and crosscutting concepts. Finally, the tasks need to include supports for "what to do next," depending on students' responses to tasks, so that they can be used to support learning (DeBarger et al., 2017).

The Contingent Pedagogies project provides evidence for the value of providing integrated supports for classroom assessment and having teachers elicit and interpret student thinking in multiple times and ways (DeBarger et al., 2017; Penuel et al., 2017). In that project, a set of formative assessment tasks was integrated into two investigation-based units in middle school earth science that aligned to the NGSS. Teachers received professional development on three-dimensional learning and how to use these tasks to elicit students' initial ideas prior to investigation and to check their understandings at the conclusion of the investigation. The assessment materials included a set of questions for teachers to ask that drew on identified problematic facets of student understanding, clicker technology for collecting student responses, and a set of talk moves to use to support student argumentation about their responses. The materials also included a set of "teaching routines" (DeBarger et al., 2010) for enacting the full cycle of formative assessment that included a set of activities teachers could use if students were having particular difficulties with understanding the focal ideas of an investigation. A quasi-experimental study of the resources that compared students in classrooms with the assessment-enhanced resources to students with the original units found students in the treatment condition scored higher on both post-unit earth science tests than control after adjusting for prior test scores[4] (Harris et al., 2015). The study also found

---

[4]For the physical science (energy) unit, the estimated effect size of 0.22 was statistically significant (z1/42.16, p1/40.03). For the earth science unit, the estimated effect size of 0.25 was statistically significant (z1/42.02, p1/40.04).

that teachers were able to use the materials to foster norms of supporting claims with evidence, which mediated student learning outcomes.

In order to provide effective foundations for these kinds of assessment conversations (Duschl and Gitomer, 1997), embedded assessments need to not only provide rich questions for teachers to ask students, but also provide formats for engaging students in self- and peer-assessment, frameworks for interpreting student ideas, and strategies for teachers to employ when student thinking reveals problematic ideas after instruction (Penuel and Shepard, 2016). Furthermore, embedded formative assessments should be based upon research into how student thinking develops in a disciplinary domain, taking into account how students' lived experiences interact with and inform their development of understandings of disciplinary core ideas and crosscutting concepts. That is, these formative assessments are not domain-general strategies for eliciting student thinking but are specific to the scientific ideas, concepts, and practices being learned. Formal, embedded assessment tasks need to be designed using evidence-centered design that specify claims of how students make use of the knowledge and evidence that is needed to support the claim (Harris et al., 2014).

FOSTER AN INCLUSIVE LEARNING ENVIRONMENT

Instructional resources can support equity by providing differentiated supports and multiple options. The science and engineering practices require students to engage in intensive forms of language use for both communication and learning (Lee, Quinn, and Valdés, 2013). Leveraging the communicative resources students bring to class and enabling them to express understanding using different modalities is critical in both instructional and assessment tasks (Brown and Spang, 2008; Buxton et al., 2013). Resources that follow principles of Universal Design for Learning (UDL; Burgstahler, 2012; Center for Universal Design, North Carolina State University, 1997; Duerstock, 2018; Rose and Meyer, 2002) can ensure that a variety of entry points and modalities are intentionally integrated. One strategy for promoting more equitable participation in science classrooms is to focus on phenomena and design challenges that connect to students' everyday lives. Instruction that builds on students' own funds of knowledge, everyday experiences, and cultural practices in families and communities shows great potential for supporting active participation in science class for all students (Calabrese Barton et al., 2005; Hudicourt-Barnes, 2003; Rosebery et al., 2010).

For specific populations, instructional resources that reflect principles of contextualization derived from ethnographic research in students' communities can support students linking everyday ways of making sense of the world and scientific and engineering practices (Sánchez Tapia, Krajcik, and

Reiser, 2018), core ideas, and crosscutting concepts. In addition, focusing on helping students navigate between these different ways of knowing—rather than expecting students to give up their everyday ways of knowing—is critical for promoting respect for different cultural worldviews and epistemologies (Aikenhead, 2001; Bang and Medin, 2010). As Lee and colleagues (2013) concluded, promoting equitable participation across different student populations means an emphasis on making meaning, on hearing and understanding the contributions of others, and on communicating ideas in a common effort to build understanding of the phenomenon or to design solutions for the system being studied.

COHERENCE

Instructional resources that develop student understanding over time provide extensive supports for continuous sense-making and incremental building of models and mechanisms, including providing guidance to teachers in how to support students in making connections between their investigations and the questions they are trying to answer and how the models they build explain and support phenomena. They provide tools that students can use to keep track of their questions and the progress they are making to answer them, to help assemble evidence they have gathered into coherent science explanations, and to help students come to consensus about key components and interactions to represent in explanatory models of phenomena and criteria for solutions to challenges (Windschitl and Thompson, 2013; Windschitl et al., 2012). Importantly, these tools and routines are introduced "just in time" rather than "just in case" students need them. They are not "front loaded" at the beginning of the school year or a unit, as has been customary in science textbooks that begin with a first chapter on the scientific method (Osborne and Quinn, 2017; Windschitl, Thompson, and Braaten, 2008).

Greater coherence is essential in attaining the new vision for science education. One can think of the three dimensions working together as a tapestry to help students conceptualize core ideas, in essence, building a platform or structure where students use the three dimensions in an integrated manner to reason and make sense of phenomena. *A Framework for K–12 Science Education* (National Research Council, 2012) asserts "successful implementation [of science standards] requires all of the components across levels cohere and work together in a harmonious or logical way to support the new vision" (p. 245). The *Framework*'s vision is students will acquire knowledge and skill in science and engineering through a carefully designed sequence of learning experiences. Each stage in the sequence will develop students' understanding of particular science and engineering practices, crosscutting concepts, and disciplinary core ideas. Coherence, therefore, means the three dimensions are connected together and lead students to an explanation of the phenomena.

Stress on isolated parts can train students in a series of routines without educating them to understand an overall picture that will ensure the development of integrated knowledge structures and information about conditions of applicability (National Research Council, 2000). The application of practices, core ideas, and crosscutting concepts to make sense of phenomena provides a way for students to internalize, conceptualize and generalize knowledge in ways that it becomes part of how they see the natural and engineered world. Understanding the three dimensions is essential, but real transformation occurs when these dimensions are integrated in a coherent instructional approach.

The principle of incremental sense-making is one implication of the *Framework's* first strategy of "a developmental progression." The notion of developmental progressions could be taken in part to reflect a logical sequence based upon the structure of the discipline as disciplinary experts see it, as Bruner (1960) argued. This approach of disciplinary coherence, for example as reflected in the *Atlas* work of the American Association for the Advancement of Science (2001, 2007), would be a major advance over many existing instructional resources that do not pay adequate attention to connecting ideas and helping students build complex ideas from more simple ones (Roseman et al., 2010). However, it would not necessarily provide students with meaningful encounters with how scientific activity unfolds in practice. The logic of walking through an already-worked out explanation (with 20-20 hindsight) is quite different from what makes sense for students to question and work on a step-by-step basis. Reiser, Novak, and McGill (2017) argued that supporting meaningful engagement in three-dimensional learning requires developing and enacting instructional resources that are coherent *from the students' perspective.* They argue that the notion of a social practice suggests that it is insufficient for instructional resources or teachers to present in a top-down fashion what questions or challenges students should work on and what practices they should engage in.

Instead, Reiser et al. (2017) argued that authentically engaging in science and engineering practices should help students address questions or challenges they have identified and committed to address. They build on earlier arguments for project-based learning (Blumenfeld and Krajcik, 2006; Blumenfeld et al., 1991) and learning-for-use (Edelson, 2001; Kanter, 2010) to argue that achieving the *Framework's* vision means that students should be partners, along with instructional resources and teachers, in figuring out what to work on next in order to progress in making sense of phenomena and solving challenges. Expectations of what it means to be competent in doing science and understanding science go beyond skillful performance and recall of factual knowledge. Contemporary views of learning value understanding and application of knowledge to new contexts, both in and beyond the classroom. Students who understand science can use and apply ideas and concepts in diverse contexts, drawing connections among multiple representations of a given concept (National Research Council, 2007). Instructional materials should provide useful tools and expectations for investigating phenomena and challenges beyond the classroom. Building understanding across time will only occur when instruction and the resources supporting them are coherent. There are a number of different ways to interpret coherence when exploring how instructional resources and teaching can support more effective approaches to science teaching and learning.

The shift in the aim of science education away from simply knowing science to *using* science and engineering ideas and practices to make sense of the world or solve challenges requires working with students' initial resources for sense-making as valuable starting points, even though they may be piecemeal and contextualized in everyday experiences rather than coherent, generalized theories (diSessa and Minstrell, 1998; Hammer and Elby, 2003; Minstrell, 1992). Therefore, instructional resources need to be organized to help students build on their prior understandings, incrementally extending and revising these understandings as the students use practices in meaningful ways to explore phenomena and design challenges. Furthermore, the target disciplinary core ideas are more than collections of facts, but are complex coherent understandings of mechanisms, such as how matter can be rearranged or how living things get the energy and matter they need. Constructing these ideas is not like simply providing a series of answers to particular questions or testing a series of hypotheses about different variables. Instead, this knowledge building occurs incrementally as students use their prior knowledge to make sense of new situations. The *Framework* argues that learning should be viewed as a progression "designed to help children continually build on and revise their knowledge and abilities, starting from their curiosity about what they see around them and their initial conceptions about how the world works" (National Research Council, 2012, p. 11). Thus, instructional resources can support students' building initial models, and continuously extending those models as they encounter new phenomena, connecting to prior explanations, deepening mechanisms to improve their explanatory power, and revising them as they uncover limitations in these models (Berland et al., 2016; Windschitl et al., 2008, 2012).

LEARNING GOALS AS PERFORMANCE EXPECTATIONS

Instructional resources help students *build toward* performance expectations by engaging learners in making sense of phenomena or solving challenges by using a variety of disciplinary core ideas and crosscutting concepts across disciplines to engage in various scientific and engineering practices. In this way, the components of three-dimensional learning are used as flexible tools (Duncan, Krajcik, and Rivet, 2016) to support students in sense-making. By focusing on phenomena and design challenges, instructional resources bring together science and engineering practices with disciplinary core ideas and crosscutting concepts into three-dimensional performances that have three-dimensional learning goals, rather than treating "content" and "process" as separate learning goals. Learning goals are articulated as performance expectations and are necessarily three-dimensional. In order to reach these expectations, the instructional sequences used in lessons must describe what students are doing in the lesson sequences using three-dimensional student performances. Integration of the *Framework*'s three dimensions means going beyond simply focusing students' attention at some point on each of the three dimensions to authentic integration around a compelling question or challenge. This structure is reflected in one of the criterion of the EQuIP[5] rubric on Integrating the Three Dimensions in NGSS lessons—"Student sense-making of phenomena and/or designing of solutions requires student performances that integrate elements of the SEPs [science and engineering practices], CCCs [crosscutting concepts], and DCIs [disciplinary core ideas]" (Achieve, 2016, p. 2).

Learning goals that gradually develop understanding toward the performance expectations need to guide the development of materials (Krajcik et al., 2014). A careful sequence of learning goals helps build coherence in a unit. Performance expectations include many components and students cannot be expected to develop understanding of these expectations in a single class period or even a single unit. Rather, learners are expected to build understanding necessary to demonstrate mastery of the performance expectations over time. In order to do so, they need to experience instruction that engages them in three-dimensional learning. As such, learning goals expressed as three-dimensional performances need to guide instruction and instructional materials.

---

[5] EQuIP stands for Educators Evaluating the Quality of Instructional Products. It provides criteria by which to measure the degree to which lessons and units are designed for the NGSS. The purpose of the rubric and review process is to (1) review existing lessons and units to determine what revisions are needed; (2) provide constructive criterion-based feedback and suggestions for improvement to developers; (3) identify examples/models for teachers' use within and across states; and (4) inform the development of new lessons, units, and other instructional materials. For more information, see http://www.nextgenscience.org/resources/equip-rubric-lessons-units-science [October 2018].

TECHNOLOGY

Technology is a tool for facilitating learning and is itself an instructional resource. It can be used for data collection, as a source of data, for data analysis, for modeling, for visualization, for simulations, and for presentations. There are important distinctions that educators must consider now between data collected through familiar modes of measurement (e.g., using common instruments in classroom laboratories, such as rulers and scales) and data collected by automated sensors, generated by simulations or other computational means, or publicly available scientific data reused by educators (Cassel and Topi, 2015; Wallis, Milojevic, and Borgman, 2006). Furthermore, many examinations of students' data use focus on one specific context, topic, and grade range. For instance, student-collected "first-hand" and educator or curriculum-provided "second-hand" data each carry different affordances for classroom practice (Hug and McNeill, 2008), with second-hand data requiring additional context creation work in the classroom for the data to be made sensible. There are also equity implications to be considered in terms of which students have access to the tools and time needed to generate and capture their own data.

The use of automated data collection sensors has become more established in science education since publication of *America's Lab Report* (National Research Council, 2006), even as research on the conditions for their effective use is still emerging. In this section, we review the latest work and emerging trends in these areas. While we refer to these data collection sensors as "automated," we do not mean to imply that they require no oversight from a student or a teacher. Indeed, these tools place new demands on teachers and students that differ from manual data collection activities. For instance, electronic probes and accompanying software allow learners to collect data that would be difficult, time-consuming, or impossible to collect without their use. Probes are electronic sensors and software that can be used to collect and analyze data. Electronic probes attached to various computer devices—including handheld devices such as smartphones and tablets and associated software—allow students to collect, graph, and visualize a variety of data, including pH, force, light, distance and speed, dissolved oxygen, and much more. Students can use probes to facilitate data collections and visualizations. Although probes have been used in science classrooms for more than 25 years as laboratory tools and can support learners in multiple scientific practices and investigations, their use is still not commonplace in most secondary science classrooms.

Metcalf and Tinker (2004) demonstrated that probeware indeed could be used with handheld computers and effectively integrated into middle school science classrooms when coupled with supportive instructional resources. In their study, teachers responded positively to the introduction of probeware in their classrooms. Beyond the classroom, field trip and field work experiences, such as water sampling and ecosystem exploration, have also served as effective and feasible spaces for probeware use (Kamarainen et al., 2013).

The effectiveness of using probeware up to grade 8 with moderate to large effect sizes in inquiry-oriented science and engineering, across a range of topics, has been documented in Zucker et al. (2008). Struck and Yerrick (2010) have also documented effectiveness of probeware with high school physics students, which can be augmented even further when those students also participate in digital video analysis. Consistent with prior research on probeware (e.g., Linn, Layman, and Nachmias, 1987), students also improved in their graph comprehension capabilities. Together, these studies affirm that the use of probeware in science and engineering classrooms, when coupled with supportive instructional resources and other tools, can be an asset for student learning. Also, see the discussion of modeling physics in Chapter 9.

Other types of technology can also be used for automated data collection, such as wearable sensors (Ching et al., 2016; Klopfer, Yoon, and Perry, 2005; Lee, Drake, and Williamson, 2015; Lyons, 2014); log data such as records of clicks on Websites or which tools are most frequently used (Rivera-Pelayo et al., 2012); and networked sensors (Hsi, Hardy, and Farmer, 2017; Martin et al., 2010). The measurements and visualizations made available by wearable sensors are not always intuitive nor easily comprehended by students (Ching, Schaefer, and Lee, 2014), largely because they were not initially designed with youth or learners' needs or familiar activities in mind (Lee, Drake, and Thayne, 2016). However, as the range of possible measurements (e.g., time spent standing, heart rate, electrodermal activity) and the ecosystem of wearable devices expands, these off-the-shelf wearable devices appear to offer familiar options for classrooms that can also produce significant gains in students' ability to reason with data (Lee and DuMont, 2010; Lee, Drake, and Thayne, 2016). One project with networked sensors, the *iSense* project, seeks to enable remote sensing and analysis of relevant proximal and local data using a network of sensors placed around a classroom or within a neighborhood (Martin et al., 2010). Students could log on to an online data repository that includes analysis and visualization tools to monitor the data generated by sensors. Similarly, the *InSPECT* project led by the Concord Consortium involves using Internet of Things (IoT) technologies and student-programmed automated data collection technologies to support high school biology lab activities (Hsi et al., 2017). These are coupled with data visualization tools, such as CODAP (Common Data Analysis Platform),[6] to support data analysis

---

[6] See http://codap.concord.org [October 2018].

activities. Another project using IoT at the University of Colorado Boulder and Utah State University is exploring the use of SparkFun's Smart School IoT platform that will obtain remote sensor data—such as temperature and air quality—for student inquiry activities (NSF Grant No. DRL-1742053). Further infrastructure work is still needed for these tools to be effectively used in educational settings. The aforementioned projects demonstrate feasibility using a range of paradigms, whether they involve students engineering their own sensor networks (Hsi et al., 2017; Martin et al., 2010) or obtaining and examining data from more public remote sensors. However, the abundance of data that can be collected from such projects yields both technological and pedagogical questions. These questions include how to effectively store and archive data for subsequent access and examination by classrooms (Wallis et al., 2006), as well as how to best support students in designing and navigating complex collections of data sources for which relationships are likely to be especially noisy, multivariate, and caused by unknown or unexpected factors.

Computer-based technology has the potential to support learners in conducting all aspects of scientific investigations. Computers, Internet access, and other widely available technologies are used in the examples above and can facilitate a broad and diverse array of investigations and design challenges by providing the means to quickly collect and analyze data, share results, and access additional data and information. The interactive features of computer-based technology have the capabilities to capture, display, and analyze data and information. Traditional formats can, of course, be used for analyzing and displaying information and are a key part of investigation and design. Learners can also use computer-based technologies to explore various complex aspects of science, including building, testing, and revising models; collecting, analyzing, and representing data; and finding, sharing, and presenting information (Krajcik and Mun, 2014). New computer-based technology tools can also scaffold learners in planning and conducting investigations (Quintana et al., 2004).

Portable technologies, including interactive tablets and cell phones, can support students conducting investigations in the field, allowing for more authentic investigations (Tinker and Krajcik, 2001). The flexibility, interactive power and networking capabilities, customization, and multiple representation functionality of computer-based tools, including portable technologies, will change the structure of science classrooms and how students engage in doing investigations. Instead of students receiving information from teachers or computer applications, students can use computer-based technology tools to take part in making sense of phenomena or solving design challenges by building models and developing explanations using evidence. Students and teachers can use tablets and other mobile devices with ubiquitous information access from cloud technologies to support students in the collection, organization, and analysis of data. They can then use these data to support the development of scientific explanations.

The full potential to promote student learning using new technology tools can only be realized when they are used in ways to support learning to do tasks that cannot be accomplished without them. For example, students can use simulations to explore and visualize the atomic world and the forces that hold atoms together.[7] When technology is used to carry out investigations that could have been done with real materials (such as a titration lab), the learning gains are less clear.

Computer-based technologies that have been designed to support students in learning have been referred to as "learning technology" (Krajcik and Mun, 2014; Krajcik et al., 2000). Learning technologies can serve as powerful tools that help learners meet important learning goals and engage in various scientific practices. But not all learning technologies are designed to support students in conducting scientific investigation. E-books that are a digital representation of a classical textbook might have certain features to support student learning, but they typically do not support learners in conducting scientific investigations.

Tools exist that are not necessarily designed to support students conducting investigations, but that can serve that purpose in the hands of skillful teacher. For example, spreadsheets can accomplish a number of challenging tasks that can be used to promote scientific investigations. Although not designed for classrooms, spreadsheets can facilitate scientific investigations by organizing and analyzing data and presenting data in graphical form. The use of presentation tools is another example. Presentation tools allow learners to create multimedia documents to share the results of their investigations. Multimedia documents can be critiqued and shared and serve to make students' thinking visible.

Computer-based technology tools support students in scientific investigation by promoting access and collect a range of scientific data and information. Krajcik and Mun (2014) discussed several ways in which computer-based technology tools allow and support students in scientific explanations: (1) use visualization, interactive, and data analysis tools; (2) collaborate and share information across remote sites; (3) plan, build, and test models; (4) develop multimedia documents that illustrate student understanding (Novak and Krajcik, 2004); (5) access information and data when needed; and (6) use remote tools to collect and analyze data. These features support students in conducting scientific investigation by expanding the range of questions that students can investigate and the variety

---

[7] See the Next Generation Molecular Workbench from the Concord Consortium at http:// mw.concord.org/nextgen/ [October 2018].

and type of phenomena and challenges that students can experience and explain.

Computer-based tools by themselves will not necessarily support learning or students' engagement in three-dimensional learning. However, when they are embedded within a learning environment in a manner that supports learners in answering meaningful questions, making sense of phenomena, and finding solutions to challenges in ways that support clear and specified learning goals, they can support students in three-dimensional learning. Scaffolds can be provided to support students in being successful with challenging tasks.

Research has also shown the critical role of cognitive tools in learning (Salomon, Perkins, and Globerson, 1991; Jonassen, 1995). Computer applications, such as databases, spreadsheets, networks, and multimedia/hypermedia construction, can function as computer-based cognitive tools with the role of an intellectual supporter to facilitate the cognitive process. With appropriate supports and instructional components, cognitive tools can amplify and expand what students can do in constructing knowledge (Jonassen, 1995). For example, the periodic table serves as a cognitive tool for many chemists as it represents important ideas and relationships about the properties of matter that chemists can use to make predictions. The chemist understands the underlying ideas and how to apply those ideas. Unfortunately, in school, the periodic table is often seen as something to memorize. However, for computer applications to promote learning, instruction needs to be designed around the relationships and use of core ideas.

Various forms of computer applications also serve as cognitive tools because they allow learners to carry out tasks not possible without the application's assistance and support. For instance, new forms of computer software allow learners to visualize complex datasets and interact with visualizations that show underlying mechanisms that explain phenomena (Edelson and Reiser, 2006; Linn and Elyon, 2011). In addition, many eLearning environments provide prompts to promote student reflection of the learning process, such as the WISE[8] project (Slotta and Linn, 2009).

TEACHER INVOLVEMENT IN THE DEVELOPMENT OF INSTRUCTIONAL RESOURCES

Designing quality instructional resources requires time, effort, intention, and different types of expertise. Instructional materials are strongest

---

[8] Web-based Inquiry Science offers a collection of free, customizable curriculum projects on topics central to the science standards as well as guidance for teachers on how these Internet-based projects can be used to improve learning and instruction in their science classrooms (grades 6-12).

when they have been developed by teams that include classroom teachers, content experts, and other experts as needed. Many classroom teachers do not have the time to design the instructional materials to support all of their classes, but they have expertise that is critical to designing materials that are effective in supporting students' sense-making. Likewise, content experts may have deep understanding of the core ideas, crosscutting concepts, and science and engineering practices, and they can identify common and persistent misconceptions and alternate conceptions that should be acknowledged in instruction (and may be educative for the teachers). Others can bring technical expertise in designing simulations and illustrations and in assembling a coherent set of investigations.

Development of a high-quality sequence of instructional resources requires significant work from a team that includes or has access to multiple types of expertise. For example, the team might include an expert in the science to be learned, in instruction for three-dimensional learning goals, in grade-level-appropriate expectations of students and their interests, in equity and inclusion for science and engineering learning, and in assessment of student learning. Instructional materials should also be designed against a rubric to meet clear goals. As highlighted earlier in this chapter, the EQuiP rubric (Achieve, 2016) provides one example that can guide materials development to align with the Next Generation Science Standards and other *Framework*-based standards and supplements. An iterative process of development allows materials to be tested in the classroom and modified as needed based on their initial use and provides teachers, principals, and districts with confidence that materials can be effectively implemented in their classrooms.

INSTRUCTIONAL RESOURCES
AND PROFESSIONAL LEARNING

To be effective, instructional resources need to be bundled with professional learning for teachers, along with assessment activities, into an integrated "curricular activity system" (Roschelle, Knudsen, and Hegedus, 2010). Of particular importance is professional learning that helps teachers to discern underlying purposes and structures of the instructional resources, so that when they select and adapt resources, they do so with integrity to the coherence of the resources (Davis and Varma, 2008). Professional learning that supports teachers in critically evaluating instructional resources to ensure that they align with classroom goals and use three-dimensional approaches to student learning is crucial.

In addition, professional learning works best when it is closely tied to what teachers will be expected to do to support students' productive disciplinary engagement with activities that are part of the resources: that is, focused on the content of the unit, its underlying theory of how to develop student understanding, and pedagogical strategies hypothesized to support learning in the unit (Ball and Cohen, 1999). Some supports for teacher learning are integrated into resources themselves, in which they support teacher learning of new practices, content, and/or resources. Instructional resources, as concrete reflections of the way instructional shifts can play out in teacher moves and in student work, are a key component of helping teachers shift their practice (Ball and Cohen, 1996; Remillard and Heck, 2014). Instructional resources that incorporate resources to support teacher learning are called *educative curriculum materials* (Davis and Krajcik, 2005). Their purpose is to help guide teachers in making instructional decisions—such as how to respond to different student ideas—when using the resources. These resources and other types of professional learning are discussed in further detail in Chapter 7.

SUMMARY

How phenomena and challenges are treated in *Framework*-aligned classrooms requires a key instructional shift in both instructional resources and teaching. Phenomena and challenges need to shift from illustrations or applications of science ideas that students have already been taught to contexts that raise questions or challenges in which students develop, reason through, and utilize these ideas to explain phenomena or develop solution to challenges. When instructional resources provide a variety of carefully chosen phenomena and design challenges, teachers can select and adapt phenomena and design challenges that are best suited to their students' backgrounds, prior knowledge and experiences, and culture and place. Instructional resources provide support to teachers in crucial areas, such as scope, sequencing, and coherence of investigation and design, gathering and use of data, and the role and use of technology. These resources can facilitate three-dimensional learning, offer phenomena that are relevant to students, support the use of data as evidence, and support development of argument for how evidence supports an explanation or design solution. They can integrate supports for equitable participation and for assessment and provide an expectation that students will apply learning to novel phenomena and design challenges beyond the classroom.

REFERENCES

Achieve. (2016). *Educators Evaluating the Quality of Instructional Products (EQuIP) Rubric for Science, Version 3.0.* Available: http://www.nextgenscience.org/sites/default/files/EQuIP Rubric for Sciencev3.pdf [October 2018].
Aikenhead, G.S. (2001). Integrating western and aboriginal sciences: Cross-cultural science teaching. *Research in Science Education, 31*(3), 337–355.

American Association for the Advancement of Science. (2001). *Atlas of Scientific Literacy.* Washington, DC: Author.

American Association for the Advancement of Science. (2007). *Atlas of Scientific Literacy* (vol. 2). Washington, DC: Author.

Bathgate, M., and Schunn, C.D. (2017). Factors that deepen or attenuate decline of science utility value during the middle school years. *Contemporary Educational Psychology, 49,* 215–225.

Ball, D.L., and Cohen, D.K. (1996). Reform by the book: What is—or might be—the role of curriculum materials in teacher learning and instructional reform? *Educational Researcher, 25*(9), 6–8.

Ball, D.L., and Cohen, D.K. (1999). Developing practice, developing practitioners: Toward a practice-based theory of professional education. In G. Sykes and L. Darling-Hammond (Eds.), *Teaching as the Learning Profession: Handbook of Policy and Practice* (pp. 3–32). San Francisco: Jossey Bass.

Bang, M., and Medin, D. (2010). Cultural processes in science education: Supporting the navigation of multiple epistemologies. *Science Education, 94*(6), 1008–1026. doi:10.1002/sce.20392.

Berland, L.K., Schwarz, C.V., Krist, C., Kenyon, L., Lo, A.S., and Reiser, B. J. (2016). Epistemologies in practice: Making scientific practices meaningful for students. *Journal of Research in Science Teaching, 53*(7), 1082–1112. doi: 10.1002/tea.21257.

Blumenfeld, P., and Krajcik, J.S. (2006). Project-based learning. In R.K. Sawyer (Ed.), *The Cambridge Handbook of the Learning Sciences* (pp. 333–354). New York: Cambridge University Press.

Blumenfeld, P., Soloway, E., Marx, R., Krajcik, J.S., Guzdial, M., and Palincsar, A. (1991). Motivating project-based learning: Sustaining the doing, supporting the learning. *Educational Psychologist, 26*(3 & 4), 369–398.

Bricker, L.A., and Bell, P. (2014). "What comes to mind when you think of science? The perfumery!": Documenting science-related cultural learning pathways across contexts and timescales. *Journal of Research in Science Teaching, 51*(3), 260–285. doi: 10.1002/tea.21134.

Brown, B.A., and Spang, E. (2008). Double talk: Synthesizing everyday and science language in the classroom. *Science Education, 92,* 708–732.

Bruner, J.S. (1960). *The Process of Education: A Searching Discussion of School Education Opening New Paths to Learning and Teaching.* Cambridge, MA: Harvard University Press.

BSCS. (2017). *Guidelines for the Evaluation of Instructional Materials in Science.* Colorado Springs, CO: Author.

Burgstahler, S. (2012). *Making Science Labs Accessible to Students with Disabilities: Application of Universal Design to a Science Lab. (DO-IT)—Disabilities, Opportunities, Internetworking and Technology.* University of Washington, College of Engineering. Available: https://www.washington.edu/doit/sites/default/files/atoms/files/Making-Science-Labs-Accessible-Students-Disabilities.pdf [October 2018].

Buxton, C.A., Allexsaht-Snider, M., Suriel, R., Kayumova, S., Choi, Y.-J., Bouton, B., and Baker, M. (2013). Using educative assessments to support science teaching for middle school English-language learners. *Journal of Science Teacher Education, 24*(2), 347–366.

Calabrese Barton, A., Koch, P.D., Contento, I.R., and Hagiwara, S. (2005). From global sustainability to inclusive education: Understanding urban children's ideas about the food system. *International Journal of Science Education, 27*(10), 1163–1186.

Cassel, B., and Topi, H. (2015). *Strengthening Data Science Education through Collaboration.* Workshop report 7-27-2016. Arlington, VA. Available: http://computingportal.org/sites/default/files/Data%20Science%20Education%20Workshop%20Report%201.0_0.pdf [October 2018].

Center for Universal Design. (1997). *Seven Principles of Universal Design for Learning*. Raleigh, NC: North Carolina State University.

Chick, H., Pfannkuch, M., and Watson, J.M. (2005). Transnumerative thinking: Finding and telling stories within data. *Curriculum Matters, 1*, 87–109.

Ching, C.C., Schaefer, S., and Lee, V. E. (2014). Identities in motion, identities at rest: Engaging bodies and minds in fitness gaming research and design. In *Learning Technologies and the Body: Integration and Implementation in Formal and Informal Learning Environments* (pp. 201–219). New York: Routledge, Taylor & Francis Group.

Ching, C.C., Stewart, M.K., Hagood, D.E., and Rashedi, R.N. (2016). Representing and reconciling personal data and experience in a wearable technology gaming project. *IEEE Transactions on Learning Technologies, 9*(4), 342–353.

Crismond, D., and Adams, R. (2012). The informed design teaching and learning matrix. *Journal of Engineering Education, 101*(4), 738–797.

Crowley, K., Barron, B.J.S., Knutson, K., and Martin, C.K. (2015). Interest and the development of pathways to science. In K.A. Renninger, M. Nieswandt, and S. Hidi (Eds.), *Interest in Mathematics and Science Learning and Related Activity* (pp. 297–313). Washington, DC: American Educational Research Association.

Davis, E.A., and Krajcik, J.S. (2005). Designing educative curriculum materials to promote teacher learning. *Educational Researcher, 34*(3), 3–14.

Davis, E.A., and Varma, K. (2008). Supporting teachers in productive adaptation. In Y. Kali, M.C. Linn, and J.E. Roseman (Eds.), *Designing Coherent Science Education* (pp. 94–122). New York: Teachers College Press.

DeBarger, A.H., Penuel, W.R., Harris, C.J., and Schank, P. (2010). Teaching routines to enhance collaboration using classroom network technology. In F. Pozzi and D. Persico (Eds.), *Techniques for Fostering Collaboration in Online Learning Communities: Theoretical and Practical Perspectives* (pp. 224–244). Hershey, PA: Information Science Reference.

DeBarger, A.H., Penuel, W.R., Moorthy, S., Beauvineau, Y., Kennedy, C.A., and Boscardin, C.K. (2017). Investigating purposeful science curriculum adaptation as a strategy to improve teaching and learning. *Science Education, 101*(1), 66–98. doi: 10.1002/sce.21249.

diSessa, A.A., and Minstrell, J. (1998). Cultivating conceptual change with benchmark lessons. In J.G. Greeno and S.V. Goldman (Eds.), *Thinking Practices in Mathematics and Science Learning* (pp. 155–187). Mahwah, NJ: Lawrence Erlbaum Associates.

Duerstock, B. (2018). *Inclusion of Students with Disabilities in the Lab*. The American Physiological Society. Available: http://www.the-aps.org/forum-disabilities [October 2018].

Duncan, R., Krajcik, J., and Rivet, A. (2016). *Disciplinary Core Ideas: Reshaping Teaching and Learning*. Arlington, VA: National Science Teachers Association Press.

Duschl, R. (2008). Science education in 3-part harmony: Balancing conceptual, epistemic and social learning goals. *Review of Research in Education, 32*, 268–291.

Duschl, R., and Gitomer, D. (1997). Strategies and challenges to changing the focus of assessment and instruction in science classrooms. *Educational Assessment, 4*(1), 37–73.

Edelson, D.C. (2001). Learning-for-use: A framework for integrating content and process learning in the design of inquiry activities. *Journal of Research in Science Teaching, 38*(3), 355–385.

Edelson, D.C., and Reiser, B.J. (2006). Making authentic practices accessible to learners: Design challenges and strategies. In R.K. Sawyer (Ed.), *The Cambridge Handbook of the Learning Sciences* (pp. 335–354). Cambridge, UK: Cambridge University Press.

Greene, K. (2016). For sale: Your lesson plans. *Educational Leadership, 74*(2), 28–33.

Hammer, D., and Elby, A. (2003). Tapping epistemological resources for learning physics. *Journal of the Learning Sciences, 12*(1), 53–90.

Harris, C.J., Penuel, W.R., DeBarger, A., D'Angelo, C., and Gallagher, L.P. (2014). *Curriculum Materials Make a Difference for Next Generation Science Learning: Results from Year 1 of a Randomized Control Trial.* Menlo Park, CA: SRI International.

Harris, C.J., Penuel, W.R., D'Angelo, C.M., DeBarger, A.H., Gallagher, L.P., et al. (2015). Impact of project-based curriculum materials on student learning in science: Results of a randomized controlled trial. *Journal of Research in Science Teaching, 52*(10), 1362–1385. doi: 10.1002/tea.21263.

Hsi, S., Hardy, L., and Farmer, T. (2017). Science thinking for tomorrow today. *@Concord, 21*(2), 10–11.

Hudicourt-Barnes, J. (2003). The use of argumentation in Haitian Creole science classrooms. *Harvard Educational Review, 73*(1), 73–93.

Hug, B., and McNeill, K.L. (2008). Use of first-hand and second-hand data in science: Does data type influence classroom conversations? *International Journal of Science Education, 30*(13), 1725–1751. doi: 10.1080/09500690701506945.

Hunter, L.J., and Hall, C.M. (2018). A survey of K-12 teachers' utilization of social networks as a professional resource. *Education and Information Technologies, 1–26.* doi: 10.1007/s10639-017-9627-9.

Jonassen, D. (1995). Computers as cognitive tools: Learning with technology, not from technology. *Journal of Computing in Higher Education, 6,* 40. doi: 10.1007/BF02941038.

Kamarainen, A.M., Metcalf, S., Grotzer, T., Browne, A., Mazzuca, D., Tutwiler, M.S., and Dede, C. (2013). EcoMOBILE: Integrating augmented reality and probeware with environmental education field trips. *Computers & Education, 68*(Supplement C), 545–556. doi: 10.1016/j.compedu.2013.02.018.

Kanter, D.E. (2010). Doing the project and learning the content: Designing project-based science curricula for meaningful understanding. *Science Education, 94*(3), 525–551.

Kerlin, S.C., McDonald, S.P., and Kelly, G.J. (2010). Complexity of secondary scientific data sources and students' argumentative discourse. *International Journal of Science Education, 32*(9), 1207–1225.

Kesidou, S., and Roseman, J.E. (2002). How well do middle school science programs measure up? Findings from Project 2061's curriculum review. *Journal of Research in Science Teaching, 39*(6), 522–549.

Klopfer, E., Yoon, S.A., and Perry, J. (2005). *Using Palm Technology in Participatory Simulations of Complex Systems: A New Take on Ubiquitous and Accessible Mobile Computing.* Available: https://repository.upenn.edu/gse_pubs/54 [October 2018].

Krajcik, J., and Mamlok-Naaman, R. (2006). Using driving questions to motivate and sustain student interest in learning science. In K. Tobin (Ed.), *Teaching and Learning Science: A Handbook* (pp. 317–327). Westport, CT: Praeger.

Krajcik, J.S., and Mun, K. (2014). Promises and challenges of using learning technologies to promote student learning of science. In *Handbook of Research on Science Education* 2 (pp. 337–360). New York: Routledge, Taylor & Francis, Group.

Krajcik, J., Blumenfeld, B., Marx, R. and Soloway. E. (2000). Instructional, curricular, and technological supports for inquiry in science classrooms. In J. Minstell and E. Van Zee (Eds.), *Inquiry into Inquiry: Science Learning and Teaching* (pp. 283–315). Washington, DC: American Association for the Advancement of Science Press.

Krajcik, J.S., Codere, S., Dahsah, C., Bayer, R., and Mun, K. (2014). Planning instruction to meet the intent of the Next Generation Science Standards. *Journal of Science Teacher Education, 25*(2), 157–175. doi:10.1007/s10972-014-9383-2.

Lee, O., and Buxton, C. A. (2008). Science curriculum and student diversity: Culture, language, and socioeconomic status. *Elementary School Journal, 109*(2), 123–137.

Lee, O., Quinn, H., and Valdés, G. (2013). Science and language for English language learners in relation to Next Generation Science Standards and with implications for Common Core State Standards for English language arts and mathematics. *Educational Researcher, 42*(4), 223–233. doi: 10.3102/0013189X13480524.

Lee, V.R., and DuMont, M. (2010). An exploration into how physical activity data-recording devices could be used in computer-supported data investigations. *International Journal of Computers for Mathematical Learning, 15*(3), 167–189. doi: 10.1007/s10758-010-9172-8.

Lee, V.R., Drake, J., and Williamson, K. (2015). Let's get physical: K-12 Students using wearable devices to obtain and learn about data from physical activities. *TechTrends, 59*(4), 46–53. doi: 10.1007/s11528-015-0870-x.

Lee, V.R., Drake, J.R., and Thayne, J.L. (2016). Appropriating quantified self technologies to improve elementary statistical teaching and learning. *IEEE Transactions on Learning Technologies, 9*(4), 354–365. doi: 10.1109/TLT.2016.2597142.

Linn, M., and Eylon, B. (2011). *Science Learning and Instruction: Taking Advantage of Technology to Promote Knowledge Integration.* New York: Routledge.

Linn, M.C., Layman, J., and Nachmias, R. (1987). Cognitive consequences of microcomputer-based laboratories: Graphing skills development. *Journal of Contemporary Educational Psychology, 12,* 244–253.

Lyons, L. (2014). Exhibiting data: Using body-as-interface designs to engage visitors with data visualizations. In V.R. Lee (Ed.), *Learning Technologies and the Body: Integration and Implementation in Formal and Informal Learning Environments* (pp. 185–200). New York: Routledge.

Martin, F., Kuhn, S., Scribner-MacLean, M., Corcoran, C., Dalphond, J., Fertitta, J., et al. (2010). iSENSE: A web environment and hardware platform for data sharing and citizen science. In *2010 AAAI Spring Symposium Series.* Available: https://www.aaai.org/ocs/index.php/SSS/SSS10/paper/download/1099/1394 [October 2018].

Metcalf, S.J., and Tinker, R. (2004). Probeware and handhelds in elementary and middle school science. *Journal of Science Education and Technology, 13*(1), 43–49.

Minstrell, J. (1992). Facets of students' knowledge and relevant instruction. In F. Duit, F. Goldberg, and H. Niedderer (Eds.), *Research in Physics Learning: Theoretical Issues and Empirical Studies* (pp. 110–128). Kiel, Germany: IPN.

Moulding, B., Bybee, R., and Paulson, N. (2015). *A Vision and Plan for Science Teaching and Learning.* Essential Teaching and Learning PD, LLC.

National Research Council. (2000). *How People Learn: Brain, Mind, Experience, and School. Expanded Edition.* Washington, DC: National Academy Press.

National Research Council. (2006). *America's Lab Report: Investigations in High School Science.* Washington, DC: The National Academies Press.

National Research Council. (2007). *Taking Science to School.* Washington, DC: The National Academies Press

National Research Council. (2012). *A Framework for K-12 Science Education: Practices, Crosscutting Concepts, and Core Ideas.* Washington, DC: The National Academies Press.

Novak, A., and Krajcik, J.S. (2004). Using learning technologies to support inquiry in middle school science. In L. Flick and N. Lederman (Eds.), *Scientific Inquiry and Nature of Science: Implications for Teaching, Learning, and Teacher Education* (pp. 75–102). The Netherlands: Kluwer.

Osborne, J.F., and Quinn, H. (2017). The framework, the NGSS, and the practices of science. In C.V. Schwarz, C.M. Passmore, and B.J. Reiser (Eds.), *Helping Students Make Sense of the World Through Next Generation Science and Engineering Practices* (pp. 23–31). Arlington, VA: NSTA Press.

Penuel, W.R., and Shepard, L.A. (2016). Assessment and teaching. In D.H. Gitomer and C.A. Bell (Eds.), *Handbook of Research on Teaching* (pp. 787–851). Washington, DC: AERA.

Penuel, W.R., Van Horne, K., Jacobs, J., Sumner, T., Watkins, D., and Quigley, D. (2017). *Developing NGSS-Aligned Curriculum that Connects to Students' Interests and Experiences: Lessons Learned from a Co-design Partnership.* Paper presented at the NARST, San Antonio, TX.

Powers, A.L. (2004). An evaluation of four place-based education programs. *The Journal of Environmental Education, 35*(4), 17–32.

Quintana, C., Reiser, B.J., Davis, E.A., Krajcik, J., Fretz, E., Duncan, R.G., Kyza, E., Edelson, D., and Soloway, E. (2004). A scaffolding design framework for software to support science inquiry. *Journal of the Learning Sciences, 13*(3), 337–386.

Reiser, B.J., Novak, M., and McGill, T.A.W. (2017). *Coherence from the Students' Perspective: Why the Vision of the Framework for K-12 Science Requires More than Simply "Combining" Three Dimensions of Science Learning.* Paper commissioned for the Board On Science Education Workshop Instructional Materials for the Next Generation Science Standards. Available: http://sites.nationalacademies.org/cs/groups/dbassesite/documents/webpage/dbasse_180270.pdf [October 2018].

Remillard, J.T., and Heck, D. (2014). Conceptualizing the curriculum enactment process in mathematics education. *ZDM: The International Journal on Mathematics Education, 46*(5), 705–718.

Rivera-Pelayo, V., Zacharias, V., L., and Braun, S. (2012). Applying quantified self approaches to support reflective learning. In *Proceedings of the 2nd International Conference on Learning Analytics and Knowledge* (pp. 111–114). New York: ACM. Available: http://dl.acm.org/citation.cfm?id=2330631 [October 2018]

Roschelle, J., Knudsen, J., and Hegedus, S.J. (2010). From new technological infrastructures to curricular activity systems: Advanced designs for teaching and learning. In M.J. Jacobson and P. Reimann (Eds.), *Designs for Learning Environments of the Future: International Perspectives from the Learning Sciences* (pp. 233–262). New York: Springer.

Rose, D.H., and Meyer, A. (2002). *Teaching Every Student in the Digital Age: Universal Design for Learning.* Washington, DC: ASCD.

Rosebery, A., Ogonowski, M., DiSchino, M., and Warren, B. (2010). "The coat traps all your body heat": Heterogeneity as fundamental to learning. *The Journal of the Learning Sciences, 19*(3), 322–357.

Roseman, J.E., Stern, L., and Koppal, M. (2010). A method for analyzing the coherence of high school biology textbooks. *Journal of Research in Science Teaching, 47*(1), 47–70.

Ruiz-Primo, M.A., Shavelson, R.J., Hamilton, L.S., and Klein, S. (2002). On the evaluation of systemic science education reform: Searching for instructional sensitivity. *Journal of Research in Science Teaching, 39*(5), 369–393.

Salomon, G., Perkins, D.N., and Globerson, T. (1991). Partners in cognition: Extending human intelligence with intelligent technologies. *Educational Research, 20*, 2–9.

Sánchez Tapia, I., Krajcik, J., and Reiser, B.J. (2018). "We don't know what is the real story anymore": Curricular contextualization principles that support indigenous students in understanding natural selection. *Journal of Research in Science Teaching.* Available: https://onlinelibrary.wiley.com/doi/full/10.1002/tea.21422 [October 2018].

Schmidt, W.H., McKnight, C.C., and Raizen, S.A. (Eds.). (1997). *A Splintered Vision: An Investigation of U.S. Science and Mathematics Education.* Boston: Kluwer.

Schmidt, W.H., Wang, H.C., and McKnight, C.C. (2005). Curriculum coherence: An examination of us mathematics and science content standards from an international perspective. *Journal of Curriculum Studies, 37*(5), 525–559.

Senechal, E. (2007). Environmental justice in Egleston Square. In D. Gruenewald and G. Smith (Eds.), *Place-Based Education in an Era of Globalization: Local Diversity* (pp. 85–111). Mahwah, NJ: Erlbaum.

Slotta, J.D., and Linn, M.C. (2009). *WISE Science: Web-Based Inquiry in the Classroom*. New York: Teachers College Press.

Sobel, D. (2005). *Place-Based Education: Connecting Classrooms and Communities*. (2nd ed.) Great Barrington, MA: Orion Society.

Stern, L., and Roseman, J.E. (2004). Can middle-school science textbooks help students learn important ideas? Findings from Project 2061's curriculum evaluation study: Life science. *Journal of Research in Science Teaching, 41*(6), 538–568.

Struck, W., and Yerrick, R. (2010). The effect of data acquisition-probeware and digital video analysis on accurate graphical representation of kinetics in a high school physics class. *Journal of Science Education and Technology, 19*(2), 199–211.

Suriel, R.L., and Atwater, M.M. (2012). From the contribution to the action approach: White teachers' experiences influencing the development of multicultural science curricula. *Journal of Research in Science Teaching, 49*(10), 1271–1295.

Tinker, R., and Krajcik, J. (2001). *Portable Technologies: Science Learning in Context. Innovations in Science Education and Technology*. Hingham, MA: Kluwer Academic.

Wallis, J.C., Milojevic, S., and Borgman, C.L. (2006). The special case of scientific data sharing with education. *Proceedings of the American Society for Information Science and Technology, 43*(1), 1–13. Available: http://onlinelibrary.wiley.com/doi/10.1002/meet.14504301169/full [October 2018].

Wilkerson, M.H., and Laina, V. (n.d.). *Reasoning about Data, Context, and Chance through Storytelling with Repurposed Local Data*.

Wilkerson, M.H., Lanouette, K.A., Shareff, R.L., Erickson, T., Bulalacao, N., Heller, J., and Reichsman, F. (2018). Data transformations: Restructuring data for inquiry in a simulation and data analysis environment. In *Proceedings of ICLS 2018*. London, UK: ISLS.

Windschitl, M., and Thompson, J. (2013). The modeling toolkit: Making student thinking visible with public representations. *The Science Teacher, 80*(6), 63–69.

Windschitl, M., Thompson, J., and Braaten, M. (2008). Beyond the scientific method: Model-based inquiry as a new paradigm of preference for school science investigations. *Science Education, 92*(5), 941–967. doi: 10.1002/sce.20259.

Windschitl, M., Thompson, J., and Braaten, M. (2018). *Ambitious Science Teaching*. Cambridge, MA: Harvard Education Press.

Windschitl, M., Thompson, J., Braaten, M., and Stroupe, D. (2012). Proposing a core set of instructional practices and tools for teachers of science. *Science Education, 96*(5), 878–903.

Wyss, V.L., Heulskamp, D., and Siebert, C.J. (2012). Increasing middle school student interest in STEM careers with videos of scientists. *International Journal of Environmental and Science Education, 7*(4), 501–552.

Xie, C., Schimpf, C., Chao, J., Nourian, S., and Massicotte, J. (2018), Learning and teaching engineering design through modeling and simulation on a CAD platform. *Computer Applications in Engineering Education, 26*(4), 824–840. doi: 10.1002/cae.21920.

Zucker, A.A., Tinker, R., Staudt, C., Mansfield, A., and Metcalf, S. (2008). Learning science in grades 3–8 using probeware and computers: Findings from the TEEMSS II project. *Journal of Science Education and Technology, 17*(1), 42–48.

7

Preparing and Supporting Teachers to Facilitate Investigation

As student learning goals and the role of the teacher are changing (Chapters 4 and 5), so must professional learning for teachers. Teachers are one of the most important elements in the educational system for influencing student learning—more important than spending levels, class size, or student demographics (Center for Public Education, 2016; Darling-Hammond, 2000), and teachers need time and support to learn how to engage students in meaningful science investigation and engineering design. Likewise, other emerging bodies of research have linked teacher certification in school subjects, including science, to positively affecting student learning (National Academies of Sciences, Engineering, and Medicine, 2015; Neild, Farley-Ripple, and Byrnes, 2009). Therefore, a sustainable, highly qualified science and engineering teaching workforce is necessary.

The professional learning of teachers forms a continuum from preservice programs, including preservice clinical work (student teaching), to distinct summer and school-year professional development sessions, to formal and informal work between colleagues, to a teacher's experience in his or her classroom. As pointed out in *Science Teachers' Learning*, the value of what teachers learn in their classrooms on a daily basis has been underappreciated (Ball and Cohen, 1999; Ball and Forzani, 2011; Luft et al., 2015; National Academies of Sciences, Engineering, and Medicine, 2015). This professional learning continuum follows a trajectory in which educators move from seeing science with a student perspective to a teacher perspective to a leadership perspective, and it is essential for educators to improve their craft, deepen their knowledge, and become masterful teachers.

There has been a change in the landscape of professional learning for science teachers since the 2006 publication of *America's Lab Report* (National Research Council, 2006) and a new context for professional learning to prepare teachers for the specifics of centering classrooms around investigation and design. The first part of this chapter looks at what is happening now for preservice and in-service teachers, and the second part looks at modern ideas for professional learning to prepare teachers to engage students in investigation and design. Inclusive pedagogy is also addressed.

THE CURRENT STATE OF TEACHING
AND TEACHER LEARNING

We begin with exploring what is currently happening in preservice learning and in-service teaching. We then turn to discuss the ways in which science education and professional learning have changed and what teachers need for the classroom.

Preservice Teacher Learning

In 2013, the most recent year for which data are available, approximately 192,500 students completed a teacher preparation program of some sort, whether a bachelor's degree, master's degree, certification program (often a 1-year post-baccalaureate program), or an alternative pathway, such as Teach for America (National Research Council, 2010; U.S. Department of Education, 2013, 2016). A large majority—around 85 percent—completed "traditional" teacher preparation programs, primarily 4-year baccalaureate degree programs (U.S. Department of Education, 2013, 2016). Within traditional and alternative programs based at institutions of higher education, fewer than 5 percent of program completers studied to teach science. At the secondary level, 38 states plus the District of Columbia, Puerto Rico, Guam, Marshall Islands, and Northern Mariana Islands set teacher standards in science. However, only six states refer to the National Science Teachers Association (NSTA) standards and two to the National Science Education Standards (NSES) in developing their standards for teachers.

Teacher preparation programs vary significantly across the country, and requirements for teacher certification differ from state to state. Not all programs have content-specific or grade level-specific requirements for certification (National Research Council, 2010; U.S. Department of Education, 2013). The Department of Education reports that 20 states require a bachelor's degree in a content area for an initial credential at the middle school level, and 28 require such a degree at the secondary level. The 2012 National Survey of Science and Mathematics Education reveals that 41 percent of practicing middle school science teachers and 82 percent of high school science teachers have a degree in science/engineering or science education (Banilower et al., 2013).

Preservice preparation for teachers typically includes coursework in science and education, preservice clinical work, and some opportunities to experience doing science and engineering through undergraduate research or internships. The committee questioned to what extent these programs start to move future teachers towards expertise as we defined it above. Recent research around practice-based teacher preparation is showing the impact that new methodologies can have on new teacher practice (Beyer and Davis, 2012; Forzani, 2014; Luft and Dubois, 2017).

Content Preparation of Science and Engineering Teachers

Introductory college STEM courses provide most middle and high school teachers with their primary instructional models and experiences for building pedagogical approaches to science and engineering investigations. The large majority of middle and high school science teachers have taken at least one class in life sciences, chemistry, physics, earth and space science, and science education, while slightly more than one-half have taken a course in environmental science (Banilower et al., 2013). Coursework in engineering is rare among science teachers: only 7 percent of middle school science teachers and 14 percent of high school science teachers report having taken a class in engineering. High school science teachers are about twice as likely as middle school teachers to have taken one or more courses beyond the introductory level in chemistry and physics and equally likely to have taken courses beyond the introductory level in earth and space science; in addition, a large majority of middle and high school teachers have taken courses beyond the introductory level in life sciences (Banilower et al., 2013). The question remains about what is known about the nature of this undergraduate coursework and how well it matches the vision for three-dimensional teaching and learning described in *A Framework for K–12 Science Education* (hereafter referred to as the *Framework*; National Research Council, 2012). Most college courses are not designed to align with K–12 standards. Below, we explore the literature to understand what practices are used in courses across the disciplines more broadly.

As states adopt *Framework*-based standards, many also are updating or revising their standards for teacher certification that influence the design of teacher preparation programs. For example, the Professional Educator Standards Board (PESB) in Washington State adopted competencies for endorsement in science content areas that match the Next Generation Science Standards (NGSS). Teacher preparation programs impact how teachers view the goals of science education. Intentionally or not, courses and practica in these programs model science instruction teacher candidates will use in their own classrooms. Teacher preparation programs have a responsibility to be on the cutting edge of research-based instruction to produce candidates able to effectively engage students in three-dimensional science investigation and engineering design experiences—which can also mean working with colleagues in the science and engineering disciplines to modify instructional practice in disciplinary courses.

Special Science Courses for Teachers

Nearly 30 years ago, McDermott (1990) called for "special science courses for teachers" that should (1) emphasize the content that teachers are expected to teach, (2) emphasize the evidence and lines of reasoning that have allowed for the development of this knowledge, (3) cultivate quantitative and qualitative reasoning, (4) engage teachers in the scientific process, (5) develop teachers' communication skills, particularly formulating and using operational definitions, (6) identify common conceptual difficulties, and (7) help teachers make sound choices about instructional practices, including choosing curricular materials and prioritizing learning objectives.

Many universities that offer teacher preparation programs also offer specialized science courses for teachers. They are primarily designed for elementary education majors, however, and the research describing the effectiveness of these courses is largely limited to individual classes. In life sciences, these are described by Tessier (2010) and Weld and Funk (2005), both of whom showed gains in elementary education majors' perceptions of their own abilities to teach science and use inquiry-based techniques. Sanger (2008) compared two groups of students' views about teaching and learning science: a group of elementary education majors who had taken an inquiry-based chemistry course and a group of secondary science (chemistry) education majors who had taken only "regular" chemistry courses but were also taking a science methods course. Coded written reflections suggested that the inquiry-based courses had a profound effect on the elementary education majors and are likely to influence the way that they teach science, while the secondary science education majors described viewing the teacher and/or the textbook as the source of all knowledge in the classroom.

Despite the demonstrated effectiveness of these science courses for teachers at the elementary level, however, few changes have occurred in courses for middle and high school science teacher preparation. At some institutions, new approaches are being developed to examine how content-specific pedagogy courses for teachers might prepare science and engineering teacher candidates to facilitate science investigation and engineering design. For example, at the University of Colorado Boulder, teacher candidates in the CU Teach secondary science, engineering, and mathematics teacher preparation program are required to take two courses on teaching and learning in a discipline, such as Teaching and Learning Chemistry, Teaching and Learning Physics, or Teaching and Learning Earth Systems.

Undergraduate Science Courses

The life sciences dominate science teacher preparation. Ninety percent of elementary teachers, 96 percent of middle school science teachers, and 91 percent of high school science teachers have taken at least one college-level course in life sciences; 65 percent of middle and 79 percent of high school science teachers have taken one or more course beyond introductory life sciences (Banilower et al., 2013). A meta-analysis conducted by Beck et al. (2014) of 142 university-based studies published between 2005 and 2012 concluded that most laboratory activities that resemble the three-dimensional investigations described in the *Framework* occur in upper-level courses that preservice teachers may not take. Buck et al. (2008) analyzed laboratory manuals across multiple disciplines focusing on chemistry. Out of 386 experiments evaluated, only 26 (6%) were determined to be guided inquiry and only 5 experiments (1%) were open inquiry.

When future teachers enroll in geosciences courses, the material they learn does not correlate well with the type of earth and space sciences that they may be expected to teach in the future or with *Framework*-style teaching approaches. Budd et al. (2013) observed 26 faculty teaching 66 introductory physical geology classrooms at 11 different institutions of higher education that span the range of Carnegie institution types. They used the Reformed Teaching Observation Protocol (RTOP), which consists of 25 items grouped into five subscales that allow an observer to holistically assess the degree to which an instructor is using evidence-based practices during a particular class period. The total possible score is 100; typical scores fall in the range of 20 to 80. Lower scores indicate more teacher-centered instruction and higher scores indicate more learner-centered instruction. On the basis of RTOP scores, Budd et al. (2013) grouped instructors into teacher-centered (n = 8 [31%], RTOP ≤ 30), transitional (n = 9 [34.6%], 31 < RTOP < 49), and student-centered (n = 9 [34.6%], RTOP ≥ 49). More recently, Teasdale et al. (2017) expanded the use of the RTOP and found similar results; even in more student-centered classrooms, they found that the large majority of instructors spend less than one-half of class time on activities, questions, and discussion, and virtually all instructors use traditional lecture (to some extent) nearly every day in class. They also looked at student-student inter-actions in class—94 percent of teacher-centered classrooms and 42 percent of transitional classrooms had no student-student interaction at all. Egger et al. (2017) analyzed chapter titles in introductory geoscience textbooks and found little alignment between the content presented in traditional introductory geoscience courses and the disciplinary core ideas of the NGSS in earth and space science. In particular, the concept of sustainability, mentioned only in the earth and space science component of the *Framework*, is nearly absent from introductory textbooks.

Despite the fact that numerous undergraduate science teaching reform efforts and assessment instruments have emerged out of physics—including peer-led team learning (Zhang, Ding, and Mazur, 2017) and the Force Concept Inventory (Savinainen and Scott, 2002)—little discipline-wide research on what actually goes on in undergraduate physics courses exists. A study by Lund et al. (2015) combined the use of the RTOP and COPUS to measure the use of reformed instructional practices across all STEM disciplines at 28 research-intensive universities. Among the disciplines, engineering has the highest percentage of time spent in lecture during class periods (averaging 75% of time), followed by physics and chemistry (both around 65%). Neither physics nor engineering included any collaborative learning time. Stains et al. (2018) found that "didactic practices are prevalent throughout the STEM curriculum despite ample evidence for the limited impact of these practices . . ." (p. 1469). Although there are some undergraduate science classrooms that are attempting to model student-centered learning approaches (Herreid and Schiller, 2013), the collective findings of these reports indicate that university course work in science does not always provide prospective science teachers with models of the instructional strategies outlined in this report.

Undergraduate Research Experiences

Ideally, teacher candidates would have the opportunities to take science course work that is consistent with how they are expected to teach, serve as apprentices to gain authentic experiences both in the classroom as a teacher and as a scientist or engineer, and conduct research and engage in authentic science investigations and engineering challenges. Practicing scientists enter the laboratory or the field with a question—or many questions—to which they do not know the answer. Yet more than half of middle and high school science teachers agree or strongly agree with the statement that "hands-on/laboratory activities should be used primarily to reinforce a science idea that the students have already learned" (Banilower et al., 2013).

Undergraduate research has been described as a high-impact practice (Kuh, 2008). Current practice is described as "diverse and complex" in the 2017 National Academies report *Undergraduate Research Experiences for STEM Students: Successes, Challenges, and Opportunities*, which stated that more systematic study of the characteristics, impacts, and participants in undergraduate research experiences (UREs) is needed. What literature exists suggests that these experiences are a net benefit for students, and include *Framework*-aligned goals such as engaging students in arguing from evidence, a focus on significant and relevant problems, and an emphasis on collaboration and teamwork (National Academies of Sciences, Engineering, and Medicine, 2017).

It is difficult to assess the extent to which preservice teachers have the opportunity to engage in UREs, which may occur as part of their undergraduate major or as an optional summer experience. Seventy-eight percent of practicing high school science teachers have a degree in the natural sciences (Snyder, deBrey, and Dillow, 2016, Table 209.50). Russell et al. (2007) found that as many as half of all STEM majors engage in UREs, while only 1 in 15 is funded by programs through the National Science Foundation (NSF), National Institutes of Health, or others. These percentages may be lower for STEM majors who enter into the teaching profession, however, as many universities have different programs for students preparing to become teachers and students planning to pursue careers in science disciplines.

Some examples of programs that facilitate undergraduate research experiences for teachers are NSF's Robert Noyce Scholarship program (Mervis, 2015) and the Science Teacher and Researcher (STAR), a partnership between universities, K–12 districts, and national laboratories (Baker and Keller, 2010). STAR[1] recruits students who are enrolled in STEM teacher preparation and STEM programs and places them, for summer research experiences, primarily in national laboratories; they are also matched with a master teacher and a science education faculty mentor at the university.

In summary, there are several opportunities for preservice teachers to engage in authentic science investigations (and possibly authentic engineering design projects as well), but it is unclear what proportion of preservice teachers actually participate in these opportunities. Even more elusive is research that assesses the influence of these experiences on professional learning. As UREs become more widespread and integrated into the curriculum, teacher preparation programs may be able to capitalize on these efforts to support teacher development. Additional opportunities to help teachers embrace investigation and design concepts include nontraditional internships in which teachers work with scientists and engineers or they receive training through engineering and technical societies.

In-Service Teacher Learning

There are about 211,000 middle and high school science teachers in the United States (National Science Foundation, 2012, Appendix Table 1-10) although not all are qualified in the science subjects they teach (see Table 7-1; Gao et al., 2018). It is important to note that fully certified

---

[1] For more information, see http://star-web.cosam.calpoly.edu/about [October 2018].

TABLE 7-1 Science Teachers and Their Certifications (percentage certified listed by grade band and discipline taught)

	Grades 6–8	Grades 9–12
Any Science Certification	56.8–60.0	85.7–85.9
In Science Subject They Teach:		
Science, general	42.7	38.5
Biology/life sciences	33.2–47.5	75.0–80.0
Chemistry	32.4	59.3–69.8
Physics	9.2	47.8–60.8
Physical sciences	16.2–21.2	36.8–67.4
Earth sciences	20.2–22.6	35.0–62.5

SOURCE: National Academies of Sciences, Engineering, and Medicine (2015, p. 75, Table 4-1).

math and science teachers were less prevalent in high-poverty schools and those with large numbers of students from groups underrepresented in science and engineering in comparison to low-poverty schools and those with low numbers of students from groups underrepresented in science and engineering (National Science Board, 2018). In light of research showing the effect of teacher certification on student achievement (Mo, Singh, and Chang, 2013), this disparate distribution of fully certified science teachers is a contributing source to inequitable science education. Of note is that one-quarter of school districts in California reported lacking sufficient numbers of credentialed teachers to teach to the new standards reflected in the *Framework* (Gao et al., 2018).

Because engineering is relatively uncommon in middle and high school and there is much variation in how engineering is addressed in the curriculum, it is difficult to find systematic information about the engineering teaching workforce. Engineering teachers make up a small fraction of the nation's teaching force; estimates from the National Center for Education Statistics Schools and Staffing Survey place the number at 20,000 to 30,000—roughly an order of magnitude less than the number of science teachers (Aud et al., 2011). Most engineering courses and concepts are taught either by science teachers or technology education (also known as industrial arts) teachers. Yet, very few middle school science teachers (7%) or high school science teachers (14%) have taken at least one college course in engineering. Therefore, it is not surprising that fewer than 10 percent of middle and high school science teachers on a national survey report feeling "very well prepared" to teach engineering concepts (Banilower et al., 2013).

High voluntary turnover has also created staffing problems within schools in hiring quality science educators (Ingersoll, Merrill, and Stuckey, 2014). A national longitudinal study revealed that more than 41 percent of beginning teachers leave teaching within the first 5 years, and already difficult-to-staff schools (i.e., high-poverty, those with large numbers of students from groups underrepresented in science and engineering, urban, and rural) have the highest rates of turnover (Ingersoll et al., 2014). Research suggests that teacher effectiveness, as measured by gains in student performance, significantly increases with additional experience over the first several years of teaching; thus, many teachers are exiting the profession prior to fully developing their skills, which has major implications for the quality of science instruction (Ingersoll et al., 2014).

Attracting new and highly qualified science teachers remains difficult, and this reality is even more pronounced in high-poverty, large numbers of students from groups underrepresented in science and engineering, and urban districts, where new hires are more likely to lack practical teaching experience and/or certification in the subjects that they teach (Center for Public Education, 2016; Metz and Socol, 2017; National Academies of Sciences, Engineering, and Medicine, 2015). Nearly 500,000 students attend schools where less than 60 percent of teachers are certified, and students from historically underrepresented groups are more likely than white students to attend schools where more than 20 percent of the teaching staff are either inexperienced or uncertified/unlicensed (U.S. Department of Education, 2014). While schools and districts make many of the decisions about recruiting, hiring, and assigning teachers, state education officials are the gatekeepers of the data systems containing this information, and thus share in the critical role of addressing disparities in teacher quality (Metz and Socol, 2017).

In 2014, the Excellent Educators for All Initiative was created by the U.S. Department of Education to provide equal access to effective teachers to all students, and particularly to students at Title I schools (Center for Public Education, 2016). As part of this initiative, states proposed strategies to address inequities in teacher quality. An analysis of the state equity plans revealed that most states outlined broad efforts to raise overall teaching quality, and a few state plans included examples that could inform the work of other states to ensure equitable distribution of quality teachers among middle and high schools in America (Metz and Socol, 2017; Williams et al., 2016). These examples discuss (1) increasing transparency about student assignments and how these assignments impact student learning, (2) targeting more resources to high-needs districts and schools, and (3) fostering district-wide coherence for collaborative problem solving among leaders (Metz and Socol, 2017; Williams et al., 2016). The *Every Student Succeeds Act* affords new opportunities for state leaders to take stronger, equity-focused action in human capital management, providing all student groups with access to the best teachers as they engage in science investigation and engineering design.

Teacher Learning in School

Comprehensive and sustained professional development can help prepare teachers for implementing investigation and design. One-quarter of middle school science teachers and one-third of high school science teachers reportedly participate in sustained professional development (35 hours or more) over the course of 3 years (Banilower et al., 2013, p. 34, Table 3.3). Fifty-three percent of middle and high school teachers reported they had received less than 6 hours of professional development in science in the previous 3 years (Banilower et al., 2013). A lower percentage of teachers in lower-achieving schools reported receiving professional development on student-centered teaching than teachers in schools with higher achieving students (Banilower et al., 2013). Typically, schools provide time for professional development in science in the form of professional days during the school year, and a slightly smaller amount provide time outside of the school year (Banilower et al., 2013, p. 47, Table 3.27).

Additionally, teachers look for time to devote to joint planning with colleagues who face similar challenges and have similar teaching assignments, as well as time for individual planning and evaluating student work. Sustained joint planning time for all science teachers within a department facilitates the professional learning that is needed to support coherence across courses. Common planning time for teachers offered by schools can support professional learning communities (PLCs) (discussed in more detail below), yet science PLC/teacher study groups, in particular, are offered in less than 50 percent of middle and high schools (Banilower et al., 2013, p. 44, Table 3.21). When asked about factors affecting instruction, the afforded time to plan individually and with colleagues was reported to be beneficial in 58 percent of classes, but was an inhibitor toward science instruction in 25 percent of classes (Banilower et al., 2013, p. 120, Table 7.18). Although each middle and high school science department will manage these needs somewhat differently, it is essential that time for managing the "components" for investigations and design is recognized as an important part of a successful science program.

It can be challenging to find time for professional learning for in-service teachers. An added complication is that science teachers, along with art or shop teachers, have an additional responsibility to manage, maintain, and move around equipment and materials so that what is needed is appropriately set up in the classroom for every class. The time demands of set-up and breakdown work, as well as planning and ordering supplies, and ensuring maintenance and refurbishment of equipment, are considerations for teachers' schedules and do not always count as official work time. Some of these tasks, such as setting up carts with the equipment and materials for the next day's classes, could be fulfilled by a paraprofessional science aide, thereby freeing valuable time for the teacher to interact with students or other teachers or to reflect upon the day to optimize their practice.

Research Experiences for Teachers

Another set of professional learning opportunities is offered outside the school and district by universities, laboratories, and other educational organizations. Research Experiences for Teachers (RETs), for example, embed practicing (in-service) teachers in college or university research labs during the summer months to expose them to cutting-edge research, some of which might be translated to the classroom curriculum (Enderle et al., 2014; Faber et al., 2014; Klein-Gardner, Johnston, and Benson, 2012; Reynolds et al., 2009). RETs provide opportunities for teachers to not only observe the various roles of scientists and their community of post-docs and graduate students, but also participate in the research lab's interactions as a novice.

In a study of 14 high school teacher participants in a 6-week summer research program, Miranda and Damico (2013) reported significant changes in teacher beliefs after participating in a summer research experience. They noted in particular that all of the teacher participants recognized that their experiences of doing science were very different from the science learning in their classrooms, and several indicated that they planned to modify their activities to include more open and guided inquiry. The study stopped short, however, of assessing actual changes in practice.

The assumption that teachers' research experiences can be easily applied to middle and high school classrooms is naïve. Teachers must be given explicit opportunities for reflection about how and why science is conducted and how to replicate the science community in their classrooms. Unfortunately, when the team leading the RET lacks expertise in education, teachers may not be supported in making explicit reflections about how to connect their experiences to their teaching practice. As Lakatos (1970) opined, "Most scientists tend to understand little more *about* science than fish about hydrodynamics" (p. 148). As scientists are deeply immersed in their practice, they may be unable to help teachers understand the most important elements of conducting high-quality investigations.

The results of this albeit limited work suggests that few future or current teachers have the opportunity to engage in authentic research, and, of those who do take part in these experiences, few are supported in explicit reflections about how to connect their experiences to their teaching practice.

PREPARING TO TEACH INVESTIGATION AND DESIGN

As discussed throughout this report, the nature of the classroom experience and the role of the teacher are dramatically different in investigation and design, and teachers need multiple opportunities to experience it themselves, ideally from both a student perspective and from a teacher perspective. Providing educators with explicit strategies for adapting curriculum materials can help them to improve science teaching and learning (Penuel, Gallagher, and Moorthy, 2011).

Less-experienced educators may benefit most from intensive workshops, whereas educators with more implementation experience may learn more from opportunities to try new strategies in the classroom and discuss their efforts with colleagues (Frank et al., 2011). By preparing educators to productively adapt instructional strategies and materials rather than simply to implement them with fidelity, professional development can help educators feel ownership over reform and feel respected by professional development providers (DeBarger et al., 2013). During professional learning experiences, the teacher will be able to reflect and discuss with colleagues the process and the decision points and use their insights to continue to improve experiences for their students.

As discussed throughout this report (especially in Chapters 4, 5, and 6), many aspects of teaching investigation and design are relatively new for many teachers. These include the selection of a phenomenon or a design challenge, helping students develop models, and facilitating the communication of reasoning to themselves and others, which are addressed here. Data and technology in investigation and design are discussed below.

Choosing a phenomenon appropriate to the scientific topic under study and appropriate for the students is crucial to the learning experience. Often teachers less experienced with this approach will use instructional resources to help make an appropriate choice. As they gain experience, teachers will begin to notice patterns in what works well and to figure out how to appropriately select and problematize phenomena for use in the classroom. Professional development experiences that actively explore curriculum through investigation, problem solving, and discussion can help teachers to develop the skills needed to effectively evaluate and adapt materials for their own classroom needs (Banilower, Heck, and Weiss, 2007).

The extent to which teachers listen to and support student reasoning matters, and through this, they learn more about student thinking, about science, and, most importantly, how to support students' meaningful science learning in the classroom (Russ, Sherin, and Sherin, 2016). Making this change requires professional learning approaches that model the science learning experiences expected in teachers' classrooms and engages teachers in reflection on the mechanisms for positive changes they value and can enact. Research on professional learning has shown that helping educators develop content knowledge through recognizing patterns of student thinking can improve both teaching and learning outcomes (Heller et al., 2012) and that it can help prepare educators to give students greater agency, that is, choice and responsibility in planning investigations that address their questions (Morozov et al., 2014).

Professional learning can provide educators with concrete strategies for building on students' cultural and community funds of knowledge to guide science investigations (Tzou and Bell, 2010). Professional development can also promote equity when providers have high expectations for all students' learning and prepare educators to engage students in all aspects of inquiry (Jeanpierre, Oberhauser, and Freeman, 2005). Promoting equity entails paying explicit attention to historical inequities, which can help students identify with the enterprise of science (Bang and Medin, 2010). Designs for professional development can also prepare educators to use discussion to develop student ideas elicited from tasks and educator questions (Doubler et al., 2011; Harris, Phillips, and Penuel, 2012; Minstrell and van Zee, 2003)

Gather and Analyze Data and Information

Working with data is a key component of investigation and design. There are some special preparations necessary for teachers, especially in the area of digital data and technological tools. Probeware is one of the more established sources of digital data in science education, and consequently also has the longest history of research and practice related to teacher professional learning. Teachers' use of probeware as part of their preservice and in-service development appears favorable (Ensign, Rye, and Luna, 2017; Metcalf and Tinker, 2004). Teacher preparation programs and professional development experiences offering sustained involvement of teachers in using probeware through full cycles of inquiry rather than as brief, single-visit in-service demonstrations are likely to be more effective.

When teachers are working with data about and from students, they may find that they are in a position of restricted expertise. For instance, when students compare activity levels of groups of students during their lunch breaks, the students often have far more to say about what activities transpired at typical lunch times than the teachers do. This represents an important opportunity for teachers to let students lead and to ask questions of the students for greater precision about their claims and how their recollections of experience and numerical data align with one another. Teacher education activities with respect to these kinds of personal data have yet to be studied extensively, but one potential model is to have preservice teachers undergo their own inquiries with their own personal data collected through automated means and reflect upon what inferences and arguments they are inclined to make (Schneiter, Christensen, and Lee, 2018).

With networked sensing and potentially large data corpora, teachers may need to develop more familiarity with computational techniques for manipulating data. They also should be aware and help set expectations with students that much of the work with large data corpora includes "data cleaning" (i.e., practices that involve making sure data are structured appropriately and that some algorithmic errors are appropriately addressed). Teachers need ample experience working with computer-based simulations and learning about effective design and integration strategies and rationale for incorporating such simulations into larger classroom units (Lin and Fishman, 2004). It is also important for teachers to recognize that simulation environments may be effective for content knowledge learning but still require additional support for students to interpret and critique data that are produced within them. Also, to support students in constructing new forms of data-supported explanations and arguments from models that involve emergent processes or are highly probabilistic, teachers themselves could benefit from having models of what such explanations and arguments would look like and how they are constructed.

While teacher familiarity with simulations and algorithmically generated data represent important areas for future teacher learning, effective teaching practice with simulation data may involve the teacher being positioned as a member of the audience and a fellow learner rather than the expert on how a given simulation works (Grimm et al., 2005). Thus, making sense of what simulations can actually tell students is a matter of collaborative meaning-making among peers (Chandrasekharan and Nersessian, 2015) such as simulation models of complex systems and video games for scientific discovery (Foldit, EteRNA etc.. Teachers should foreground questions of what role simulations play as tools for experimentation and model-based reasoning alongside argumentation, observation, measurement, and so forth (Greca, Seoane, and Arriassecq, 2014).

Teachers should be aware of the appeal and high levels of engagement that accompany the use of video, images, and spatial data in middle and high school classrooms. This can lead to active and enthusiastic participation from students, but increased participation may not lead to learning targeted scientific practices. It becomes incumbent on the teacher to model for students how to examine and inspect such data and to utilize scaffolds, whether they are embedded in a tool, curriculum, or in teacher actions, to guide students. Professional development experiences that help teachers notice student thinking as it relates to the content and practices that are targeted may help teachers best support students' use of such data in the classroom (Sherin and Van Es, 2009).

As with other emerging forms of data, we expect that one critical component of teacher learning related to public datasets and data visualizations lies in developing teachers' experience and comfort with these artifacts. Preliminary work by Lee and Wilkerson (commissioned paper) with teachers found that providing case-study examples (through video or transcript) of students reasoning through complex datasets and visualizations can be inspiring and motivating for teachers. Drawing from known findings in more established areas such as probeware and simulations, we expect that providing teachers with opportunities to engage with data and visualizations as a part of their own inquiry, as well as helping them to "step back" and understand these resources as sources of information rather than as objective truth, can also be effective. Given the novelty of complex data and visualizations in the classroom, and their primarily *supportive* role as resources embedded within larger, goal-oriented inquiry or modeling activity, this is also an area that may benefit from educative curriculum materials (Davis, Palincsar, and Arias, 2014) that support teacher learning at the same time as they support instruction. This could take the form, for instance, of specialized annotations and images of classroom interactions around visualizations embedded in curriculum materials. Certainly, however, more research is needed in this area.

Technology

Many aspects of using technology for investigation and design were discussed above in the context of data use. Another aspect of technology is the potential to use it for professional learning itself. The capacity to use video-conferencing software is nearly ubiquitous with current computer cameras, and many online tools are available with high-definition resolution, quality audio, and supplementary tools. Video-conferencing programs allow teachers who cannot meet in person to share scanned images of student work, play videos, or review digital copies of lesson plans and student tasks. Although unique online group norms must be established, video conferencing provides a legitimate PLC experience for isolated science teachers.

Whether in person or through video conferencing, video-capture software and multimedia digital portfolios can provide the raw materials for analysis and reflection in PLCs. Video capture software allows teachers to film their classroom while introducing a phenomenon or eliciting questions for students that are worthy of exploration. Many video-capture systems also include annotation systems that allow the teacher, a coach, or the PLC to watch the video ahead of time and raise questions, suggest changes, or highlight effective moves. These tools can streamline PLC meetings so that time can be focused on growth and not on watching the video during the limited synchronous meeting time. Unlike video-conferencing tools, however, most current video-capture and annotation systems are currently more costly.

Multimedia portfolio tools may provide a more cost-effective alternative. Electronic portfolios have been shown to aid teacher growth through the collection of artifacts that reflect teacher practice and student engagement (Stefani, Mason, and Pegler, 2007).[2] More contemporary digital portfolios, created as tablet-based applications, expand on the types of artifacts collected from classrooms, including images of classroom space, short videos of student and teacher interactions, digital versions of lesson plans, and scanned images of student work and teacher feedback. In combination with PLCs, these digital tools may provide the structure and support necessary to change how investigations are facilitated in middle and high school classrooms.

CHANGES IN THE LANDSCAPE OF PROFESSIONAL LEARNING

Professional learning across all stages of the teacher development continuum can be guided by the same theories of learning that guide the conceptualization of what students should be able to do in classrooms, described in *How People Learn* (National Research Council, 1999) and *A Framework for K–12 Education* (National Research Council, 2012) and discussed in Chapter 3 of this report. Indeed, these foundational theories describe learning as a fundamental process of human development at all ages, not just for children (e.g., Wenger, 1998). Putnam and Borko (2000) encouraged the field to consider what these conceptualizations of learning implied for the ways to think about and design for learning. Like the way to think about learning in schools for children, our committee considers teachers as participants in a multifaceted system of activity that involves contexts, tools, multiple roles, and changes in practice over time. This assertion is consistent with the theoretical framing used previously in this report to describe what students know and are able to do. This experiential view of learning helps shift the focus of professional learning from teacher knowledge to enacting professional learning experiences that are centered on engaging educators in science investigation and engineering design to build the context for learning.

This way of thinking about professional learning is a shift from the approach taken by *America's Lab Report* (National Research Council, 2006). The 2006 report defined four realms of knowledge for teachers—science content knowledge, pedagogical content knowledge (PCK), general

---

[2] For example, see https://activatelearning.com/engineering-the-future/videos or https://www. eie.org/engineering-elementary/engineering-education-videos [September 2018].

pedagogical knowledge, and knowledge of assessment. It described how these realms interact in a teacher's daily work and the general lack of adequate preparation for most teachers in all four areas. *America's Lab Report* focused on teacher *knowledge* and other factors that influence implementation of teaching reforms, such as teachers' preparation, the grade-level and content areas they teach, and the contexts in which they work (e.g., Gess-Newsome et al., 2017; Jacob, Hill, and Corey, 2017).

Science Teachers' Learning (National Academies of Sciences, Engineering, and Medicine, 2015) identified three important areas in which science teachers need to develop expertise: (1) the knowledge, capacity, and skill required to support a diverse range of students; (2) content knowledge, including understanding of disciplinary core ideas, crosscutting concepts, and scientific and engineering practices; and (3) pedagogical content knowledge for teaching science, including a repertoire of teaching practices that support students in rigorous and consequential science learning.

Therefore, in this update, we examine professional learning through a new lens and in the specific context of preparing teachers to engage students in investigation and design. Professional learning is key to implementation of investigation and design because teachers are not likely to have experienced this approach themselves in their K–12 or undergraduate education, and it is a dramatic change from current expectations. Preservice and in-service teachers need opportunities to experience investigation and design themselves and to understand why the approach is important. The dramatic change in the role of the teacher necessitates multiple opportunities to prepare by trying the approaches in a supportive environment where teachers can have multiple rounds of iteration and learn from their experiences which techniques are more likely to work for them in the classroom.

The Guide to Implementing the NGSS (National Research Council, 2015) recommends a gradual approach to change, advocating that three-dimensional teaching will require long-term, incremental, and curriculum-supported change that provides opportunities for science teachers to identify problems in their practice and take risks on the way to realizing new instructional practices. It is unreasonable to expect teachers to completely transform their instruction during the course of one academic year or to come into the profession with the same repertoire of practices possessed by experienced teachers. Changes require ongoing support as teachers share effective strategies and collaborate to develop and/or assemble new instructional units aligned to three-dimensional learning. Similarly, teacher preparation programs can make gradual changes to ensure that new teachers entering the workforce share the vision and goals of the *Framework*.

After the release of the *Framework*, the Council of State Science Supervisors (CSSS) developed the *Science Professional Learning Standards*

(*SPLS*)[3] (Council of State Science Supervisors, 2015) specific to that new vision of K–12 science education. The *SPLS* address three aspects of professional learning experiences: (1) attributes of high-quality professional learning opportunities, (2) implementing and sustaining a professional development infrastructure, and (3) evaluating professional learning opportunities. CSSS provides expectations for both the professional development provider and the professional learner (the teacher), including ideas for engaging educators in professional development that is sustained, coherent, and models three-dimensional teaching and learning.

ENSURING TEACHERS HAVE OPPORTUNITIES FOR PROFESSIONAL LEARNING

Successful leadership for professional learning includes state, district, and school leaders who understand the role of continuous and sustained professional learning consistent with the goals of science education and honors educators as professionals; it also includes leaders of teacher preparation programs and professional development providers. A clear understanding of the underlying principles of effective professional learning will help leaders to make informed decisions. Effective professional learning is predicated on educators and administrators at various levels of the educational system taking responsibility for making and using opportunities for professional learning. An underlying belief that educators make a difference in students' lives and learning and that this is "a cause beyond oneself" is the key to sustaining a commitment to continuous professional improvement (Bryk and Schneider, 2002; Lee and Smith, 1996).

In science education, professional learning requires that educators see and engage in models of instruction consistent with investigations and problem solving (Harris et al., 2012; McNeill and Knight 2013; Putnam and Borko, 2000). Administrators play a key role in the extent to which these opportunities are readily available to teachers and the extent to which the school culture welcomes change efforts. Administrators can arrange opportunities for teachers to work collaboratively to choose phenomena and contexts relevant to their students, and to engage in and learn about inclusive pedagogies to promote equitable participation in science investigation and engineering design. They are also crucial for ensuring that appropriate facilities, equipment, and supplies are available for teachers to engage their students in science investigation and engineering design. These issues are discussed further in Chapters 8 and 9.

Ongoing professional learning (in-service professional development) is a common part of most teachers' lives. More than 80 percent of both

---

[3] See http://cosss.org/Professional-Learning [December 2018].

middle and high school science teachers participated in professional development in the 3 years prior to a 2012 survey, although high school science teachers generally spent more time on professional development than middle school teachers (Banilower et al., 2013). Research provides a clear picture that effective professional learning experiences must be sustained, coherent, and connected to the classroom work of the teachers; much of this research is discussed in the recent *Science Teachers' Learning* report (National Academies of Sciences, Engineering, and Medicine, 2015). Professional learning opportunities can provide teachers with information about the research on student learning and what it means for instruction, including how to best engage students in learning to make sense of phenomena and engineering challenges. Teachers can have experiences aligned with standards, based upon pedagogical theory, and gain experience meeting diverse learning styles. Whether teachers participate in building or district-sponsored development or seek development programs through their professional associations, they need to have support to effectively implement innovations. Teacher capacity is nurtured in school environments where professional collegiality and a shared vision exist. The vision for science education may not be accomplished without sufficient professional development and meaningful opportunities for educators to interact with a community of practice (Kloser, 2017).

Professional learning is one of the key elements for a successful transformation of a school system. As Moon, Michaels, and Reiser (2012) said in a commentary piece in *Education Week*, effective professional development programs build "on deep subject-matter knowledge, knowledge of students' progressive conceptual development, and the use of evidence to inform instructional judgments. . . . Indeed, we know that one-shot, topic-oriented, technique-driven, one-size-fits-all professional 'training' is not effective." The vision of instruction centered around phenomena that requires students to engage in the use of science and engineering practices, core disciplinary ideas, and crosscutting concepts to develop scientific sound understanding of science will require rethinking the way that most professional development is constructed. Teachers will need new tools and strategies to weave the three dimensions into a seamless instructional experience for the students. Darling-Hammond and colleagues (2017) defined effective professional development as "structured professional learning that results in changes in teacher practices and improvements in student learning outcomes" (p. v). Moon and colleagues (2012) identified five research-based principles to consider in developing professional development models (see Box 7-1).

In summary, the Professional Development model described here is content focused, uses effective practices, incorporates active learning, offers feedback and reflection, supports collaboration, provides coaching

---

BOX 7-1
Principles of Professional Development

According to Moon, Michaels, and Reiser (2012), five research-based principles should be considered for supporting productive and positive teacher-learning practices:

1. Teacher-learning experiences should include what the *Framework* and the standards are asking all students to learn. Student learning and teacher learning are inextricably linked; teachers cannot teach what they themselves cannot do.
2. Teacher-learning experiences need to be close to the classroom. They must be relevant, recognizable, and realistic. Teachers should see, hear, and feel what this new vision of science looks like with students that compare to their own, over extended periods of time, in order to recognize the implications and adapt their practice.
3. Teacher learning requires working with rich images of desired practice. These shifts in teaching and learning go beyond modifications of instruction. They call for an ability to engage students in building and refining scientific knowledge.
4. Teacher-learning experiences should provide educators with models of expertise in different formats. Examples include videos of real classrooms, scientists' and engineers' perspectives on the role of particular practices such as modeling, and print and technology-based resources.
5. Resources and teacher-learning experiences must be scalable, widely accessible, and interwoven into a well-coordinated system of expertise, resources, tasks, and tools adaptable to different learning contexts.

Any new genre of teacher professional development should bring together these principles in a highly specific, mutually reinforcing, coherent system of learning. The strength of a system-based model is twofold: to provide usable resources, tools, and classroom images in meaningful teacher-learning contexts; and to expose problems in practice within a classroom context and then to support teachers as they investigate those problems.

SOURCE: Moon, Michaels, and Reiser (2012).

---

and expert support, and is of sustained duration. These principles align well with the characteristics of effective professional development identified by Darling-Hammond and colleagues (2017) in their review of 35 studies, which demonstrated a positive link between teacher professional development, teaching practices, and student outcomes. There are multiple approaches to engaging teachers in professional learning: educative instructional resources; summer or special workshops with appropriate follow-up; extended professional learning across a school year, especially when done in partnership with communities of colleagues; and teacher participation in research practice partnerships.

Some supports for teacher learning are integrated into resources themselves; they support teacher learning of new practices, content, and/or resources. Instructional resources, as concrete reflections of the way instructional shifts can play out in teacher moves and in student work, are a key component of helping teachers shift their practice (Ball and Cohen, 1996; Remillard and Heck, 2014). As noted in Chapter 6, instructional resources that incorporate resources to support teacher learning are called educative curriculum materials (Davis and Krajcik, 2005). Their purpose is to help guide teachers in making instructional decisions—such as how to respond to different student ideas—when using the resources. They may be targeted toward developing teachers' subject matter knowledge; their pedagogical content knowledge with respect to particular core ideas, practices, or crosscutting concepts; and their knowledge of typical student patterns of student thinking and problem solving. The use of highly specified (designed by using research-based principles that promote learning) and developed (fully articulated and clear to follow) educative resources can be beneficial and cost-effective (see the work of Ball and Cohen).

When the resources also are educative for teachers, they can be highly beneficial to all learners and, in many respects, support more equitable instruction. Professional development to support teachers in learning about students' cultural practices at home and making adaptations to instructional resources that strengthen connections between scientific and engineering practices and those practices may be one strategy for supporting the process (Tzou and Bell, 2009). Learning about the cultural practices of students can be facilitated by professional development experiences that involve the students' communities. Such efforts alter teachers' beliefs and practices about their ability to teach science to diverse populations and result in gains in science learning for students (Grimberg and Gummer, 2013).

Another opportunity for professional learning is through targeted summer professional development that allows teachers to work on complex parts of instructional practice in a low-stakes, easily manipulated setting with students, such as a summer camp (see Box 7-2). Lotter et al. (2018) researched a program in which teachers engaged in ongoing cycles of practice-teaching and reflection. Surveys and observations at multiple points throughout the year indicated increased self-efficacy in using inquiry teaching methods and changes to instructional practice that reflected inquiry-based teaching methods. The authors cited the importance of the practice component as central to this change.

A critical component of teachers' professional learning and instructional practices is the support of the communities in which teachers work. As described in *Science Teachers' Learning* (National Academies of Sciences,

---

BOX 7-2
Professional Learning: Chemistry

Rushton and colleagues (2011) researched the impact of professional development with 23 chemistry teachers in which the teachers took part, as learners, in a series of investigations (representation), engaged in discussions and reflections about the work (decompositions), and had an opportunity to approximate their new understandings in a summer setting with high school students. The authors found that the representations and decompositions shifted teachers' initially naïve views about scientific inquiry toward views that align more with what has now been defined in *A Framework for K–12 Science Education*. However, the opportunity to "try out" elements of their new understandings was seen as essential by teachers to taking the practice back to their own schools and classrooms. The conceptual shift occurred in the original professional development, but teachers needed the opportunity for an approximation. Ultimately, observations of teachers' practice in their school-year classrooms indicated that 75 percent of the teachers reached the "inquiry threshold" identified by the RTOP observation protocol, which is a holistic measure of the presence/absence of specific teaching strategies divided into five subscales (lesson design and implementation, propositional knowledge, procedural knowledge, student-teacher classroom interaction, student-student classroom interaction).

SOURCE: Rushton et al. (2011).

Engineering, and Medicine, 2015), "Teacher quality is dependent not only on individual teachers but also on their communities" (p. 94). Cultivating opportunities for teachers to participate in professional learning communities focused on productive instructional practices also supports change. Together, the results of this research point in the direction of building preservice programs and professional development programs with the primary outcome of improving the quality of teachers' classroom practice in addition to developing teacher knowledge.

Teachers need time with colleagues to create and implement science curriculum materials that allow them to expand content meaning and implement inclusive pedagogies. An example of inclusive pedagogies (see Box 7-3) for teacher professional development that has shown both positive teacher and student gains was teaching that took into account the culture of science, the culture of science education, and the culture of the American Indian Tribe of the students, referred to as the cultural points of intersection of the three cultures (Grimberg and Gummer, 2013). Teacher practice and the quality of student science investigation and engineering design are improved when teachers are willing to make their practice public in a professional culture of learning (Gibbons, 1993; Darling-Hammond et al.,

---

BOX 7-3
Professional Learning: Cultures

Another professional development project centered cultural points of inter-section for a unit on accelerated motion. Grimberg and Gummer (2013) studied a professional development program for science teachers near or on Native American reservations in Montana. Two cohorts of teachers participated over 2 years, including face-to-face interactions at day-long academies once a month, a 2-week summer institute, a 3-day summer cultural camp, and an ongoing year-long online component.

Framed by culturally relevant pedagogy, instructional strategies focused on the intersection of three cultures—tribal, science teaching, and science. The pro-fessional development program utilized several inclusive pedagogies. Specifically, culturally relevant pedagogy was used as the conceptual framework; culturally responsive models assisted in the identification of topics relevant to the tribal communities; and culturally congruent instruction guided the design of the activi-ties by determining which tribal cultural elements and practices would be matched to science content. The researchers reported that after 2 years in the program, the teachers "steadily and significantly increased their confidence in the ability to teach science content and to reach non-mainstream students" (p. 28). The class-room instructional time also increased, allowing students to make connections between science content and topics relevant to their life, communities, and real-world hands-on experiences. The teachers in the study increased their confidence to teach science content and to implement equitable teaching approaches over their 2 years of participation in the professional development program.

SOURCE: Grimberg and Gummer (2013).

2009; Lewis and Tsuchida, 1998; Ma, 1999).[4] Safe professional cultures provide educators with a nurturing place to experiment with their profes-sional practice.

In recent years, PLCs have emerged as one structure for supporting the kinds of long-term changes in practice necessary to realize the *Framework* vision in science classrooms. Approximately three-quarters of practicing middle and high school science teachers report that they have participated in a PLC as part of their professional development (Banilower et al., 2013). In PLCs, small groups of teachers work in subject-specific groups (see McLaughlin and Talbert, 2001, 2006) and create space for teachers to critically examine their classroom practices and improve student outcomes (Seashore, Anderson, and Riedel, 2003). Effective PLCs vary in structure,

---

[4] See *Making Practice Public: Teacher Learning in the 21st Century* by Lieberman and Mace at http://www.ccte.org/wp-content/pdfs-conferences/ccte-conf-2013-spring-Final-version-JTE.pdf [October 2018].

but all include shared goals and norms, collaborative opportunities for making public one's instructional practices, and dedicated time for reflective dialogue (Turner et al., 2017).

Facilitation of PLCs requires significant teaching experiences and facilitation expertise. The literature on PLCs has shown that improvement in practice can result from facilitation within or from an outside expert, but in cases where the target practice is lacking expertise within the community, then expert facilitation is required (Horn and Kane, 2015). In the case of improving classroom investigations, many science teachers will need an expert to provide evidence of high-quality practice that can be used as a goal for others in the community to reach. Lacking such expertise and a clear focus, PLC meetings can devolve into "talking shop" about happenings within the school without focusing on practice (Turner et al., 2017). Expert-facilitated PLCs that are carefully structured to address the classroom work of the teachers provide opportunities for a community of teachers to see representations of high-quality practice, analyze their own practice, and focus the change to incrementally focus on learnable aspects of teaching and learning over time.

For instance, a PLC might focus an entire semester on analyzing artifacts and videos of classroom interactions that help teachers establish community norms for collaborative work and collective understanding. Another PLC might implement a yearlong, highly effective curriculum that presents relevant phenomena to students, allowing teachers to focus on the facilitation of productive, sense-making talk related to that curriculum. PLC participants can focus on both the teacher's role and the resulting interactions with students by analyzing classroom videos of discussions and student work samples (National Academies of Sciences, Engineering, and Medicine, 2015). Existing frameworks might also be adopted by PLCs, such as the TAGS framework developed by Tekkumru-Kisa and colleagues (2015). The TAGS framework is composed of two dimensions: (1) the cognitive demand of the science learning task and (2) the level of integration of science content and practices. As a *Framework*-influenced vision of investigations includes both high cognitive demand and an integration of the three dimensions, PLCs could benefit from analyzing tasks associated with investigations before, during, and after they are presented to students.

Teachers interested in improving investigations within their science classrooms cannot merely collaborate with other teachers. They must collaborate with teachers open to change and committed to a long-term investment of time and effort (Turner et al., 2017). For teachers in rural school settings with fewer teachers or in contexts with little commitment to growth, finding this community can be difficult. Contemporary technologies may play a significant role in providing access for all teachers to necessary professional development (National Academies of Sciences,

Engineering, and Medicine, 2015). Digital tools such as video conferencing, shared online documents for collaboration during lesson development, video capture and annotation software, and multimedia digital portfolios may be useful.

EQUITY AND INCLUSION

As noted in *Science Teachers' Learning* and suggested throughout this report, teachers need the knowledge, capacity, and skill to support diverse learners—all of which should be embedded in teacher preparation programs and improved during in-service teaching. They need support to learn strategies for cultural sensitivity and valuing the contributions of all their students. Chapter 5 described some ways of thinking about inclusive pedagogies as methods of teaching that incorporate diverse and dynamic instructional practices to address the needs of all learners. Multicultural content and multiple strategies for assessing learning can help with the goal of success in learning science in a culturally relevant and socially consistent setting. Professional learning can give teachers experience implementing these approaches, and science investigation and engineering design provide unique opportunities for their use to bring a broader spectrum of students into relevant and motivating learning environments. Professional learning can assist teachers with how to focus attention on equity, equality, and cultural relevance to support the inclusion of diverse perspectives and kinds of knowledge. This has the potential to positively affect both student interest in and identity with science and engineering. Box 7-4 describes an effort to support preservice teacher professional learning about inclusive pedagogy.

Inclusive pedagogies can be used to make science education and engineering design more culturally and socially relevant. As discussed earlier, in order to teach in these ways, preservice teachers and in-service teachers, with assistance and support from committed stakeholders, will need time and resources to work in collaborative partnerships to address equity, diversity, and social justice in science teaching. Inclusive pedagogies for science education require both policy and administrative decision making to set structures that will allow these inclusive pedagogies to serve the best interests of all students (see the discussion of Systems in Chapter 9).

SUMMARY

The shifts necessary to realize three-dimensional science investigation and engineering design in middle and high school classrooms that are equally and equitably accessible, as well as culturally inclusive and responsive, require changes in both preservice teacher education and in ongoing in-service professional learning. This includes not only helping students

---

BOX 7-4
Professional Learning: Pollution

In teacher education, Mensah (2011) used culturally relevant teaching when three preservice teachers worked together in co-planning and co-teaching a Pollution Unit in a New York City school. Though the study took place in one classroom, the researcher had support from the principal to place preservice teachers in all classrooms in the school. All the preservice teachers in the science methods course created lessons using tenets of culturally relevant teaching and taught their lessons in every classroom in the school. The findings of the study revealed the importance of having supportive collaborations (i.e., teacher education faculty, classroom teachers, the school administration, and preservice teacher peers) in planning, teaching, and assessing students' learning and teachers' implementation of inclusive pedagogies. While this work was done in a 4th- and 5th-grade classroom in an elementary school, it can inform thinking about middle schools.

The preservice teachers challenged their notions of what science teaching should look like in the classroom and what topics could be covered that would broaden students' and their understanding of culturally relevant teaching and science concepts that connected to their daily lives. The decision to teach a Pollution Unit had personal meaning to the preservice teachers and the students because of high asthma rates and low school attendance. The preservice teachers realized the amount of time and effort necessary in planning and addressing the learning needs of diverse students and teaching science with critical perspectives. Working in a partnership school with support from teachers and administration who placed science as a priority in the elementary school strengthened the potential for inclusive pedagogies.

SOURCE: Mensah (2011).

---

choose and reason through a particular phenomenon, but also concrete strategies for building on students' cultural and community funds of knowledge to guide science investigations. Teachers need not just science content knowledge, but also personal experience with the process of investigation and design and time to reflect upon their improvement efforts with colleagues. Professional learning communities may play an important role in supporting teachers as they work towards providing high-quality instructional practices critical to science investigation and engineering design. These opportunities would provide a space for teachers to see representations of high-quality practice and the use of technology, analyze their own practice, and focus the incremental change to learnable aspects of teaching and learning over time.

In addition, social and cultural knowledge is needed so that teachers can better understand and address the inequities in and exclusion from science education that persists today. Professional development with a focus on equity ensures that teachers have high expectations for all students' learning and prepares them to engage students in all aspects of inquiry. Sustained, coherent, and focused professional development opportunities are essential for practicing teachers to make these meaningful instructional changes. Administrators play a key role in the extent to which these opportunities are available to teachers as well as whether the school culture would welcome such changes. Professional development should inspire, as well as inform, educators to make positive instructional changes. Understanding the role of science investigation and engineering design in science and science education is paramount to educators developing the value for making changes in their instructional practice.

Beginning with the types of courses and experiences future teachers have as undergraduates and continuing through the professional development experiences new and senior teachers have during their teaching tenure, it is important to consider the full trajectory of teacher learning. As shifts occur in these learning opportunities, being conscious of this learning continuum would begin to answer questions such as: (1) what courses/experiences are crucial for preservice teachers? (2) what are good "starting points" for in-service teachers? and (3) what can novice teachers learn once they are in the classroom?

REFERENCES

Aud, S., Hussar, W., Kena, G., Bianco, K., Frohlich, L., Kemp, J., and Tahan, K. (2011). *The Condition of Education 2011*. (NCES 2011-033). U.S. Department of Education, National Center for Education Statistics. Washington, DC: U.S. Government Printing Office. Available: https://nces.ed.gov/pubs2011/2011033.pdf [October 2018].

Baker, W., and Keller, J. (2010.) Science Teacher and Researcher (STAR) program: Strengthening STEM education through authentic research experiences for preservice and early career teachers. *Peer Review, 12*(2), 22–26.

Ball, D.L., and Cohen, D.K. (1996). Reform by the book: What is—or might be—the role of curriculum materials in teacher learning and instructional reform? *Educational Researcher, 25*(9), 6–8.

Ball, D.L., and Cohen, D.K. (1999). Developing practice, developing practitioners: Toward a practice-based theory of professional education. In G. Sykes and L. Darling-Hammond (Eds.), *Teaching as the Learning Profession: Handbook of Policy and Practice* (pp. 3–32). San Francisco: Jossey Bass.

Ball, D.L., and Forzani, F.M. (2011). Building a common core for learning to teach, and connecting professional learning to practice. *American Educator, 35*(2), 17–21, 38–39.

Bang, M., and Medin, D. (2010). Cultural processes in science education: Supporting the navigation of multiple epistemologies. *Science Education, 94*(6), 1008–1026.

Banilower, E.R., Heck, D., and Weiss, I. (2007). Can professional development make the vision of standards a reality? The impact of the National Science Foundation's Local Systemic Change Through Teacher Enhancement Initiative. *Journal of Research in Science Teaching, 44*(3), 375–395.

Banilower, E.R., Smith, P.S., Weiss, I.R., Malzahn, K.A., Campbell, K.M., and Weis, A.M. (2013). *Report of the 2012 National Survey of Science and Mathematics Education.* Chapel Hill, NC: Horizon Research.

Beck, C., Butler, A., and Burke da Silva, K. (2014). Promoting inquiry-based teaching in laboratory courses: Are we meeting the grade? *CBE-Life Sciences Education, 13*(3), 444–452.

Beyer, C.J., and Davis, E.A. (2012). Learning to critique and adapt science curriculum materials: Examining the development of preservice elementary teachers' pedagogical content knowledge. *Science Teacher Education, 96*(1), 130–157.

Bryk, A.S., and Schneider, B. (2002). *Trust in Schools: A Core Resource for Improvement.* New York: Russell Sage Foundation.

Buck, L.B., Towns, M.H., and Bretz, S.L. (2008). Characterizing the level of inquiry in the undergraduate laboratory. *Journal of College Science Teaching, 38*(1), 52–58.

Budd, D.A., van der Hoeven Kraft, K.J., McConnell, D.A., and Vislova, T. (2013). Characterizing teaching in introductory geology courses: Measuring classroom practices. *Journal of Geoscience Education, 61*(4), 461–475.

Center for Public Education. (2016). *Educational Equity: What does it mean? How do we know when we reach it?* Available: http://www.centerforpubliceducation.org/system/files/Equity Symposium_0.pdf [October 2018].

Chandrasekharan, S., and Nersessian, N.J. (2015). Building cognition: The construction of computational representations for scientific discovery. *Cognitive Science, 39,* 1727–1763.

Council of State Science Supervisors. (2015). *Science Professional Learning Standards.* Available: http://www.csss-science.org/SPLS.shtml [October 2018].

Darling-Hammond, L. (2000). Teacher quality and student achievement: A review of state policy evidence. *Educational Policy Analysis Archives, 8*(1), 1–44. Available: https://epaa.asu.edu/ojs/article/view/392/515 [October 2018].

Darling-Hammond, L., Hyler, M.E., and Gardner, M. (2017). *Effective Teacher Professional Development.* Palo Alto, CA: Learning Policy Institute. Available: https://learningpolicyinstitute.org/sites/default/files/product-files/Effective_Teacher_Professional_Development_REPORT.pdf [October 2018].

Darling-Hammond, L., Chung-Wei, R., Andree, A., Richardson, N., and Orphanos, S. (2009). *Professional Learning in the Learning Profession: A Status Report on Teacher Development in the U.S. and Abroad.* Stanford, CA: National Staff Development Council and School Redesign Network, Stanford University. Available: https://learningforward.org/docs/default-source/pdf/nsdcstudy2009.pdf [October 2018].

Davis, E.A., and Krajcik, J.S. (2005). Designing educative curriculum materials to promote teacher learning. *Educational Researcher, 34*(3), 3–14. doi: 10.3102/0013189X034003003.

Davis, E., Palincsar, A., and Arias, A. (2014). Designing educative curriculum materials: A theoretically and empirically driven process. *Harvard Educational Review, 84,* 24–52.

DeBarger, A.H., Choppin, J.M., Beauvineau, Y., and Moorthy, S. (2013). Designing for productive adaptations of curriculum interventions. *National Society for the Study of Education Yearbook, 112*(2), 298–319.

Doubler, S., Carraher, D., Tobin, R., and Asbell-Clarke, J. (2011). *The Inquiry Project: Final Report Submitted to the National Science Foundation.* Cambridge, MA: TERC.

Egger, A.E., Kastens, K.A., and Turrin, M.K. (2017). Sustainability, the Next Generation Science Standards, and the education of future teachers. *Journal of Geoscience Education, 65*(2), 168–184.

Enderle, P., Dentzau, M., Roseler, K., Southerland, S., Granger, E., Hughes, R., Golden, B., and Saka, Y. (2014). Examining the influence of RETs on science teacher beliefs and practice. *Science Education, 9*(6), 1077–1108.

Ensign, T.I., Rye, J.A., and Luna, M.J. (2017). Embedding probeware technology in the context of ocean acidification in elementary science methods courses. *Journal of Science Education and Technology, 26*(6), 646–656.

Faber, C., Hardin, E., Klein-Gardner, S., and Benson, L. (2014). Development of teachers as scientists in research experiences for teachers programs. *Journal of Science Teacher Education, 25,* 785–806. doi: 10.1007/s10972-014-9400-5.

Forzani, F.M. (2014). Understanding "core practices" and "practice-based" teacher education: Learning from the past. *Journal of Teacher Education, 65*(4) 357–368.

Frank, K.A., Zhao, Y., Penuel, W.R., Ellefson, N.C., and Porter, S. (2011). Focus, fiddle and friends: A longitudinal study of characteristics of effective technology professional development. *Sociology of Education, 84*(2), 137–156.

Gao, N., Adan, S., Lopes, G. and Lee, G. (2018). *Implementing the Next Generation Science Standards: Early Evidence from California.* Public Policy Institute of California. Available: http://www.ppic.org/wp-content/uploads/r-0317ngr.pdf [October 2018].

Gess-Newsome, J., Taylor, J.A., Carlson, J., Gardner, A.L., Wilson, C.D., and Stuhlsatz, M. (2017). Teacher pedagogical content knowledge, practice, and student achievement. *International Journal of Science Education,* 1–20.

Gibbons, F. (1993). Self-attention and behavior: A review and theoretical update. *Advances in Experimental and Social Psychology, 23,* 249–295.

Greca, I.M., Seoane, E., and Arriassecq, I. (2014). Epistemological Issues concerning computer simulations in science and their implications for science education. *Science & Education, 14*(23), 897–921. doi: 10.1007/s11191-013-9673-7.

Grimberg, B.I., and Gummer, E. (2013). Teaching science from cultural points of intersection. *Journal of Research in Science Teaching, 50*(1), 12–32.

Grimm, V., Revilla, E., Berger, U., Jeltsch, F., Mooij, W.M., Railsback, S.F., and DeAngelis, D.L. (2005). Pattern-oriented modeling of agent-based complex systems: Lessons from ecology. *Science, 310*(5750), 987–991. doi: 10.1126/science.1116681.

Harris, C., Phillips R., and Penuel, W. (2012). Examining teachers' instructional moves aimed at developing students' ideas and questions in learner-centered science classrooms. *Journal of Science Teacher Education, 23*(7), 769.

Heller, J., Daehler, K., Wong, N., Shinohara, M., and Miratrix, L. (2012). Differential effects of three professional developments models on teacher knowledge and student achievement in elementary science. *Journal of Research in Science Teaching, 49,* 333–362.

Herreid, C.F., and Schiller, N.A. (2013). Case studies and the flipped classroom. *Journal of College Science Teaching, 42*(5), 62–66. Available: http://archive.aacu.org/pkal/regional-networks/documents/CRWG-SPEE-REF-01.pdf [September 2018].

Horn, I.S., and Kane, B.D. (2015). Opportunities for professional learning in mathematics teacher workgroup conversations: Relationships to instructional expertise. *Journal of the Learning Sciences, 24*(3), 373–418.

Ingersoll, R., Merrill, L., and Stuckey, D. (2014). *Seven Trends: The Transformation of the Teaching Force.* CPRE Report (#RR-80). Philadelphia: Consortium for Policy Research in Education, University of Pennsylvania.

Jacob, R., Hill, H., and Corey, D. (2017). The impact of a professional development program on teachers' mathematical knowledge for teaching, instruction, and student achievement. *Journal of Research on Educational Effectiveness, 10*(2), 379–407.

Jeanpierre, B., Oberhauser, K., and Freeman, C. (2005). Characteristics of professional development that effect change in secondary science teachers' classroom practices. *Journal of Research in Science Teaching, 42*(6), 668–690.

Klein-Gardner, S., Johnston, M., and Benson, L. (2012). Impact of RET teacher-developed curriculum units on classroom experiences for teachers and students. *Journal of Pre-College Engineering Education Research, 2,* 21–35. doi: 10.5703/1288284314868.

Kloser, M. (2017). *The Nature of the Teacher's Role in Supporting Student Investigations in Middle and High School Science Classrooms: Creating and Participating in a Community of Practice.* Paper commissioned for the Committee on Science Investigations and Engineering Design for Grades 6-12. Board on Science Education, Division of Behavioral and Social Sciences and Education. National Academies of Sciences, Engineering, and Medicine.

Kuh, G.D. (2008). *High-Impact Educational Practices: What They Are, Who Has Access to Them, and Why They Matter.* Report from the Association of American Colleges and Universities. Available: https://provost.tufts.edu/celt/files/High-Impact-Ed-Practices1.pdf [October 2018].

Lakatos, I. (1970). Falsification and the methodology of scientific research programmes. In I. Lakatos and A. Musgrave (Eds.), *Criticism and the Growth of Knowledge* (pp. 91–96). Cambridge, UK: Cambridge University Press.

Lee, V.E., and Smith, J.B. (1996). Collective responsibility for learning and its effects on achievement for early secondary school students. *American Journal of Education, 104*(2), 103–147.

Lewis, C., and Tsuchida, I. (1998). A lesson is like a swiftly flowing river: Research lessons and the improvement of Japanese education. *American Educator, 22*(4), 12–17, 50–52.

Lin, H.T., and Fishman, B. J. (2004). Supporting the scaling of innovations: Guiding teacher adaptation of materials by making implicit structures explicit. In Y.B. Kafai, W.A. Sandoval, N. Enyedy, A.S. Nixon, and F. Herrera (Eds.), *Proceedings of the 6th International Conference of the Learning Sciences* (p. 617). Mahwah, NJ: Lawrence Erlbaum.

Lotter, C.R., Thompson, S., Dickenson, T.S., Smiley, W.F., Blue, G., and Rea, M. (2018). The impact of a practice-teaching professional development model on teachers' inquiry instruction and inquiry efficacy beliefs. *International Journal of Science and Mathematics Education, 16*(2), 255–273.

Luft J.A., and Dubois S.L. (2017). Essential instructional practices for science teaching. In K.S. Taber and B. Akpan (Eds.), *Science Education. New Directions in Mathematics and Science Education.* Rotterdam, Netherlands: Sense.

Luft, J.A., Dubois, S.L., Nixon, R.S., and Campbell, B.K. (2015). Supporting newly hired teachers of science: Attaining teacher professional standards. *Studies in Science Education, 51*(1), 1–48. doi: 10.1080/03057267.2014.980559.

Lund, T.J., Pilarz, M., Velasco, J.B., Chakraverty, D., Rosploch, K., Undersander, M., and Stains, M. (2015). The best of both worlds: Building on the COPUS and RTOP observation protocols to easily and reliably measure various levels of reformed instructional practice. *CBE Life Sciences Education, 14*(2), 1–12.

Ma, L.P. (1999). *Knowing and Teaching Elementary Mathematics: Teacher's Understanding of Fundamental Mathematics in China and the United States.* Mahwah, NJ: Erlbaum Associates.

McDermott, L.C. (1990). A perspective on teacher preparation in physics and other sciences: The need for special science courses for teachers. *American Journal of Physics, 58*(8), 734–742.

McLaughlin, M.W., and Talbert, J.E. (2001). *Professional Communities and the Work of High School Teaching.* Chicago: University of Chicago Press.

McLaughlin, M.W., and Talbert, J.E. (2006). *Building School-Based Teacher Learning Communities: Professional Strategies to Improve Student Achievement.* Chicago: University of Chicago Press.

McNeill, K.L., and Knight, A.M. (2013). Teachers' pedagogical content knowledge of scientific argumentation: The impact of professional development on K–12 teachers. *Science Education, 96*, 936–972.

Mensah, F.M. (2011). A case for culturally relevant teaching in science education and lessons learned for teacher education. *The Journal of Negro Education, 80*(3), 296–309.

Mervis, J. (2015). A classroom experiment. *Science, 347*(6222), 602–605.

Metcalf, S.J., and Tinker, R.F. (2004). Probeware and handhelds in elementary and middle school science. *Journal of Science Education and Technology, 13*(1), 43–49.

Metz, R., and Socol, A.R. (2017). *Tackling Gaps in Access to Strong Teachers: What State Leaders Can Do*. Washington, DC: The Education Trust.

Minstrell, J., and van Zee, E. (2003). Using questioning to assess and foster student thinking. In J.M. Atkin and J. Coffee (Eds.), *Everyday Assessment in the Science Classroom* (pp. 61–74). Arlington, VA: NSTA Press.

Miranda, R.J., and Damico, J.B. (2013). Science teachers' beliefs about the influence of their summer research experiences on their pedagogical practices. *Journal of Science Teacher Education, 24*(8), 1241–1261.

Mo, Y., Singh, K., and Chang, M. (2013). Opportunity to learn and student engagement: A HLM study on 8th grade science achievement. *Educational Research for Policy and Practice, 12*, 3–19

Moon, J., Michaels, S., and Reiser, B.J. (2012). Science standards require a teacher-learning rethink. *Education Week, 32*(13). Available: https://www.edweek.org/ew/articles/2012/11/30/13moon.h32.html [October 2018]

Morozov, A., Herrenkohl, L., Shutt, K., Thummaphan, P., Vye, N., Abbott, R.D., and Scalone, G. (2014). Emotional engagement in agentive science environments. In J.L. Polman, E. Kyza, K. O'Neill, and I. Tabak (Eds.), *Proceedings of the 11th International Conference of the Learning Sciences* (pp.1152–1156). Boulder, CO: International Society of the Learning Sciences.

National Academies of Sciences, Engineering, and Medicine. (2015). *Science Teachers' Learning: Enhancing Opportunities, Creating Supportive Contexts*. Washington, DC: The National Academies Press.

National Academies of Sciences, Engineering, and Medicine. (2017). *Undergraduate Research Experiences for STEM Students: Successes, Challenges, and Opportunities*. Washington, DC: The National Academies Press.

National Research Council. (1999). *How People Learn: Brain, Mind, Experience, and School*. Washington, DC: The National Academies Press.

National Research Council. (2006). *America's Lab Report: Investigations in High School Science*. Washington, DC: The National Academies Press.

National Research Council. (2010). *Preparing Teachers: Building Evidence for Sound Policy*. Washington, DC: The National Academies Press.

National Research Council. (2012). *A Framework for K-12 Science Education: Practices, Crosscutting Concepts, and Core Ideas*. Washington, DC: The National Academies Press.

National Research Council. (2015). *Guide to Implementing the Next Generation Science Standards*. Washington, DC: The National Academies Press.

National Science Board. (2018). *Science and Engineering Indicators, 2018. NSB-2018-1*. Alexandria, VA: National Science Foundation. Available: https://www.nsf.org/statistics/indicators [October 2018].

National Science Foundation. (2012). *National Center for Science and Engineering Statistics, Special Tabulations (2011) of 2007–08 Schools and Staffing Survey*. Arlington, VA: Author.

Neild, R.C., Farley-Ripple, E.N., and Byrnes, V. (2009). The effect of teacher certification on middle grades achievement in an urban district. *Educational Policy, 23*(5), 732–760.

Penuel, W.R., Gallagher, L.P., and Moorthy, S. (2011). Preparing teachers to design sequences of instruction in Earth science: A comparison of three professional development programs. *American Educational Research Journal, 48*(4), 996–1025.

Putnam, R.T., and Borko, H. (2000). What do new views of knowledge and thinking have to say about research on teacher learning? *Educational Researcher, 29*(1), 4–15.

Remillard, J.T., and Heck, D. (2014). Conceptualizing the curriculum enactment process in mathematics education. *ZDM: The International Journal on Mathematics Education, 46*(5), 705–718.

Reynolds, B., Mehalik, M.M., Lovell, M.R., and Schunn, C.D. (2009). Increasing student awareness of and interest in engineering as a career option through design-based learning. *International Journal of Engineering Education, 25*(1), 788–798.

Rushton, G. T., Lotter, C., and Singer, J. (2011). Chemistry teachers' emerging expertise in inquiry teaching: The effect of a professional development model on beliefs and practice. *Journal of Science Teacher Education, 22*(1), 23–52.

Russ, R. S., Sherin, B.L., and Sherin, M.G. (2016). What constitutes teacher learning? In D.H. Gitomer, and C.A. Bell (Eds.), *Handbook of Research on Teaching* (5th ed., pp. 391–438). Washington, DC: American Educational Research Association.

Russell, S., Hancock, M., and McCullough, J. (2007). The pipeline—Benefits of undergraduate research experiences. *Science, 316*(5824), 548–549.

Sanger, M.J. (2008). How does inquiry-based instruction affect teaching majors' views about teaching and learning science? *Journal of Chemical Education, 85*(2), 297.

Savinainen, A., and Scott, P. (2002). Using the Force Concept Inventory to monitor student learning and to plan teaching. *Physics Education, 37*(1), 53–58.

Schneiter, K., Christensen, L., and Lee, V.R. (2018). *Using Personal Activity Data in an Undergraduate Statistics Course.* Paper presented at the 10th International Conference on the Teaching of Statistics (ICOTS10), Kyoto, Japan.

Seashore, K.R., Anderson, A.R., and Riedel, E. (2003). Implementing arts for academic achievement: The impact of mental models, professional community and interdisciplinary teaming. Available: https://conservancy.umn.edu/bitstream/handle/11299/143717/Report.pdf?sequence=1&isAllowed=y [October 2018].

Sherin, M.G., and Van Es, E.A. (2009). Effects of video club participation on teachers' professional vision. *Journal of Teacher Education, 60*(1), 20–37.

Stains, M., Harshman, J., Barker, M.K., Chasteen, S.V., Cole, R., DeChenne-Peters, S.E., and Young, A.M. (2018). Anatomy of STEM teaching in North American universities. *Science, 359*(6383), 1468–1470. doi: 10.1126/science.aap8892.

Stefani, L., Mason, R., and Pegler, C. (2007). *The Educational Potential of E-Portfolios.* London: Routledge.

Snyder, T.D., de Brey, C., and Dillow, S.A. (2016). *Digest of Education Statistics 2015.* (NCES 2016-014). Washington, DC: National Center for Education Statistics, Institute of Education Sciences, U.S. Department of Education.

Teasdale, R., Viskupic, K., Bartley, J.K., McConnell, D., Manduca, C., Bruckner, M., Farthing, D., and Iverson, E. (2017). A multidimensional assessment of reformed teaching practice in geoscience classrooms. *Geosphere, 13*(2), 608–627.

Tekkumru Kisa, M., Stein, M.K., and Schunn, C. (2015). A framework for analyzing cognitive demand and content practices integration: Task analysis guide in science. *Journal of Research in Science Teaching, 52*(5), 659–685.

Tessier, J. (2010). An inquiry-based laboratory improves preservice elementary teachers' attitudes about science. *Journal of College Science Teaching, 4,* 84–90.

Turner, J.C., Christensen, A., Kackar-Cam, H.Z., Fulmer, S.M., and Trucano, M. (2017). The development of professional learning communities and their teacher leaders: An activity systems analysis. *Journal of the Learning Sciences, 27*(1), 49–88.

Tzou, C.T., and Bell, P. (2009). *Design Collaborations as Professional Development: Orienting Teachers to Their Students' Everyday Expertise.* Paper presented at the International Conference of the Association for Science Teacher Education, Hartford, CT.

Tzou, C.T., and Bell, P. (2010). Micros and me: Leveraging home and community practices in formal science instruction. In K. Gomez, L. Lyons, and J. Radinsky (Eds.), *Proceedings of the 9th International Conference of the Learning Sciences* (pp. 1135–1143). Chicago, IL: International Society of the Learning Sciences.

U.S. Department of Education, Office for Civil Rights. (2014). *Civil Rights Data Collection Data Snapshot: Teacher Equity.* Washington, DC: Author.

U.S. Department of Education, Office of Postsecondary Education. (2013). *Preparing and Credentialing the Nation's Teachers: The Secretary's Ninth Report on Teacher Quality.* Washington, DC: Author.

U.S. Department of Education, Office of Postsecondary Education. (2016). *Preparing and Credentialing the Nation's Teachers: The Secretary's Tenth Report on Teacher Quality.* Washington, DC: Author.

Weld, J., and Funk, L. (2005). "I'm not the science type": Effect of an inquiry biology content course on preservice elementary teachers' intentions about teaching science. *Journal of Science Teacher Education, 16*(3), 189–204.

Wenger, E. (1998). *Communities of Practice: Learning, Meaning, and Identity.* Cambridge, UK: Cambridge University Press.

Williams, W., Adrien, R., Murthy, C., and Pietryka, D. (2016). *Equitable Access to Excellent Educators: An Analysis of States' Educator Equity Plans.* Rockville, MD: Westat.

Zhang, P., Ding, L., and Mazur, E. (2017). Peer instruction in introductory physics: A method to bring about positive changes in students' attitudes and beliefs. *Physical Review Physics Education Research,* 010104.

8

Space, Time, and Resources

In Chapter 7, we began the discussion on how to practically support science investigations and engineering design with an emphasis on professional learning for teachers. In the language of this chapter, the teachers are the human resources. In addition to these crucial human resources and the instructional resources discussed in Chapter 6, many other types of resources are needed to provide a three-dimensional science program that effectively engages *all* middle and high school students in investigation and design. For instance, sufficient and equitable physical space, instructional time, and fiscal resources for materials, equipment, and technology are other important components of safe and effective science teaching and learning environments.

In this chapter, we focus on the practical needs of students to successfully engage in science investigation and engineering design. We highlight the current state of America's public school facilities, propose a more flexible design for science learning spaces, review safety considerations and practices for the science classroom and outdoors, describe time for instruction and equitable funding for space and technologies as the means to best support science learning, and provide examples of opportunities for fidelity to the current vision for science teaching and learning when resources are limited.

PROVIDING FACILITIES TO SUPPORT SCIENCE INVESTIGATION AND ENGINEERING DESIGN

America's Lab Report (National Research Council, 2006) established that an integrated laboratory-classroom space best supports laboratory experiences in high school to follow the principles for science teaching and learning developed in that report. This integrated design affords shared space for teacher planning, instruction, and preparation of investigations alongside student activities. Additionally, the flexible layout (i.e., movable benches, chairs, and desks) allows seamless transition from data gathering to other forms of sense-making instructional strategies, such as small group and whole-class discussions. Given the goal to provide students with experiences that resemble the activities of professional scientists, this space also includes secured storage for supplies and long-term/cumulative student projects. Finally, with consideration for the costs associated with constructing or renovating a laboratory space, the report recommended that combined laboratory-classroom spaces (1) accommodate multiple science disciplines instead of being discipline-specific spaces that remain unused at times, (2) leverage the use of natural sunlight and access to outdoor science learning spaces, and (3) support a future-oriented vision for a school's science curriculum, one that is developed for use over a decade or more (National Research Council, 2006, pp. 170–171). When the report was written in 2006, there was little comprehensive data on integrated and flexible laboratory spaces within high schools, aside from survey responses from members of the National Science Teachers Association (NSTA) and the International Technology Education Association (ITEA), indicating that some forms of combined laboratory-classrooms were fairly common at the time (National Research Council, 2006, p. 172).

The State of Middle and High School Science Learning Spaces

School facilities matter for science teaching and learning, and there is a growing body of evidence linking physical spaces and overall school experience. In fact, the environmental and physical quality of school facilities is said to impact student attendance, student learning, student achievement, teacher turnover, student and staff health, and school finances (Barrett et al., 2015; Filardo, 2016; U.S. Department of Education, 2016a; Wall, 2016). In the 2012–2013 school year, the average functional age of public secondary school facilities was 19 years (U.S. Department of Education, 2016a). The functional age reflects the age of the school at the time of the most recent major renovation or the year of construction of the main instructional facility if no renovations occurred. Large school facilities (600 or more students enrolled; average functional age: 15 years) were newer than both medium-sized (300–599 students; average functional age: 20 years) and small (less than 300 students; average functional age: 23 years) schools by 5 years and 8 years, respectively.

In 2007, the NSTA released a position statement emphasizing the integral role of laboratory investigations within science curriculum and instruction, and concurrently established guidelines informed by *America's Lab Report* (National Research Council, 2006) for building and/or renovating school facilities, including science labs, that support effective science teaching and learning (Motz, Biehle, and West, 2007; National Science Teachers Association, 2007). Since that time, the integrated lab-class space design outlined in *America's Lab Report* has been used by states and school districts as a guide for improving their science educational program(s). For example, the Massachusetts School Building Authority (MSBA) provided $60 million to fund its Science Laboratory Initiative, which supports new construction of science labs in high schools across school districts in Massachusetts (Grossman and Craven, 2010). Additionally, Massachusetts created a task force to develop a prototype for the new science lab and instructional spaces with the following design requirements: curriculum-driven, flexible (i.e., affording reconfiguration via movable furnishings), combined laboratory/lecture room layout, accommodation to multiple science disciplines, attentiveness to characteristics of a safe learning environment (e.g., an allotment of 60 net square feet per student), and forward-looking (equipped with water and gas systems to allow for potential future uses different from originally intended) (Grossman and Craven, 2010). Similar to Massachusetts, the Washington State Legislature established a STEM Pilot Program as part of the 2015–2017 capital budget for construction of science classrooms and labs (Washington State Office of Superintendent of Public Instruction, 2016), and North Carolina established prototype designs for science program and facilities as a supplement to public school facilities guidelines (North Carolina Department of Public Instruction, 2010). Utah conducted research to determine students' experience in science laboratories and the needs of teachers facilitating them across the state, while audits of middle and high school science labs across 30 school districts in the greater Kansas City region were conducted as part of an agenda to improve student achievement in STEM subjects (Campbell and Bohn, 2008; Success Link, 2007). Collectively, these examples reflect different initiatives underlying transformations in science learning spaces across America's secondary public schools.

Typically, local districts carry the responsibility of making the critical decisions about public school educational facilities standards and investments, guided in part by frameworks established by building science professionals (Filardo, 2016). One report examining district plans for construction proposed to be completed in 2015 projected the inclusion of science labs in all newly constructed middle/junior high school buildings and a slight reduction in the inclusion of science lab facilities within newly constructed high schools compared to the construction plans in 2005 (Abramson, 2005, 2015). The same report revealed that 4.9 percent of middle/junior high schools being retrofitted or modernized in 2015 included the addition of a science lab as part of their plans, and it could only be inferred that less than 8.8 percent of high school plans did. Within these data, schools are represented as part of regional groups, which likely masks cases where progress in this area is lacking. For example, in California, 54 percent of districts reported insufficient access to science labs, in terms of quantity, and an even higher share of districts (60%) reported that the quality of the science labs was outdated and did not support 21st century science learning (Gao et al., 2018).

In science, facilities-related issues are common, with 19 to 30 percent of public secondary schools reporting that lack of science facilities was a serious problem for science instruction (Banilower et al., 2013). The 2017 Infrastructure Report Card assigned a D+ for the condition of America's public school buildings, with 24 percent of the structures rated as being in "fair" to "poor" condition (American Society of Civil Engineers, 2017). In years prior to the release of *America's Lab Report*, the condition of public school buildings in America was assigned a cumulative grade of D (American Society of Civil Engineers, 2005), so while efforts to improve the state of school facilities are indeed underway, conditions overall have progressed very little in over a decade.

A More Flexible Science and Engineering Class Design

The three-dimensional instructional model used in the standards in *A Framework for K-12 Science Education* (hereafter referred to as the *Framework*; National Research Council, 2012) and described in this report can be accommodated within the vision for science learning spaces outlined in *America's Lab Report* (National Research Council, 2006). However, this science classroom design was optimized for "integrated" laboratory and lecture-based science instruction, and not for full transition to investigation and design as the central feature of science classes. Additionally, this design did not consider features specific to engineering design activities and middle school contexts. Thus, an even more flexible design is proposed.

For both middle school and high school, there are elements of the classroom design that are important to facilitate aspects of science investigation and engineering design. Students spend much of their time working in small groups and undertake design projects and science investigations that are open-ended and student-planned, and thus need flexible workspace in which they can access the materials and equipment that they need, as they need it (Neill and Etheridge, 2008). They work together, not just to investigate or build design prototypes, but also to develop group design plans and system models and to construct explanations of the phenomena they are studying using those models. This means that their workspace and classroom layout need flexible furnishings that are designed for small group work, but can be rearranged to accommodate a variety of instructional approaches and group sizes (Neill and Etheridge, 2008). Additionally, flexible design spaces with adjustable-height workstations afford comparable access to all students, and particularly to students with disabilities.

Students bring needed materials to their group area, which supports both the "hands-on" work of manipulating materials and the "minds-on" work of model or design development, data analysis, and simulation manipulation(s) to construct explanations. There is also a greater need for display wall space, where, for example, a display board can be used to capture student questions related to the overall driving question of a unit, or where student groups can display their models as they discuss and share them (Beichner, 2008). This means that the room is comprised of open wall space with display capability. In contrast, less space is needed for large black or white boards solely for teacher use. When the class functions as a whole group, it is because the students are sharing ideas from their group work, rather than because the teacher is presenting information for an extended period of time (i.e., lecture-based instruction) (Beichner, 2008). Therefore, the seating arrangement remains in a "student-centered" layout that supports group work, instead of the traditional front-facing classroom organization. In fact, it may be difficult to define "the front of the room" as both teachers and students, and indeed the furniture, frequently move around in the flexible space.

As in the 2006 design, storage space is important, not only for equipment and materials, but also for students' works in progress, as projects will often extend over multiple class periods (Wall, 2016). Therefore, internal storage spaces within each classroom containing materials that can be easily accessed by students to work on projects inside and outside of class time are ideal. Central storage space that is readily accessible from multiple classrooms is another important design element. This adds to the flexible class design by removing equipment when it is not needed, and provides the restricted access necessary for lockable storage of chemicals, hazardous materials, or power tools, especially during periods when unsupervised student work is underway.

Rather than science learning spaces defined by discipline, a high school needs two basic types of science classrooms, all flexible, but only some (the second type) equipped specifically for chemistry and biology needs, including facilities such as an exhaust-capable fume hood and possibly temperature-controlled incubator spaces (U.S. Department of Defense Education Activity, 2014). The spaces needed for both middle and high school science are similar, although the relative number and distribution of chemistry/biology equipped spaces that are needed may differ depending on the course sequences (e.g., in an integrated course sequence model, science courses are taken every year and each course covers multiple scientific disciplines) and the number of students taking each course. Yet, a middle school may not need the second type of space, as it is less likely that middle school chemistry investigations would require a fume hood, gas connections, or safety shields, since many of the chemical substances used at this level are common household items (American Chemical Society, 2018).

Flexible laboratory classrooms are not the only spaces where investigation and design occur, as some middle and high schools are introducing "maker spaces" that have additional design and build capabilities, such as laser cutters and 3D printers, and the associated computer technology and software to use them (Blikstein, 2013; Cohen et al., 2016; Moorefield-Lang, 2014). Career and technical education courses have long had "shop" spaces that include additional equipment, such as a computer-controlled milling machine in a metal shop or a lathe in a wood shop. These spaces facilitate a larger range of engineering design projects, and ideally high school students will have access to such spaces in addition to the more flexible science learning spaces described above. Even without such dedicated spaces, many engineering projects require student access to different tools, technologies (including software), and materials separate from those used in science classes, which means that engineering-specific needs are also considered when planning and designing science learning spaces.

Outdoor learning spaces are also important adjacencies to both foster and reinforce science learning, particularly within middle school contexts. We use the phrase "outdoor learning spaces" rather than "the field" because of the widespread use of the term "field trip," which generally means any expedition away from the school and generally conjures images of loading up students and chaperones on buses. In contrast, outdoor learning spaces include school gardens, woods, or other natural environments within walking distance of the school, and at times, other outdoor spaces that require transportation to get to. These spaces can be leveraged to increase environmental literacy, develop health and social skills, and encourage environmental responsibility and agency, by connecting and engaging students with the natural environment (U.S. Department of Defense Education Activity, 2017). For example, school gardens can provide learning opportunities around human impact and food production, plants and soil, lifecycles and chemical change, and many other connections within a given three-dimensional science curriculum (University of Georgia College of Agricultural and Environmental Sciences, 2017).

Preferably, site-specific affordances within the local school environment are considered for outdoor learning spaces, and these spaces are accessible from the main instructional space via pedestrian connections that meet ADA[1] standards and display appropriate signage to highlight the site's loca-

---

[1]Americans with Disabilities Act of 1990, P.L. 101-336, 42 U.S.C. § 12101 is a civil rights law that prohibits discrimination based on disability.

tion (U.S. Department of Defense Education Activity, 2017). Additionally, the location would allow teachers to observe students in an unobstructed manner (Wall, 2016). Other important considerations for this design space include temporary seating, which can be incorporated as built-in benches or raised plant beds, and low-cost/maintenance site features, such as sundials, themed walkways, nature paths, and bioswales, which would extend opportunities to learn in outdoor environments to a more diverse range of students (U.S. Department of Defense Education Activity, 2017).

Budgeting for Science Learning Spaces

The cost of newly constructed or renovated science lab spaces in an existing public school building is more expensive than other types of school spaces (National Research Council, 2006). In fact, budget plans to renovate and expand high school science spaces within one school district in New York revealed an estimated costs range from $325–375 per square feet, which at the highest end is about 1.25 times more expensive than the cost of renovating regular classroom spaces, estimated at $300 per square feet (Voorheesville Central School District, 2017). Various factors are considered in these budget plans including, but not limited to: the location of the school as it relates to degree of accessibility and proximity to an urban environment; the age of the building and planned construction type; the availability of services required to renovate the building area to support the new and modern space; the impact the space will have upon adjacent program areas within and outside of the building; the science discipline(s) for the space(s); and the projected length of time to completion, given possible conflicts may arise with other building projects and unforeseeable setbacks (American Society of Professional Estimators, 2014).

In 2014–2015 (the most recent available data), the total per pupil expenditure for public schools was $13,119. Of this amount, $1,029 per pupil was allocated for capital outlay, which are the expenditures used to build and improve school facilities (U.S. Department of Education, 2016b). The federal government provides very little capital support (about 0.2 percent) toward K–12 facilities; therefore, the funding roles and responsibilities are primarily fulfilled at the state and district levels (Filardo, 2016). The *State of Our Schools 2016* report revealed that 5 states pay for nearly all of their school districts' capital costs and 12 others provide no direct support for their districts (American Society of Civil Engineers, 2017; Filardo, 2016). The average cost of construction of a high school was $132 per square foot in 2003, and in 2013 the reporting cost had risen to $235.29 per square foot. A similar trend was seen in construction costs for middle schools, going from $130 per square foot in 2003 to $243 per square foot in 2013 (Abramson, 2015). An important point made in *State of Our Schools* is that school facilities such as science labs are generally designed with consideration for only the initial student population attending the school, which could create significant problems in light of growing enrollment observed each year in the majority of middle and high schools.

At the local level, school districts spent almost $7.8 billion on new schools, $3.2 billion on additions to existing buildings, and $3.14 billion on retrofitting and modernization of existing structures (Abramson, 2015). However, ASCE reported that persistent underinvestment in school facilities has resulted in an estimated $38 billion annual investment gap (American Society of Civil Engineers, 2017). Closing the investment gap for facilities will not only require additional revenue, but also planning reform, given 4 in 10 public schools currently lack long-term education facilities plans to address operations and maintenance needs (American Society of Civil Engineers, 2017). Future spending and planning that reflect the current national system for facilities will unfortunately result in districts that are underprepared to provide adequate and equitable school facilities for all students.

SAFETY CONSIDERATIONS FOR ENGAGING IN SCIENCE INVESTIGATION AND ENGINEERING DESIGN

Throughout this report, we have shown how engaging in science investigation and engineering design affords high-quality instruction to all students; however, active involvement in investigation and design could increase risks to students if steps are not taken to ensure student safety during these experiences. In *America's Lab Report*, student safety was briefly explored, and at that time, many U.S. high schools were underprepared to provide safe laboratory experiences to students (National Research Council, 2006). In this section, we review the science and engineering lab safety standards and policies for safe instructional classroom and outdoor spaces, articulated by the NSTA, the American Chemical Society (ACS), and others. Additionally, we discuss important safety considerations for science and engineering teaching and learning, specifically calling attention to current safety practices within middle and high schools across America.

Safety Standards for Science Classroom Spaces

As professionals, teachers of science are legally held to a "duty of care" obligation, whereby they must ensure the safety of students, teachers, and staff (National Science Teachers Association, 2014a; Prosser et al., 1984). Additionally, they are required to justify engaging in any educational activity with associated safety risks and must act as a "reasonable and prudent person" would to provide and maintain a safe learning environment with both students and staff considered. The Maryland Department of Education (1999) states that a reasonable and prudent teacher

- provides prior warning of any hazards associated with an activity,
- demonstrates the essential portions of the activity,
- provides active supervision,
- provides sufficient instruction to make the activity and its risks understandable,
- ensures that all necessary safety equipment is available and in good working order,
- has sufficient training and equipment available to handle an emergency, and
- ensures that the place of the activity is as safe as reasonably possible.

Failure to exercise any of the above duties may result in a charge of negligence, and while several parties can be implicated in the charge of negligence arising from a science laboratory experience (e.g., teacher, state, school district, school board, school administration), liability most likely falls to the classroom teacher. It is presumed that the classroom teacher is the expert and, therefore, is responsible for ensuring that students work in a prudent and safe manner. No distinction is made between teachers of science in elementary, middle, and high school classrooms or outdoor education facilities (Maryland Department of Education, 1999). Therefore, any science classroom teacher is deemed responsible for the welfare of the students.

The ACS is one of many professional organizations that have established guidelines and recommendations for laboratory and classroom safety. For example, the ACS recommends that teacher certification in chemistry includes training on good safety practices for setting up and conducting laboratory activities and demonstrations. Ongoing professional development is recommended as part of the teachers' practice, covering information about yearly changes in safety procedures, particularly those that are frequently used by teachers and more likely to result in laboratory accidents (American Chemical Society, 2018; National Science Teachers Association, 2007). In fact, effective professional development for chemistry teachers characterized by the ACS comprised "accessible alerts to [chemistry teachers of] accidents that occur when common laboratory activities and/or demonstrations are carried out, with access to recommended modifications" (American Chemical Society, 2018). The ACS also states that secure communications with school administration and emergency response personnel is needed within science instructional spaces along with the following safety equipment: a hands-free, plumbed-in eyewash station; a fire extinguisher; a safety shield; a first-aid kit; a goggle UV-sanitizer; and a class set of goggles (American

Chemical Society, 2018). The ACS recommends that this safety equipment be near the demonstration area when in use and at all other times be accessible, but in storage spaces that are separate from the main demonstration/work area (American Chemical Society, 2018).

Periodically, training in the management and operation of materials and equipment is also recommended to ensure that students and teachers are protected in the event of a resource malfunction (National Science Teachers Association, 2007). Moreover, for safe lab preparation and maintenance, it is advised that the science lab space be vacant at least one period per day and restricted from uses other than science and engineering (American Chemical Society, 2018). Schools and districts are encouraged to prioritize support for professional development in safety, but in cases where funding may be restricted, alternatives are still available (American Chemical Society, 2018). For example, the American Association of Chemistry Teachers (AACT) provides safety resources in the form of periodicals, blogs, and webinars (American Chemical Society, 2018). In addition, vendors of laboratory equipment and supplies, such as Flinn Scientific, offer lengthy online training courses, including courses on middle and high school laboratory safety.[2]

Data demonstrating that the number and frequency of laboratory accidents increase as class size increases (National Science Teachers Association, 2014b; Stephenson, West, and Westerlund, 2003; West and Kennedy, 2014) have led to established parameters for class size. This relationship was observed in both middle and high school science classes, and is particularly evident when there is less than 60 square feet of workspace per student (National Science Teachers Association, 2014b). Classroom size is recommended to be at a minimum 60 square feet per student in a classroom/lab facility, and this size is set for classes of a maximum of 24 students (American Chemical Society, 2018; National Science Teachers Association, 2014b). Both class size and workspace per student influence the teacher's classroom management ability and active supervision of students while engaged in science investigation and engineering design. Workspace per student is not simply due to room size limitations; a smaller classroom space can still have sufficient space per student if enrollment is small. The number of students within the space (i.e., elbow space) is what matters, and even a large classroom would be insufficient at accommodating too large of a class size (National Science Teachers Association, 2014b).

Occupant load, which is the number of people who can safely occupy a building or portion at any one time, is another safety concern for science class spaces (NFPA 101-2012: section 3.3.162.2). International Building

---

[2]For example, a single course can be taken free of charge at https://labsafety.flinnsci.com/ [October 2018]. Courses cover aspects of science lab safety, including right-to-know laws, SDS requirements, proper use of personal protective equipment, and safe laboratory practices.

Codes are used to determine this value; for pure educational science laboratory spaces, the standard is 50 square feet net per person (NFPA 101-2012 Occupant Load Factor table 7.3.12-Shops, laboratories, vocational rooms, pp. 101–174).[3] However, this number may vary based on different state mandates requiring additional footage and based on the special needs of students in the class (American Chemical Society, 2018). Occupant load standards are also used to determine the number and means of egress required for a particular space, and while the occupancy load limit may accommodate more students, the NSTA recommends that science class spaces still have a maximum of 24 students (Motz, Biehle, and West, 2007). A more detailed discussion of all standards related to safety in science classroom spaces is beyond the scope of this report; nevertheless, several organizations (see Box 8-1) provide Internet-accessible general safety guidelines and practices that are commonly accepted for secondary science and engineering education to provide and maintain safe learning and working environments for students and staff.

Safety Standards for Engineering Education

In addition to all of the safety considerations outlined for science classroom spaces, there are a few specific considerations for student safety when engaging in engineering design. Hand and power tools are often utilized to construct prototypes in designing solutions to engineering challenges, which increases the risk of accidents that involve hand injuries (Love, 2014). Safety videos that demonstrate the proper way to use required tools and equipment are valuable resources for teachers to show students. However, due to variations in features and appearances, students may have trouble making connections between the tools and machines in the video and those in the actual lab space. Therefore, it is recommended that teachers regularly demonstrate how to safely use the specific tools and equipment before the start of every design project, in addition to showing the safety videos (Love, 2014). Moreover, because not all criteria may apply in a given video or within general engineering safety guidelines, it is recommended that teachers be adept at choosing the best resources or carefully adapting available resources to ensure that all students understand safety within the specific laboratory environment. For example, in the flexible design discussed in this chapter, the laboratory and classroom spaces are not separate. Therefore, if any student is using a tool or machine, then all students within the space must wear eye protection regardless of proximity to the tool or machine

---

[3] For more information, see the NSTA Issue Papers document on Overcrowding in the Instructional Space available at http://static.nsta.org/pdfs/OvercrowdingInTheInstructional-Space.pdf [October 2018].

BOX 8-1
Science and Engineering Teaching and Learning:
Safety Guidelines and Recommendations

Council of State Science Supervisors: Science Education Safety
(http://www.csss-science.org/safety.shtml)

Connecticut State Department of Education: High School Science Safety
(http://portal.ct.gov/SDE/Publications/Connecticut-High-School-Science-Safety/
Science-Education-Safety)

Connecticut State Department of Education: Middle School Science Safety
(http://portal.ct.gov/SDE/Publications/Connecticut-Middle-School-Science-Safety)

International Technology and Engineering Education Association-Council for
Supervision and Leadership: ITEEA-CSL Safety Website
(http://iteea-csl.org/pages/safetywebsite.html)

Maryland State Department of Education: Science Safety Manual
(http://mdk12.msde.maryland.gov/instruction/curriculum/science/safety/index.
html)

National Science Teachers Association: Liability of Science Teachers for Laboratory Science Position Statement
(http://www.nsta.org/about/positions/liability.aspx)

National Science Teachers Association: Safety and School Science Instruction
Position Statement
(http://www.nsta.org/about/positions/safety.aspx)

Technology and Engineering Education Association of Pennsylvania (TEEAP):
Safety Guides and Information
(https://www.teeap.org/Safety)

U.S. Department of Health and Human Services: Enviro-Health Links-Laboratory
Safety
(https://sis.nlm.nih.gov/enviro/labsafety.html)

(Haynie, 2009). Technology and engineering educators possess deep expertise in tool and machine safety, and thus can work with science educators
to safely integrate engineering content and practices embedded in the design
process (Love, 2014).

Safety Standards for Outdoor Learning Spaces

As mentioned earlier in this chapter, learning experiences in outdoor spaces can be a valuable, positive addition to any three-dimensional science program. As with all investigations, effective planning and preparation for these experiences include attention to student safety. But while many organizations have developed safety protocols and liability documents around science laboratories, use of chemicals, and specific equipment, few have done so for conducting field investigations. NSTA, one of the few, has developed a Field Trip Safety resource (National Science Teachers Association, 2015, see section V) that specifically addresses safety considerations for outdoor field experiences with some of the following guidelines:

- Before the field trip, field trip supervisors should create a checklist of needs that may occur outdoors. These include, but are not limited to, parking, availability of drinking water, washing and lavatory facilities, trash disposal or recycling, and other needs. These needs can best be determined by a visit to the site prior to the field trip.
- Before the field trip, field trip supervisors should determine the ability to use a mobile telephone or another device such as walkie-talkies, the presence of unexpected harmful substances in the site (flooding, broken glass, fallen trees), and the local flora and fauna that are present. In particular, the presence of poisonous plants, stinging insects, and pests should be assessed. In some outdoor experiences, acoustics can be a problem. Supervising adults and instructors may wish to bring a voice amplification device, especially in locales where there is interfering background noise, such as machinery or running water. Hand signals may also be needed in these circumstances.
- Accounting for all students regularly in outdoor experiences is crucial. Students' understanding of danger and physical limits may vary, causing some to stray from the group into other areas when outdoors (Wall, 2016). If organizing students into separate groups is most suitable for the field experience, then field trip supervisors should establish rendezvous procedures and locations, and should plan to meet as a whole group regularly and take roll. During travel, adults should be placed at the front and rear of the group, even for older students.
- Field trip supervisors need to account for weather and other outdoor conditions. In particular, students may need to be protected to excessive sun exposure, water, and environmental hazards by wearing appropriate attire and using appropriate safeguards (e.g., broad-brimmed hats, sunscreen, sunglasses, insect repellent).

Furthermore, the North American Association for Environmental Education (NAAEE) has developed core competencies for environmental educators, and candidates in teacher certification programs that are recognized by the NAAEE must demonstrate proficiency within these competencies. These competencies include settings for instruction, such as, "A certified environmental educator will analyze one of his or her teaching environments citing three ways to address potential safety issues . . ." (North American Association for Environmental Education, 2006). However, few practicing teachers have received certification from NAAEE-approved programs, and overall, there is very little guidance provided for middle and high school science teachers to safely implement investigations in outdoor learning spaces.

Current Patterns in Science and Engineering Lab Safety

Many of today's public schools remain under-resourced and ill-equipped to safely provide students with quality science learning experiences (Baker, Farrie, and Sciarra, 2018; Filardo and Vincent, 2017). Indoor air quality (IAQ) is a major source of concern within schools, in part due to the age and poor conditions of buildings (Occupational Health and Safety Administration, n.d.). It is estimated that one-half of schools in the United States are characterized by poor IAQ (Environmental Protection Agency, n.d.). These conditions are especially concerning in light of engaging in science investigations, where lack of proper air flow may jeopardize safety while working with chemicals that pose inhalation hazards. Additionally, student performance and achievement are negatively impacted when learning and productivity are impaired due to health and comfort issues (Environmental Protection Agency, n.d.; Filardo, 2016). Other possible areas that have been identified as safety concerns while teaching science include overcrowding, inadequate science equipment and facilities, and lack of safety training experience in teachers (National Science Teachers Association, 2014b).

According to the Schools and Staffing Survey (SASS), the class size for teachers in departmentalized instruction in 2011–2012 was on average 25.5 in middle schools and 24.2 in high schools (U.S. Department of Education, 2014, Table 7).[4] Departmentalized instruction refers to instruction to several classes of different students most or all of the day in one or more subjects, which is the typical structure for instruction at the middle and high school levels. Although these data are not disaggregated by subject matter, the average class sizes are comparable to the recommended maximum class size of 24 students, though states such as California and Nevada show patterns of overcrowding with class averages of at least 30 students per class at both the middle and high school levels (U.S. Department of Education,

---

[4]See https://nces.ed.gov/surveys/sass/tables/sass1112_2013314_t1s_007.asp [September 2018].

2014, Table 7). Overcrowding reduces allotted workspace for both teachers and students, thereby increasing risk for injury and negatively impacting the quality of science instruction. Additionally, it has been found that students from low-income families benefit from smaller class sizes (defined by a small teacher-to-student ratio); therefore, the negative effects of overcrowding on student learning may be exacerbated in schools serving the highest percentages of students from low-income families (Baker et al., 2018). As part of its Science Laboratory Initiative, the MSBA listed safety as a top priority, specifically recommending that overcrowding be limited within these spaces. At the time that this initiative was launched, average class sizes in Massachusetts were 25 for middle school and 22 for high school (U.S. Department of Education, 2014, Table 7).

Inadequate teacher safety training has also been a concern for both science and engineering classrooms. In 2006, a high school student was severely burned during a demonstration of the classic "rainbow" chemistry experiment in which a flammable solvent such as methane is used on an open bench to show the spectrum of visible light (Kemsley, 2015). In response to this accident, the U.S. Chemical Safety & Hazard Investigation Board (CSB) released a video entitled "After the Rainbow" illustrating how this incident could have been preventable with safer practices exercised by the teacher (U.S. Chemical Safety & Hazard Investigation Board, 2013). This video warning proved insufficient to prevent further accidents of this kind, given two high school students from New York City and six high school students in Virginia were burned during a demonstration of the same experiment in 2014 and 2015, respectively. In 2014, ACS officially released a safety alert, advising chemistry teachers of the dangers of this educational demonstration when carried out in this way, adding that even though demonstrating this experiment in a properly functioning chemical hood is safer than on an open bench, this, too, poses risks if fuel sources are not controlled (Hill, 2014). Therefore, ACS called for the discontinuation of this experiment performed with flammable solvents and suggested alternative ways to demonstrate the same rainbow phenomenon. For example, the teacher could soak wooden splints in salt solutions and then place the splints in a Bunsen burner, which affords a safer way for students to observe the salt's characteristic color.

The state of Utah reported that on average 160 students per year are injured in technology and engineering education laboratory accidents, and over half of these accidents (56%) were hand injuries while using saws and sanders (Love, 2014). Unfortunately, lack of training in hazard recognition and safety as it relates to implementing the use of hand and power tools has been reported for science teachers, who are those primarily teaching engineering at the K–12 level (Roy, 2012). Ensuring that science teachers remain informed about the most current safety practices and liabilities is the responsibility of both pre- and in-service institutions, and a case study approach during professional development is suggested as a promising model to promote safer teaching practices and policies (Love, 2014). It appears that current safety policies and practices for science and engineering tend to be reactive in nature, rather than reflecting proactive measures to prevent accidents and injury.

MAKING SCIENCE LEARNING A PRIORITY
IN MIDDLE AND HIGH SCHOOLS

In addition to physical space, budgetary, and safety considerations, effectively supporting students in science investigation and engineering design warrants an increase in emphasis on science learning. Historically, science has fallen behind English Language Arts (ELA) and mathematics in its precedence within public K–12 education. Recently, the amount of time that 8th graders spend on science has increased in a typical week but is still significantly less than the time they spend on ELA or mathematics instruction (U.S. Department of Education, 2011). Federal accountability policies, such as the *No Child Left Behind Act*[5] and *Every Student Succeeds Act,*[6] focused on standardized assessments in ELA and mathematics rather than in science, and in some states, student performance in science is not weighed equally with performance in mathematics and English (Gao et al., 2018). Even some parents in America view science as less important than reading, writing, or math are to their children's education and future career paths (Gao et al., 2018).

In this final section of the chapter, we discuss student time and technology needs that best support science investigation and engineering design. Additionally, we highlight areas of historic inequities that pose serious problems when attempting to provide quality science instruction to *all* middle and high school students. Lastly, we illustrate a few ways to immediately begin to modify instruction to align to the vision of the *Framework* at the classroom level, on the path to building sufficient resource capacity at the district level.

Student Time

Time spent doing science in appropriately structured instructional frames is a crucial part of science education. The degree of instructional time in science influences preparedness for the rigor of high school level science for middle school students, and college and career-readiness for high school

---

[5]No Child Left Behind Act of 2001, P.L. 107-110, 20 U.S.C.§ 6319 (2002).
[6]Every Student Succeeds Act of 2015. P.L. 114-95, 20 U.S.C.§ 6301 (2015-2016).

students. Additionally, time for instruction influences the level of skills that students develop and their capacity to actively engage in science and engineering learning, as it relates to thinking about the quality of evidence, interpreting evidence, and planning and refining a subsequent approach based on this evidence (National Research Council, 2007).

Standards aligned with the *Framework* lead to changes in course-taking patterns for science within middle and high schools (i.e., science every semester in grades 6–8 and at least 3 years of science in grades 9–12) and bring added scheduling demands along with space needs. Given current course scheduling patterns, these expectations may be difficult to implement or may restrict time available for students to take elective courses. Lack of time for science instruction has previously been reported as problematic within approximately one-third of middle and high schools (Banilower et al., 2013, p. 118, Table 7.15). Currently, class period timing patterns within public secondary schools range from 45-minute periods, with every subject every day, to longer class periods via a block-scheduling model (i.e., alternate day schedule, 4 x 4 semester plan, trimester plan). The latter types of schedules have advantages for any course where students are engaged in design project work or investigations; longer class periods mean that a single project or investigation spans fewer class periods, and less time is consumed by set-up and putting away of the work materials. School schedules are complicated by the diverse needs of various subjects and are influenced by advising and budget constraints; nevertheless, longer period options are compatible with investigation and design. As educators continue to develop strategies to implement the *Framework* with fidelity and to increase levels of academic performance for all students, each must be supported to use instructional time in different and more effective ways. When middle school science teachers were asked to estimate the time breakdown for each component within a recent science lesson, 40 percent of time on average was allocated to whole-class activities, 31 percent to small group work, and 20 percent to individual student work (Weiss, 2013, p. 18, Table 28). The remaining 10 percent of time was spent on non-instructional activities, such as attendance taking and classroom management duties. The same allocation patterns in time were reported by high school science teachers (Banilower et al., 2013, p. 79, Table 5.18). Approximately one-third of all middle and high schools use a block scheduling model (Banilower et al., 2013), and in science, this model might allow students to more easily move from one concept to the next and plan and carry out an investigation to enhance a concept, while still having time for follow-up discussion (Day, 1995). However, across districts, there may be different approaches to block scheduling, including those that deviate from a "consecutive minutes" model. So, while there are some advantages to implementing a block schedule, there are still many questions regarding this type of scheduling approach.

Technology

Technology is a key component of science investigations and engineering design. In *America's Lab Report*, the topic of computer technologies in laboratory experiences was briefly addressed, and a distinction was made between computer technologies designed to support *learning* and those designed to support *science* (National Research Council, 2006, pp. 103–106). Technologies designed to support *learning* include software programs developed specifically for the classroom, affording exploration of particular natural phenomena that may otherwise be inaccessible. Those designed to support *science* include Internet access to large databases that are more commonly designed for scientific communities, but can be utilized or repurposed for the K–12 science classroom (National Research Council, 2006). Within the last decade, computer technology has changed radically, along with access both inside and outside of the classroom by individual students and teachers.

More recent studies suggest that the availability of technologies in the classroom has become even more prevalent, in response to legislative initiatives such as ConnectED (McKnight et al., 2016). Schools and districts across the country have implemented 1:1 (1 laptop or tablet per student) or BYOD (bring your own device) programs, and as a result the use of handheld devices is growing faster than laptop use (Sung, Chang, and Liu, 2016). The low-cost Chromebook—a laptop designed to be used when connected to the Internet—was launched in 2011 and, by 2016, had become the majority of devices shipped to schools in the United States (Singer, 2017). Additionally, Google Classroom—a document-sharing application designed for the classroom environment—was launched in 2014 and is used by around 15 million students in the United States today (Singer, 2017). Table 8-1 below highlights the different technologies that are available for student use in schools by grade level, as reported by current teachers from 46 states and the District of Columbia who participated in a Web-based survey conducted by Simba Information in 2016.

As of 2016, and within science classes specifically, laptops and tablets are predominantly used to create student work and to access content during class (Simba Information, 2016, Table 3.7 and Table 3.8). Chromebook laptops in particular have become a popular choice for deployment of student technology, and 28.2 percent of educators reported that at least one Chromebook device is available for student use, with availability comparable between middle and high schools (as shown in Table 8-1). Additionally, smartphones have become more widely available for student use in the classroom, and not surprisingly, are most often utilized in high schools (Table 8-1).

Computer-based technology can support learners in conducting many aspects of scientific investigation and engineering design. Students can use

TABLE 8-1 Availability of Technological Devices for Student Use by Grade Level (in percentage)

Device	Middle School	High School	Total
Any Desktop Computer	36.1	35.1	53.4
iPad	22.9	23.4	36.9
Chromebook	33.7	33.0	28.2
Non-Chromebook Laptop	19.3	31.9	24.8
Student Response System	15.7	20.2	14.7
Smartphone	14.5	31.9	11.7
Non-iPad Tablet	1.2	5.3	4.4
eReader	3.6	2.1	3.4

SOURCE: Modified from Simba Information (2016).

these tools to gather, organize, and analyze data; develop models and scientific explanations to make sense of phenomena; and solve engineering design problems supported by the gathered evidence. For example, tablets and other portable devices with ubiquitous information access can be used for these purposes, as well as to link graphs, tables, and various images (e.g., photos of investigations, photos of data, and movies with text that describe the graphs and videos). Electronic probes with compatible software allow learners to collect, graph, and visualize a variety of data, including pH, force, light, distance and speed, and dissolved oxygen data (i.e., heart rate and blood pressure) that would be difficult, time consuming, or impossible to collect without their use. Although probes were introduced into science classrooms more than 25 years ago as useful laboratory tools, they have not been utilized to their full potential by middle and high school students in investigations due to lack of funding for equipment and professional development for teachers (Cayton, 2018). It is clear that modern technologies, supplies, and equipment can expand and support the domain of interest that can be explored in a science class. Therefore, provision for long-term use of these tools and for specialists to provide ongoing professional development for science teachers to use modern technologies effectively in their instruction is a critical component to successfully offer opportunities to learn through the utility of these resources.

For students with disabilities (SWD), the use of assistive technology or providing materials in alternate formats, following the principles of universal design for learning (UDL), are important accommodations to maximize access to science investigation and engineering design experiences (Burgstahler, 2012, Table 8-2). Other technology accommodations required for investigation and design may be inherent within the schools where

TABLE 8-2 Seven Principles of Universal Design for Learning

Principle	Descriptor
Equitable Use	The design is useful and marketable to people with diverse abilities.
Flexibility in Use	The design accommodates a wide range of individual preferences and abilities.
Simple and Intuitive Use	The design is easy to understand, regardless of the user's experience, knowledge, language skills, or current concentration level, when in use.
Perceptible Information	The design communicates necessary information effectively to the user, regardless of ambient conditions or the user's sensory abilities.
Tolerance for Error	The design minimizes hazards and the adverse consequences of accidental or unintended actions.
Low Physical Effort	The design can be used efficiently and comfortably and with a minimum of fatigue.
Size and Space for Approach and Use	Appropriate size and space is provided for approach, reach, manipulation, and use, regardless of user's body size, posture, or mobility.

SOURCE: Adapted from Center for Universal Design (1997).

these students are enrolled, such as Braille technology or tactile printouts of documents, captioning, or audio amplification technologies (Duerstock, 2018). Additionally, lab equipment, like a video camera mounted to a light microscope, helps students with visual and mobility impairments to view specimens without needing to use microscope eyepieces (Duerstock, 2018; Mansoor et. al., 2010). In the same way, technical accommodations for operating equipment exists, such as the use of Braille labels on lab equipment. The committee was unable to locate systemic data verifying the degree of implementation of these accommodations in U.S. middle and high schools, but it is likely that some UDL strategies are already in place. For instance, in response to the *Individuals with Disabilities Education Improvement Act of 2004,*[7] some districts have expanded their facilities to support students with special needs and disabilities by modifying building and grounds, along with class sizes and other programmatic changes (Filardo, 2016).

Disparities in Funding for Science Learning Needs

The goal of making science learning accessible to all students is complex and can require special knowledge, skill, authority, and resources. The beliefs and policies of the National School Boards Association (NSBA) on

---

[7]Individuals with Disabilities Education Improvement Act of 2004, P.L. 108-446, 20 U.S.C. § 1400 (2004).

equity state that "public schools should provide equitable access and ensure that all students have the knowledge and skills to succeed as contributing members of a rapidly changing, global society, regardless of factors, such as race, gender, sexual orientation, ethnic background, English proficiency, immigration status, socioeconomic status, or disability" (Center for Public Education, 2016). Additionally, NSBA defines educational equity as *intentionally* allocating resources, instruction, and opportunities according to need (National School Boards Association, 2018). This committee recognizes that disparities in funding for science learning needs (i.e., supplies, equipment, and technologies) continue to pose serious problems for providing quality science instruction to the most vulnerable populations of students. Quality science facilities, specialized equipment, and supplies facilitate science investigation and engineering design opportunities for *all* students, which prepare them to be college- and/or career-ready and informed 21st-century citizens.

Historically, school districts that serve large populations of students of color and students from low-income families have consistently received far less funding than those serving white and more affluent students. For example, a study of school facilities improvement projects between 1995 and 2004 found that projects emerging from schools located in high-wealth areas received greater than three times more in capital investments than schools in the lowest wealth areas (Filardo, 2016). More specifically, high-poverty districts receive about $1,000 less per student than low-poverty districts, and when adjusted based on the federal Title I formula, which accounts for the fact that educating students in poverty costs 40 percent more than the basic per pupil allocation, this funding gap widens (Center for Public Education, 2016; Morgan and Amerikaner, 2018). Moreover, this gap increases to $1,800 less per student when comparing funding allocated to districts serving the most students of color and those serving the fewest (Morgan and Amerikaner, 2018). In 2015, the funding distribution measure was classified as either flat or regressive for 37 states, meaning that these states did not allocate at least 5 percent more in funding to districts with high student poverty compared to low-poverty districts, which was determined to be the minimum additional support to ensure fair school funding (Baker et al., 2018). Still, these reported gaps are likely underestimations when considering the notion that many students in poverty start academically behind their more affluent peers and may need additional supports to reach comparable levels of achievement. For example, the Education Law Center developed a teacher-to-student fairness measure associated with improved student outcomes, and defined fairness as a greater distribution of teachers to schools with greatest need, such as those that service a large number of students living in poverty (Baker et al., 2017, 2018). The most recent data revealed that only 19 states have a progressive distribution of teachers (at least 5% more teachers per students) in high-poverty districts compared to low-poverty districts, which is a decrease from 2013–2014, when 22 states were reported to do so (Baker et al., 2017, 2018). Thus, failure to distribute teachers equitably remains a challenge and likely decreases opportunities to create safer and effective learning environments for conducting science investigation and engineering design. Furthermore, fiscal resources determine teacher salaries, the extent and frequency of professional development, the length of the school day, and the number of students in the classroom among a great number of other factors, demonstrating the potential systemic effects of funding inequities.

Maintenance and operations (M&O) budgets support the ongoing costs of equipment, materials, supplies, and technologies, as well as any required maintenance, upgrades, and repair (Filardo, 2016). In *America's Lab Report,* disparities in science lab equipment and supplies were found to pose serious problems, particularly in high schools with the largest populations of students in poverty and students from historically underrepresented groups. Additionally, it was mentioned that while, in some cases, there may be a sufficient capital budget to build a science lab space, only limited funds may be set aside in the M&O budget to provide the equipment and supplies to use the lab over subsequent years (National Research Council, 2006). Since the 2006 report, student access to learning tools has increased in some ways, but disparities in both quantity and quality of science labs, equipment, materials, and supplies in middle and high schools persist (Banilower et al., 2013, p. 118, Table 7.15 and Table 7.16; Gao et al., 2018). More than 57 percent of districts in California reported that the quantity of science equipment was a big issue in middle and high schools, and was most concerning in 69 percent of low-performing districts (Gao et al., 2018, p.13, Figure 7).[8] Additionally, only 54 percent of districts reported that the conditions of more than half of the science labs in their districts were sufficient (Gao et al., 2018, p.13, Figure 7).

Median spending per pupil, specifically for science equipment (e.g., microscopes, beakers, Bunsen burners) and consumable supplies (e.g., chemicals, batteries, paper), are not distributed equally across schools. Schools in rural areas spend $3.78 per pupil on equipment and supplies (including software) compared to $1.91 per pupil spent in urban areas, which is consistent with the finding that the smallest schools spend almost twice as much, $3.94/pupil, on these materials compared to the largest schools that spend $2.04/pupil (Banilower et al., 2013, p. 105, Table 6.21). Spending was also found to be 2.3 times more in schools where the lowest quartile of students

---

[8] District performance was defined by degree of participation in Advanced Placement courses, whereby low-performing districts fall in the bottom quartile for participation.

eligible for free or reduced-price lunch are enrolled ($3.56/pupil) compared to spending in schools with the highest quartile of these students enrolled ($1.54/pupil) (Banilower et al., 2013, p. 105, Table 6.21). Science facilities (e.g., lab tables, electric outlets, faucets, and sinks) were reported to be adequate for instruction by 57 percent of teachers in middle schools and 71 percent of teachers in high schools (Banilower et al., 2013, p. 106, Table 6.23).

On the contrary, instructional technologies (e.g., computers, calculators, probes/sensors) were reported to be inadequate for instruction by more than 50 percent of science teachers in both middle and high schools (Banilower et al., 2013, p. 106, Table 6.23). In terms of technology-related issues, aged computers and lack of access to computers were reported as a serious problem for instruction, particularly in middle school science classes, but Internet access and reliability, and the availability of software were generally nonproblematic across middle and high schools (Banilower et al., 2013, p. 108, Table 7.21). More recently, access to desktop computers has been observed at above-average levels in districts with high proportions of students eligible for free or reduced-price lunch, and in the majority of districts in rural locations (Simba Information, 2016). On the contrary, tablets and laptops are still most often accessible in higher socioeconomic districts and suburban areas (Simba Information, 2016). Overall, modern and adequate resources for science instruction are more likely to be available in classes with mostly high achievers and in schools with the lowest quartiles of students eligible for free or reduced-priced lunch (Banilower et al., 2013, p. 108, Table 6.26).

Making Incremental Progress Toward the Ideal

Throughout this chapter, we have discussed associated needs (i.e., physical space, time, fiscal resources, and equipment/technologies) for investigation and design. What we have outlined can be considered the ideal, in which each element is optimally supplied. The committee recognizes that there are many barriers to designing, constructing, and equipping schools with the needed supplies and equipment that are discussed in this chapter. Furthermore, the multiple levels of oversight and accountability within districts and schools suggest that for many schools, building full resource capacity will require several months to years. However, engaging *all* students in science investigation and engineering design in the classroom is necessary even when access to the full range of resources is limited.

Science investigation and design can still take place in the absence of the most sophisticated facilities; however, they must remain purposeful, substantial, student-centered, and three-dimensional. Additionally, all components of these experiences should align to at least one of four features: a question based on a phenomenon in the natural or engineered world, engagement with empirical evidence to develop models and explanations, involvement of discourse and development of ideas, and placement within a coherent sequence. By starting with a few strategic initial investments in teachers' professional learning and quality equipment, there are opportunities to immediately shift toward more student-centered work and make incremental progress toward the ideal. There are ways to begin engaging students in science investigation and engineering design in the classroom now concurrently with district-level coordination of larger shifts in funding allocation for science learning that will be required for alignment to all recommendations in this report.

For example, there are a variety of ways to modify a water quality project to fit local needs and currently available resources. Even in the absence of optimal resources, students can still ask questions, collect and analyze data, and write an explanation about the water quality of a local body of water. Chiefly, it is important for students to be engaged in a phenomenon, such as the health of a local body of water, that provides opportunities to explain findings and potentially design solutions to problems that are uncovered based on these explanations. Time and equipment constraints present real challenges, but it is possible to introduce students to three-dimensional science learning, even if these barriers limit students to only vicarious experiences to build on. Whether students can physically travel to the body of water or if the body of water must be brought to them to facilitate student-led questions and sense-making of water quality measures, adapting and personalizing projects to the local community can help to motivate learners. Situating the investigation in the context of a waterway and water issues relevant in the community and taking instruments to the site to gather data over time can make the project more meaningful.

Sophisticated technology can allow students to ask complex questions and produce interesting models as they study a body of water over time. However, students can observe some measures of water quality (e.g., color, smell, amount of trash) without a need for instruments, and simple water quality kits can also be used for data collection. In some cases, thermometers and pH paper are the only available tools. These laboratory tools can be used to measure water quality, and although these tools offer limited measures of water quality, students can still be engaged in figuring out the quality of their body of water. Additionally, adaptations can be made when only a limited number of tools for students are available. For example, a teacher can set up stations for students to visit in rotations throughout the course of the investigation. One station might contain an electronic dissolved oxygen probe or dissolved oxygen kit, another station might contain an electronic pH probe, pH paper, or a pH kit, and yet another, a probe for dissolved solids, or nitrate and phosphate testing kits.[9]

Another example of an accessible solution to get students engaged with investigation and design quickly as resources are gathered is to have them start creating ideas for models that could explain their results. Modeling is an essential aspect of doing science and engaging learners in making sense of phenomena. Students, as professional scientists, should develop, revise, and use models to predict and explain phenomena. If computers or tablets are accessible, then students can use these technologies along with freely available modeling software to create dynamic models. These tools allow students to validate their models by comparing the outputs from their own models with data they collected from their experiments or from other sources. Although there are advantages to using dynamic modeling, the use of such sophisticated technology is not a requirement for constructing an explanatory model or using models to engage in the doing of science.

SUMMARY

More flexible science and engineering class spaces are ideal for supporting a three-dimensional model of instruction that is student-centered as envisioned by the *Framework* (National Research Council, 2012). Additionally, increases in new construction and renovation of existing spaces are needed to provide all students with quality science and engineering learning experiences. While some schools have appropriate facilities, over one-half of the nation's public schools still need extensive improvements to meet the needs for students to effectively engage in science investigation and engineering design. Moreover, consistent and increased investment in facilities is needed to sufficiently provide adequate spaces for 21st-century science learning.

To ensure student safety that affords adequate supervision, the square footage of science classroom spaces must meet regulations, along with class size. While each state may require its own safety requirements based on building and fire safety codes and the special needs of students in the class, NSTA recommends a maximum of 24 students in a classroom with a minimum of 60 square feet per student. Better comprehensive training in safety and safety enforcement for science teachers are needed to establish preventive measures against accidents and injuries, while engaging in science investigation and engineering design. Likewise, though outdoor spaces present invaluable opportunities to enhance science learning experiences

---

[9]A variety of water-quality testing kits may be obtained from companies such as Hach at https://www.hach.com [October 2018] or LaMotte at http://www.lamotte.com/en/education/water-monitoring/5870-01.html [October 2018].

for students, more guidance is needed for safe and effective teaching and learning in these spaces.

Specifically, in middle school, time spent on science instruction continues to fall behind time allocated for math and English Language Arts, which may contribute to the problem of student unpreparedness for the rigor of science in high school. Additionally, longer instructional periods may be most compatible with investigation and design experiences that need to span multiple class periods. Technology and specialized equipment greatly enhance science investigation and engineering design experiences and improve the ability of students to gather meaningful and accurate data to support explanations. Growing access to learning technologies, such as desktop computers, laptops, and other portable devices, has been observed in recent years, but similar to the case with human resources described in Chapter 7, instructional resources and funding are disproportionately allocated, leaving many schools under-resourced and specific populations of students underserved and underprepared. Short-term strategies afford immediate shifts toward the vision for science teaching and learning outlined in this report, but continuous investments in route to building full resource capacity are greatly warranted.

REFERENCES

Abramson, P. (2005). *10th Annual School Annual Construction Report. National Statistics, Building Trends & Detailed Analysis.* Springboro, OH: School Planning and Management.

Abramson, P. (2015). *20th Annual School Construction Report National Statistics, Building Trends & Detailed Analysis.* Springboro, OH: School Planning and Management.

American Chemical Society. (2018). *ACS Guidelines and Recommendations for Teaching Middle and High School Chemistry.* Washington, DC: Author.

American Society of Civil Engineers. (2005). *Infrastructure Report Card.* Washington, DC: Author.

American Society of Civil Engineers. (2017). *Infrastructure Report Card.* Washington, DC: Author.

American Society of Professional Estimators. (2014). *A Technical Paper: How to Estimate the Cost of a High School Laboratory at Conceptual Level.* Available: https://cdn. ymaws.com/www.aspenational.org/resource/resmgr/Techical_Papers/2014_June_Tp.pdf [October 2018].

Baker, B., Farrie, D., Johnson, M., Luhm, T., and Sciarra, D.G. (2017). *Is School Funding Fair? A National Report Card* (6th Edition). Education Law Center. Available: http://www. edlawcenter.org/assets/files/pdfs/publications/National_Report_Card_2017.pdf [October 2018].

Baker, B., Farrie, D., and Sciarra, D.G. (2018). *Is School Funding Fair? A National Report Card* (7th Edition). Education Law Center. Available: http://www.edlawcenter.org/assets/ files/pdfs/publications/Is_School_Funding_Fair_7th_Editi.pdf [October 2018].

Banilower, E.R., Smith, P.S., Weiss, I.R., Malzahn, K.A., Campbell, K.M., and Weis, A.M. (2013). *Report of the 2012 National Survey of Science and Mathematics Education.* Chapel Hill, NC: Horizon Research.

Barrett, P., Davies, F., Zhang, Y., and Barrett, L. (2015). The impact of classroom design on pupil's learning: Final results of a holistic, multi-level analysis. *Building and Environment, 89*, 118–133.

Beichner, R. (2008). *The SCALE-UP Project: A Student-Centered, Active Learning Environment for Undergraduate Programs*. An invited white paper for the National Academy of Sciences. Available: https://sites.nationalacademies.org/cs/groups/dbassesite/documents/webpage/dbasse_072628.pdf [October 2018].

Blikstein, P. (2013). Digital fabrication and 'making' in education: The democratization of invention. In J. Walter-Herrmann and C. Büching (Eds.), *FabLabs: Of Machines, Makers and Inventors*. Bielefeld, Germany: Transcript.

Burgstahler, S. (2012). *Making Science Labs Accessible to Students with Disabilities: Application of Universal Design to a Science Lab*. (DO-IT)- Disabilities, Opportunities, Internetworking and Technology. University of Washington, College of Engineering. Available: https://www.washington.edu/doit/sites/default/files/atoms/files/Making-Science-Labs-Accessible-Students-Disabilities.pdf [October 2018].

Campbell, T., and Bohn, C. (2008). Science laboratory experiences of high school students across one state in the U.S.: Descriptive research from the classroom. *Science Educator, 17*(1), 36–48.

Cayton, E.M. (2018). *Exploring Funding for Instructional Materials in Secondary Science Classrooms*. Dissertation submitted to North Carolina State University. Available: https://repository.lib.ncsu.edu/bitstream/handle/1840.20/35088/etd.pdf [October 2018].

Center for Public Education. (January 2016). *Educational Equity: What does it mean? How do we know when we reach it?* Available: http://www.centerforpubliceducation.org/system/files/Equity Symposium_0.pdf [October 2018].

Center for Universal Design. (1997). *Seven Principles of Universal Design for Learning*. Raleigh: North Carolina State University.

Cohen, J., Jones, W.M., Smith, S., and Calandra, B. (2016). Makification: Towards a framework for leveraging the maker movement in formal education. *Journal of Educational Multimedia and Hypermedia, 26*(3), 217–229.

Day, T. (1995). New class on the block. *The Science Teacher, 62*(4), 28–30.

Duerstock, B. (2018). *Inclusion of Students with Disabilities in the Lab*. The American Physiological Society. Available: http://www.the-aps.org/forum-disabilities [October 2018].

Environmental Protection Agency. (n.d.). *Healthy Schools and Indoor Air Quality*. Available: https://www.epa.gov/schools-air-water-quality/healthy-schools-and-indoor-air-quality [October 2018].

Filardo, M. (2016). *State of Our Schools: America's K–12 Facilities 2016*. Washington, DC: 21st Century School Fund.

Filardo, M., and Vincent, J.M. (2017). *Adequate & Equitable U.S. PK–12 Infrastructure: Priority Actions for Systemic Reform*. Washington, DC: 21st Century School Fund, Center for Cities + Schools, National Council on School Facilities, and Center for Green Schools.

Gao, N., Adan, S., Lopes, G., and Lee, G. (2018). *Implementing the Next Generation Science Standards: Early Evidence from California*. Stanford: Public Policy Institute of California.

Grossman, S., and Craven, K. (2010). *MSBA Guidelines for Science Labs*. Massachusetts School Building Authority. Boston: Massachusetts School Building Authority. Available: http://www.massschoolbuildings.org/sites/default/files/edit-contentfiles/Documents/SLI/Science_Lab_Guideline_Presentation.pdf [October 2018].

Haynie, W.J., III. (2009). Safety and liability in the new technology laboratory. *The Technology Teacher, 69*(3), 31–36.

Hill, R. (2014). Safety alert: The rainbow demonstration. *Chemical & Engineering News, 92*(11), 43. Available: https://cen.acs.org/articles/92/i11/Safety-Alert-Rainbow-Demonstration.html [October 2018].

Kemsley, J. (2015). Teaching safely. *Chemical & Engineering News*, 93(46), 37–39. Available: https://cen.acs.org/content/dam/cen/93/46/09346-educ.pdf [October 2018].

Love, T.S. (2014). Safety and liability in STEM education laboratories: Using case law to inform policy and practice. *The Technology and Engineering Teacher, 73*(5), 1–13.

Mansoor, A., Ahmed, W.M., Samarapungavan, A., Cirillo, J., Schwarte, D., Robinson, J.P., and Duerstock, B.S. (2010). AccessScope project: Accessible light microscope for users with upper limb mobility or visual impairments. *Disability and Rehabilitation: Assistive Technology, 5*(2), 143–152.

Maryland Department of Education. (1999). Legal aspects of laboratory safety. In *Science Safety Manual*. Available: http://mdk12.msde.maryland.gov/instruction/curriculum/science/safety/index.html [October 2018].

McKnight, K., O'Malley, K., Ruzic, R., Horsley, M.K., Franey, J.J., and Bassett, K. (2016). Teaching in a digital age: How educators use technology to improve student learning. *Journal of Research on Technology in Education, 48*(3), 194–211.

Moorefield-Lang, H. (2014). Makers in the library: Case studies of 3D printers and maker spaces in library settings. *Library Hi Tech, 32*(4), 583–593.

Morgan, I., and Amerikaner, A. (2018). *Funding Gaps 2018: An Analysis of School Funding Equity Across the U.S. and Within Each State.* Washington, DC: The Education Trust.

Motz, L., Biehle, J., and West, S. (2007). *The NSTA Guide to Planning School Science Facilities, 2nd Edition.* Arlington, VA: National Science Teachers Association.

National Research Council. (2006). *America's Lab Report: Investigations in High School Science.* Washington, DC: The National Academies Press.

National Research Council. (2007). *Taking Science to School: Learning and Teaching Science in Grades K-8.* Washington, DC: The National Academies Press.

National Research Council. (2012). *A Framework for K–12 Science Education: Practices, Crosscutting Concepts, and Core Ideas.* Washington, DC: The National Academies Press.

National School Boards Association. (2018). *NSBA's Vision for Equity in Public Education* Available: https://www.nsba.org/about-us/equity [October 2018].

National Science Teachers Association. (2007). *The Integral Role of Laboratory Investigations in Science Instruction: A Position Paper.* Available: https://www.nsta.org/about/positions/laboratory.aspx [October 2018].

National Science Teachers Association. (2014a). *Duty or Standard of Care.* Paper by the NSTA Safety Advisory Board. Available: http://static.nsta.org/pdfs/DutyOfCare.pdf [October 2018].

National Science Teachers Association. (2014b). *Overcrowding in the Instructional Space.* Paper by the NSTA Safety Advisory Board. Available: http://static.nsta.org/pdfs/OvercrowdingInTheInstructionalSpace.pdf [October 2018].

National Science Teachers Association. (2015). *Field Trip Safety.* Paper by the NSTA Safety Advisory Board. Available: http://static.nsta.org/pdfs/FieldTripSafety.pdf [October 2018].

Neill, S., and Etheridge, R. (2008). Flexible learning spaces: The integration of pedagogy, physical design, and instructional technology. *Marketing Education Review, 18*(1), 47–53.

North American Association for Environmental Education. (2006). *Core Competencies for NAAEE Certification Programs.* Available: https://naaee.org/eepro/resources/certification-based-individuals [October 2018].

North Carolina Department of Public Instruction. (2010). *School Science Facilities Planner.* Raleigh: Author. Available: http://www.schoolclearinghouse.org/pubs/SCIENCE.PDF [October 2018].

Occupational Safety & Health Administration, U.S. Department of Labor. (n.d.). *Indoor Air Quality: Schools.* Available: https://www.osha.gov/SLTC/indoorairquality/schools.html [October 2018].

Prosser, W.L., Keeton, W.P., Dobbs, D.B., Keeton, R.E., and Owen, D.G. (Eds.) (1984). *Prosser and Keeton on Torts.* 5th ed. Eagan, MN: West Group.

Roy, K. (2012). STEM: A question of safety. *Science Scope, 36* (1), 84–85.

Simba Information. (2016). *K-12 Classroom Technology Survey Report 2016.* Stanford, CT: Author.

Singer, N. (2017). How Google took over the classroom. *The New York Times.* Available: https://www.nytimes.com/2017/05/13/technology/google-education-chromebooks-schools.html?_r=0 [October 2018].

Stephenson, A.L., West, S., and Westerlund, J. (2003). An analysis of incident/accident reports from the Texas Secondary school Science Safety Survey, 2001. *School Science and Mathematics, 103*(6), 293–303.

Success Link. (2007). *The State of Middle School and High School Science Labs in the Kansas City Region.* doi: 10.2139/ssrn.2355018.

Sung, Y.T., Chang, K.E., and Liu, T.C. (2016). The effects of integrating mobile devices with teaching and learning on students' learning performance: A meta-analysis and research synthesis. *Computers & Education, 94*(Suppl. C), 252–275.

University of Georgia College of Agricultural and Environmental Sciences. (2017). *School Garden Initiative-Sixth, Seventh, and Eight Grade Curriculum.* Atlanta, GA: Author.

U.S. Chemical Safety & Hazard Investigation Board. (2013). *After the Rainbow.* Available: https://www.csb.gov/videos/after-the-rainbow/ [October 2018].

U.S. Department of Defense Education Activity. (2014). *DoDEA Education Facilities Specification for 21st Century Schools. Space Types and Requirements-Science Laboratory.* Available: https://www.dodea.edu/edSpecs/upload/20140204_ScienceLab.pdf [October 2018].

U.S. Department of Defense Education Activity. (2017). *DoDEA Education Facilities Specifications–Middle School.* Available: https://www.dodea.edu/edSpecs/upload/20170208_V5_MS.pdf [October 2018].

U.S. Department of Education. (2011). *National Center for Education Statistics. Schools and Staffing Survey, 2011–12.* Available: https://nces.ed.gov/pubs2016/2016817_1.pdf [October 2018].

U.S. Department of Education. (2014). *Schools and Staffing Survey,* Public School Teacher Data File, 2011–12. Washington, DC: Author.

U.S. Department of Education. (2016a). *Changes in America's Public School Facilities: From School Year 1998-99 to School Year 2012-13. Stats in Brief.* National Center for Education Statistics 2016-074. Washington, DC: Author.

U.S. Department of Education. (2016b). *National Public Education Financial Survey, 2000–01 through 2014–15.* Available: https://nces.ed.gov/programs/coe/indicator_cmb.asp [October 2018].

Voorheesville Central School District. (2017). *2020 Capital Project: Science Lab Cost Estimates.* Voorheesville, NY. Available: https://www.voorheesville.org/cms/lib/NY01914012/Centricity/Domain/248/Science Labs Cost Estimates.pdf [October 2018].

Wall, G. (2016). *The Impact of Physical Design on Student Outcomes.* Commissioned for the New Zealand Ministry of Education. Wellington, New Zealand.

Washington State Office of Superintendent of Public Instruction (June 2016). *STEM Pilot Project Grant Program.* Available: http://www.k12.wa.us/LegisGov/2016documents/2015-16-STEMPilotProgram.pdf [October 2018].

Weiss, A.M. (2013). *2012 National Survey of Science and Mathematics Education: Status of Middle School Science.* Chapel Hill, NC: Horizon Research.

West, S., and Kennedy, L. (2014). Science safety in secondary Texas schools: A longitudinal study. *Proceedings of the 2014 Hawaiian International Conference on Education,* Honolulu, HI.

9

The Education System and Investigation and Design

Making science investigation and engineering design the center of science and engineering learning in middle and high school classrooms is a dramatic change to the status quo. As described throughout the report, engaging all students in investigation and design requires significant effort by teachers and can only happen if the complex factors outside the classroom support their work. Influences come from the policies and practices at the school, district, regional, state, and national levels. While science education reform has been happening almost as long as science has been taught in schools, this constant quest for improvement had several turning points in the history of science education (see Chapter 2). As this report has illustrated, since the 2006 release of *America's Lab Report* (National Research Council, 2006), the education community has been increasing the extent to which knowledge of how students learn is applied to teaching and has been paying more attention to including a diverse range of students in the kinds of science learning that prepare all students for the future (Krajcik and Shin, 2014; Lee, Quinn, and Valdés, 2013).

Previous chapters of this report have looked at the student experience with investigation and design and some of the more closely related parts of the system. In this chapter we turn to consider the system as a whole. Implementation of investigation and design is impacted by multiple other factors: the availability of classrooms well equipped with tools, technology, equipment, and supplies (see Chapter 8); teachers who have access to high-quality instructional resources and professional learning experiences (see Chapters 6 and 7); and the time to prepare and use available resources (touched on in Chapters 7 and 8). Many other interacting factors influence implementation as well, such as the culture of the school and district; state requirements for curriculum, testing, and graduation; and the perspectives and priorities of the local community. There is not a significant research base on systemic issues related to implementation of investigation and design. Therefore, the committee considers here several ways of thinking about the education system and education reform. This serves to inform the discussion of selected efforts to reform education and what might be learned from those experiences that could be applied to the context of investigation and design.

This chapter contains discussion of interacting components of the education system relevant to implementation of investigation and design, a continuous improvement model applied to investigation and design, potential lessons from previous efforts to improve education, and the importance of considering equity and inclusion during reform.

THE INTERACTING COMPONENTS
OF THE EDUCATION SYSTEM

The U.S. education system includes control from various levels: school, district, regional, state, and federal. Through the passing of the *Elementary and Secondary Education Act* (1965) and codified in the *No Child Left Behind Act* (2001), test-based accountability policies were put into place to ensure that all students were held to the same rigorous academic standards in core subjects (Penfield and Lee, 2010). There have been many analyses of the complex educational system in the United States (e.g., Cohen, 1995; Ghaffarzadegan, Larson, and Hawley, 2016; Hamilton, Stecher, and Yuan, 2009; Mital, Moore, and Llewellyn, 2014), and it is beyond the committee's charge to delve into a deep consideration of all the levels and components. However, we have worked to identify some of the key aspects of the system that influence implementation of science investigation and engineering design. Figure 9-1 presents one interpretation of the complex interactions that influence each other in the ways that impact science education in the classroom. As noted in Figure 9-1, the committee identified many factors at different levels that influence what students encounter in the classroom. States often determine the standards that must be met as well as play a significant role in funding of schools. Districts often make decisions about instructional time, space, facilities, and other resources, as well as about course sequences. In addition to these key components, it is important to consider the influences of federal policies, national efforts, and perspectives from the local communities and cultures where schools exist.

Some components that more closely influence what students encounter include teachers who enter the classroom, teacher preparation programs, teacher preparation regulations, how teachers are evaluated, and state and

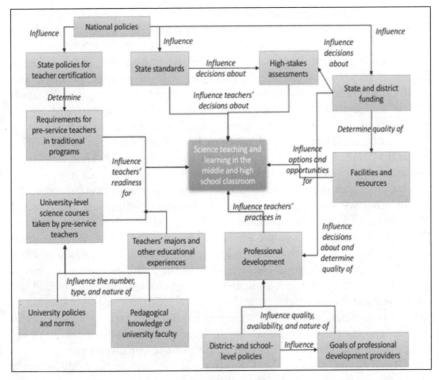

FIGURE 9-1 Committee's representation of some interactions within the U.S. education system.
NOTE: These interactions occur within and are influenced by the social, political, economic, and cultural milieu of the United States.

local certification requirements. Others impact the content and focus of the material used in classrooms, such as the curriculum and instructional resources. Assessment policies, including state and federally mandated tests, also influence what happens in the classroom. Standardized tests impact what is perceived as important and this can be challenging when the focus or format of the tests do not align well with the instructional approach chosen. The tests can also constrain course sequencing options because students need to enroll in the expected courses before the relevant required exams. Other components that influence classroom experiences include the approach taken to professional learning and the opportunities and incentives for teachers to participate in professional leaning and to apply their learning to their daily work. In addition, school leaders and teachers' expectations, priorities, and degree of commitment to equity together create an instructional climate that encourage or discourage particular pedagogical approaches. The literature about how teacher evaluation influences teachers' values and practices is informative and can provide insight for administrators who observe and evaluate teachers (Firestone, 2014; Harris and Harrington, 2015; Hinchey, 2010).

Other important factors that need to be considered and have been discussed in previous chapters include the role of parents, families, and communities that help to shape a student's learning. By leveraging the funds of knowledge that these constituents bring to the classroom and school environment, the potential for more equitable learning environments can be attended to. That is, there needs to be greater attention to the socio-cultural system. Unfortunately, although the committee acknowledges the importance, they are not included in Figure 9-1 as the influence has multiple touch points and should be a pervasive component of the system overall.

In other words, what goes on in classrooms is influenced and affected by a variety of factors within and beyond a single school, district, and state. Decisions are made at multiple levels and interact in various ways to influence the education students receive. Therefore, thinking about education and education reform requires a consideration of the complex interacting pieces of the system that can affect implementation of changes. Efforts to bring science investigation and engineering design to all students must be cognizant of the constraints and opportunities coming from many directions. Thoughtful analysis can contribute to the ability to leverage opportunities for improvement and to address challenges that might impede improvement.

Of particular note in the U.S. education system is how education is primarily a state and local responsibility. Although the components of the education system interact mostly at the state level, federal regulations and programs do have an impact on focus and priorities. The federal government's role in education has varied over time but is relatively minimal in terms of funding, providing only about 8 percent of the money spent on elementary and secondary education (U.S. Department of Education, 2017). The system is also influenced by the participation of many other stakeholders. Public and private organizations develop standards, curriculum, and instructional resources. Often, state colleges and universities prepare and provide continuing education to teachers.

The interaction between K–12 and higher education is complex and multidirectional. In addition to the role of higher education in preparing future teachers and providing some professional learning for in-service teachers, higher education also provides a model for teachers of how science and engineering are taught. When teachers have experiences with separate laboratory sections that do not closely relate to their in-class learning, it can influence their expectations for how K–12 students learn science and what they see as optimal to prepare their students for college coursework. Undergraduate experiences are slowly moving away from these traditional approaches, with more of these students being exposed to evidence-based pedagogy and other new approaches such as course-based undergraduate research experiences (National Academies of Sciences, Engineering, and Medicine, 2017).

State standards have a large influence on the type of instruction that takes place in the classroom. Interactions between standards, curriculum, and resources have a significant influence on what is taught and how it is taught. Whereas policy makers may choose standards, the interpretations of the standards and the enacted curriculum are influenced on a more local level. The fidelity of implementation of the intended curriculum is also influenced by the support that teachers receive either via in-service professional development or in their teacher preparation programs and by the funding allocated for the acquisition of instructional resources and construction of instructional spaces that facilitate the type of instruction conductive to the learning outcomes described in this report.

A Framework for K–12 Science Education (hereafter referred to as the *Framework*; National Research Council, 2012) calls for substantial changes in science teaching and learning that are impacted by and have implications for many of the components of the education system described above. Specific changes needed to put investigation and design in the center of the middle and high school classroom require changes to instruction and the nature of the student experience. They should also build on the experiences students have in elementary school where they begin learning progressions of the *Framework*. A high priority needs to be placed on professional learning and the selection and use of appropriate high-quality instructional resources, as well as ensuring access to adequate space and suitable equipment and supplies.

CONTINUOUS IMPROVEMENT MODEL

Implementation of investigation and design as the central focus of middle and high school science and engineering courses requires many significant changes and is not expected to happen at once. A continuous improvement model can be applied to the ongoing and sustained efforts that will be needed to enact change. A coherent strategy is more likely to emerge if decision makers have a mechanism for considering the various components of the system and how they interact. In this section, we group the components into three interrelated areas used by scholars who study systemic science education reform in the United States: organizational culture, capability, and policy and management (Blumenfeld et al., 2000). Work in each of these areas can be aligned, and efforts in each area can combine to foster continuous improvement.

The first area is organizational culture, which includes expectations for collaboration and reflection by educators and the local context of school and school district norms, routines, and practices. When considering science investigation and engineering design, key aspects of this area include leadership, accountability, data-driven decision making, and collaboration. School leaders and teachers' expectations, priorities, and degree of commitment to equity together create an instructional climate that encourages or discourages particular pedagogical approaches. For example, schools and districts will vary in the expectations for teachers to spend time gaining information about new approaches to teaching. District leaders play key roles in supporting and encouraging sincere efforts to improve or being satisfied with the status quo. Reciprocal accountability where teachers and administrators are together and separately responsible for continued improvement can enhance progress. That is, it may be beneficial to make decisions and base district policies on an expectation of good instruction and not merely on compliance with policies and regulations.

The second area is capability, which includes the ability to implement curriculum and strategies and is dependent on educators' beliefs and expertise. When considering science investigation and engineering design, key aspects of this area include familiarity with *Framework*-aligned approaches, instructional resources of the type described in Chapter 6, and qualified educators with access to quality professional learning experiences such as described in Chapter 7. Another important aspect of educators' beliefs is their perspectives about who can and should do science and engineering, and their knowledge about inequality and inequity in science and engineering. Districts vary in their focus on providing high-quality science and engineering experiences for all students, as well as the number and qualifications of their educators and the access provided for teachers to process and utilize instructional resources. The opportunity to collaborate with other teachers and form professional learning communities to work together on implementation and refinement of teaching affects capability for change.

Policy and management make up the third area, which concerns funding, resources, scheduling, staffing, and allocation of responsibility, including monitoring and guidance. In the context of investigation and design, this area would include many of the topics discussed in Chapter 8, such as space, equipment, supplies, time, and scheduling, as well as staffing policies. Decisions about instructional time, resources, and course sequences are made at different levels of the system and have a direct impact on and are impacted by the availability and types of instructional spaces and teacher expertise. As such, states and districts may need to consider instructional strategies that have shown the greatest promise when making decisions about courses and teacher expertise. Policies on assigning teachers, courses, and spaces impact the success of implementation of investigation and design. Smaller-scale decisions about equipment and supplies and time to order, prepare, and clean them up can also be important.

POTENTIAL LESSONS FROM PREVIOUS IMPROVEMENT EFFORTS

As described in Chapter 2, throughout history various stakeholders in science education have pursued transformations in science instruction. Different stakeholders have led these pursuits, and the pursuits have targeted different levers in science education. For example, starting in the 1950s and spanning several decades, the National Science Foundation (NSF) spearheaded efforts to change science curriculum; it initiated similarly structured efforts commencing in the 1970s geared toward the professional development of teachers (National Research Council, 2007; National Science Foundation, 2000). Likewise, states instituted a wave of initiatives to raise high school graduation requirements in science in the 1980s (Clune and White, 1992; Lee and Ready, 2009). These pre-1990 reforms generally addressed facets of science education in isolation of other aspects of the system. This section identifies several education reform efforts in the context of their interactions with the system via consideration of the areas in the continuous improvement structure described above.

The observations made about the examples we present are based on available literature and the experiences of the committee. As discussed in Chapter 1, the committee is confident in making different types of conclusions depending on the strength of the supporting evidence. The examples here rely mainly on evaluation studies or summary documents as supporting evidence, most of which have not been subject to peer review. They are nevertheless informative for considering the factors that must be considered in making efforts to implement investigation and design. In addition, most of these efforts pre-date the *Framework* and the Next Generation Science Standards (NGSS). However, to the extent possible, we have chosen examples in which the general pedagogical approach is similar to, and reflects the intellectual underpinnings of, the *Framework*. Finally, because research on investigation and design in the way the committee is conceiving of it is scarce, most of the examples focus on the broader idea of science instruction rather than on investigations per se. The examples also do not include engineering because research on K–12 engineering education was even scarcer before the *Framework* and NGSS. For the sake of the discussion, we use improving instruction as a proxy for improving investigation and design, though we acknowledge that further research is needed to confirm the strength of that connection.

REFORM EFFORTS

We consider the ways that these past efforts can provide lessons for achieving *Framework*- style classrooms with investigation and design at the center. It is important to note that not all of these efforts enjoyed total or sustained success and that many happened in schools and classrooms where the vision of the *Framework* had not yet been realized. However, they are instructive because they show the complexity and difficulty of meaningful and lasting change, and this can inform attempts to secure science investigation and engineering design for all students.

Policy and Management: San Diego City Schools

In the early 2000s, San Diego City Schools in California began an ambitious effort to improve science instruction at scale (Bess and Bybee, 2004). This effort had strong leadership support and coupled instructional materials with professional development to improve instruction. It also involved a redesign of course sequencing to better serve students.

The instructional materials used by San Diego during this time (*BSCS A Human Approach*, *Active Physics*, *Living by Chemistry*) were all based on NSF-funded research and were developed by practitioners and academic researchers with a robust understanding of the current science education context and research. Yet even when coupled with extensive professional development (2 weeks in- the summer, 7 days during the academic year) and supports from the district and curriculum developers, the improvement work of the district was challenging. Writing about the professional development challenges, leaders of the effort expressed a pessimistic view about the amount of work needed to generate improvements (Bess and Bybee, 2004, p. 7):

> Most teachers were unprepared to support an inquiry-based curriculum. Few had any concrete grasp of a sound instruction model. The management of the instructional materials and equipment for use by all students to develop conceptual understanding overwhelmed many teachers. Many teachers hold deep-seated doubt about the capabilities of their students. They are challenged in evaluating conceptual understanding.

Discussing the outcomes of this effort, Bess and Bybee (2004, p. 9) went on to say:

> Teachers report that they struggle with classroom and materials management, questioning strategies, assessment tools (other than multiple choice), and supporting English learners. The standards test score data show some improvement on moving students to higher performance bands and some

success in moving students from the lowest performance band into to the basic level performance band. There is, however, a great deal of room for improvement.

These findings are sobering for those seeking to implement three-dimensional learning at scale. Quality, research-based instructional materials, strong central support, and extensive professional development resulted in modest improvements in student learning as measured on standardized tests, and only after extensive effort and time.

Consideration of course offerings and course sequencing are important aspects of high school science improvement. In San Diego, leaders addressed this challenge by moving the district to a "physics first" model where students in 9th grade took physics, in 10th grade chemistry, and 11th grade biology. While initially this change had broad support, as the work progressed the change management process became overwhelming. Five years after the change was made, the district reversed itself (Gao, 2006). For science educators seeking to advance instruction along the lines of Chapter 5 of this report, course-taking and course-sequencing are important levers for change, but because of issues connected to teacher credentials and college admissions requirements, making or sustaining the change can be difficult.

The San Diego example also shows the importance of local leadership capacity and some of the pitfalls of centrally directed leadership efforts. In San Diego, "Relying on the constituents to come to consensus on what improvements need to be made, gathering support, creating a model that represents the views of all is a formidable task. (That approach was deemed inappropriate for the identified needs.)" (Bess and Bybee, 2004, p. 11). Instead, the superintendent was "quite direct" and "geared to making immediate changes," resulting in a hierarchical structure where, ultimately "teachers were expected to follow prescribed daily agendas using curriculum materials selected to meet the needs of their students" (Bess and Bybee, 2004, p. 7).

The three-dimensional science learning described in this report is new—so "relying on the constituents" to generate and embrace the necessary changes could be difficult. However, as the results of the San Diego effort show, a top-down or externally driven agenda will also generate its own set of challenges.

In returning to our continuous improvement model, this example shows the importance of organizational change and especially the role of leadership. It illustrates how school districts are the locus of considerable control. While states set funding levels, standards, and curriculum, districts are important fulcrums of change because they sit at the intersection of policy and practice. District leaders can be important actors in efforts to improve science instruction at scale because they are in a position to exert a strong influence on the instructional approaches that are used, the guidance that is given about using and evaluating those approaches, and the type and level of supports that are provided to implement those approaches. The importance of capability is also illustrated here in the impact of instructional resources and professional learning.

Organizational Change and Capability: Brockton High School Transformation

The difficulties of change in three schools struggling to improve achievement for student groups that have historically underperformed (i.e., African American and Latino students, students with disabilities, and low socioeconomic disadvantaged students) were analyzed by Noguera (2017). One of these schools is Brockton High School (BHS), the largest high school in Massachusetts. In 1999, BHS was described by the *Boston Globe* as "the cesspool of education," but by 2010 it was considered a national example of turnaround success.[1]

In contrast to the San Diego example, the policies that drove the changes at BHS started with teachers. A group of teachers calling themselves the "Restructuring Committee" began meeting to analyze the causes of BHS student failure and develop a plan to address those causes. This effort was supported by the school administration and eventually by the school district central office. The group did not initially include all teachers in the school, but it sought to use evidence of its success to entice more teachers to participate (Noguera, 2017).

Working together, the teachers and school administration identified a series of changes that needed to occur within the instructional program and the school schedule to support students' academic and nonacademic needs. Key elements of the reform included adopting a curriculum that emphasized "deeper learning" to engage and motivate students, providing targeted support where students needed it the most, and modifying the school schedule to allow sufficient class time to provide that support. Teachers realized that to implement the planned changes, they needed to learn and practice pedagogical strategies such as the Socratic Method, project-based learning, and literacy in the content areas. School administrators monitored professional development and conducted nonevaluative classroom observations to provide the appropriate support to teachers. To help students in need of extra support, teachers also made themselves available before and after school and during lunch periods (Noguera, 2017).

Teachers and school administrators recognized several nonschool factors that were influencing student achievement, such as poverty, trauma,

---

[1] See https://www.studeri.org/blog/lessons-from-brockton-high-school [September 2018].

and homelessness. To address the various effects of these issues on the learning process, the school partnered with community and social service organizations to connect students with services that would address their nonacademic needs. The changes in BHS gradually spread to other schools in the district (Noguera, 2017). But the turnaround was not fast or easy. It was the result of a concerted effort by all levels of the system, starting with teachers and strongly supported by the school administration, the school district central office, and the community. Noguera (2017, p. 29) identified some essential elements that are needed to support this type of turnaround:

- Clear understanding of the academic needs of students and design of the "intervention" to address those needs.
- Differentiated training and support for teachers so that particular teachers or groups of teachers receive supports targeted to their particular needs.
- Collaborative problem solving between central office teams and site leaders to devise strategies for building the capacity of schools. This approach is particularly important for schools that have struggled to meet lower state standards in the past.
- New systems of support at the state and district levels, combined with equity-based funding policies that provide supplemental social supports to school in high-poverty communities.

Capability: Chicago Public Schools Transformation Efforts

Managing large urban school districts like Chicago is challenging. From roughly 2006 through 2010, the Chicago Public Schools undertook an extensive high school transformation effort that focused on nearly every aspect of high schools including governance, school incubation, enrollment, and accountability (Elmore, Grossman, and King, 2007). A key component of this effort was a focus on providing curriculum and professional development to schools (Gewertz, 2006). An extensive evaluation of this effort was conducted by SRI International and the Chicago Consortium on School Research (Humphrey and Shields, 2009). Most relevant to this discussion of science investigations in middle and high schools was the effort to create "instructional development systems" (IDSs), which were tightly combined combinations of curricula and school supports (Sporte et al., 2009, p. 1), which they described as follows:

[Chicago Public Schools] worked with educational experts to develop two to three comprehensive curricula in each of three subjects: English, mathematics, and science from which participating schools could choose. Each subject area IDS includes curricular strategies, classroom materials, formative and summative assessments, targeted professional development, and personalized coaching. The goal of each IDS curriculum is to prepare students for college and the workforce, and each will be aligned to both state and college readiness standards.

The IDS models in science were selected via competitive bid and all led by university partners with considerable science and science education expertise. While all predated the *Framework*, two of the three science models featured curricula developed from an extensive research base, built in part with funding from the National Science Foundation. The third featured popular if traditional instructional materials. Schools could choose the option that suited them best, and the work was phased in over several years adding one grade level at a time. All included a full suite of laboratory equipment for each classroom, summer workshops for teachers based on the particular instructional materials chosen by the school, in-classroom coaching by expert science teachers, and extensive data to support implementation. The entire high school transformation effort had quite strong financial and administrative resources.

The evaluation found the IDS intervention was well implemented. Generally, teachers generally liked the instructional materials they received. The effort created coherence and enhanced collaboration. Most teachers thought the professional development and in-school coaching was beneficial (Sporte et al., 2009). However, outcomes of this intervention were mixed, and the limitations in these results have the potential to be instructive to subsequent reformers interested in increasing the quality and quantity of investigations in high schools. Observations of instruction showed that even after implementation, "instruction in IDS classrooms generally needed improvement" (Sporte et al., 2009, p. 17) Teacher expectations of student learning and achievement were "generally low" among IDS teachers. Questioning techniques remained challenging for most teachers, even when supported by instructional materials with questioning supports built in and accompanying professional development sessions. Student outcomes were slightly improved in grade point average, mirroring the system as a whole, with slightly fewer failed courses. In the first few years of implementation, standardized test performance was not different between IDS schools and non-IDS schools (Humphrey and Shields, 2009), though according to internal district records, IDS schools outperformed other schools in later years on standardized tests (Michael Lach, personal communication). Like most large-scale improvement efforts, there was more variance of performance within schools than across schools (Lesnick et al., 2009). And issues of attendance and classroom management were found to be particularly vexing challenges: the engaging, well-supported instructional materials, coaching, and professional development were unable to counter the poor attendance patterns of many schools and unable to balance the challenging discipline issues facing many classrooms (Sporte et. al., 2009).

Findings from this work highlight the challenges facing reformers seeking to advance the vision of science instruction described in Chapter 4:

- In many high schools, issues of attendance and classroom management dominate the experience of the adults and children. To resolve these issues, a solution focused on instructional improvement is likely necessary but insufficient.
- Because school-specific issues dominated the data, attention to local school structures, routines, and leadership capacity is essential.
- Providing equipment and materials at scale is not easy, but necessary (Humphrey and Shields, 2009, pp. 14–16).
- Given the racial make-up of Chicago, and the fact that observed teacher expectations of students remained low throughout the intervention, future reformers should be reminded of the importance of issues of diversity and equity.

This example shows a strong focus on the continuous improvement areas of capability (providing the units and professional development). It also illustrates that even well-designed and well-implemented curriculum and instructional supports can be drowned out by adult expectations, school culture, and classroom management background if not attended to.

Collaboration and Organizational Change: The Case of Modeling

Collaboration between teachers can facilitate change efforts. In cases where local peers are not numerous links to a larger group can be helpful. For example, many high schools have only one physics teacher and therefore lack a pool of colleagues to form a professional learning community focused on physics (Tesfaye and White, 2012). Modeling is a science teaching approach and a community of science teachers that can in some ways serve as a professional community.[2] In modeling, teachers present carefully selected phenomena (such as a ball rolling down an inclined plane) and through a series of experiments, students create a model (often mathematical, but not always) that describes that phenomena and can be used to make predictions about new situations and contexts, much like the "developing

---

[2]In the mid-1980s, modeling grew into a method of teaching high school physics (Jackson, Dukerich, and Hestenes, 2008; Wells, Hestenes, and Swackhamer, 1995); a method of teaching other high school science courses and topics; a set of instructional materials; a community; and a professional organization called the American Modeling Teachers Association. For more information, see https://modelinginstruction.org/sample-page/synopsis-of-modeling-instruction/ [October 2018].

and using models" practice from the *Framework*. Modeling classrooms typically feature extensive group work, lots of student discussion and debate, and a focus on precise communication of scientific ideas.

While modeling initially expanded thanks to an NSF Teacher Enhancement Grant in 1994 (Hestenes et al., 1994), the subsequent expansion of modeling has generally occurred without the direct support of states, districts, or schools that many other middle and high school improvement efforts benefit from. This follows from the context: in more than 80 percent of U.S. schools where physics is taught, there is only one person teaching the subject (White and Tesfaye, 2010). An approach designed to forge connections across schools between individual practitioners makes sense. Generally, modeling workshops are organized by teachers and partners at local universities, often using competitive math-science partnership grant funding or some sort of fee-for-service configuration. The community is deeply distributed and nearly all online, sharing lessons, activities, and insights through a variety of email lists and social media.

Several factors likely contribute to this decentralized and significant expansion. The community is driven to a large degree by a focus on assessment and data. A set of conceptually focused assessment instruments, including the Force Concept Inventory (FCI) (Hestenes, Malcolm Wells, and Swackhamer, 1992) and the Mechanics Baseline Test (MBT) (Hestenes and Wells, 1992), were used to drive the change process. Physics teachers using traditional pedagogies were generally amazed at how poorly their students do on this exam, which focuses on conceptual understanding, leading them to be more open to suggestions from teachers who use the different conceptual and student-centered approaches as described earlier in this report. A design-test-iterate cycle, using concept inventories as the benchmark, resulted in ever-improving sets of lessons, tasks, and units that are shared online within the community. By routinely collecting and sharing outcome data (for instance, Hake, 1998), the modeling community was able to both spread the word about their efforts and make it easier for interested scholars and practitioners to build on existing efforts. Efforts to increase the quality and quantity of *Framework*-based investigations could learn from this teacher-focused, data-rich, distributed community approach to improving instruction at scale.

This example shows how the continuous improvement area of organizational change can expand to include collaboration across schools and between K–12 educators and universities, and provide another viewpoint to illustrate the many interconnections between K–12 and higher education. The development of instructional resources and the organization of multiple types of ongoing professional learning show the importance of attention to capability.

Challenges of Alignment: State Systemic Initiatives

In the early 1990s, NSF supported a series of systemic initiatives—first, in 1991, focused on states (state systemic initiatives, or SSIs), and later, in 1994, focused on urban districts and rural regions:

> NSF specified a set of key "drivers" of systemic reform, asking each SSI to report its progress in terms of: (1) implementation of comprehensive, standards-based curricula; (2) development of a coherent set of policies to support high quality science and mathematics education; (3) convergence of the use of resources in support of science and mathematics education; (4) broadbased support for the reforms; (5) evidence that the program is enhancing student achievement; and (6) evidence that the program is improving the achievement of all students, including those that have historically been underserved (Webb et al., 2003, p. 2).

This concept of engaging entire systems was chosen in an effort to align different parts of the system (e.g., requirements mandated by policy, curriculum, assessment, administrator and teacher professional development) toward a common goal. The SSIs made some inroads toward these goals. They created conditions for improvement (Horn, 2004; Huffman and Lawrenz, 2004; National Science Foundation, 2000; Zucker et al., 1998), provided needed capacity in challenging regions (Heck et al., 2003), and contributed to improvements in student mathematics performance (Webb et al., 2003). However, sustaining the SSIs became impossible after nearly a decade in part due to lack of support from local and state policy makers to sustain these initiatives (Hoff, 2001).

There is much to learn from the SSIs that might be relevant to current efforts to change the instruction of science teachers at scale. Perhaps the key lesson is that coherence matters. When components of the system—including, at the district level, for instance curriculum, instruction, assessment, and professional development—articulate with one another clearly and cleanly, improvement accelerates. As the final evaluation of SSIs indicates:

> Change is most effective when multiple components are addressed in concert: i.e., when the SSIs served as catalysts for other reform efforts that states had initiated, they achieved optimum impact. When state policies are aligned with the goals of a systemic initiative and when state infrastructure supports teachers and schools as they change their practices, reform can result in substantial achievement gains in a relatively short time (Heck et al., 2003, p. v).

In revisiting the continuous improvement model, this example illustrates the challenge of alignment and the opportunities and challenges that lie in efforts to focus all the components on shared goals and approaches.

Lessons Learned from Previous Efforts

The examples discussed illustrate that coordinating states, local educational agencies, and schools to increase the quality and quantity of science investigations in the context of supporting three-dimensional science learning is a multifaceted effort. Paradigmatic instructional changes (such as shifting to three-dimensional learning) are difficult to achieve at scale and even more difficult to sustain. There are no silver bullets or magic formulas. Moreover, as the examples illustrate, although instructional change manifests at the classroom level, it does not happen in the isolation of a classroom. A myriad of other changes within the education system are necessary to support a shift toward the desired instructional approach. Identifying, planning for, making, and sustaining these changes takes time, patience, and commitment from the parties who have a stake in the success of the reform and who, by working together, have the different types of expertise to make it happen.

The successes and challenges of the efforts described in this chapter, together with research from other reform efforts, reveal elements that seem to be important when changing science instruction at scale. These include the following:

1. **High-capacity leadership that brings both resources and political cover.** The onus of changing how students engage in investigations and design in science classrooms should not fall solely on individual teachers. Whether at the federal, state, or district level, reformers who are savvy about the change process, skilled in the art of compromise and making difficult tradeoffs, and able to balance the needs of often-competing interests can have impact. School and district administrators provide time, curricular, and professional resources for growth. If they also understand the goals and highly effective practices envisioned within three-dimensional science classrooms (National Academies of Sciences, Engineering, and Medicine, 2015), they can facilitate implementation of science and investigation in the classroom. If administrators are not aware of innovations of *Framework*-based standards, teachers may become hesitant to implement those innovations if they receive conflicting messages or guidance about what constitutes effective instruction (Allen and Penuel, 2015). If administrators are not focused on understanding and addressing the impediments to equality and equity, it is difficult to alleviate persistent disparities between groups of students. In short, this vision of investigation and design for all demands leaders who know both science education and who are able to deftly lead schools and districts.

2. **Science-specific (as opposed to content-agnostic) strategies.** Some instructional practices, such as inclusive pedagogies and the use of formative assessment, are essential ingredients of quality teaching. Although there is some evidence that these types of strategies also are effective in science, they might be operationalized differently in science instruction, because science is different. As the previous chapters have shown, science instruction has its own set of considerations that should be integrated into any improvement effort from the beginning. Given the specialized content knowledge and instructional strategies required in science, efforts to improve instruction at scale might require collaboration and partnerships to bridge gaps in expertise between partners who are more expert in science and science education and partners who are more expert in educational systems and structures.

3. **Iterative improvement.** The efforts described above unfolded with careful planning, development, and coordination, and many took years to reach their full maturity. They encountered challenges that slowed their intended progress (e.g., classroom management issues in Chicago) and that required adjustments to respond to local contextual factors. These kinds of unexpected setbacks and ongoing adaptations mean that change will be incremental and require a long view to recognize the progress that is being made along the way.

Several of these efforts also focused on providing professional learning for educators that was coupled with well-designed instructional materials enacted in line with the local context. These strategies recognize the centrality of teachers to any instructional improvement effort, and the need to ensure that they have sufficient supports and capacity to improve their practices.

PULLING THE PIECES TOGETHER

Beyond these general principles for improving science instruction at scale, this committee's specific focus on investigation and equality and equity intersect with different aspects of the education system in ways that warrant additional consideration. Teaching science in the ways described in this report requires that students and teachers have access to ongoing investigations, appropriate space for students to work in small groups with real materials, appropriate tools to make the measurements needed, curriculum and assessment resources aligned to the teaching goals including appropriate video and simulation resources, and the technology for students to access and manipulate these resources at the level of small groups or individually. It is especially important for under-resourced schools and districts to have these tools and resources available to all of their students. Chapters 6 and 8 of this report explore the issues of instructional resources and space and facilities in more detail. These chapters point out numerous instances of inequitable resource distribution and its potential for large effects on student learning. These inequities impact all three of the continuous improvement areas discussed here. Equity audits can be a useful tool for ensuring accountability to equitable education. Organizational culture will impact the way stakeholders respond to the audits and to the underlying situation. Qualified educators are key to having the capability to work towards science investigation and engineering design for all, but these educators require funding for salaries, space, equipment and supplies, all items that fall under the area of policy and management.

Schools that serve primarily groups underrepresented in science rarely have the best space, equipment, and instructional resources, but even these are of little value unless the teacher knows how to use them effectively. Thus, as we have discussed in Chapter 7, teacher preparation and ongoing professional learning are keys to effective science teaching. Teachers not only need a sound understanding of the science being taught, but also they need to have experienced the type of science learning that they are being asked to deliver—for example, to have developed their own models and explanations for phenomena or planned their own experiments. These experiences allow them to develop their own understanding of the science and engineering practices and of the role of the crosscutting concepts; alongside an understanding of how to teach science in this way. Coordination between schools of education, science departments, and state education policies on science teacher qualification could achieve better science teacher preparation and certification for secondary science teaching that achieves *Framework*-based standards, without diminishing the importance of science teachers knowing the science they are teaching. Teacher preparation programs that integrate science learning and learning about appropriate science pedagogy can provide teachers with the types of experiences they will be providing to their students. Significant change at the K–12 level and the undergraduate level will not happen without attention to the way that courses offered to undergraduates impact the future teaching of K–12 students.

Students' ability to participate in and learn from investigations is determined, in part, by the courses they are enrolled in and the design of those courses. As discussed in Chapter 3, current high school course structures do not support the breadth of topics addressed in *Framework*-based standards. Moreover, states that require fewer than three high school science courses for graduation might not be adequately preparing students for the performance expectations of *Framework*-based standards (NGSS Lead States, 2013, App. K).

Thus, broader changes to the scope and sequence of high school course offerings are needed to achieve three-dimensional learning at scale. A severe constraint on this reorganization is that the majority of high school science teachers and even many middle school science teachers are certified to teach in only a single disciplinary area (see Chapter 3). In addition, few high school science teachers have sufficient experience or background in teaching engineering design, so the incorporation of engineering projects across all disciplines of science will further stretch the capacity of most education systems. If high school course offerings are revised, it is likely that eventually graduation requirements and college entrance requirements would need to be rewritten to move away from requiring a certain number of "laboratory science" courses to instead include descriptions that more closely reflect the role of investigation in three-dimensional learning.

Bringing these changes to scale so that *all* students engage in high-quality science investigation and design will require changes to assessment systems in addition to the many other changes already discussed. New approaches to state testing of science that takes into account how students learn through science investigation and engineering design and is aligned to the *Framework* would facilitate change. *Framework* alignment would mean inclusions of earth systems science, physical sciences (both chemistry and physics concepts), and life sciences (including both biology and ecology concepts) as well as engineering. Appendix A discusses some specific issues related to designing assessments that capture three-dimensional learning.

Finally, any effort to take three-dimensional learning to scale must take into account how policies of tracking students into particular course options and sequences has limited participation of students from under-represented groups in advanced courses and contributed to the well-documented inequities in science and engineering majors and careers. Students perceived as college bound have traditionally taken a biology-chemistry-physics sequence, plus possible honors or AP science courses, all including laboratory. Students with lower scores (particularly in mathematics) are often assigned a lower track where they take a different sequence with fewer science courses overall, no access to advanced courses, and fewer laboratory opportunities. For some students, career and technical education courses count toward science requirements for graduation. These courses may or may not include opportunities for learning rigorous science content, although recent reforms such as "linked-learning" academies attempt to design career-linked and project-based course sequences that integrate standards across all disciplines and prepare the students for college entry (e.g., the University of California Curriculum Integration Program to include academic content needed for university admission in high school career and technical courses).[3] Notwithstanding these types of academies, career and technical education generally does not meet the entry requirements of the top-level state university systems. The career and technical education track, together with differentiated mathematics course sequences, have long acted as gatekeepers for college entry and preparation to major in a science or engineering area in college.

SUMMARY

Systemic reform is needed to ensure access to science investigation and engineering design for all students. Policies at all levels can impact opportunities and requires attention to potential sources of inequity and decision points that limit opportunities for historically underrepresented groups. Moreover, it is important to consider the changing role of the teacher and to provide access to appropriate instructional resources, professional learning, funding, space, equipment, supplies, and student safety. This chapter presented a framework for continuous improvement that focused on organizational culture, educatory capability, and policy and management. Although discussed as separate components, it is crucial to recognize the interrelationships among the components of the continuous improvement model to ensure that schools provide high-quality access to science investigations and engineering design.

REFERENCES

Allen, C., and Penuel, W.R. (2015). Studying teachers' sensemaking to investigate teachers' responses to professional development focused on new standards. *Journal of Teacher Education 6*(2), 136–149. Available: http://journals.sagepub.com/doi/pdf/10.1177/0022487114560646 [October 2018].

Bess, K., and Bybee, R. (2004). *Systemic Reform of Secondary School Science: A Review of an Urban U.S. School District, San Diego City Schools.* Presented at the AAAS/UNESCO International Conference of Science Technology Education, Paris, France.

Blumenfeld, P., Fishman, B.J., Krajcik, J., Marx, R.W., and Soloway, E. (2000). Creating usable innovations in systemic reform: Scaling up technology-embedded project-based science in urban schools. *Educational Psychologist, 35*(3), 149–164.

Clune, W.H., and White, P.A. (1992). Education reform in the trenches: increased academic course taking in high schools with lower achieving students in states with higher graduation requirements. *Educational Evaluation and Policy Analysis, 14*(1), 2–20.

Cohen, D.K. (1995). What is the system in systemic reform? *Educational Researcher, 24*(9), 11–17.

Elmore, R.F., Grossman, A.S., and King, C. (2007). *Managing The Chicago Public Schools.* Available: http://pelp.fas.harvard.edu/files/hbs-test/files/pel033p2.pdf [October 2018].

Firestone, W. (2014). Teacher evaluation policy and conflicting theories of motivation. *Educational Researcher, 43*(2), 100–107.

---

[3] See https://www.ucop.edu/agguide/career-technical-education/ucci/index.html [October 2018].

Gao, H. (2006). S.D. subtracts physics requirement: High school students given leeway in science. *San Diego Union Tribune.* Available: http://legacy.sandiegouniontribune.com/uniontrib/20060524/news_7m24science.html [October 2018].

Gewertz, C. (2006). Getting down to the core: The Chicago school district takes an 'intentional approach' to high school courses. *Education Week*, 26–29. Available: https://www.edweek.org/ew/articles/2006/11/29/13hscurric.h26.html?r=1276917344 [October 2018].

Ghaffarzadegan, N., Larson, R., and Hawley, J. (2016). Education as a complex system. *Systems Research and Behavioral Science* 34(3), 211–215.

Hake, R.R. (1998). Interactive-engagement vs traditional methods: A six-thousand-student survey of mechanics test data for introductory physics courses. *American Journal of Physics(66)*, 64–74. doi: 10.1119/1.18809.

Hamilton, L., Stecher, B., and Yuan, K. (2008). *Standards-Based Reform in the United States: History, Research, and Future Directions.* (No. RP-1384). Santa Monica, CA: Rand Education. Available: https://www.rand.org/pubs/reprints/RP1384.html [October 2018].

Harris, D., and Herrington, C. (Eds.). (2015). Value added meets the schools: The effects of using test-based teacher evaluation on the work of teachers and leaders [Special issue]. *Educational Researcher*, 44(2), 71–76.

Heck, D.J., Weiss, I.R., Boyd, S.E., Howard, M.N., and Supovitz, J.A. (2003). *Lessons Learned About Designing, Implementing, and Evaluating Statewide Systemic Reform.* Chapel Hill, NC: Horizon Research.

Hestenes, D., and Wells, M. (1992). A mechanics baseline test. *The Physics Teacher, 30*, 159–166.

Hestenes, D., Dukerich, L., Swackhamer, G., and Wells, M. (1994). *Modeling Instruction in High School Physics.* Arizona State University, National Science Foundation Grant Award No. 9353423.

Hestenes, D., Wells, M., and Swackhamer, G. (1992). Force Concept Inventory. *The Physics Teacher, 30*, 141–158.

Hinchey, P.H. (2010). *Getting Teacher Assessment Right: What Policymakers Can Learn from Research.* National Education Policy Center, School of Education, University of Colorado. Available: https://nepc.colorado.edu/sites/default/files/PB-TEval-Hinchey_0.pdf [October 2018].

Hoff, D. (2001). NSF plots new education strategy. *Education Week Online.* Available: https://www.edweek.org/ew/articles/2001/11/07/10nsf.h21.html [October 2018].

Horn, J. (2004). *The Rural Systemic Initiative of the National Science Foundation: An Evaluative Perspective at the Local School and Community Levels.* Evaluation Center. Available: https://files.eric.ed.gov/fulltext/ED486077.pdf [October 2018].

Huffman, D. and Lawrenz, F. (2004). The impact of a state systemic initiative on U.S. science teachers and students. *International Journal of Science and Mathematics Education 1(3)*, 357–377.

Humphrey D.C., and Shields, P. M. (2009). *High School Reform in Chicago Public Schools: An Overview.* Available: https://consortium.uchicago.edu/sites/default/files/publications/Overview.pdf [October 2018].

Jackson, J., Dukerich, L., and Hestenes, D. (2008). Modeling instruction: An effective model for science education. *Science Educator, 17*(1), 10–17.

Krajcik, J.S., and Shin, N. (2014). Project-based learning. In R.K. Sawyer (Ed.), *The Cambridge Handbook of the Learning Sciences* (2nd ed., pp. 275–297). New York: Cambridge University Press.

Lee, O., Quinn, H., and Valdés, G. (2013). Science and language for English language learners in relation to Next Generation Science Standards and with implications for Common Core State Standards for English language arts and mathematics. *Educational Researcher*, 42(4), 223–233.

Lee, V.E., and Ready, D.D. (2009). U.S. high school curriculum: Three phases of contemporary research and reform. *The Future of Children, 19*(1), 135–156.

Lesnick, J.K., Sartain, L., Sporte, S.E., and Stoelinga, S.R. (2009). *High School Reform in Chicago Public Schools: A Snapshot of High School Instruction.* Available: https://consortium.uchicago.edu/sites/default/files/publications/Part%205%20-%20Instruction.pdf [October 2018].

Mital, P., Moore, R., and Llewellyn, D. (2014). Analyzing K–12 education as a complex system. *Procedia Computer Science 28,* 370–379.

National Academies of Sciences, Engineering, and Medicine. (2015). *Science Teachers' Learning: Enhancing Opportunities, Creating Supporting Contexts.* Washington, DC: The National Academies Press.

National Academies of Sciences, Engineering, and Medicine. (2017). *Undergraduate Research Experiences for STEM Students: Successes, Challenges, and Opportunities.* Washington, DC: The National Academies Press.

National Research Council. (2006). *Taking Science to School: Learning and Teaching Science In Grades K-8.* Washington, DC: The National Academies Press.

National Research Council. (2007). *America's Lab Report: Investigations in High School Science.* Washington, DC: The National Academies Press.

National Research Council. (2012). *A Framework for K-12 Science Education.* Washington, DC: The National Academies Press.

National Science Foundation. (2000). Education: Lessons about learning. In *America's Investment in the Future* (pp. 32–47). Arlington, VA: Author.

NGSS Lead States. (2013). *Next Generation Science Standards: For States, By States.* Washington, DC: The National Academies Press.

Noguera, P. (2017). *Taking Deeper Learning to Scale.* Palo Alto, CA: Learning Policy Institute. Available: https://learningpolicyinstitute.org/sites/default/files/product-files/Taking_Deeper_Learning_Scale_REPORT.pdf [October 2018].

Penfield, R.D., and Lee, O. (2010). Test-based accountability: Potential benefits and pitfalls of science assessment with student diversity. *Journal of Research in Science Teaching, 47*(1), 6–24.

Sporte, S.E., Correa, M., Hart, H.M., and Wechsler, M.E. (2009). *High School Reform in Chicago Public Schools: Instructional Development Systems.* Available: https://consortium.uchicago.edu/sites/default/files/publications/Part%202%20-%20IDs.pdf [October 2018].

Tesfaye, C.L., and White, S. (2012). *High School Physics Teacher Preparation,* American Institute for Physics Reports on High School Physics. Available: https://www.aip.org/sites/default/files/statistics/highschool/hs-teacherprep-09.pdf [October 2018].

U.S. Department of Education. (2017). *The Federal Role in Education.* Available: https://www2.ed.gov/about/overview/fed/role.html [October 2018].

Webb, N.L., Kane, J., Yang, J.-H., Kaufman, D., Cohen, A., Kang, T., Park, C., and Wilson, L. (2003). *Final Report on the Use of State NAEP Data to Assess the Impact of the Statewide Systemic Initiatives.* Wisconsin Center for Education Research. Available: https://files.eric.ed.gov/fulltext/ED497577.pdf [October 2018].

Wells, M., Hestenes, D., and Swackhamer, G. (1995). A modeling method for high school physics instruction. *American Journal of Physics, 63,* 606–619.

White, S., and Tesfaye, C.L. (2010). *Who Teaches High School Physics? Results from the 2008-09 Nationwide Survey of High School Physics Teachers.* Statistical Research Center. Available: https://photos.aip.org/sites/default/files/statistics/highschool/hs-whoteaches-09.pdf [October 2018].

Zucker, A.A., Shields, P.M., Adelman, N.E., Corcoran, T.B., and Goertz, M.E. (1998). *A Report on the Evaluation of the National Science Foundation's Statewide Systemic Initiatives (SSI) Program.* Menlo Park, CA: SRI International.

10

Conclusions, Recommendations, and Research Questions

This report looks at the available information on science investigation and engineering design in middle and high schools and the approaches and strategies that can be used by teachers, professional development providers, administrative leaders, education researchers, and policy makers to help provide all students with high-quality learning experiences. Engaging all students in science investigation and engineering design requires significant changes to what both students and teachers do in the classroom. Because many aspects of science and engineering are part of students' daily lives, contextualizing science learning by integrating what students bring to the classroom into science investigation and engineering design can facilitate learning. In addition, using inclusive pedagogies can make science and engineering learning accessible to all students. This chapter summarizes the conclusions the committee has made from the available evidence and provides recommendations for action as well as questions for future research. Substantial progress in optimal student learning and motivation is more likely when reform at various levels of the system (e.g., federal, state, district) through its diverse functions (e.g., resource distribution, establishment of policy) act in concert to provide high-quality educational experiences to support and nurture the learning of all students. This includes attention to the resources needed to prepare for, implement, and evaluate science and engineering learning that is three-dimensional and engages students with science and engineering practices, disciplinary core ideas, and crosscutting concepts simultaneously (the three dimensions described in *A Framework for K–12 Science Education*; hereafter referred to as the *Framework*).

CONCLUSIONS

In reviewing the available information on science investigation and engineering design in middle and high schools, the committee made the following conclusions, which inform the interconnected recommendations that follow.

CONCLUSION 1: Engaging students in learning about natural phenomena and engineering challenges via science investigation and engineering design increases their understanding of how the world works. Investigation and design are more effective for supporting learning than traditional teaching methods. They engage students in doing science and engineering, increase their conceptual knowledge of science and engineering, and improve their reasoning and problem-solving skills.

Well-designed and implemented science investigation and engineering design experiences foster three-dimensional science learning in accordance with the ideas of the *Framework*. Although teachers generally select topics for investigations, the specifics of what the students do result from student questions that build on their own prior knowledge and experiences, including their local context, culture, and identity. Students grapple with data/ information and using science ideas and concepts to support explanations of the causes of phenomena and to solve problems. Teachers attend to and respond to students' thinking (classroom discourse and arguing from evidence), and guide students in using evidence from multiple sources to support their science explanations and/or solutions to engineering problems. Teachers and students recognize that there may be multiple acceptable explanations, outcomes, solutions, models, or designs. Investigation provides an opportunity for students to apply their thinking in new ways. They can learn about multiple related phenomena, see a known phenomenon in a new context, or identify analogous or related phenomena that share similar underlying causes. In addition, the same core ideas and crosscutting concepts can be relevant for multiple phenomena and this extension can provide an opportunity for students to apply their science and engineering knowledge.

CONCLUSION 2: Teachers can use students' curiosity to motivate learning by choosing phenomena and design challenges that are interesting and engaging to students, including those that are locally and/or culturally relevant. Science investigation and engineering design give middle and high school students opportunities to engage in the wider world in new ways by providing agency for them to develop questions and establish the direction for their own learning experiences.

Students' curiosity about the world around them can serve as a motivating factor to their learning. One way that science investigation and engineering design are valuable is that they can provide opportunities to connect to locally and culturally relevant experiences through phenomena that build on students' prior knowledge and actively engage students in learning and reasoning about the natural and designed world. By keeping in mind the diverse backgrounds and experiences of the students and situating science and engineering topics in contexts relevant to students' lives, investigation and design can increase motivation and engagement, increase a sense of belonging, deepen students' understanding of science and engineering, and lead to more effective continued learning. When students have the opportunity to participate in multiple sustained experiences with investigation and design, those experiences provide a way to learn that explicitly engages students in science and engineering contexts that support understanding of the nature of science and engineering.

CONCLUSION 3: Science investigation and engineering design entail a dramatic shift in the classroom dynamic. Students ask questions, participate in discussions, create artifacts and models to show their reasoning, and continuously reflect and revise their thinking. Teachers guide, frame, and facilitate the learning environment to allow student engagement and learning.

In the classroom, student engagement in investigation and design is not separate from the main flow of the instruction, but instead pervades the entire teaching of science and engineering in middle and high schools. Engaging in the three-dimensional approach of the *Framework* requires shifts in what goes on in the classroom that alter the teaching and learning relationship between teacher and students. Teachers provide structure and skillful guidance to engage students while building on the assets the students bring to the classroom. Students do not receive knowledge; they build understanding through three-dimensional performances in which they examine phenomena, ask questions, collect and analyze data, and construct explanations to deepen their understanding of science and engineering. The teacher provides a structure for learning and builds on students' current understanding of science and engineering through classroom discourse, investigation/design experiences, and in response to students' thinking (reasoning). Teachers establish the criteria for learning and engage students in gathering the information and ideas needed to construct scientifically accurate explanation(s) or design solutions. During the classroom discussions, teachers support the use of accurate science language and ideas by building on the preliminary explanations of the students.

CONCLUSION 4: Inclusive pedagogies can support the learning of all students by situating differences as assets, building on students' identities and life experiences, and leveraging local and dynamic views of cultural life for the study of science and engineering.

Inclusive pedagogies help contextualize science learning by integrating what students bring to the classroom into science investigation and engineering design. Repositioning students' differences as assets instead of deficits allows new approaches to teaching and learning that are more receptive and respectful of students' cultures, identities, languages, literacies, and communities. Inclusive pedagogies can work to intentionally remove barriers limiting full participation in investigation and design. This approach supports students' meaningful and rigorous learning, helps sustains their interest in and positive perceptions of science and engineering, increases their sense of belonging, and impacts their self-perceptions as science and engineering learners. Changing pedagogical approaches to integrate science investigation and engineering design into instruction is a significant change but is especially important because today's students are the most diverse student population ever educated in U.S. public schools.

CONCLUSION 5: Centering classes on science investigation and engineering design means that teachers provide multiple opportunities for students to demonstrate their reasoning and show understanding of scientific explanations about the natural world. Providing opportunities for teachers to observe student learning and embed assessment into the flow of learning experiences allows students as well as teachers to reflect on learning.

Teachers organize students' experiences so that the students can construct explanations for the causes of phenomena and design solutions to human challenges as the focus of the class experience. In this type of learning instructionally embedded three-dimensional assessments look different than many traditional lab reports or tests because the new assessments mirror what happens during class. The embedded as well as the post-instructional assessments provide evidence of students' ability to demonstrate three-dimensional learning, including rich evidence of what students can and cannot do, and areas where students have not yet achieved understanding. Such information can inform and support ongoing modifications to teaching and learning. Embedding assessment in instruction allows teachers to monitor progress toward learning goals while students are engaged in science investigation and engineering design. It also allows both the teacher and student to use assessment as a tool to reflect on and improve learning.

CONCLUSION 6: Instructional resources are key to facilitating the careful sequencing of phenomena and design challenges across units and grade levels in order to increase coherence as students become increasingly sophisticated science and engineering learners.

Instructional resources to support science investigation and engineering design that are based upon research-based principles of learning and engagement can be designed to promote learning for all students. The resources can include groups of carefully chosen phenomena and design problems that all relate to a science or engineering topic and that together will help students learn and gradually develop a deeper understanding of science and engineering. These phenomena can tie to topics of interest to students to increase motivation. Resources can provide ideas for tying investigation and design to students' prior knowledge to build on it and provide structures for students to organize their learning, as well as opportunities for students to reflect upon and use what they have learned. In addition to providing materials to help students make sense of phenomena and the designed world around them, well-designed instructional resources can provide strategies to support educators in adapting them to fit the local culture and place. Instructional resources that support science investigation and engineering design can provide support for learning by presenting a coherent structure for the exploration of phenomena or design challenges in a way that facilitates sense-making by the students across lessons, units, grades, and disciplines, ideally as part of a well-designed curriculum. Furthermore, instructional resources to support science investigation and engineering design can bring coherence to system-level issues, connecting and organizing assessments, professional learning, and classroom instruction around key learning experiences for students and teachers.

CONCLUSION 7: Teachers' ability to guide student learning can be improved by preservice education on strategies for investigation and design as well as opportunities for professional learning at many stages of their inservice teaching careers. Intentionally designed and sustained professional learning experiences that extend over months can help teachers prepare, implement, and refine approaches to investigation and design.

Teacher learning takes place along a continuum that begins with their own experiences as students, includes their undergraduate courses in science as well as education, and continues throughout their career in education. Existing professional development opportunities, as well as most current undergraduate science classes, do not generally provide teachers and future teachers with three-dimensional experiences as science learners of the type that is expected for their students. These opportunities also do not often provide guidance on how to teach engineering. Multiple sustained professional learning opportunities in investigation and design can provide a learning experience for teachers that continues across a career trajectory from pre-service to experienced educator.

Teachers' knowledge of pedagogy, how students learn, and ways to recognize and honor the needs of their diverse groups of students is as important as their knowledge of science and engineering concepts. High-quality professional learning opportunities are sustained experiences that engage teachers in coherent professional learning experiences that model teaching and learning through investigation and design. These experiences engage teachers in science in ways that are consistent with how students learn science, are culturally relevant for the local context, and allow teachers to engage in using the three dimensions to make sense of phenomena and reflect on their own learning. As a component of their professional learning, teachers accumulate a large "tool-box" of materials and resources they can apply in their own classrooms. It includes opportunities for teachers to examine student artifacts drawn from the context of science investigation and engineering design and examines how to draw from these artifacts to assess student learning and provide next-step suggestions for three-dimensional learning. Professional learning experiences allow teachers to work with each other to develop learning communities and they help teachers improve how they attend and respond to the nature and quality of student thinking. Teachers consider how they and their students can learn from and build upon evidence from assessment as they participate in three-dimensional science and engineering learning that includes a range of student work illustrating what progress and success look like.

As teachers learn and implement new instructional approaches, the classroom, school, and community expectations can change. Professional learning communities can provide support for teachers during this transition as they reflect on their own practice in the context of science investigation, engineering design, and issues of equity and inclusion. The National Research Council report *Science Teachers' Learning* and the *Science Professional Learning Standards* prepared by the Council of State Science Supervisors both provide guidance for professional development providers and professional learners, as well as state and local leaders, on the attributes of effective science professional learning experiences to support teachers.

CONCLUSION 8: Engaging students in investigation and design requires attention to facilities, budgets, human resources, technology, equipment, and supplies. These resources can impact the quantity and quality of investigation and design experiences in the classroom and the students who have access to them.

If the space, technology, equipment, and supplies currently available are insufficient for the number of students who need to engage in science investigation and engineering design, then creative plans can be developed to achieve gradual incremental progress towards the goal. For example, improved access to appropriate space (such as studio classrooms and outdoor areas such as natural space and gardens); technology (such as computers and Internet); adequate equipment (such as computer-linked probes for measuring temperature, pressure, and speed); and supplies (such as chemicals and safety items) can be phased in over time if necessary so that all students can experience meaningful science investigation and engineering design throughout their school years. Flexible studio-style space provides a venue for student engagement in doing science and engineering that allows for group work, space to capture student discussion, easy access to a variety of material and technologies, and room for long-term projects. These resources can enrich student experiences with science investigation and engineering design.

CONCLUSION 9: Changes in the teaching and learning of science and engineering in middle and high schools are occurring within a complex set of systems. Classroom-level change is impacted in various and sometimes conflicting ways by issues related to funding and resources, local community priorities, state standards, graduation requirements, college admission requirements, and local, state, and national assessments. When incentives do not align, successful implementation of investigation and design is hindered.

Changing classroom instruction at scale does not just happen at the classroom or school level. Instead, what happens in classrooms is influenced and affected by a variety of factors within and beyond a single school, district, or state. For instance, decisions about instructional time, resources, and course sequences are made at different levels of the system and have direct impact on and are impacted by the availability and types of instructional spaces and teacher expertise. School leaders' and teachers' expectations, priorities, and commitment to equity create an instructional climate that encourage or discourage particular pedagogical approaches. School leadership and a willingness to work iteratively to continue improvements over time are crucial.

CONCLUSION 10: There are notable inequities within and among schools today in terms of access to educational experiences that engage students in science investigation and engineering design. Many policies and structures tend to perpetuate these inequities, such as disparities in facilities and teacher expectations, experiences, and qualifications across schools and districts.

There are many under-resourced schools, and research shows disparities in low-wealth and high-wealth districts and schools serving students differing in race/ethnicity, language, culture, and socioeconomic status. On average schools serving primarily students of color (with the exception of some schools with large numbers of Asians) and students from low socioeconomic status (SES) backgrounds receive fewer resources and have less adequate facilities than the schools for their Asian and white, high-SES counterparts. A large, complex social-political system influences teaching of science and engineering in middle and high schools. Current inequities, inequalities, and exclusionary mechanisms in the teaching of science and engineering are rooted in the sociopolitical and historical origins of schools and schooling, in which the educational opportunities offered to any student were heavily dependent on the socioeconomic and racial groups from which that student came.

There are many schools, particularly in low SES areas, where teachers do not have the necessary certifications and experiences to support students in science investigation and engineering design. This is particularly true in areas of high school physics and chemistry. In all areas, teachers need depth of subject matter and research experiences to support students in scientific investigations. In school districts in which teachers lack appropriate qualifications, rigorous course-taking opportunities are either limited or unavailable. As a result, students do not have access to high-quality educational experiences that will engage them in science investigation and engineering design.

In addition to obstacles due to limited rigorous course-taking opportunities or a lack of teachers with the necessary certifications and experiences, students may also be excluded if they are not seen as the science type, because of implicit bias and assumptions about their abilities, or because the school has focused on their lack of mastery of preliminary skills. While attention to increasing opportunity for all students has increased, inequalities and inequities associated with traditionally underrepresented groups in science and engineering (e.g., females, English language learners, students with disabilities, traditionally underserved racial groups) have persisted over time and seem intractable. Therefore, particular attention and intentional efforts to make these science investigation and engineering design experiences available and accessible are warranted.

If participation in doing science investigation and engineering design is considered as an expectation for *all* students, then positive steps must be taken to support *all* students as they learn to engage with phenomena and solve problems using a three-dimensional approach to build increasingly more sophisticated understanding of science and engineering. School and district staff cannot ensure that these opportunities are available to all students unless they analyze enrollment and success in science and engineering courses and work to improve the current inequities and inequalities in science and engineering education. Conscious alignment of goals and intentionality in addressing equality, equity, and inclusion by the various stakeholders (on the federal, state, district, and classroom levels) can facilitate improvements in curriculum, instruction, assessment, and professional development needed to support science investigation and engineering design for all students.

RECOMMENDATIONS

In light of the evidence discussed throughout the report and the conclusions above, the committee recommends the following actions to improve science and engineering education in middle and high schools. Short- and long-term changes by educators, administrative leaders, and policy makers will be needed to immerse students in three-dimensional science investigations and engineering design so that the students can make sense of phenomena in order to learn science. The first two recommendations discuss changes to the nature of the classroom experience and the later recommendations focus on how instructional resources, professional learning, preservice preparations, and policy decisions can support these changes.

RECOMMENDATION 1: Science investigation and engineering design should be the central approach for teaching and learning science and engineering.

- Teachers should arrange their instruction around interesting phenomena or design projects and use their students' curiosity to engage them in learning science and engineering.
- Administrators should support teachers in implementation of science investigation and engineering design. This may include providing teachers with appropriate instructional resources, opportunities to engage in sustained professional learning experiences and work collaboratively to design learning sequences, choose phenomena with contexts relevant to their students, and time to engage in and learn about inclusive pedagogies to promote equitable participation in science investigation and engineering design.

RECOMMENDATION 2: Instruction should provide multiple embedded opportunities for students to engage in three-dimensional science and engineering performances.

- Teachers should monitor student learning through ongoing, embedded, and post-instruction assessment as students make sense of phenomena and design solutions to challenges.

- Teachers should use formative assessment tasks and discourse strategies to encourage students to share their ideas, and to develop and revise their ideas with other students.
- Teachers should use evidence from formative assessment to guide instructional choices and guide students to reflect on their own learning.

RECOMMENDATION 3: Instructional resources to support science investgation and engineering design need to use approaches consistent with knowledge about how students learn and consistent with the *Framework* to provide a selection of options suitable for many local conditions.

- Teachers and designers of instructional resources should work in teams to develop coherent sequences of lessons that include phenomena carefully chosen to engage students in the science or engineering to be learned. Instructional resources should include information on strategies and options teachers can use to craft and implement lessons relevant to their students' backgrounds, cultures, and place.
- Administrators should provide teachers with access to high-quality instructional resources, space, equipment, and supplies that support the use of *Framework*-aligned approaches to science investigation and engineering design.

RECOMMENDATION 4: High-quality, sustained, professional learning opportunities are needed to engage teachers as professionals with effective evidence-based instructional practices and models for instruction in science and engineering. Administrators should identify and encourage participation in sustained and meaningful professional learning opportunities for teachers to learn and develop successful approaches to effective science and engineering teaching and learning.

- Professional development leaders should provide teachers with the opportunity to learn in the manner in which they are expected to teach, by using *Framework*-aligned methods during professional learning experiences. Teachers should receive feedback from peers and other experts while working throughout their careers to improve their skills, knowledge, and dispositions with these instructional approaches.
- Professional development leaders should prepare and empower teachers to make informed and professional decisions about adapting lessons to their students and the local environment.

- Administrators and education leaders should provide opportunities for teachers to implement and reflect on the use of *Framework*-aligned approaches to teaching and learning.

RECOMMENDATION 5: Undergraduate learning experiences need to serve as models for prospective teachers, in which they experience science investigation and engineering design as learners.

- College and university faculty should design and teach science classes that model the use of evidence-based principles for learning and immerse students in *Framework*-aligned approaches to science and engineering learning.
- Faculty should design and teach courses on pedagogy of science and engineering that use instructional strategies consistent with the *Framework*.
- College and university administrators should support and incentivize design of new courses or redesign of existing courses that use evidence-based principles and align with the ideas of the *Framework*.

RECOMMENDATION 6: Administrators should take steps to address the deep history of inequities in which not all students have been offered a full and rigorous sequence of science and engineering learning opportunities, by implementing science investigation and engineering design approaches in all science courses for all students.

- School and district staff should systematically review policies that impact the ability to offer science investigation and engineering design opportunities to all students. They should monitor and analyze differences in course offerings and content between schools, as well as patterns of enrollment and success in science and engineering courses at all schools. This effort should include particular attention to differential student outcomes, especially in areas in which inequality and inequity have been well documented (e.g., gender, socioeconomic status, race, and culture). Administrators should use this information to construct specific, concrete, and positive plans to address the disparities.
- State and national legislatures and departments of education should provide additional resources to schools with significant populations of underserved students to broaden access/opportunity and allow all students to participate in science investigation and engineering design.

RECOMMENDATION 7: For all students to engage in meaningful science investigation and engineering design, the many components of the system must become better aligned. This will require changes to existing policies and procedures. As policies and procedures are revised, care must be taken not to exacerbate existing inequities.

- State, regional, and district leaders should commission and use valid and reliable summative assessment tools that mirror how teachers measure three-dimensional learning.
- States, regions, and districts should provide resources to support the implementation of investigation and engineering design-based approaches to science and engineering instruction across all grades and in all schools, and should track and manage progress towards full implementation. State, regional, and district leaders should ensure that the staff in their own offices who oversee science instruction or science educators have a deep knowledge of *Framework*-aligned approaches to teaching and learning.

RESEARCH QUESTIONS

While the work in this report draws on existing empirical research studies, this report also serves as a stage for the production of a range of research questions. The questions below are an invitation for continued dialogue and a guide for funders or researchers engaged in learning more about the role of science investigation and engineering design for advancing student understanding of three-dimensional science and engineering knowledge. Addressing these questions in classes, schools, districts, and states that are using *Framework*-based approaches provides an opportunity to track successes and failures and to refine the implementation efforts and address any observed weaknesses. Future research can help understand the ways that learning via science investigation and engineering design is most effective and provide more information on long-term effects and on causality. Research that examines the impact of *Framework*-based reform should address what is implemented, how it is implemented, under what conditions implementation occurs, why the implementation works or does not work, and for whom does it work.

The Classroom Experience with Science
Investigation and Engineering Design

The selection of topics for science investigation and engineering design is key to engaging students and focusing their learning on science and engineering concepts that educators want them to learn. Choosing topics and resources that allow students to see the relevance appears to be an approach that can motivate student learning. More information on these approaches and how instructional resources can facilitate the process are needed.

1. How does the relevance, contextualization, and locality of a phenomenon or design challenge relate to what students learn as they engage in science investigation and engineering design? Which aspects of relevance and contextualization are most important, under what conditions do they operate, what are their impacts, and what is the duration of impact?

2. What types of instructional resources best support teachers and students as students engage in science investigation and engineering design? How are these similar/different to resources used for prior ways of thinking about curriculum materials and laboratory reports?

Discourse

Students sharing ideas and understanding through productive discourse can allow students to build off each other's ideas and for students and teachers to monitor and reflect upon their evolving understanding of science and engineering practices and concepts. Discourse is a more prominent tool for learning in *Framework*-aligned classrooms and especially for investigation and design, and more research is needed on how it can be best used.

3. Under what conditions are classroom discourse most productive, and how is productive classroom discourse related to what students learn as they engage in science investigation and engineering design?

4. What are the most effective instructional strategies for being inclusive in engaging students in classroom discussions?

Inclusive Pedagogies

As described previously in this report, a broad range of approaches can create more inclusive learning environments for the increasingly diverse population of students in the United States. Additional research on the design and engagement of these ideas and interventions has the potential to help the field better address many of the challenges in achieving equity and equality in science learning via science investigation and engineering design that this report describes.

5. In what ways are students' experiences, lived histories, and other assets most meaningfully engaged in support of their participation of science investigation and engineering design? How can teachers honor and connect these experiences during science investigation and engineering design?
6. How can teachers and administrators best learn to enact inclusive pedagogies in science investigation and engineering design? How does their effectiveness compare to other pedagogical interventions? How can these approaches be infused as an essential component in professional learning experiences?
7. In what ways does school design influence the use and effectiveness of inclusive pedagogies for science investigation and engineering design? What sorts of school design—and accompanying community engagement—have the greatest potential to both accelerate student learning in science and engineering and to close gaps among groups of students?

Technology

Recent years have seen dramatic shifts in the technology available in classrooms and in students' daily lives. There are many new ideas on how to use these technologies in science and engineering classrooms and a need to evaluate the technologies and the ways they can be used in education to determine how they can best contribute to student learning.

8. In what ways do particular technology-enhanced investigations help and hinder student engagement and learning in science investigation and engineering design? What are the appropriate roles within particular science investigation and engineering design environments for student use of technology to collect, analyze, interpret, and communicate data?
9. In what ways are particular technologies utilized by professional scientists, such as small- or large-scale visualizations or modeled data simulations, useful as a component of investigation and design? What adaptations of professional data and technology-rich tools are needed for effective use in science investigation and engineering design?

Working with Data and Models

Working with data is at the heart of science investigation and engineering design. Research shows that students can respond differently to data they have gathered themselves versus data that comes from another source.

More information can help determine which approaches and experiences will best help students use data to make sense of the world around them.

10. What are good strategies for helping students work with and understand data, the strengths and limits of models, and the concept of uncertainty in the context of science investigation and engineering design?
11. What are best practices for supporting students in complex practices such as modeling? How does modeling relate to and support other science investigation and engineering design practices?

Outcomes

Measuring student motivation and student learning tells the field about the success of new efforts to teach science and engineering. Traditional approaches to this measurement do not often get at the heart of student understanding of the practices and nature of science and engineering. New tools and techniques for monitoring learning can provide insight into the best ways to gather this type of information in ways that can help improve use of investigation and design to foster learning.

12. What are best practices for three dimensional assessment design? What kinds and range of evidence do these three dimensional assessment tasks generate? How are three-dimensional assessment tasks best used for formative or summative purposes?
13. What are the most effective strategies for helping students to use the results of formative assessment to support learning?
14. How does participation in science investigation and engineering design affect student interest in science and engineering?
15. What are the short- and long-term impacts of engagement in engineering for both students and teachers?
16. Does increased science investigation and engineering design experience affect student outcomes such as GPA, graduation rates, enjoyment of learning, jobs, college entrance, or college success?

Professional Learning

Professional learning is the key to preparing teachers to use investigation and design to foster student understanding. Teachers need practice in how to structure, guide, and facilitate these new approaches. It is known that sustained professional learning experiences have the most impact, but more information is needed on the professional learning that will most improve teachers' abilities to engage students in investigation and design.

17. How does professional learning affect instructional practices in the classroom? How do resulting changes in teacher behavior impact student outcomes?
18. How does engaging preservice and in-service teachers as learners in three-dimensional science and engineering learning influence the development of their own content knowledge, classroom practices, and beliefs about student learning?
19. What tools, resources, and professional learning experiences help teachers develop the repertoire of practices necessary to facilitate productive classroom discourse?
20. What kinds of preservice teacher preparation programs (as opposed to later during their teaching careers) do science and engineering teachers need in order to effectively engage their students in science investigation and engineering design?

The Education System

Factors outside the classroom can limit the impact of attempts to reform classroom instruction. The complex interactions that make up the system of K–12 education in the United States do not always work in concert to advance improvement. More information is needed on how to implement and sustain reform efforts that improve student learning.

21. What practices and policies at the school, district, and/or state levels support or hinder widespread implementation of science investigation and engineering design projects for all students?
22. Have efforts to make science education available to all decreased the impact of historical inequities?
23. Does professional development for administrators influence school culture and the implementation or sustainability of investigation and design in the classroom?

FINAL REFLECTIONS

Science education provides students with a powerful set of tools to understand the world in which they live. Engaging students in science investigation and engineering design is the central strategy for helping students to connect learning to their own experiences and develop deep and sustained knowledge and abilities to use science as a way of knowing. Hence, science investigation and engineering design should be the central instructional approach for teaching and learning science to *all* students.

All students deserve the opportunity to engage in relevant and interesting science investigation and engineering design. This requires educators to develop the skills and knowledge to make science engaging, relevant, and inclusive, which requires systemic changes by the education system. This includes changes to disposition about science education so that *science education is seen as a pump and not a filter*: that is, science education should lift up all students and not act as a barrier or hurdle to all but a few. Science education should be relevant, engaging, and fun in ways that empower all students to develop interest and identity with science.

New standards are an opportunity for the education system to change teaching to be consistent with how students learn, to make investigation and design central to science learning, and to make changes to the system to better embrace equity practices for all students. New standards provide an opportunity to change the structure of instruction and shift toward more student-centered teaching and learning. They are an opportunity to engage educators in professional learning that is focused on principled improvements to teaching and learning and is sustained, engaging, and relevant to the work of the classroom and student learning.

Appendix A

The Role of Assessment in Supporting Science Investigation and Engineering Design

A reader of this report may notice the absence of a chapter titled Assessment. This was a deliberate choice by the committee, first recognizing the contribution of the report *Developing Assessments for the Next Generation Science Standards* (National Research Council, 2014), and second, noting the importance of seamlessly integrating assessment throughout the vision of science investigation and engineering design articulated throughout the report. Table A-1 below provides a guide to the reader of the places in the report most relevant to assessment. The next section contains an overview of three empirically supported ideas for assessment systems that provide strong evidence of student learning in science investigations and engineering design. We then provide some worked examples of the design and enactment of classroom assessment that can be used to support science investigation and engineering design (Kang, Thompson, and Windschitl, 2014) to illustrate ways that this approach can be used with investigation and design. Finally, the last section includes an example of how discourse can be used as assessment (Coffey et al., 2011). This approach can also be applied to assessment of engineering design (Alemdar et al., 2017; Purzer, 2018).

EMPIRICALLY SUPPORTED IDEAS FOR ASSESSMENT SYSTEMS

1. The Assessment Triangle (National Research Council, 2001) identifies three components of an assessment system that when aligned provides strong evidence of student learning: the learning goals (cognition), the tasks (observation), and the system of interpretation,

including the coding rubric (interpretation). As learning goals have shifted to Framework-inspired (National Research Council, 2014) three-dimensional (3D) learning, modifications to assessment tasks and interpretation systems that maintain this alignment must be considered.

2. Classroom-based investigation and design assessment systems have the following characteristics, regardless of whether they are used for formative or summative purposes:

    a. The student's performance on the tasks reveal evidence of progress on 3D learning along a continuum between expected beginning and ending points relative to the learning expectations.
    b. The coding rubric and system of interpretation provide evidence of students' progress across a range of student abilities (Gotwals and Songer, 2013).
    c. The tasks and coding rubric provide a range of opportunities for students to demonstrate 3D learning with and without guidance, such as scaffolds (e.g., Kang, Thompson, and Windschitl, 2014; Songer, Kelcey, and Gotwals, 2009).
    d. The coding rubric and system of interpretation are specific enough to be useful in guiding teachers in either next instructional steps (formative) or in determining the amount and rate of progress in 3D learning (summative) (National Research Council, 2014).

3. Research studies demonstrate that three-dimensional assessment tasks of a short answer and/or scaffold-rich format can provide stronger evidence of 3D learning than multiple choice items. For example, a research study conducted with 1,885 Detroit Public School sixth graders in 22 classrooms evaluated the relative amount of information on 3D learning demonstrated through embedded, multiple choice (called standardized) and 3D learning tasks (called complex) in association with a 3D learning-fostering 8-week unit on ecology and biodiversity. Results demonstrated that the embedded assessment tasks revealed both the largest amount of information and the greatest range of information across student abilities (Songer, Kelcey, and Gotwals, 2009). A similar study also demonstrated that 3D assessment systems provided opportunities for students at a range of ability levels to demonstrate evidence of both successes and challenges in 3D learning along a unit learning progression (Gotwals and Songer, 2013).

TABLE A-1 Where Is Assessment in This Volume?

Chapter	Subject	Focus	Pages
4	How Students Engage with Investigation and Design	Communicate reasoning to self and others	97–98
5	How Teachers Support Investigation and Design	Embedded assessment	127–129
		Features come together for investigation and design	131–138
6	Instructional Resources for Supporting Investigation and Design	Assessment and communicating reasoning to self and others	162–163
7	Preparing and Supporting Teachers to Facilitate Investigations	Equity and inclusion	205
10	Conclusions and Recommendations	Conclusion #5	270
		Conclusion #7	271–272
		Recommendation #2	275–276
		Research questions	278

Worked Examples of the Design and Enactment of Classroom Assessment

Kang and colleagues (2014) described five different types of scaffolding in formative assessment tasks. These scaffolds appear to show promising benefit for student learning. They help to support students in making their ideas explicit and providing guidance to students as they develop higher-quality explanations. Examples of each of these different scaffolding types for formative assessment tasks are shared here from Kang, Thompson, and Windschitl (2014):

1. **Allowing students to draw in combination with writing to explain focal phenomena**

When students were asked to draw unobservable underlying mechanisms that caused an observable phenomenon or event, they engaged in the scientific practice of modeling and in more challenging intellectual work. The example shown below (see Figure A-1), taken from a 9th-grade biology classroom (p. 679), illustrates how students are asked to show how a paramecium gets everything it needs to survive.

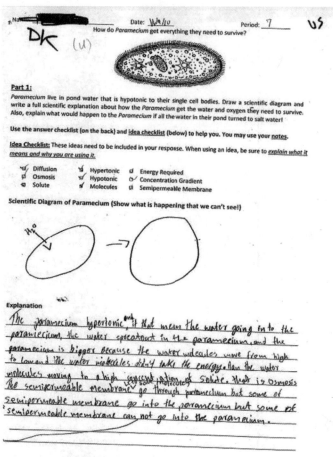

FIGURE A-1 Worked example of Paramecium questions.
SOURCE: Kang et al. (2014)

2. Asking a question with a contextualized phenomenon

Contextualized phenomena also help students provide better explanations. That is, rather than asking students to explain a generic event or scientific idea, these tasks ask students to place the idea in context. An example is provided below (p. 679):

> A skater girl is flying down the big hill on 102nd (right in front of Steve Cox Memorial Park, where that cabin is, behind McLendon's Hardware) when she realizes that some jerk has built a huge brick wall across the road. She knows that she won't be able to stop in time. What should she do to minimize, or decrease, her injuries? Explain why this is the best option for the skater girl.

3. **Providing sentence frames**

Teachers used both focusing and connecting sentence frames to help students draw their students to focal phenomena and lead in to explanations. While some sentence frames helped students get started with their explanation (e.g., "What I saw was _____" . . . "I know this because_____,") higher-quality, connecting sentence frames helped students to more deeply connect evidence and reasoning to make scientific explanations. These sentence frames included, for example, starters such as "Evidence for _____ comes from the [activity on] _____ because _____."

4. **Scaffolding by providing students with a checklist**

An additional form of scaffolding is a checklist, which can either provide students with a word bank to use when creating an explanation or a model (called a "simple checklist") or an "explanation checklist" that prompts students to provide information about aspects of a model or explanation or relationships among ideas (see Figure A-2).

Gotta-have checklist

▸ **You need to include in your explanation:**
   ☐ How molecules cause pressure
   ☐ About differences in conditions inside versus outside the tanker at every phase
   ☐ About heat energy and how it affects parts of the system
   ☐ About how changes in the volume of a container affects pressure

FIGURE A-2 Checklist.
SOURCE: Kang et al. (2014)

5. Scaffolding by providing a rubric

Consistent with studies performed in other disciplinary areas (e.g., Andrade, 2010; Kang, Thompson, and Windschitl, 2014) found that providing a rubric in a task also helped explicitly provide students with criteria that helped raise the quality of their explanation. The example of the "skater girl" assessment, shown below (see Figure A-3), illustrates how such a rubric with points for higher-quality work can be embedded into a task, making clear the ways in which students' work will be evaluated by the teacher (p. 680).

Name _____ Period __L__ Date _____   Score: ____ /14

Final Explanation: The Skater Girl

THE SITUATION: A skater girl is flying down the big hill on 102nd (right in front of Steve Cox Memorial Park, where that cabin is, behind McLendon's Hardware) when she realizes that some jerk has built a huge brick wall across the road. She knows that she won't be able to stop in time. What should she do to minimize, or decrease, her injuries?

FINAL EXPLANATION: Use your journal, the Word Wall, and your Evidence Buckets to answer Questions 1–3.

1. What should the skater girl do to minimize her injuries? (1 point) *Steer towards the pond or grass for a softer landing than the wall*

2. Explain, using words and pictures, why this is the best option for the skater girl. Use as many words from the word wall as you can. Use the space below to draw a picture that helps you answer if you need it. (3 points)

Word Bank			
Velocity	Vector	Acceleration	Momentum
Force	Net force	Friction	Mass

- 1 point: <u>Describe</u> the forces acting on the skater girl in #1.
- 1 point: <u>Use at least 3 words</u> from the Word Bank/Word Wall.
- 1 point: <u>Explain why</u> this is better than another choice she has.
- 1 point: <u>Draw a picture</u> that helps explain your answer.

• The skater girl should try to (slowly) steer towards the grass, pond, or other surface to avoid the wall because steering (slowly) away would result in her accelerating in such a way that her velocity decreases & force upon impact isn't as great as it would be when hitting the wall.
• She shouldn't hit the wall because the sudden change in momentum would hurt her. & She shouldn't drag her feet/butt because of the friction from the coarse cement would hurt her & she would still hit the wall.

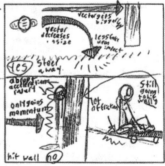

USING EVIDENCE: Use your Evidence Bucket to answer this question.

3. Give at least one piece of evidence from a class activity that supports your ideas in #2. (2 points)
   The egg video thing shows that when momentum is changed very slowly, the stopping force upon said body is also very low. However, if momentum is changed abruptly, the stopping force is very high. Therefore, we know it would be a good idea for the girl to slowly change her momentum, so that her stopping force is small & injuries acquired are also fairly minor.

FIGURE A-3 Worked force and motion assessment.
SOURCE: Kang et al. (2014)

Combining multiple scaffolds in one assessment

These different forms of scaffolds can be combined in one assessment, as illustrated by the task shown below (see Figure A-4), which illustrates a contextualized phenomenon, a sentence frame, and the combination of drawing plus writing (Kang et al. 2014, Figure 5, p. 692).

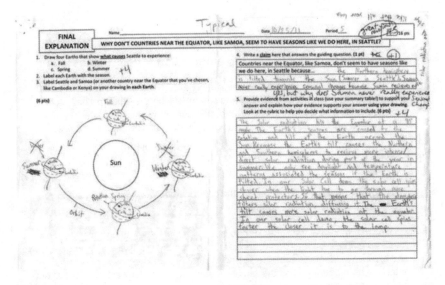

FIGURE A-4 Worked assessment on seasonal change.
SOURCE: Kang et al. (2014)

INFORMAL ASSESSMENT THROUGH CLASSROOM DISCOURSE: THE EXAMPLE OF TERRY'S CLASSROOM DISCUSSION

Assessment does not need to use a formal instrument. It can occur by way of classroom discourse. Box A-1 provides an example of how this was done in a high school chemistry course.

BOX A-1
Assessing Student Thinking During Classroom Discussion

Terry was a 9th-grade teacher initiating a conversation with his students about the difference between mass and weight, which the students had studied previously. These ideas were relevant to their current work around the chemistry of life, which built on basic understandings of matter, atoms, and molecules.

Terry: What influences your weight? Do you weigh more on the earth or on the moon?

Barb: Gravity!

Terry: Ohhh. (quietly). And. So what's the difference between your weight and your mass. Standing right here. [silence for several seconds] Nothing.

At this moment, Terry decided to set the topic aside, stating that he didn't "think it's going to be that significant" for the lesson they were about to engage in, and allowed students to continue saying "weight." He asked the students whether a table was matter, and all the students said yes, and then asked them about water. Barb answered, "No."

Terry took a key opportunity to follow up on Barb's response to further unpack her thinking. Rather than moving ahead with the lesson, he chose to ask her a follow-up question to elicit the reason for her claim that water was not matter.

Terry: Why?

Barb: I think it's composed of molecules.

Terry: OK, which are?

Barb: Matter? [barely audible]

Terry: Are they? Perhaps it doesn't matter, but you kind of went, "Matter?" [mimicking the tentative tone] [quiet laughter]

Barb: Yes. [clearly stated]

At this point, Terry guided the students to apply the definition of matter—it has weight and takes up space —to water, and the students quickly agreed. A student suggested, "Doesn't matter have to do with a state? Like liquid and solid and gasses?" The implication was that, since water is a liquid or a gas, it must also be matter. Terry then asked the students whether air was also matter, and several students simultaneously responded "No," following up with "You can't weigh it" and "You can't see it."

BOX A-1 Continued

Barb: It takes up space but you can't feel it, Like you can't bump into it . . . 'Cause air is everywhere, except for in water . . . well actually, no, there is air in water.

Terry: Adria. Shh. Adria, did you have your hand up?

Adria: I was gonna say you could feel it. Or you can't feel it.

Barb: Yeah, well you can feel wind. [overlapping talk]

Terry: Yeah, What's wind?

Brianna: Air . . . air blowing [overlapping talk]

Terry: So can we weigh it?

Students: No . . . no

Terry: Those are the issues we've got to resolve. Can we weigh it?

Maggie: No [multiple students] [emphatic]

Terry: How could I weigh it? What could you do to weigh it?

Barb: You could like put it in a balloon or something but there's the weight of the balloon so you couldn't weigh it.

Terry: I haven't got a scale with me today. [walks over to his desk and pulls out a bag of balloons] . . . So I have balloons, right? [tosses Barb a balloon.] Blow it up.

In this first part of the conversation, Coffey and colleagues note, Terry has used questions to draw out students' understanding of what does and does not count as matter and, as a result, has uncovered that the students exhibit some basic confusion about the meaning of the concept of matter. They were not sure whether water is matter, or whether air is matter. Rather than focusing on the "correct" definition of ideas that had previously been covered, Terry used open-ended questions to encourage the students to talk through their ideas with the class, and Terry held them accountable for their ideas and followed their lead. When he asked if they should weigh air, despite some students saying no, he encouraged students to perform an investigation, scrapping his original instructional plan to seize on the moment to respond to students' ideas.

In this way, Terry has used a moment of informal formative assessment in which he listened and attended to student ideas in order to create a basis for conducting an investigation, which in turn generated evidence relevant to the disagreement that had surfaced in the classroom conversation through the questions Terry had asked.

Barb inflated the balloon, and Mikela commented, "That one's stretching because she's blowing air into it." Terry asked if this was because there was a different "amount of stuff in it." Students disagreed, saying "yes" and "no" at the same time. Lauren argued, "Air and matter is closed up," and Barb said that air was "occupying space in there," referring to the balloon. Terry asked if air was "occupying space in the room," and students spoke over each other with a mix of responses.

continued

BOX A-1 Continued

Terry: Are you saying? And I'm asking, I'm not telling. That it takes up space when it's in HERE [in the balloon], but it doesn't take up space when it's in the room.

India: No.

Terry: Is that the general consensus?

Barb: No! Actually that's right cause you can't put something inside that balloon with air in it. [several students speaking at once]

Terry: OK. What would happen to the air in the balloon, if I put water in it too?

Barb: There wouldn't be as much air.

Terry: Because?

India: The water's taking up space.

Terry: OK. What would happen to the air in the balloon, if I put water in it, too?

Barb: There wouldn't be as MUCH air.

Terry: Because?

India: The water's taking up space.

Terry: OK, so . . .

Laura: The air is the space.

Terry: Say it again.

Laura: The air IS the space.

Terry: So air IS the space. Are you saying it takes up space? Is that the idea?

Ari: The air is the space that gets taken up.

Terry: So it's an empty space until I put water in it? I'm trying, I'm trying to work your way. I'm not trying to say you're right or wrong, I'm asking. This is not a graded assignment or anything.

Ari: Yes.

Terry: Yes? How many people agree with that? Air is empty space that the water is going to take up when I pour water in. If I were more daring, I would've brought a couple of water balloons too. I'm afraid they'll blow up in here . . . So think about this, some of you have this look on your face like "I don't know for sure," is this just empty space which we filled up with water, or is there something in there?

Brianna and Laura (simultaneously): There's something in there.

Terry: Okay, what's the something?

Students: Air! Air!

Terry: So, does it take up space?

Students: Yes!

Laura: I'm confused!

India: Oh my god!

Terry: You don't sound convinced, you're giving me "ummmm." Yea, go ahead.

India: But when, when something else goes in there, doesn't some of the air leave?

In this exchange, we see Terry clearly letting students know that they are safe to let him know what they know, and that they are not being evaluated on

BOX A-1 Continued

their ideas at this moment. ("I'm not trying to say you're right or wrong, I'm ask-ing. This is not a graded assignment or anything.") He also uses a mixture of eliciting questions ("What's the something?") with more directed questions that mark particular student ideas and help to push students in their thinking. ("Say it again . . . so the air IS the space. Are you saying it takes up space? Is that the idea?") Toward the end of the conversation, he encourages students to come to a consensus. ("How many people agree with that?")

Later in the class, the students compared the weights of an empty balloon and an inflated balloon, and found no difference. When they discussed this re-sult, they concluded that the scale may not have been sensitive enough, so they tried again on the next day with a more sensitive scale, and found the inflated balloon to be slightly heavier than the uninflated balloon. Ultimately, through the combination of guided questioning and empirical data collected and analyzed in response to ideas that emerged through the conversation, the class concluded that air was indeed matter.

SOURCE: Adapted from Coffey et al. (2011, pp. 1124–1127).

REFERENCES

Alemdar, M., Lingle, J.A., Wind, S.A., and Moore, R.A. (2017). Developing an engineer-ing design process assessment using think-aloud interviews. *International Journal for Engineering Education, 33*(1), 441–452

Andrade, H., Du, Y., and Mycek, K. (2010). Rubric-referenced self-assessment and middle school students' writing. *Assessment in Education: Principles, Policy & Practice, 17,* 199–214.

Coffey, J.E., Hammer, D., Levin, D.M., and Grant, T. (2011). The missing disciplinary substance of formative assessment. *Journal of Research in Science Teaching, 48*(10), 1109–1136.

Gotwals, A.W., and Songer, N.B. (2013) Validity evidence for learning progression-based assessment items that fuse core disciplinary ideas and science practices. *The Journal of Research in Science Teaching, 50*(5), 597–626.

Kang, H., Thompson, J., and Windschitl, M. (2014). Creating opportunities for students to show what they know: The role of scaffolding in assessment tasks. *Science Education, 98*(4), 674–704.

National Research Council. (2001). *Knowing What Students Know: The Science and Design of Educational Assessment.* Washington. DC: The National Academies Press.

National Research Council. (2014). *Developing Assessments for the Next Generation Science Standards.* Washington, DC: The National Academies Press.

Purzer, S. (2018). *Engineering Approaches to Problem Solving and Design in Secondary School Science: Teachers as Design Coaches.* Paper commissioned for the Committee on Science Investigations and Engineering Design for Grades 6–12. Board on Sci-ence Education, Division of Behavioral and Social Sciences and Education. National Academies of Sciences, Engineering, and Medicine. Available: http://www.nas.edu/Science-Investigation-and-Design [October 2018].

Songer, N.B., Kelcey, B., and Gotwals., A.W. (2009). When and how does complex reasoning occur? Empirically driven development of a learning progression focused on complex reasoning about biodiversity. *Journal of Research in Science Teaching, (46)*6, 610–631.

Appendix B

Public Agenda for
Meeting #1—May 2017

11:15 am   **Welcome and Overview of the Study**
Heidi Schweingruber, Director, Board on
    Science Education
Nancy Songer and Brett Moulding, Study Cochairs

11:25 am   **Discussion of the Charge with the Sponsors**
Scott Heimlich, Amgen Foundation
Jim Short, Carnegie Corporation of New York

12:15 pm   **Lunch and Small Group Discussion of the Study**

1:15 pm   **Panel on Needs of Educators and the Field**
Tiffany Neill, Council of State Science Supervisors
    and Oklahoma State Department of Education
Al Byers, National Science Teachers Association
Donna Barrett-Williams, Georgia Science Teachers
    Association and STEM Director-Science at
    Fulton County Schools

1:45 pm   Panel Discussion and Questions for the Panel from
the Committee

2:15 pm   Questions for the Panel from the Audience

2:30 pm   **Adjourn Open Session**

Appendix C

Public Agenda for
Meeting #2—July 2017

OPEN SESSION

12:30 pm   Lunch

1:15 pm   **Welcome and Overview of the Study**
              Nancy Songer and Brett Moulding, Study Cochairs

1:25 pm   **Introduction of Session on Equity**
              Eileen Parsons, Committee Member

1:35 pm   **Engineering, Identity, and African American Males**
              Christopher Wright, Drexel University

2:00 pm   **Science Education and Culturally Marginalized
              and Economically Disadvantaged Children**
              Rowhea Elmesky, Washington University in St. Louis

2:25 pm   **Under-Represented Girls in STEM**
              Kimberly Scott, Arizona State University

2:50 pm   **Discussion with Three Presenters on Equity**
              Moderated by Eileen Parsons

3:20 pm   **Break**

3:30 pm   **Investigations & Nature of Science: Beyond Planning
                 and Carrying Out Investigations**
                 Rick Duschl, The Pennsylvania State University
                 Moderated by Brett Moulding

3:55 pm   **Adjourn Open Session**

Appendix D

Agenda for Workshop at Meeting #3—November 2017

10:00 am   **Welcome**
Heidi Schweingruber, Director, Board on
    Science Education
Overview of the Workshop
Nancy Songer and Brett Moulding, Study Cochairs

10:10 am   **Engaging Students in Investigations-How Students Use Evidence**
Ravit Golan Duncan, Rutgers University

10:45 am   **The Teacher Role**
Matt Kloser, University of Notre Dame
Commentary by Stacey van der Veen,
    NGSSPD Consultants

12:00 pm   **Lunch**

1:00 pm   **Inclusive Pedagogy for Investigations**
Megan Bang, University of Washington, Seattle
    (participating virtually)

1:35 pm   **Panel on Professional Development**
Lizette Burks, Kansas State Department of Education
    (participating virtually)

Susan Gomez Zwiep, California State University,
    Long Beach
Wil van der Veen, Raritan Valley Community College

3:05 pm   **Break**

3:30 pm   **The Role and Impact of Technology on Teaching
           Investigations**
           Scott McDonald, The Pennsylvania State University

4:05 pm   **Panel on Engineering Design**
           Christian Schunn, University of Pittsburgh
           Tamara Moore, Purdue University
           John Kamal, Science Leadership Academy @ Center City

5:20 pm   **Thank You, Reflections, and Concluding Remarks**
           Nancy Songer and Brett Moulding

5:45 pm   **Reception and Networking (Lecture Room and
           East Court)**

7:30 pm   **Adjourn**

Appendix E

Biographical Sketches of Committee Members and Staff

BRETT MOULDING (Cochair) is the director of the Partnership for Effective Science Teaching and Learning. He was the state of Utah science education specialist and coordinator of curriculum from 1993 to 2004 and then director of curriculum and instruction until 2008. He taught chemistry for 20 years at Roy High School in the Weber District Science and served as the district teacher leader for 8 years. He also served on the board of the Triangle Coalition, the National Assessment of Educational Progress 2009 Framework Committee, and as president of the Council of State Science Supervisors from 2003–2006. He has received the Governor's Teacher Recognition Award, the Presidential Award for Excellence in Mathematics and Science Teaching, the Award of Excellence from the Governor's Science and Technology Commission, and the National Science Teachers Association's Distinguished Service to Science Education Award. He served on the the National Academies of Sciences, Engineering, and Medicine's committee that developed the Framework for K–12 Science Education, as well as on three committees related to education at the National Aeronautics and Space Administration. He was a member of the Board on Science Education from 2005–2011. He was a lead writers on the Next Generation Science Standards and currently provides professional development for teachers throughout the nation. He graduated from the University of Utah with a bachelor's degree in chemistry with minors in biology, math, and physics. He also has a master's degree in education from Weber State University and an administrative supervisory certificate from Utah State University.

NANCY SONGER (Cochair) is the dean and distinguished university professor in the School of Education at Drexel University. Prior to this, she was a professor of science education and learning technologies at the University of Michigan for 18 years and the director of the Center for Essential Science. Her areas of expertise include STEM education, urban education, and educational assessment, and her research focuses on the design of education innovations for promoting critical thinking in science, environmental awareness, increased interactivity, and participation in science careers. She is renowned for her research on how to engage and support complex scientific reasoning among students ranging from elementary to high school ages. Her scholarship has received frequent recognition, including a Presidential Faculty Fellowship awarded by President Clinton. Songer is now leading urban STEM initiatives investigating new definitions of public school-university partnerships with several West Philadelphia public schools within the Drexel University School of Education's neighborhood. She served on the National Academies of Sciences, Engineering, and Medicine's Committee on a Framework for Assessment of Science Proficiency in K–12. Songer earned a bachelor's degree in biological sciences from the University of California, Berkeley, master's degree in developmental biology from Tufts University, and doctorate degree in science education and learning technologies from the University of California, Davis.

JUAN-CARLOS AGUILAR is the director of innovated programs and research at the Georgia Department of Education. He serves as liaison between the department and science organizations, and with the Georgia University System in science. He serves on the board of directors for the Georgia Youth Science and Technology Centers and board of advisors for Valdosta STEAM. He served as the Department of Education science program manager for 9 years, when he oversaw state policy in science education, coordinated K–12 science curriculum development, co-directed Georgia's K–12 STEM initiative, and supervised the alignment of state assessments with the Georgia Performance Standards for science. He led the revision and adoption of the new Georgia Standards of Excellence in Science. He is the past president of the Council of State Science Supervisors. He is an advisor for the NIH SEPA 2015 Emory grant titled Experiential Citizen Science Training for the Next Generation. He previously taught, including 10 years as a science and mathematics teacher at a Spanish-immersion middle school and 5 years as a high school physics teacher, both in Fayette County, Georgia. He also taught science and mathematics for 4 years at a high school in Guatemala City. He has a Licenciature in Physics from the University Del Valle of Guatemala. He received a principal certification from Morehead State University, an M.S. in physics from the University of Louisville, and a Ph.D. in physics from the University of Kentucky.

ANNE EGGER is an associate professor at Central Washington University (CWU), where she has a joint appointment in Geological Sciences and Science Education. She has served as director of the office of undergraduate research at CWU and as president of the National Association of Geoscience Teachers (NAGT). Through NAGT and other projects, she has led numerous professional development workshops on building skills in teaching through active learning. As an author, editor, and co-project director for Visionlearning, Egger develops freely available, Web-based, peer-reviewed readings for learning about science. Additionally, she is involved in developing rigorously tested curricular materials that integrate geoscience and societal issues across the curriculum at the undergraduate level. She has conducted research on how prepared future teachers are to teach about the sustainability concepts of the NGSS, and on the mismatch between introductory college earth science courses taken by future teachers and the material they will be expected to teach in their own classrooms. Prior to her appointment at CWU, she was a lecturer and undergraduate program coordinator in the School of Earth Sciences at Stanford University. She earned a bachelor's degree in geology and geophysics from Yale University and a master's degree and doctorate in geological and environmental sciences from Stanford University.

ERIN MARIE FURTAK is professor of science education and associate dean of faculty in the school of education at the University of Colorado Boulder. Previously, she was a public high school biology and earth science teacher. Her current research focuses on how to support secondary science teachers in improving formative assessment practices. She was principal investigator for a CAREER grant from the National Science Foundation to investigate how a long-term professional development program centered on a learning progression for natural selection supported high school teachers in iteratively designing, enacting, and revising formative assessments. Recently, she has extended this work in a long-term research-practice partnership supporting formative assessment design with high school physics, chemistry, and biology teachers in a large school district. She received the Presidential Early Career Award for Scientists and Engineers in 2011 and the German Chancellor Fellowship from the Alexander von Humboldt Foundation in 2006. She is involved in professional development partnerships with school districts and organizations within Colorado and across the United States. She earned a bachelor's degree in environmental, population, and organismic biology from the University of Colorado Boulder, a master's degree in education from the University of Denver, and a doctorate in science education from Stanford University.

KENNETH L. HUFF is a National Board Certified Teacher in early adolescence science and a middle school teacher in the Williamsville Central School District in Williamsville, New York. He is a member of the New York State Education Department's Science Education Steering Committee, and he founded and leads a Young Astronaut Council for 5th- through 8th-grade students at his school. He is also a National STEM Teacher Ambassador, president-elect of the Science Teachers Association of New York State, and member of the National Science Education Leadership Association Professional Development Committee. He is past president of the Association of Presidential Awardees in Science Teaching, served as a member of the National Science Teachers Association (NSTA) Board of Directors-Division Director Middle Level Science Teaching; co-chaired the Teacher Advisory Council of the National Academies of Sciences, Engineering, and Medicine; and was a member of the writing team for the Next Generation Science Standards. His awards include the Presidential Award for Excellence in Mathematics and Science Teaching, Empire State Excellence in Teaching Award, NSTA Robert E. Yager Foundation Excellence in Teaching Award, Educator Achievement Award from the American Institute of Aeronautics and Astronautics, and National Congress on Aviation and Space Education Crown Circle for Aerospace Education Leadership Award. He earned his B.S. and M.S. degrees from the State University of New York College at Buffalo.

JOSEPH KRAJCIK is Lappan-Phillips professor of science education and director of the CREATE for STEM Institute. Previously, he taught high school chemistry and physical science in Milwaukee for 8 years, and taught at the University of Michigan for 21 years. His expertise includes curriculum and instruction; science education; and teacher education, learning, and policy. He works with science teachers to reform teaching practices to promote students' engagement in and learning of science. He is currently principal investigator and co-principal investigator for two National Science Foundation grants to design, develop, and test middle school assessments and curriculum materials aligned with the Next Generation Science Standards. He served as lead writer for developing NGSS Physical Science Standards and lead writer for the Physical Science Design team that developed the Framework for K–12 Science Education. He was co-editor of the *Journal of Research in Science Teaching* and has authored and co-authored curriculum materials, books, software, and manuscripts. He held a distinguished professorship from Ewha Woman's University in Seoul and guest professorship from Beijing Normal University. He has presented on reforming science education in Chile, Singapore, China, Thailand, Brazil, and South Korea. He is a fellow of the American Association for the Advancement of Science; and was president of the National Association for

Research in Science Teaching, from which he received the Distinguished Contributions to Science Education Through Research Award. He earned a doctorate in science education from the University of Iowa.

MICHAEL LACH is the director of STEM education policy and strategic initiatives at UChicago STEM Education at the University of Chicago, where he conducts research and provides technical assistance on large-scale improvements in U.S. mathematics and science education. Previously, he led science and mathematics education efforts at the U.S. Department of Education. He taught high school biology and general science at Alceé Fortier Senior High School in New Orleans as a charter member of Teach For America. He then joined the national office of Teach For America as director of program design. He returned to the classroom in New York City and Chicago. He was named one of Radio Shack's Top 100 Technology Teachers, earned National Board Certification, and was Illinois Physics Teacher of the Year. He served as an Albert Einstein Distinguished Educator Fellow and was lead curriculum developer for the *Investigations in Environmental Science* curriculum developed at Northwestern University. As a Chicago Public Schools administrator, he led instructional improvement efforts in science and mathematics between 2003 and 2009, ultimately becoming chief officer of teaching and learning. He is a former members of the Board on Science Education and has served on multiple National Academies of Sciences, Engineering, and Medicine committees. He earned a bachelor's degree in physics from Carleton College, master's degrees from Columbia University and Northeastern Illinois University, and doctorate from the University of Illinois at Chicago.

RONALD LATANISION (NAE) is a senior fellow at Exponent, Inc. and an emeritus professor at the Massachusetts Institute of Technology (MIT). At MIT, he held joint faculty appointments in the Department of Materials Science and Engineering and Department of Nuclear Engineering. He directed the School of Engineering's Materials Processing Center from 1985 to 1991. He is a fellow of ASM International, NACE International, and the American Academy of Arts and Sciences. His research interests are focused largely in the areas of materials processing and corrosion of metals and other materials in aqueous environments. He has served as a science advisor to the U.S. House of Representatives Committee on Science and Technology. He was appointed by President George W. Bush to the U.S. Nuclear Waste Technical Review Board and was reappointed by President Barack Obama. He chaired the Council on Primary and Secondary Education at MIT, founded the MIT Science and Engineering Program for High School Teachers, and cochaired the Network of Educators in Science and Technology. He was a co-principal investigator of Project PALMS, a

National Science Foundation-sponsored educational reform initiative in Massachusetts. Over the past 30 years, he served on over 20 technical and education-related National Academies committees. In 2011, he was named editor-in-chief of the NAE quarterly, *The Bridge*. He received a B.S. in metallurgy from The Pennsylvania State University and a Ph.D. in metallurgical engineering from Ohio State University.

MITCHELL NATHAN is Vilas distinguished achievement professor of educational psychology in the School of Education at the University of Wisconsin–Madison. Additionally, he directs the Center on Education and Work; directs the IES Postdoctoral Fellowship Program in Mathematical Thinking, Learning, and Instruction; and holds faculty appointments in several other university departments. He is a member of the University of Wisconsin–Madison Cognitive Science Cluster and an affiliate of the interdisciplinary program in learning, understanding, cognition, intelligence, and data science. He uses experimental design and video-based discourse analysis methods to study learning and teaching. He investigates the role of prior knowledge and invented strategies in the development of algebraic thinking and the notion of Expert Blind Spot to explain teachers' instructional decision making, and how teachers use gestures, embodiment, and objects to convey abstract ideas during STEM instruction. He is on the editorial boards of several journals and advisory board for The INSPIRE Research Institute for Pre-College Engineering at Purdue. He is principal researcher for projects funded by the National Science Foundation, Institute for Education Sciences, and National Institutes of Health and served on several National Academies committees. He earned bachelor's degrees in electrical and computer engineering, mathematics, and history from Carnegie Mellon and a doctorate in cognitive psychology from the University of Colorado Boulder.

EILEEN PARSONS is a professor of science education in the School of Education at the University of North Carolina at Chapel Hill. She studies the influences of sociocultural factors, specifically race and culture, on learning in science and participation in STEM. Her research uses primarily, but not exclusively, qualitative methods to investigate the cultural and racial responsiveness of practices with respect to African American students in K–12 learning environments, with a focus on middle school. Additionally, she studies cultural and racial inclusiveness for traditionally underrepresented students of color in undergraduate STEM. She has served on several editorial boards for science education research journals including associate editor of the *Journal of Research in Science Teaching* and section editor for *Science Education*. Additionally, she served on the Board of Directors for the National Association for Research in Science

Teaching and the Association for Science Teacher Education. As a science policy fellow for the American Association for the Advancement of Science, she worked on the congressionally mandated strategic plan for STEM Education. She taught high school science and math; instructed elementary, middle school, and high school science methods courses in undergraduate and master's teacher preparation programs; coached lateral-entry teachers; and facilitated the professional development of practicing teachers. She earned a bachelor's degree in science teaching (chemistry) from the University of North Carolina at Chapel Hill. Her master's and doctorate degrees in science education are from Cornell University.

CYNTHIA PASSMORE is a professor specializing in science education in the School of Education at the University of California, Davis. Her areas of expertise include models and modeling in student learning, curriculum design, and teacher professional development. As part of the Sacramento Area Science Project—an education partnership between the University of California, Davis, and California State University, Sacramento—she has focused on investigating model-based reasoning in a range of contexts and is particularly interested in understanding how the design of learning environments interacts with students' reasoning practices. She is a member of the American Educational Research Association, National Association for Research in Science Teaching, National Science Teachers Association, and Association for the Education of Teachers of Science. She earned her Ph.D. in curriculum and instruction from the University of Wisconsin. Prior to her doctoral studies, she was a high school science teacher.

HELEN QUINN (NAS) is professor emerita of particle physics and astrophysics at SLAC National Accelerator Laboratory at Stanford University. Previously, she completed a postdoctoral fellowship at Deutsche Elektronen-Synchrotron in Germany, taught high school physics, and was on the staff and faculty of Harvard University. Her research focused on theoretical particle physics with an emphasis on phenomenology of the weak interactions, and her work with Robert Peccei resulted in what is now called the Peccei-Quinn symmetry. She was elected to the National Academy of Sciences in 2003 and was president of the American Physical Society in 2004. Her involvement in science education includes contributing to the California State Science Standards development process. She chaired the Committee on a Conceptual Framework for New K–12 Science Education Standards and served on other National Academies' committees focused on physics and space, and on science education. She was a member of the Board on Science Education from 2005–2009 and its chair from 2009–2014. Additionally, she has taught and done outreach to encourage interest in physics. She was awarded the Karl Taylor Compton Medal for

Leadership in Physics by the American Institute of Physics in 2016. She earned a bachelor's degree in physics and a doctorate in elementary particle physics from Stanford University.

ANDREA TRACY is assistant principal at Lawton High school in Lawton, Oklahoma. Prior to that, she taught biology, physical science, and AP physics at MacArthur High School, also in Lawton. She has an extensive background in middle school science teaching, curriculum development, and assessment. Previously, she was an adjunct professor at the University of Phoenix-Okinawa, Japan, where she held an appointment in the Masters of Education in Teaching Department, specializing in teaching and professional development. She is a member of the National Science Teachers Association and the Association for Supervision and Curriculum Development. She did the course work for a master's degree in teaching from Hamline University, holds an Oklahoma School Principal certification, and is currently pursuing her doctoral studies in educational leadership and management at Capella University. She earned a bachelor's degree in biology from the University of North Dakota, Grand Forks, and a master's degree in education administration from Lamar University.

STAFF BIOS

KERRY BRENNER (Study Director) is a senior program officer for the Board on Science Education. She was the study director for the 2017 consensus report *Undergraduate Research for STEM Students: Successes, Challenges, and Opportunities* and the 2017 workshop on service learning in undergraduate geosciences education. She is the director of the *Roundtable on Systemic Change in Undergraduate STEM Education*. She previously worked for the National Academies of Sciences, Engineering, and Medicine's Board on Life Sciences, serving as the study director for the project that produced *Bio2010: Transforming Undergraduate Biology Education for Future Research Biologists*. As an outgrowth of that study, she participated in the founding of the National Academies Summer Institutes for Undergraduate Education. Along with other projects, she has led a standing committee for the U.S. Department of Defense on Medical Technologies, multiple studies related to microbiology and biosecurity, and one on the decision-making process for reopening facilities contaminated in biological attacks. She earned her bachelors' degree from Wesleyan University in Middletown, Connecticut and her Ph.D. in molecular biology from Princeton University.

JESSICA COVINGTON is a senior program assistant with the Board on Science Education and is currently supporting the American's Lab Report

Update and Citizen Science projects. Before joining the National Academies of Sciences, Engineering, and Medicine, she was the administrative assistant to an architectural and interior design firm in Metro Center called VOA Associates, which is now known as Stantec Consulting. In 2015, she received her undergraduate degree in psychology.

GREG PEARSON is a scholar with the National Academy of Engineering. He currently serves as the responsible staff officer for a National Science Foundation-funded project examining issues related to capacity building for K–12 engineering educators in the United States. He also directs the Chevron-funded LinkEngineering online resource that is helping guide implementation of PreK–12 engineering education in the United States. Previously, he has overseen projects addressing postsecondary engineering technology education; STEM integration in K–12 education; standards for K–12 engineering education; the status and prospects for engineering in K–12 education; new messaging for the field of engineering (*Changing the Conversation*); technological literacy; and content standards for the field of technology education. He has degrees in biology and journalism.

AMY STEPHENS is a program officer for the Board on Science Education of the National Academies of Sciences, Engineering, and Medicine. She is also an adjunct professor for the Southern New Hampshire University Psychology Department, teaching graduate-level online courses in cognitive psychology and statistics. She was the study director for the recent report *English Learners in STEM Subjects: Transforming Classrooms, Schools, and Lives* and for the workshop on *Graduate Training in the Social and Behavioral Sciences*. She has an extensive background in behavioral and functional neuroimaging techniques and has examined a variety of different populations spanning childhood through adulthood. She has worked at the Center for Talented Youth on producing cognitive profiles of academically talented youth in an effort to develop alternative methods for identifying such students from underresourced populations. Additionally, she has explored the effects of spatial skill training on performance in math and science classes as well as overall retention rates within science, technology, engineering, and mathematics (STEM)-related fields for students entering the engineering program at the Johns Hopkins University. She holds a Ph.D. in cognitive neuroscience from Johns Hopkins University.

HEIDI SCHWEINGRUBER is the director of the Board on Science Education at the National Academies of Sciences, Engineering, and Medicine. She has served as study director or costudy director for a wide range of studies, including those on revising national standards for K–12 science education, learning and teaching science in grades K–8, and mathematics learning in early childhood. She also co-authored two award-winning books for practitioners that translate findings of National Academies' reports for a broader audience, on using research in K–8 science classrooms and on information science education. Prior to joining the National Academies, she worked as a senior research associate at the Institute of Education Sciences in the U.S. Department of Education. She also previously served on the faculty of Rice University and as the director of research for the Rice University School Mathematics Project, an outreach program in K–12 mathematics education. She has a Ph.D. in psychology (developmental) and anthropology and a certificate in culture and cognition, both from the University of Michigan.

TIFFANY TAYLOR is a research associate for the Board on Science Education (BOSE) at the National Academies of Sciences, Engineering, and Medicine. Prior to this position, she was a Christine Mirzayan Science and Technology Policy Fellow at the National Academies. As a Mirzayan Fellow, she also worked with BOSE providing research support across various projects. In addition to her commitment to academic research, she is concerned about the legacy of science education and its inclusion of persons of diverse backgrounds. Throughout her graduate tenure, she tutored and mentored underserved youths to encourage their pursuit of studies and careers in STEM. As a member of the Graduate Student Association Lobby Corps, she advocated for state support to accommodate recruitment and retention of renowned faculty, and support for building infrastructure and maintenance. She received a doctorate degree in biomedical sciences from the University of California, San Diego.